Media Arabic Vocabulary

Book 2

ISBN: 978-1-949650-98-3

website: www.lingualism.com

email: contact@lingualism.com

Written by Ahmad Al-Masri and Matthew Aldrich
Edited by Hend Khaled and Matthew Aldrich
Cover design by Matthew Aldrich

Disclaimer:

This publication is designed exclusively as a language educational resource. The contents of this book, which include sentences and texts, typically do not reflect or comment on real situations, whether historical or contemporary. When real events, individuals, or organizations are referenced, the specifics may not always uphold factual accuracy.

Where certain names or trademarks may appear, they are used strictly for educational purposes. They do not imply any affiliation with or endorsement by the respective rights holders and should not be considered as infringement.

Opinions expressed in the content are ascribed to fictional characters and journalists and do not necessarily reflect the views of the book's contributors or publisher. These opinions are included solely to mimic realistic language use in media settings and do not intend to endorse, critique, or influence real-world ideologies.

By using this book, readers acknowledge that it is for language education, not a source of reliable real-world information. Any errors or inaccuracies are unintentional and do not detract from the book's purpose as a language-learning tool.

Table of Contents

Introduction

Media Arabic Vocabulary is a series specially designed to bridge the gap between **intermediate** learning and reading real-world Arabic news articles. These books are intended to make the often-daunting journey into Arabic media literacy not only accessible, but engaging and enjoyable.

In our experience, many learners find themselves stuck in a language learning plateau, where they can handle classroom scenarios but are left feeling overwhelmed by the complexity of authentic, native-speaker materials, such as news articles. That is exactly where this book series comes in. Each volume is structured to help you scale that seemingly daunting wall by presenting carefully selected vocabulary and controlled texts that emulate the style and complexity of real-world Arabic media.

In this second book of the series, we will navigate through three distinct units: Economics, Science, and Sports. Each unit is further broken down into manageable sections and subsections. Subsections introduce you to key vocabulary in context, helping you understand not only the meaning of the words but also their appropriate use. As an additional aid to word recognition and correct pronunciation, all Arabic content in the book contains **diacritics** (tashkeel). You will find **English translations** for all Arabic content, which allows for better comprehension and learning, plus **audio tracks** to help you get a firm grasp on pronunciation and listening comprehension.

This dynamic approach, combining the introduction of **topical vocabulary** with **example sentences** and end-of-section practice **texts**, ensures you are not just memorizing words, but actively learning to use them in context. Over time, this exposure will greatly increase your confidence and proficiency in reading actual media Arabic-style texts.

While the volumes are numbered, they are not incremental in learning level. They simply cover different topics. Feel free to pick any book from the series that aligns with your interest in a particular theme or topic. We hope you find this approach as empowering and rewarding as we do.

Acknowledgments

This series would not have been possible without the dedicated work of some exceptional individuals. I would like to express my deepest gratitude to Ahmad Al-Masri for his invaluable contributions in compiling the extensive vocabulary list and crafting the example sentences and texts. Ahmad's insights and expertise in the Arabic language have been fundamental in shaping this book.

Likewise, I would like to extend my heartfelt thanks to Hend Khaled for her meticulous editing and proofreading of our materials. Her thoughtful feedback and suggestions have significantly elevated the quality and usability of this series. Likewise, her diligence and dedication have been indispensable in shaping the final product.

–Matthew Aldrich

How to Use This Book

Media Arabic Vocabulary is a versatile, flexible tool that can adapt to your personal learning style, immediate needs, and specific interests. Here's how to make the most of it:

Follow Your Interests

The organization of the book allows you to chart your own learning path. Feel free to delve into any unit that piques your interest or aligns with your immediate learning needs. There is no strict order to follow; every path leads to enrichment.

Understand the Structure

Vocabulary Lists: Vocabulary lists serve as your first contact with the topic-specific words and phrases. Each vocabulary item appears on the right-hand side, while its English translation appears on the opposite side. Sometimes you will notice word forms between them, preceded by a large dot. These are irregular plurals of nouns or verbal nouns (masdars) of verbs. Following each vocabulary item, in a shaded box, is an example sentence to demonstrate its use in context. Dozens of note boxes appear throughout the book with lexical and grammatical notes, learning tips, and references to other vocabulary items.

End-of-Section Texts: Following the vocabulary lists, you'll encounter different kinds of texts, including mini-articles, news reports, interviews, and more. These texts aim to immerse you in a variety of real-world contexts, further reinforcing the vocabulary and enhancing your reading proficiency.

Engage in Self-Discovery

We've consciously decided not to include traditional exercises such as multiple-choice or true-false questions. Instead, we promote a self-discovery approach, empowering you to actively engage with the material.

To effectively analyze the texts, try to identify the vocabulary from the lists in the actual context. Notice how these words interact with each other, what collocations they form, and how they contribute to the overall meaning of the text. As you progress through the content, you may notice that the English translations for certain vocabulary items in the example sentences and texts sometimes differ from those presented in the vocabulary lists. Far from an oversight, this is an intentional aspect of the methodology. Our aim here is to encourage you to ponder more deeply on the meanings of words and the nuances in their usage.

As for vocabulary organization, we encourage you to keep a dedicated notebook. Classify and group words according to logical categories that make sense to you – be it themes, synonyms, antonyms, or even roots for Arabic words. This personalized lexical resource will greatly aid your recall and application of vocabulary.

Utilize the Audio Tracks

The accompanying audio tracks can be used in conjunction with the text or separately for additional listening practice. You can listen before, during, or after reading the texts, depending on your individual preference. They are designed to help improve your listening comprehension and pronunciation. Each section in the book is preceded by its track number.

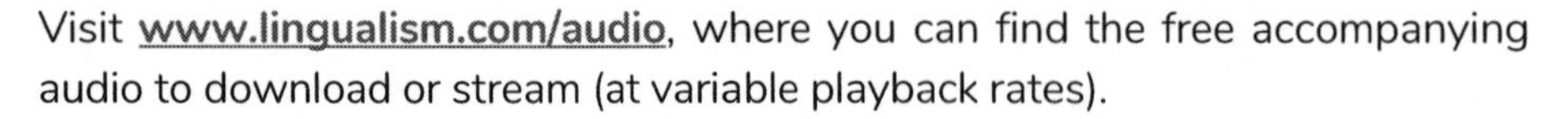

Visit www.lingualism.com/audio, where you can find the free accompanying audio to download or stream (at variable playback rates).

Expand Your Vocabulary

One of the key strengths of this book is the wealth of vocabulary embedded within its pages beyond the given lists. Each section is filled with relevant vocabulary items not explicitly listed as vocabulary items. These additional vocabulary treasures can be found within the example sentences and texts. We encourage you to be an active explorer, seeking them out and adding them to your notes. The more you interact with the texts, the more you will uncover additional topical vocabulary to bolster your Arabic language repertoire.

Happy Learning!

Remember, the journey of language learning is not a linear one. It's a process of exploration, discovery, and personal growth. We hope this book will serve as your faithful companion on this fascinating voyage into the vibrant world of Arabic media.

Unit 4
Economics and Business

In today's interconnected global society, economics and business exert a profound influence on our daily lives and the functioning of nations. This unit seeks to impart an in-depth understanding of the complex terminology and phrases encountered in Arabic media related to these domains. This is a critical foundation for anyone looking to dissect economic articles, reports, and debates in Arabic, and by extension, to gain insight into the fiscal, industrial, and commercial currents that shape the Arab world.

Our first focus within this unit is 'Macroeconomics and Finance.' Here, we explore the cornerstone concepts of Monetary Policy and Central Banking, Fiscal Policy and Public Finance, and International Trade and Exchange Rates. This section will arm you with the vocabulary and context to understand macroeconomic indicators, governmental fiscal measures, and global trade dynamics, all as they are discussed and analyzed in Arabic media.

Our journey continues into the sphere of 'Industry and Manufacturing.' In this section, we will delve into specialized vocabulary related to various industries such as the Automotive Industry, Electronics and Telecommunications, Textile and Fashion, Food and Beverage, and Construction and Building Materials. These subtopics will enable you to grasp industry-specific jargon, allowing you to engage in more nuanced and informed discussions or analyses of Arabic media's coverage of these sectors.

Mastering the vocabulary and concepts presented in this unit will not just expand your Arabic language skills; it will also deepen your understanding of the economic and business landscapes in the Arab world. These landscapes are inextricably linked to the social, political, and cultural frameworks that shape the region. Therefore, acquiring the language to discuss them is crucial for a well-rounded understanding of Arabic media and the world it reports on.

Track **1**

economy | **اِقْتِصادٌ**

عَلى الرَّغْمِ مِنَ الأَزَماتِ المُتَتالِيَةِ، تَمَكَّنَ الاِقْتِصادُ البَرازيلِيُّ مِنَ الاِسْتِقْرارِ وَتَحْقيقِ نُمُوٍّ مُسْتَدامٍ.

Despite successive crises, the Brazilian economy was able to stabilize and achieve sustainable growth.

economic | **اِقْتِصادِيٌّ**

يُؤَكِّدُ الخُبَراءُ الاِقْتِصادِيّونَ أَنَّ التَّضَخُّمَ المُفْرِطَ قَدْ يُؤَدّي إِلى تَدَهْوُرِ الوَضْعِ الاِقْتِصادِيِّ في البِلادِ.

Economic experts confirm that excessive inflation may lead to a deterioration of the country's economic situation.

4.1 Macroeconomics and Finance

4.1.1 Monetary Policy and Central Banking

Track **2**

to stabilize | اِسْتِقْرارٌ • | **اِسْتَقَرَّ**

اِسْتَقَرَّتْ أَسْعارُ النِّفْطِ بَعْدَ تَراجُعِها لِمُدَّةِ ثَلاثَةِ أَيّامٍ مُتَتالِيَةٍ.

Oil prices stabilized after falling for three consecutive days.

independence of central banks | **اِسْتِقْلالِيَّةُ البُنوكِ المَرْكَزِيَّةِ**

حافَظَتِ البُنوكُ المَرْكَزِيَّةُ فِي الدُّوَلِ الأوروبِّيَّةِ عَلى اسْتِقْلالِيَّتِها بِالرَّغْمِ مِنَ الضُّغوطِ السِّياسِيَّةِ.

Central banks in European countries maintained their independence despite political pressure.

bank | بُنوكٌ • | **بَنْكٌ**

أَعْلَنَ بَنْكُ بارْكليزْ عَنْ نَتائِجِهِ المالِيَّةِ لِلرُّبْعِ الأَوَّلِ مِنَ العامِ الحالِيِّ.

Barclays Bank announced its financial results for the first quarter of the current year.

the World Bank | **البَنْكُ الدَّوْلِيُّ**

مَنَحَ البَنْكُ الدَّوْلِيُّ قَرْضًا لِمِصْرَ لِتَطْويرِ مَناطِقِها الرّيفِيَّةِ.

The World Bank granted a loan to Egypt to develop its rural areas.

central bank **بَنْكٌ مَرْكَزِيٌّ**

رَفَعَ البَنْكُ المَرْكَزِيُّ الأَمْريكِيُّ أَسْعارَ الفائِدَةِ لِمُواجَهَةِ التَّضَخُّمِ.

The U.S. central bank raised interest rates to combat inflation.

money transfer **تَحْويلُ أَمْوالٍ**

أَصْدَرَتْ شَرِكَةُ بايْ بالْ بَيانًا يُشَدِّدُ عَلى أَمانِ تَحْويلِ الأَمْوالِ عَبْرَ مِنَصَّتِها.

Paypal issued a statement emphasizing the security of money transfers through its platform.

inflation **تَضَخُّمٌ**

تَوَقَّعَ خُبَراءُ الِاقْتِصادِ ارْتِفاعَ مُعَدَّلاتِ التَّضَخُّمِ في الهِنْدِ بِسَبَبِ الأَزْمَةِ الرّاهِنَةِ.

Economic experts predicted an increase in inflation rates in India due to the current crisis.

adjusted inflation **تَضَخُّمٌ مُعَدَّلٌ**

بَلَغَ التَّضَخُّمُ المُعَدَّلُ في اليابانِ 0.8% خِلالَ الرُّبْعِ الأَوَّلِ مِنَ العامِ.

Adjusted inflation in Japan reached 0.8% during the first quarter of the year.

As you engage with this unit, you may notice that the learning extends beyond the primary keywords we've highlighted. For instance, the term رُبْعٌ (quarter) appears twelve times in this unit alone. We strongly recommend that you highlight such recurring terms and consider adding them to your personal vocabulary notebook. These terms are not merely supplementary; they are integral to a comprehensive understanding of the topic. By being vigilant, you will uncover many more vocabulary words that are crucial to this subject matter.

banking regulation **تَنْظيمُ العَمَلِ المَصرِفيِّ**

دَعا مَسْؤولونَ إِلى تَنْظيمِ العَمَلِ المَصرِفيِّ أَكْثَرَ فَأَكْثَرَ لِمُواجَهَةِ التَّحَدِّياتِ المُسْتَقْبَلِيَّةِ.

Officials called for further regulation of banking activities to meet future challenges.

to lower • خَفْضٌ **خَفَضَ**

قَرَّرَ البَنْكُ المَرْكَزِيُّ السُّعوديُّ خَفْضَ أَسْعارِ الفائِدَةِ بِنِسْبَةِ 0.25%.

The Saudi Central Bank decided to lower interest rates by 0.25%.

رَفَعَ • رَفْعٌ **to raise**

رَفَعَ البَنْكُ المَرْكَزِيُّ اليابانِيُّ أَسْعارَ الفائِدَةِ لِلْمَرَّةِ الأولى مُنْذُ عامَيْنِ.

The Japanese Central Bank raised interest rates for the first time in two years.

سِياسَةُ الفائِدَةِ **interest rate policy**

كَشَفَتْ سِياسَةُ الفائِدَةِ الَّتي اعْتَمَدَتْها البُنوكُ المَرْكَزِيَّةُ عَنْ مُسْتَوى التَّحَفُّظِ الكَبيرِ لَدى صانِعي القَرارِ.

The interest rate policy adopted by central banks revealed a high level of caution among decision-makers.

سِياسَةٌ تَحْفيزِيَّةٌ **stimulus policy**

أَعْلَنَتِ الحُكومَةُ الكَنَدِيَّةُ عَنْ سِياسَةٍ تَحْفيزِيَّةٍ جَديدَةٍ لِتَعْزيزِ الاقْتِصادِ المَحَلِّيِّ.

The Canadian government announced a new stimulus policy to boost the local economy.

سِياسَةٌ نَقْدِيَّةٌ **monetary policy**

أَثَّرَتِ السِّياسَةُ النَّقْدِيَّةُ الفَعّالَةُ مِنْ قِبَلِ البَنْكِ المَرْكَزِيِّ البِريطانِيِّ في تَحْقيقِ الاسْتِقْرارِ الاقْتِصادِيِّ.

An effective monetary policy from the Bank of England contributed to economic stability.

سِياسَةٌ نَقْدِيَّةٌ شامِلَةٌ **comprehensive monetary policy**

طَبَّقَ البَنْكُ المَرْكَزِيُّ الأوروبِّيُّ سِياسَةً نَقْدِيَّةً شامِلَةً لِمُواجَهَةِ تَحَدِّياتِ التَّضَخُّمِ.

The European Central Bank implemented a comprehensive monetary policy to address inflation challenges.

سِياسَةٌ نَقْدِيَّةٌ مُيَسِّرَةٌ **accommodative monetary policy**

تَبَنّى بَنْكُ الصّينِ الشَّعْبِيُّ سِياسَةً نَقْدِيَّةً مُيَسِّرَةً لِتَحْفيزِ النُّمُوِّ الاقْتِصادِيِّ.

The People's Bank of China adopted an accommodative monetary policy to stimulate economic growth.

to encourage • تَشْجيعٌ **شَجَّعَ**

شَجَّعَتِ السِّياسَةُ النَّقْدِيَّةُ الجَديدَةُ الِاسْتِثْمارَ في القِطاعاتِ الخَضْراءِ.

The new monetary policy encouraged investment in green sectors.

Islamic bond • صُكوكٌ **صَكٌّ إِسْلامِيٌّ**

بَدَأَتِ البُنوكُ في الإماراتِ العَرَبِيَّةِ المُتَّحِدَةِ في إِصْدارِ الصُّكوكِ الإِسْلامِيَّةِ لِجَمْعِ الأَمْوالِ.

Banks in the United Arab Emirates began issuing Islamic bonds to raise funds.

International Monetary Fund • صَناديقُ **صُنْدوقُ النَّقْدِ الدَّوْلِيُّ**

وافَقَ صُنْدوقُ النَّقْدِ الدَّوْلِيُّ عَلى مِنْحَةٍ لِلُبْنانَ لِمُساعَدَتِهِ في تَخَطّي الأَزْمَةِ الِاقْتِصادِيَّةِ.

The International Monetary Fund approved a grant for Lebanon to help it overcome the economic crisis.

money printing **طِباعَةُ نُقودٍ**

أَعْلَنَ البَنْكُ المَرْكَزِيُّ الزِّيمْبابْوِيُّ عَنْ طِباعَةِ نُقودٍ جَديدَةٍ لِمُكافَحَةِ التَّضَخُّمِ.

The Zimbabwean Central Bank announced the printing of new money to combat inflation.

to adjust • تَعْديلٌ **عَدَّلَ**

عَدَّلَ البَنْكُ المَرْكَزِيُّ التُّرْكِيُّ تَوَقُّعاتِهِ لِلنُّمُوِّ الِاقْتِصادِيِّ في الرُّبْعِ الثّاني مِنَ العامِ.

The Turkish Central Bank adjusted its economic growth forecasts for the second quarter of the year.

interest rate • فَوائِدُ **فائِدَةٌ**

أَعْلَنَ بَنْكُ الإماراتِ دُبَيَّ الوَطَنِيُّ عَنْ تَقْليلِ فائِدَةِ القُروضِ الشَّخْصِيَّةِ لِعُمَلائِه.

Emirates NBD Bank announced a reduction in the interest rate on personal loans for its customers.

to offer • تَقْديمٌ **قَدَّمَ**

قَدَّمَ البَنْكُ الدَّوْلِيُّ مُقْتَرَحاتٍ لِتَحْسينِ سِياسَةِ الفائِدَةِ في البِلادِ.

The World Bank put forth suggestions to improve the country's interest rate policy.

decision to lower interest rates قَرارُ تَخْفيضِ الفائِدَةِ

أَثارَ قَرارُ البَنْكِ المَرْكَزِيِّ الأَمْريكِيِّ بِتَخْفيضِ الفائِدَةِ الكَثيرَ مِنَ التَّساؤُلاتِ حَوْلَ تَأْثيرِهِ عَلى الاِقْتِصادِ.

The U.S. central bank's decision to cut interest rates raised many questions about its impact on the economy.

central bank loan قَرْضُ بَنْكٍ مَرْكَزِيٍّ • قُروضٌ

تَوَصَّلَتِ الحُكومَةُ الإيطالِيَّةُ إِلى اتِّفاقٍ لِلْحُصولِ عَلى قَرْضِ بَنْكٍ مَرْكَزِيٍّ لِتَفادي الأَزْمَةِ الاِقْتِصادِيَّةِ.

The Italian government reached an agreement to secure a central bank loan to avoid the economic crisis.

incentive مُحَفِّزٌ

كَشَفَتِ الحُكومَةُ الأَلْمانِيَّةُ عَنْ مُحَفِّزاتٍ اقْتِصادِيَّةٍ جَديدَةٍ لِدَعْمِ قِطاعِ الطّاقَةِ المُتَجَدِّدَةِ.

The German government unveiled new economic incentives to support the renewable energy sector.

high مُرْتَفِعٌ

كانَتْ أَسْعارُ الفائِدَةِ مُرْتَفِعَةً لِلْغايَةِ خِلالَ الأَزْمَةِ الاِقْتِصادِيَّةِ العالَمِيَّةِ في 2008.

Interest rates were extremely high during the global economic crisis in 2008.

stable مُسْتَقِرٌّ

ظَلَّتْ أَسْعارُ العُمُلاتِ مُسْتَقِرَّةً في الأَسْواقِ العالَمِيَّةِ رَغْمَ التَّقَلُّباتِ الاِقْتِصادِيَّةِ.

Currency prices remained stable in global markets despite economic volatility.

adjusted; rate مُعَدَّلٌ

كَشَفَ البَنْكُ المَرْكَزِيُّ عَنْ مُعَدَّلِ النُّمُوِّ المُعَدَّلِ بَعْدَ الأَخْذِ بِعَيْنِ الاِعْتِبارِ التَّضَخُّمَ وَالتَّغَيُّراتِ الاِقْتِصادِيَّةَ.

The Central Bank revealed the adjusted growth rate, taking into account inflation and economic changes.

In the example above, the word مُعَدَّل appears as both an adjective and a noun. As an adjective, it describes the 'adjusted' growth rate, and as a noun, it refers to the 'rate' itself. This may seem confusing at first, but by identifying the part of speech, you can discern the meaning more clearly.

inflation rate مُعَدَّلُ تَضَخُّمٍ

سَجَّلَ مُعَدَّلُ التَّضَخُّمِ في الولاياتِ المُتَّحِدةِ ارْتِفاعًا خِلالَ الشَّهْرِ الماضي.

The inflation rate in the United States recorded an increase over the past month.

interest rate مُعَدَّلُ فائِدَةٍ

أَبْقى البَنْكُ المَرْكَزِيُّ الأُسْتُرالِيُّ عَلى مُعَدَّلِ الفائِدَةِ دونَ تَغْيير.

The Australian Central Bank kept the interest rate unchanged.

low مُنْخَفِضٌ

أَعْلَنَ البَنْكُ المَرْكَزِيُّ الأوروبِّيُّ أَنَّ مُعَدَّلاتِ الفائِدَةِ سَتَظَلُّ مُنْخَفِضَةً لِتَحْفيزِ الاِقْتِصادِ في ظِلِّ الجائِحَة.

The European Central Bank has announced that interest rates will remain low to stimulate the economy amid the pandemic.

regulated مُنَظَّمٌ

أَعْرَبَ الخُبَراءُ عَنْ قَلَقِهِمْ مِنْ أَنَّ النِّظامَ المالِيَّ غَيْرَ المُنَظَّمِ قَدْ يُؤَدّي إِلى أَزْمَةٍ اقْتِصادِيَّةٍ.

Experts expressed concern that the unregulated financial system could lead to an economic crisis.

The terms مُنَظَّمٌ and مُعَدَّلٌ are both past participles formed from the measure-II verbs نَظَّمَ (to regulate) and 'عَدَّلَ' (to adjust), respectively. They serve primarily as adjectives, with مُنَظَّمٌ meaning 'organized' and مُعَدَّلٌ meaning 'adjusted.' Identifying the part of speech helps you discern their meanings more clearly. Keep an eye out for these morphological patterns; they're common in Arabic.

to regulate نَظَّمَ • تَنْظيمٌ

نَظَّمَ البَنْكُ المَرْكَزِيُّ الهِنْدِيُّ عَمَلِيَّةَ إِصْدارِ النُّقودِ لِتَجَنُّبِ الأَزْمَةِ النَّقْدِيَّة.

The Indian Central Bank organized the money issuance process to avoid a currency crisis.

4.1.1.1 Mini-Articles

Track **3**

في إِطارِ سِياسَةٍ نَقْدِيَّةٍ مُيَسَّرَةٍ، أَعْلَنَ البَنْكُ المَرْكَزِيُّ عَنْ خَفْضِ مُعَدَّلِ الفائِدَةِ بِنِسْبَةِ 1.5% في مُحاوَلَةٍ لِتَحْفيزِ النَّشاطِ الاِقْتِصادِيِّ. وَقَدِ اتَّخَذَ البَنْكُ هَذا القَرارَ بِتَخْفيضِ الفائِدَةِ بَعْدَ أَنْ أَظْهَرَتِ البَياناتُ اسْتِقْرارَ مُعَدَّلِ

التَّضَخُّم. تَهْدِفُ هَذِهِ السِّياسَةُ التَّحْفيزِيَّةُ إلى تَشْجيعِ التَّحْويلاتِ المالِيَّةِ وَالقُروضِ المَصْرِفِيَّةِ، مِمّا يُؤَدّي بِالتّالي إلى زِيادَةِ الاِسْتِثْماراتِ وَالإِنْفاقِ الاِسْتِهْلاكِيِّ.

In the context of an accommodative monetary policy, the central bank has announced a 1.5% reduction in the interest rate in an attempt to stimulate economic activity. The bank made this decision to lower the interest rate after data showed inflation stability. This stimulative policy aims to encourage financial transfers and bank loans, thus leading to increased investments and consumer spending.

قَدَّمَ صُنْدوقُ النَّقْدِ الدَّوْلِيُّ وَالبَنْكُ الدَّوْلِيُّ قَرْضًا مُشْتَرَكًا لِدَعْمِ اسْتِقْلالِيَّةِ البُنوكِ المَرْكَزِيَّةِ في البِلادِ النّامِيَةِ. يَهْدِفُ القَرْضُ إلى تَحْسينِ تَنْظيمِ العَمَلِ المَصْرِفِيِّ وَتَعْزيزِ الاِسْتِقْرارِ المالِيِّ. في ظِلِّ هَذِهِ السِّياسَةِ النَّقْدِيَّةِ الشّامِلَةِ، يَتِمُّ تَشْجيعُ البُنوكِ عَلى طِباعَةِ النُّقودِ بِمُعَدَّلٍ مُنَظَّمٍ لِلْحَدِّ مِنَ التَّضَخُّمِ.

The International Monetary Fund and the World Bank have provided a joint loan to support the independence of central banks in developing countries. The loan aims to improve banking organization and enhance financial stability. Under this comprehensive monetary policy, banks are encouraged to print money at a regulated rate to curb inflation.

عَلى الرَّغْمِ مِنْ أَنَّ سِياسَةَ الفائِدَةِ تُعَدُّ أَداةً رَئيسِيَّةً في السِّياسَةِ النَّقْدِيَّةِ، فَإِنَّ البَنْكَ المَرْكَزِيَّ قَدْ أَعْلَنَ أَيْضًا عَنِ اسْتِخْدامِ صُكوكٍ إِسْلامِيَّةٍ كَجُزْءٍ مِنْ أَدَواتِهِ الاِقْتِصادِيَّةِ. هَذا وَتُعَدُّ الصُّكوكُ الإِسْلامِيَّةُ بَديلًا لِلْفائِدَةِ التَّقْليدِيَّةِ وَتَتَوافَقُ مَعَ قَواعِدِ الشَّريعَةِ الإِسْلامِيَّةِ. وَقَدْ تَمَّ تَقْديمُ هَذِهِ السِّياسَةِ كَرَدِّ فِعْلٍ لِتَزايُدِ مُطالَبَةِ العُمَلاءِ المُسْلِمينَ بِخِياراتٍ مَصْرِفِيَّةٍ مُتَوافِقَةٍ مَعَ الشَّريعَةِ.

Although interest rate policy is a key tool in monetary policy, the central bank has also announced the use of Islamic bonds as part of its economic instruments. Islamic bonds, known as "sukuk," serve as an alternative to conventional interest and comply with Islamic Sharia principles. This policy has been introduced in response to growing demands from Muslim customers for Sharia-compliant banking options.

مَعَ تَصاعُدِ الضُّغوطِ الاِقْتِصادِيَّةِ، أَعْلَنَ البَنْكُ المَرْكَزِيُّ عَنْ سِياسَةٍ نَقْدِيَّةٍ جَديدَةٍ تَهْدِفُ إلى الحِفاظِ عَلى اسْتِقْرارِ العُمْلَةِ وَمُحارَبَةِ التَّضَخُّمِ. قَرَّرَ البَنْكُ رَفْعَ مُعَدَّلِ الفائِدَةِ لِتَجَنُّبِ خَطَرِ التَّضَخُّمِ المُفْرِطِ. في الوَقْتِ ذاتِهِ، فَإِنَّ البَنْكَ يُخَطِّطُ لِتَنْظيمِ العَمَلِ المَصْرِفِيِّ وَمُراقَبَةِ تَحْويلِ الأَمْوالِ بِشَكْلٍ أَكْثَرَ صَرامَةً لِضَمانِ احْتِرامِ اللَّوائِحِ المالِيَّةِ.

Amid mounting economic pressures, the central bank has announced a new monetary policy aimed at maintaining currency stability and combating inflation. The bank has decided to raise the interest rate to avoid the risk of excessive inflation. At the same time, the bank plans to regulate banking operations and monitor money transfers more strictly to ensure compliance with financial regulations.

أَصْدَرَ البَنْكُ المَرْكَزِيُّ قَرارًا مُهِمًّا بِخُصوصِ سِياسَةِ الفائِدَةِ. هَذا القَرارُ، الَّذي يَشْمَلُ تَخْفيضَ مُعَدَّلِ الفائِدَةِ بِمِقْدارِ نِصْفِ نُقْطَةٍ نِسْبِيَّةٍ، مِنَ المُتَوَقَّعِ أَنْ يُشَجِّعَ النُّمُوَّ الاِقْتِصادِيَّ وَأَنْ يَعْمَلَ كَمُحَفِّزٍ لِلاِسْتِثْمارِ. عَلى الرَّغْمِ مِنْ أَنَّ

مُعدَّلَ التَّضخُّمِ مُرْتَفِعٌ نِسْبيًا، إلّا أنَّ البَنْكَ يَأْمُلُ أَنْ يَتَمَكَّنَ مِنْ تَحقيقِ التَّوازُنِ بَيْنَ النُّمُوِّ الِاقْتِصادِيِّ وَاسْتِقْرارِ الأَسْعارِ مِنْ خِلالِ هَذِهِ الخُطْوَةِ.

The central bank has issued an important decision regarding the interest rate policy. This decision, which includes a half percentage point reduction in the interest rate, is expected to stimulate economic growth and act as an investment incentive. Despite relatively high inflation, the bank hopes to achieve a balance between economic growth and price stability through this step.

4.1.1.2 Informative Article: IMF Support in Arab Countries

Track **4**

دَعْمُ صُنْدوقِ النَّقْدِ الدَّوْليِّ في الدُّوَلِ العَرَبيَّةِ

صُنْدوقُ النَّقْدِ الدَّوْليُّ، المَعْروفُ اخْتِصارًا بِ IMF، هُوَ مُنَظَّمَةٌ دَوْليَّةٌ تَأَسَّسَتْ في عامِ 1944 بِهَدَفِ تَعْزيزِ النُّمُوِّ الِاقْتِصاديِّ العالَميِّ وَالِاسْتِقْرارِ الماليِّ. يُساهِمُ صُنْدوقُ النَّقْدِ الدَّوْليُّ في تَنْظيمِ العَمَلِ المَصْرِفيِّ الدَّوْليِّ وَتَقْديمِ المَشورَةِ لِلْبُلْدانِ في مَجالِ السِّياسَةِ النَّقْديَّةِ. بِالإِضافَةِ إِلى ذَلِكَ، يُقَدِّمُ الصُّنْدوقُ القُروضَ وَالمُساعَداتِ الماليَّةَ لِلْبُلْدانِ الَّتي تُواجِهُ صُعوباتٍ اقْتِصاديَّةً.

في الدُّوَلِ العَرَبيَّةِ، يَتَعاوَنُ صُنْدوقُ النَّقْدِ الدَّوْليُّ مَعَ الحُكوماتِ وَالبُنوكِ المَرْكَزيَّةِ لِتَحْقيقِ اسْتِقْلاليَّةِ البُنوكِ المَرْكَزيَّةِ وَالِاسْتِقْرارِ الِاقْتِصاديِّ. عَلى سَبيلِ المِثالِ، في عامِ 2016، أَقَرَّ الصُّنْدوقُ قَرْضًا بِقيمَةِ 12 مِلْيارَ دولارٍ لِمِصْرَ لِدَعْمِ بَرْنامَجِها الِاقْتِصاديِّ، في ظِلِّ سِياسَةٍ نَقْديَّةٍ تَهْدِفُ إِلى تَحْقيقِ الِاسْتِقْرارِ الِاقْتِصاديِّ. تَمَّ تَوْجيهُ القَرْضِ صَوْبَ تَحْفيزِ الِاقْتِصادِ عَبْرَ تَحْويلِ أَمْوالٍ لِلْقِطاعاتِ الأَكْثَرِ احْتِياجًا وَتَقْديمِ مُحَفِّزاتٍ لِلْمَشْروعاتِ الصَّغيرَةِ وَالمُتَوَسِّطَةِ.

في الأُرْدُنِّ، قَدَّمَ الصُّنْدوقُ الدَّعْمَ عِدَّةَ مَرّاتٍ لِلْمُساعَدَةِ في تَخْفيفِ تَأْثيرِ النِّزاعاتِ الإِقْليميَّةِ وَالكَوارِثِ. فَعَلى سَبيلِ المِثالِ، في عامِ 2020، وافَقَ عَلى تَقْديمِ 1.5 مِلْيارِ دولارٍ لِلْأُرْدُنِّ لِمُساعَدَتِهِ في التَّعامُلِ مَعَ تَأْثيرِ جائِحَةِ كوفيد - 19.

في تونِسَ، قَدَّمَ صُنْدوقُ النَّقْدِ الدَّوْليُّ الدَّعْمَ في السَّنَواتِ الَّتي أَعْقَبَتِ الثَّوْرَةَ في عامِ 2011. قُدِّمَتِ القُروضُ بِشُروطٍ مُيَسَّرَةٍ لِتَعْزيزِ الِاسْتِقْرارِ الِاقْتِصاديِّ وَالمُساعَدَةِ في التَّحَوُّلِ إِلى اقْتِصادٍ أَكْثَرَ ليبْراليَّةً.

مِنْ خِلالِ هَذِهِ الأَمْثِلَةِ، يُمْكِنُ أَنْ نَرى كَيْفَ يَعْمَلُ صُنْدوقُ النَّقْدِ الدَّوْليُّ لِدَعْمِ الِاسْتِقْرارِ الِاقْتِصاديِّ وَالنَّقْديِّ في العالَمِ، مَعَ تَحْقيقِهِ سِياسَةً نَقْديَّةً شامِلَةً تَتَناوَلُ القَضايا الِاقْتِصاديَّةَ في الدُّوَلِ الأَعْضاءِ.

IMF Support in Arab Countries

The International Monetary Fund, commonly abbreviated as the "IMF," is an international organization founded in 1944 with the aim of promoting global economic growth and financial stability. The IMF contributes to the regulation of international banking and provides policy advice to countries in the field of monetary policy. Additionally, the IMF provides loans and financial assistance to countries facing economic difficulties.

In Arab countries, the IMF collaborates with governments and central banks to achieve the independence of central banks and economic stability. For example, in 2016, the IMF approved a $12 billion loan to Egypt to support its economic program, under a monetary policy aimed at achieving economic stability. The loan was directed towards stimulating the economy by channeling funds to the neediest sectors and providing incentives for small and medium-sized projects.

In Jordan, the IMF has provided support on multiple occasions to help alleviate the impact of regional conflicts and catastrophes. For instance, in 2020, it agreed to provide $1.5 billion to Jordan to assist in dealing with the impact of the COVID-19 pandemic.

In Tunisia, the IMF has provided support in the years following the 2011 revolution. Loans were provided on favorable terms to enhance economic stability and assist in transitioning to a more liberalized economy.

Through these examples, we can see how the International Monetary Fund works to support economic and monetary stability worldwide, implementing comprehensive monetary policies that address economic issues in member countries.

4.1.2 Fiscal Policy and Public Finance

Track **5**

أَصْدَرَ مِنْحَةً • إِصْدارٌ **to issue a grant**

أَصْدَرَتِ الحُكومَةُ الأَمْريكِيَّةُ مِنْحَةً بِقيمَةِ مِلْيارِ دولارٍ لِدَعْمِ البُلْدانِ النّامِيَةِ.

The U.S. government issued a grant worth a billion dollars to support developing countries.

أَعْلَنَ عَنْ ميزانِيَّةٍ • إِعْلانٌ **to announce a budget**

أَعْلَنَتِ الحُكومَةُ الأَلْمانِيَّةُ عَنْ ميزانِيَّةِ العامِ المُقْبِلِ، وَالَّتي تَضَمَّنَتْ تَّخْصيصاتٍ كَبيرَةً لِلتَّعْليمِ.

The German government announced the budget for the coming year, which included significant allocations for education.

أَنْفَقَ عَلى بِنْيَةٍ تَحْتِيَّةٍ • إِنْفاقٌ **to spend on infrastructure**

أَنْفَقَتِ الحُكومَةُ الهِنْدِيَّةُ مَبْلَغًا كَبيرًا عَلى البِنْيَةِ التَّحْتِيَّةِ لِتَحْسينِ شَبَكاتِ النَّقْلِ العامِّ.

The Indian government spent a large sum on infrastructure to improve public transport networks.

In media Arabic, certain verbs frequently appear to describe actions related to specific topics. In this section on fiscal policy and public finance, you'll find أَصْدَرَ (to issue), أَعْلَنَ (to announce), and أَنْفَقَ (to spend) as keywords (just above). But more verbs, such as وافَقَ (to agree), أَجْرى (to conduct), اِعْتَمَدَ (to approve), and سَجَّلَ (to record) can be found in other examples. While we're pointing out these verbs for you in this section, it's up to you to notice and learn such useful verbs in other sections and units to enrich your vocabulary.

إعادَةُ هَيْكَلَةِ دَيْنٍ عامٍّ
public debt restructuring

تُجْري اليونانُ مُحادَثاتٍ حَوْلَ إعادَةِ هَيْكَلَةِ دَيْنِها العامِّ لِتَخْفيفِ العِبْءِ عَلى اقْتِصادِها.

Greece is in talks to restructure its public debt to alleviate the burden on its economy.

إعانَةٌ اجْتِماعِيَّةٌ
social subsidy

وافَقَ البَرْلَمانُ البِريطانِيُّ عَلى زِيادَةِ الإعانَةِ الاجْتِماعِيَّةِ لِلْعائِلاتِ مَحْدودَةِ الدَّخْلِ.

The British Parliament agreed to increase social assistance for low-income families.

إنْفاقٌ إجْمالِيٌّ
total spending

واصَلَ الإنْفاقُ الإجْمالِيُّ في الوِلاياتِ المُتَّحِدَةِ الارْتِفاعَ بِسَبَبِ السِّياساتِ الحُكومِيَّةِ الجَديدَةِ.

Total spending in the United States continued to rise due to new government policies.

إنْفاقٌ حُكومِيٌّ
government spending

أَثارَ الإنْفاقُ الحُكومِيُّ العالي الكَثيرَ مِنَ الجَدَلِ في البَرْلَمانِ الأَلْمانِيِّ.

High government spending sparked a lot of debate in the German parliament.

إنْفاقٌ عامٌّ
public spending

أَثارَ الإنْفاقُ العامُّ المُرْتَفِعُ في إيطالْيا مَخاوِفَ مِنْ تَفاقُمِ الدَّيْنِ العامِّ.

High public spending in Italy raised fears of escalating public debt.

إيرادٌ ضَريبِيٌّ
tax revenue

سَجَّلَتِ السُّويدُ ارْتِفاعًا في الإيراداتِ الضَّريبِيَّةِ بِفَضْلِ الإصْلاحاتِ الاقْتِصادِيَّةِ الحَديثَةِ.

Sweden recorded an increase in tax revenues thanks to recent economic reforms.

expected tax revenue **إيرادٌ ضَريبِيٌّ مُتَوَقَّعٌ**

تَتَوَقَّعُ الحُكومَةُ المِصْرِيَّةُ زِيادَةَ الإيراداتِ الضَّريبِيَّةِ بِنِسْبَةِ 15% في العامِ القادِمِ.

The Egyptian government expects tax revenues to increase by 15% next year.

public revenue **إيرادٌ عامٌّ**

تَعْتَمِدُ الحُكومَةُ اللُّبْنانِيَّةُ عَلى الإيراداتِ العامَّةِ لِتَمْويلِ خُطَطِها الاِسْتِثْمارِيَّةِ.

The Lebanese government relies on public revenues to fund its investment plans.

appropriation **اِعْتِمادٌ**

لَمْ يُطْلَبْ أَيُّ اعتِمادٍ إِضافِيٍّ بِالميزانِيَّةِ لِتَمْويلِ النَّفَقاتِ.

No additional budgetary appropriation was requested to finance the expenditure.

to approve a budget • اِعْتِمادٌ **اِعْتَمَدَ ميزانِيَّةً**

اِعْتَمَدَ البَرْلَمانُ الكُوَيْتِيُّ ميزانِيَّةَ الحُكومَةِ لِلْعامِ الجَديدِ.

The Kuwaiti Parliament approved the government's budget for the new year.

In the example sentence two entries above, اِعْتَمَدَ means to rely on or to depend on, and it commonly requires the preposition عَلى to indicate what is being relied upon. This is the more common meaning of the verb. In contrast, in the example sentence just above, اِعْتَمَدَ means to approve or to adopt, and it doesn't require the preposition عَلى. Understanding the context and the presence or absence of عَلى can help you discern which meaning of اِعْتَمَدَ is intended.

economic contraction **اِنْكِماشٌ اقْتِصادِيٌّ**

تُعاني الجَزائِرُ مِنَ انْكِماشٍ اقْتِصادِيٍّ بِسَبَبِ القُيودِ المَفْروضَةِ عَلى صادِراتِ النِّفْطِ.

Algeria is suffering from an economic contraction due to restrictions imposed on oil exports.

unemployment **بِطالَةٌ**

واجَهَتْ تونِسُ مُعَدَّلاتِ بِطالَةٍ عالِيَةٍ بَيْنَ الشَّبابِ في السَّنَواتِ الأَخيرَةِ.

Tunisia has faced high unemployment rates among the youth in recent years.

economic stimulus — **تَحْفيزٌ اقْتِصاديٌّ**

تَعْتَزِمُ الحُكومَةُ المَغْرِبِيَّةُ زِيادَةَ الإِنْفاقِ العامِّ كَجُزْءٍ مِنْ خُطَّةِ التَّحْفيزِ الاقْتِصاديِّ.

The Moroccan government intends to increase public spending as part of an economic stimulus plan.

tax reduction — **تَخْفيضُ ضَرائِبَ**

أَعْلَنَتِ السُّعودِيَّةُ عَنْ تَخْفيضِ الضَّرائِبِ عَلى الشَّرِكاتِ لِجَذْبِ المَزيدِ مِنَ الاِسْتِثْماراتِ الأَجْنَبِيَّةِ.

Saudi Arabia announced a reduction in corporate taxes to attract more foreign investments.

expenditure reduction — **تَخْفيضُ مَصْروفاتٍ**

بَدَأَتِ الحُكومَةُ العِراقِيَّةُ في تَخْفيضِ مَصْروفاتِ الإِدارَةِ العامَّةِ لِتَقْليلِ العَجْزِ في الميزانِيَّةِ.

The Iraqi government has started reducing public administration expenses to reduce the budget deficit.

tax measures — *pl.* — **تَدابيرُ ضَريبِيَّةٌ**

تَبَنَّتِ الحُكومَةُ الأُرْدُنِيَّةُ تَدابيرَ ضَريبِيَّةً جَديدَةً لِزِيادَةِ الإيراداتِ.

The Jordanian government has adopted new tax measures to increase revenues.

public debt reduction — **تَقْليلُ دَيْنٍ عامٍّ**

تَعَهَّدَتِ الحُكومَةُ اللُّبْنانِيَّةُ بِتَقْليلِ الدَّيْنِ العامِّ مِنْ خِلالِ سِلْسِلَةٍ مِنَ الإِصْلاحاتِ المالِيَّةِ.

The Lebanese government pledged to reduce public debt through a series of financial reforms.

to set a tax — • تَحْديدٌ — **حَدَّدَ ضَريبَةً**

حَدَّدَتِ الحُكومَةُ المِصْرِيَّةُ ضَريبَةً جَديدَةً عَلى الخِدْماتِ الرَّقْمِيَّةِ.

The Egyptian government has set a new tax on digital services.

governmental — **حُكوميٌّ**

تُقَدِّمُ المُبادَرَةُ الحُكومِيَّةُ السُّعودِيَّةُ قُروضًا لِدَعْمِ الشَّرِكاتِ الصَّغيرَةِ وَالمُتَوَسِّطَةِ.

The Saudi government initiative provides loans to support small and medium-sized companies.

خاصٌّ — **private**

تُعْتَبَرُ شَرِكَةُ اتِّصالاتِ الإماراتِ الخاصَّةِ واحِدَةً مِنْ أَكْبَرِ شَرِكاتِ الاتِّصالاتِ في الشَّرْقِ الأَوْسَطِ.

Emirates Private Telecommunications Company is considered one of the largest telecommunications companies in the Middle East.

خَفَّضَ الإِنْفاقَ • تَخْفيضٌ — **to reduce spending**

خَفَّضَتِ الحُكومَةُ التّونِسِيَّةُ الإِنْفاقَ عَلى الخِدْماتِ العامَّةِ لِتَحْقيقِ التَّوازُنِ المالِيِّ.

The Tunisian government reduced spending on public services to achieve fiscal balance.

خَفَّضَ ضَريبَةً — **to lower a tax**

خَفَّضَتِ الحُكومَةُ العِراقِيَّةُ ضَريبَةَ الشَّرِكاتِ لِتَشْجيعِ الاِسْتِثْمارِ المَحَلِّيِّ.

The Iraqi government reduced the corporate tax to encourage domestic investment.

دَيْنٌ عامٌّ • دُيونٌ عامَّةٌ — **public debt**

يُعاني اليَمَنُ مِنْ دَينٍ عامٍّ كَبيرٍ يُعيقُ جُهودَ التَّنْمِيَةِ.

Yemen suffers from a large public debt that hampers development efforts.

رَفَعَ ضَريبَةً • رَفْعٌ — **to raise a tax**

رَفَعَتِ الحُكومَةُ الجَزائِرِيَّةُ ضَريبَةَ الدَّخْلِ لِتَمْويلِ الإِنْفاقِ العامِّ.

The Algerian government raised the income tax to finance public spending.

رُكودٌ اقْتِصادِيٌّ — **economic recession**

يُواجِهُ السّودانُ فَتْرَةً مِنَ الرُّكودِ الاِقْتِصادِيِّ بِسَبَبِ العُقوباتِ الدَّوْلِيَّةِ وَالصِّراعاتِ المَحَلِّيَّةِ.

Sudan is facing a period of economic recession due to international sanctions and local conflicts.

زادَ الإِنْفاقَ الحُكومِيَّ • زِيادَةٌ — **to increase government spending**

زادَتِ الإماراتُ العَرَبِيَّةُ المُتَّحِدَةُ الإِنْفاقَ الحُكومِيَّ في القِطاعاتِ التَّعْليمِيَّةِ وَالصِّحِّيَّةِ لِتَعْزيزِ النُّمُوِّ المُسْتَدامِ.

The United Arab Emirates increased government spending in the educational and health sectors to boost sustainable growth.

زِيادَةُ إِنْفاقٍ
spending increase

تَنْظُرُ فَرَنْسا في شَأْنِ زِيادَةِ الإِنْفاقِ الحُكومِيِّ عَلى الرِّعايَةِ الصِّحِّيَّةِ في أَعْقابِ تَفَشّي فَيْروسِ كورونا.

France is seeing an increase in government spending on healthcare in the wake of the coronavirus outbreak.

زِيادَةُ ضَرائِبَ
tax increase

أَثارَتِ الحُكومَةُ المِصْرِيَّةُ جَدَلًا واسِعًا بَعْدَ أَنْ أَعْلَنَتْ عَنْ زِيادَةِ ضَرائِبِ القيمَةِ المُضافَةِ.

The Egyptian government sparked widespread controversy after it announced an increase in value-added taxes.

سِياسَةُ تَحْفيزٍ اقْتِصادِيٍّ
economic stimulus policy

أَطْلَقَتِ الصّينُ سِياسَةَ تَحْفيزٍ اقْتِصادِيٍّ لِتَعْزيزِ القِطاعاتِ التِّكْنولوجِيَّةِ وَالاِبْتِكارِ.

China launched an economic stimulus policy to boost the technology and innovation sectors.

سِياسَةُ تَحْفيزٍ مالِيٍّ
monetary stimulus policy

تُطَبِّقُ الحُكومَةُ الأُرْدُنِّيَّةُ سِياسَةَ تَحْفيزٍ مالِيٍّ لِدَعْمِ الشَّرِكاتِ الصَّغيرَةِ وَالمُتَوَسِّطَةِ خِلالَ الأَزْمَةِ الاِقْتِصادِيَّةِ.

The Jordanian government is implementing a fiscal stimulus policy to support small and medium enterprises during the economic crisis.

سِياسَةُ تَيْسيرٍ نَقْدِيٍّ
monetary easing policy

يُطَبِّقُ البَنْكُ المَرْكَزِيُّ البِريطانِيُّ سِياسَةَ تَيْسيرٍ نَقْدِيٍّ لِتَحْقيقِ الاِسْتِقْرارِ المالِيِّ.

The Bank of England is implementing a monetary easing policy to achieve financial stability.

سِياسَةٌ مالِيَّةٌ
fiscal policy

تُرَكِّزُ السِّياسَةُ المالِيَّةُ الأَلْمانِيَّةُ عَلى تَحْقيقِ التَّوازُنِ بَيْنَ الإِنْفاقِ الحُكومِيِّ وَالإيراداتِ الضَّريبِيَّةِ.

German fiscal policy focuses on achieving a balance between government spending and tax revenues.

صادَقَ عَلى دَيْنٍ عامٍّ • تَصْديقٌ
to approve public debt

صادَقَ البَرْلَمانُ اللُّبْنانيُّ عَلى دَيْنٍ عامٍّ جَديدٍ لِلْحُكومَةِ في مُحاوَلَةٍ لِلْخُروجِ مِنَ الأَزْمَةِ الاقْتِصادِيَّةِ.

The Lebanese parliament ratified a new public debt for the government in an attempt to get out of the economic crisis.

صُنْدوقٌ سِيادِيٌّ • صَناديقُ
sovereign wealth fund

قامَ صُنْدوقُ الثَّرْوَةِ السِّيادِيُّ النَّرْويجِيُّ، وَهُوَ أَكْبَرُ صُنْدوقٍ سِيادِيٍّ في العالَمِ، بِتَحْقيقِ عَوائِدَ كَبيرَةٍ مِنَ اسْتِثْماراتِهِ في الأَسْهُمِ خِلالَ الرُّبْعِ الأَخيرِ.

The Norwegian Sovereign Wealth Fund, the world's largest sovereign fund, made significant returns from its equity investments in the last quarter.

ضَريبَةٌ • ضَرائِبُ
tax

أَعْلَنَتِ الحُكومَةُ البِريطانِيَّةُ عَنْ زِيادَةٍ في ضَريبَةِ الدَّخْلِ لِلشَّريحَةِ الأَعْلى لِجَمْعِ المَزيدِ مِنَ الإيراداتِ.

The British government announced an increase in the income tax for the top bracket to raise more revenue.

عامٌّ
public

وافَقَ البَرْلَمانُ الجَزائِرِيُّ عَلى التَّعْديلاتِ العامَّةِ عَلى قانونِ العَمَلِ لِتَحْسينِ ظُروفِ العُمّالِ.

The Algerian parliament approved the public amendments to the labor law to improve the conditions of workers.

عَجْزُ ميزانِيَّةٍ = عَجْزُ مُوازَنَةٍ
budget deficit

يُواجِهُ العِراقُ عَجْزًا في المِيزانِيَّةِ بِسَبَبِ انْخِفاضِ أَسْعارِ النِّفْطِ عالَمِيًّا.

Iraq is facing a budget deficit due to a drop in global oil prices.

فائِدَةٌ • فَوائِدُ
interest

قَدَّمَ البَنْكُ الدَّوْلِيُّ قَرْضًا بِفائِدَةٍ مُنْخَفِضَةٍ لِلْهِنْدِ لِدَعْمِ بَرْنامَجِها في الطّاقَةِ المُتَجَدِّدَةِ.

The World Bank offered a low-interest loan to India to support its renewable energy program.

budget surplus فائِضٌ ماليٌّ

تَمَكَّنَت السُّعوديَّةُ مِنْ تَحْقيقِ فائِضٍ ماليٍّ في الميزانيَّةِ لِلْعامِ الثَّاني عَلى التَّوالي.

Saudi Arabia managed to achieve a fiscal surplus in the budget for the second year in a row.

loan قَرْضٌ • قُروضٌ

تَلَقَّتْ مِصْرُ قَرْضًا مِنَ البَنْكِ الدَّوْليِّ لِدَعْمِ البِنْيَةِ التَّحْتِيَّةِ لِلتَّعْليمِ.

Egypt received a loan from the World Bank to support the infrastructure for education.

to reduce government spending قَلَّلَ الإِنْفاقَ الحُكوميَّ • تَقْليلٌ

في ظِلِّ الأَزْمَةِ الِاقْتِصاديَّةِ، قَلَّلَتِ الحُكومَةُ الأَرْجَنْتينيَّةُ الإِنْفاقَ الحُكوميَّ عَلى الخِدْماتِ العامَّةِ.

Amid the economic crisis, the Argentine government cut government spending on public services.

financial, monetary ماليٌّ

تُواجِهُ اليونانُ صُعوباتٍ ماليَّةً بِسَبَبِ دَيْنِها العامِّ الكَبيرِ.

Greece is facing financial difficulties due to its large public debt.

public expenses مَصْروفاتٌ عامَّةٌ *pl.*

قامَتِ الحُكومَةُ الإِسْبانيَّةُ بِزِيادَةِ المَصْروفاتِ العامَّةِ لِلرِّعايَةِ الصِّحِّيَّةِ وَالتَّعْليمِ.

The Spanish government increased public expenditures for healthcare and education.

budget ميزانِيَّةٌ = مُوازَنَةٌ

قَدَّمَتِ الحُكومَةُ الأَلْمانيَّةُ ميزانيَّةً لِلْعامِ 2024 تُرَكِّزُ عَلى التَّعْليمِ وَالصِّحَّةِ العامَّةِ.

The German government submitted a budget for the year 2024 focusing on education and public health.

state budget ميزانِيَّةُ الدَّوْلَةِ

تُرَكِّزُ ميزانِيَّةُ الدَّوْلَةِ الفَرَنْسيَّةِ لِعامِ 2023 عَلى النُّمُوِّ الِاقْتِصاديِّ وَالتَّحْفيزِ الِاقْتِصاديِّ.

The French state budget for 2023 focuses on economic growth and economic stimulus.

general budget **مِيزانِيَّةٌ عامَّةٌ**

طَرَحَتِ الحُكومَةُ الأُسْتُرالِيَّةُ ميزانِيَّةً عامَّةً تُرَكِّزُ عَلى تَعْزيزِ الصِّحَّةِ العامَّةِ وَالتَّعْليمِ.

The Australian government put forth a public budget focused on bolstering public health and education.

In the term ميزانِيَّةُ الدَّوْلَةِ (state budget), الدَّوْلَةُ is a noun that describes the kind of budget, functioning similarly to an adjective. It's part of an idaafa construction, which usually indicates possession but here serves more to specify the type of budget.

In contrast, in ميزانِيَّةٌ عامَّةٌ (general budget), عامَّةٌ is an actual adjective that directly modifies ميزانِيَّةٌ, describing the type of budget.

So, while both terms use different grammatical structures—a noun in an idaafa construction and an adjective—they both serve the same purpose of describing the kind of budget being discussed.

public expenditures *pl.* **نَفَقاتٌ عامَّةٌ**

اِعْتَبَرَتِ الحُكومَةُ المَكْسيكِيَّةُ زِيادَةَ النَّفَقاتِ العامَّةِ ضَرورِيَّةً لِتَحْسينِ الخِدْماتِ الصِّحِّيَّةِ وَالبِنْيَةِ التَّحْتِيَّةِ.

The Mexican government deemed an increase in public expenditures necessary to improve health services and infrastructure.

monetary **نَقْدِيٌّ**

تَتَّخِذُ البُنوكُ المَرْكَزِيَّةُ العالَمِيَّةُ سِياساتٍ نَقْدِيَّةً لِمُواجَهَةِ التَّأْثيرِ الاقْتِصادِيِّ لِلْجائِحَةِ.

Global central banks are taking monetary policies to counter the economic impact of the pandemic.

economic growth **نُمُوٌّ اقْتِصادِيٌّ**

شَهِدَتِ الصّينُ نُمُوًّا اقْتِصادِيًّا مُسْتَمِرًّا رَغْمَ التَّحَدِّياتِ العالَمِيَّةِ.

China has experienced sustained economic growth despite global challenges.

4.1.2.1 Mini-Articles

Track **6**

في ضَوْءِ الانْكِماشِ الاقْتِصادِيِّ الحالِيِّ، أَعْلَنَتِ الحُكومَةُ عَنْ خُطَّةٍ لِزِيادَةِ الإِنْفاقِ الحُكومِيِّ عَلى البِنْيَةِ التَّحْتِيَّةِ في مُحاوَلَةٍ لِتَحْفيزِ الاقْتِصادِ. لَقَدْ أَصْدَرَتْ مِنْحَةً بِقيمَةِ 500 مِلْيونِ دولارٍ لِلْمَشْروعاتِ الخاصَّةِ وَالحُكومِيَّةِ المُتَعَلِّقَةِ بِالطّاقَةِ المُسْتَدامَةِ وَالنَّقْلِ العامِّ. تَأْمُلُ الحُكومَةُ أَنْ تُسْتَخْدَمَ هَذِهِ الإِعانَةُ الاجْتِماعِيَّةُ لِتَوْفيرِ فُرَصِ عَمَلٍ جَديدَةٍ وَتَقْليلِ مُعَدَّلاتِ البِطالَةِ الرّاهِنَةِ.

In light of the current economic contraction, the government has announced a plan to increase government spending on infrastructure in an attempt to stimulate the economy. They have issued a grant of $500 million for private and government projects related to sustainable energy and public transportation. The government hopes that this social assistance will be used to provide new employment opportunities and reduce current unemployment rates.

مَعَ بِدايَةِ العامِ الجَديدِ، أَعْلَنَتِ الحُكومَةُ عَنْ ميزانِيَّةٍ جَديدَةٍ تَهْدُفُ إِلى تَخْفيضِ الدَّيْنِ العامِّ. تَتَضَمَّنُ الإِجْراءاتُ خَفْضَ الإِنْفاقِ الحُكومِيِّ وَتَخْفيض مَصاريفِ الأُجورِ وَالتَّقاعُدِ. بِالإِضافَةِ إِلى ذَلِكَ، تَمَّ تَقْديمُ تَدابيرَ ضَريبِيَّةٍ جَديدَةٍ، تَشْمَلُ رَفْعَ ضَريبَةِ القيمَةِ المُضافَةِ مِنْ 5% إِلى 7%. يَأْمُلُ المَسْؤولونَ أَنْ يُؤَدِّيَ هَذا الإِجْراءُ إِلى تَقْليلِ عَجْزِ الميزانِيَّةِ وَزِيادَةِ الإِيرادِ الضَّريبِيِّ المُتَوَقَّعِ.

With the start of the new year, the government has announced a new budget aimed at reducing public debt. The measures include cutting government spending, reducing wage and retirement expenses. In addition to that, new tax measures have been introduced, including raising the value-added tax (VAT) from 5% to 7%. Officials hope that these measures will lead to reducing the budget deficit and increasing the expected tax revenue.

مَعَ النُّمُوِّ الاِقْتِصادِيِّ البَطيءِ وَالرُّكودِ الاِقْتِصادِيِّ، قَرَّرَتِ الحُكومَةُ تَقْليلَ الدَّيْنِ العامِّ عَنْ طَريقِ إِعادَةِ هَيْكَلَةِ الدَّينِ وَبَيْعِ حِصَصٍ في الصُّنْدوقِ السِّيادِيِّ. وَقَدْ صادَقَتِ الحُكومَةُ عَلى تَقْديمِ قَرْضٍ بِقيمَةِ مِلْيارَيْ دولارٍ لِلْمُساهَمَةِ في هَذِهِ العَمَلِيَّةِ. يَتَوَقَّعُ المُحَلِّلونَ أَنْ يُؤَدِّيَ هَذا الإِجْراءُ إِلى زِيادَةِ الإِيرادِ العامِّ وَالفائِضِ المالِيِّ في السَّنَواتِ المُقْبِلَةِ.

With slow economic growth and an economic recession, the government has decided to reduce public debt through debt restructuring and selling stakes in the sovereign wealth fund. The government has approved a $2 billion loan to contribute to this process. Analysts expect that this measure will lead to an increase in general revenue and financial surplus in the coming years.

في خُطْوَةٍ غَيْرِ مُتَوَقَّعَةٍ، أَعْلَنَتِ الحُكومَةُ عَنْ تَحْفيزٍ اقْتِصادِيٍّ جَديدٍ تَحْتَ سِياسَةِ تَحْفيزٍ مالِيٍّ جَديدَةٍ. تَتَضَمَّنُ الحِزْمَةُ الجَديدَةُ إِصْدارَ مِنْحَةٍ بِقيمَةِ مِلْيارِ دولارٍ لِتَحْفيزِ الصِّناعاتِ المَحَلِّيَّةِ وَتَعْزيزِ الإِنْفاقِ العامِّ. تَتَضَمَّنُ الخُطَّةُ أَيْضًا خَفْضَ الضَّرائِبِ عَلى الشَّرِكاتِ الصَّغيرَةِ وَالمُتَوَسِّطَةِ لِتَشْجيعِ النُّمُوِّ الاِقْتِصادِيِّ. مِنَ المُتَوَقَّعِ أَنْ تُؤَدِّيَ هَذِهِ الخُطْوَةُ إِلى زِيادَةِ الإِيرادِ الضَّريبِيِّ وَتَقْليلِ مُعَدَّلاتِ البِطالَةِ.

In an unexpected move, the government announced a new economic stimulus under a new fiscal stimulus policy. The new package includes the issuance of a billion-dollar grant to stimulate local industries and boost public spending. The plan also includes a tax reduction for small and medium-sized companies to encourage economic growth. This step is expected to increase tax revenue and reduce unemployment rates.

واجَهَتِ الحُكومَةُ مُؤَخَّرًا انْتِقاداتٍ حادَّةً بِسَبَبِ الزِّيادَةِ المُسْتَمِرَّةِ في الدَّيْنِ العامِّ. في مُحاوَلَةٍ لِلتَّصَدّي لِهَذا، أَعْلَنَتْ عَنْ خُطَّةٍ لِتَقْليلِ الدَّينِ عَنْ طَريقِ خَفْضِ الإِنْفاقِ الحُكومِيِّ وَزِيادَةِ الضَّرائِبِ عَلى الأَمْلاكِ الفاخِرَةِ. في نَفْسِ

الوَقْتِ، تُقَدِّمُ الحُكومَةُ قَرْضًا بِقيمَةِ مِلْيونِ دولارٍ لِدَعْمِ الأُسَرِ الأَكْثَرِ فَقْرًا .هَذا وَيَتَوَقَّعُ الخُبَراءُ أَنْ تُؤَدّيَ هَذِهِ الخُطْواتُ إِلى إِعادَةِ التَّوازُنِ في الميزانِيَّةِ العامَّةِ وَتَحْقيقِ فائِضٍ مالِيٍّ في الأَعْوامِ المُقْبِلَةِ.

The government has recently faced sharp criticism due to the continuous increase in public debt. In an attempt to address this, it announced a plan to reduce debt by cutting government spending and increasing taxes on luxury properties. At the same time, the government is offering a one-million-dollar loan to support the most impoverished families. Experts predict that these measures will lead to rebalancing the overall budget and achieving a financial surplus in the coming years.

4.1.2.2 Interview with the Minister of Finance

Track **7**

المُذيعُ: مَرْحَبًا بِكَ مَعالي وَزيرِ المالِيَّةِ، شُكْرًا لَكَ عَلى انْضِمامِكَ إِلى بَرْنامَجِنا اليَوْمَ. هَلْ يُمْكِنُكَ التَّحَدُّثُ عَنِ الإِجْراءاتِ الجَديدَةِ الَّتي أَعْلَنَتْها الحُكومَةُ لِمُواجَهَةِ الانْكِماشِ الاقْتِصادِيِّ؟

وَزيرُ المالِيَّةِ: بِالتَّأْكيدِ، نَحْنُ نَقومُ بِتَطْبيقِ سِياسَةِ تَحْفيزٍ اقْتِصادِيٍّ جَديدَةٍ. هَذا يَتَضَمَّنُ زِيادَةَ الإِنْفاقِ الحُكومِيِّ عَلى البِنْيَةِ التَّحْتِيَّةِ، وَقَدْ أَصْدَرْنا مِنْحَةً كَبيرَةً لِدَعْمِ هَذِهِ المَشاريعِ. نَأْمُلُ أَنْ يُؤَدِّيَ ذَلِكَ إِلى نُمُوٍّ اقْتِصادِيٍّ وَخَلْقِ فُرَصِ عَمَلٍ جَديدَةٍ لِلْحَدِّ مِنَ البِطالَةِ.

المُذيعُ: وَماذا عَنِ الميزانِيَّةِ الجَديدَةِ؟ ما تَأْثيرُها عَلى الدَّيْنِ العامِّ؟

وَزيرُ المالِيَّةِ: تَهْدُفُ الميزانِيَّةُ الجَديدَةُ إِلى تَقْليلِ الدَّيْنِ العامِّ. بِإِعادَةِ هَيْكَلَةِ الدَّيْنِ العامِّ وَخَفْضِ الإِنْفاقِ، نَأْمُلُ أَنْ نُحَقِّقَ تَوازُنًا في ميزانِيَّةِ الدَّوْلَةِ وَأَنْ نُقَلِّلَ مِنَ العَجْزِ في الميزانِيَّةِ.

المُذيعُ: هَلْ يُمْكِنُكَ أَنْ تَشْرَحَ التَّدابيرَ الضَّريبِيَّةَ الجَديدَةَ الَّتي تَمَّ تَقْديمُها؟

وَزيرُ المالِيَّةِ: نَعَمْ، جُزْءٌ مِنَ السِّياسَةِ المالِيَّةِ الجَديدَةِ يَتَضَمَّنُ تَدابيرَ ضَريبِيَّةً مِثْلَ رَفْعِ ضَريبَةِ القيمَةِ المُضافَةِ. نَتَوَقَّعُ أَنْ يُؤَدِّيَ ذَلِكَ إِلى زِيادَةِ الإيرادِ الضَّريبِيِّ المُتَوَقَّعِ، وَأَنْ يُساعِدَ في تَقْليلِ الدَّيْنِ العامِّ.

المُذيعُ: ما هُوَ الدَّوْرُ المُتَوَقَّعُ لِلصُّنْدوقِ السِّيادِيِّ في هَذا السِّياقِ؟

وَزيرُ المالِيَّةِ: يَلْعَبُ الصُّنْدوقُ السِّيادِيُّ دَوْرًا هامًّا في إِعادَةِ الهَيْكَلَةِ المالِيَّةِ. مِنَ المُتَوَقَّعِ بَيْعُ حِصَصٍ في الصُّنْدوقِ السِّيادِيِّ، مِمّا سَيَزيدُ الإيرادَ العامَّ وَيُساهِمُ في تَخْفيفِ الدَّيْنِ العامِّ.

المُذيعُ: شُكْرًا لَكَ عَلى الإجاباتِ الشّامِلَةِ وَالمُفَصَّلَةِ. نَتَطَلَّعُ إِلى رُؤْيَةِ تَأْثيرِ هَذِهِ السِّياساتِ عَلى اقْتِصادِنا فِي المُسْتَقْبَلِ.

Announcer: Welcome, Minister of Finance. Thank you for joining our program today. Can you talk about the new measures announced by the government to address the economic contraction?

Minister of Finance: Certainly, we are implementing a new economic stimulus policy. This includes increasing government spending on infrastructure, and we have issued a large grant to support these projects. We hope this will result in economic growth and create new job opportunities to reduce unemployment.

Announcer: And how about the new budget? How will it affect the public debt?

Minister of Finance: The new budget aims at reducing the public debt. Through debt restructuring and expenditure reduction, we hope to achieve a balance in the state budget and reduce the budget deficit.

Announcer: Can you explain the new tax measures that have been introduced?

Minister of Finance: Yes, part of the new financial policy includes tax measures such as increasing the value-added tax. We expect this to lead to an increase in expected tax revenue and help reduce the public debt.

Announcer: What is the expected role of the sovereign wealth fund in this context?

Minister of Finance: The sovereign wealth fund plays an important role in financial restructuring. It is expected that shares in the sovereign wealth fund will be sold, which will increase general revenue and contribute to reducing the public debt.

Announcer: Thank you for the comprehensive and detailed answers. We look forward to seeing the impact of these policies on our economy in the future.

4.1.3 International Trade and Exchange Rates

Track **8**

economic crisis أَزْمَةٌ اقْتِصادِيَّةٌ

تُواجِهُ اليونانُ أَزْمَةً اقْتِصادِيَّةً خَطيرَةً بِسَبَبِ الدُّيونِ المُتَزايِدَةِ.

Greece is facing a severe economic crisis due to mounting debt.

Don't confuse this with أَزْمَةٌ مالِيَّةٌ, which specifically refers to a financial crisis. An economic crisis is broader and can encompass financial, industrial, and social aspects.

gross national income إِجْماليُّ دَخْلٍ قَوْمِيٍّ

شَهِدَ إِجْمالِيُّ الدَّخْلِ القَوْمِيِّ نُمُوًّا ثابِتًا في السَّنَواتِ الخَمْسِ الماضِيَةِ بِفَضْلِ الاِسْتِثْماراتِ في البِنْيَةِ التَّحْتِيَّةِ.

The Gross National Income has seen steady growth in the last five years, thanks to investments in infrastructure.

This term is distinct from النّاتِجُ المَحّلِّيُّ الإِجْماليُّ (Gross Domestic Product, GDP). GNI includes income from overseas investments.

debt restructuring إِعادَةُ هَيْكَلَةِ دُيونٍ

تُعْقَدُ الجَلَساتُ المالِيَّةُ لِبَحْثِ إِعادَةِ هَيْكَلَةِ الدُّيونِ الكَبيرَةِ المُسْتَحَقَّةِ عَلى البِلادِ.

Financial sessions are being held to discuss the restructuring of the country's large outstanding debts.

customs exemption إِعْفاءٌ جُمْرُكِيٌّ

مَنَحَتِ الحُكومَةُ الفَرَنْسِيَّةُ إِعْفاءً جُمْرُكِيًّا لِلْبَضائِعِ القادِمَةِ مِنْ موزَمْبيق.

The French government granted a customs exemption for goods coming from Mozambique.

global trade trends *pl.* اِتِّجاهاتُ تِجارَةٍ عالَمِيَّةٌ

تُشيرُ اتِّجاهاتُ التِّجارَةِ العالَمِيَّةِ الحَديثَةِ إِلى تَنامي الطَّلَبِ عَلى الطّاقَةِ المُتَجَدِّدَةِ.

Recent global trade trends point to increasing demand for renewable energy.

trade agreement اِتِّفاقِيَّةُ تَبادُلٍ تِجارِيٍّ = اِتِّفاقِيَّةٌ تِجارِيَّةٌ

تَمَّ تَوْقيعُ اتِّفاقِيَّةِ تَبادُلٍ تِجارِيٍّ بَيْنَ الوِلاياتِ المُتَّحِدَةِ وَالإِماراتِ.

A trade exchange agreement was signed between the United States and the UAE.

The verb تَمَّ (literally, to be completed) followed by a verbal noun (masdar) is often used in formal Arabic to indicate the passive voice, particularly for actions completed recently. Here, تَمَّ تَوْقيعُ means 'was signed,' emphasizing that the action (the signing of the agreement) was completed and is equivalent to the passive verb وُقِّعَ.

foreign direct investment اِسْتِثْمارٌ أَجْنَبِيٌّ مُباشِرٌ

شَهِدَتِ البَرازيلُ زِيادَةً في الِاسْتِثْمارِ الأَجْنَبِيِّ المُباشِرِ في قِطاعِ الطّاقَةِ النَّظيفَةِ.

Brazil has seen an increase in foreign direct investment in the clean energy sector.

investment- اِسْتِثْمارِيٌّ

تَمَّ تَشْجيعُ الأَنْشِطَةِ الِاسْتِثْمارِيَّةِ في قِطاعِ الطّاقَةِ البَديلَةِ في اليابانِ.

Investment activities in the alternative energy sector have been encouraged in Japan.

to invest • اِسْتِثْمارٌ اِسْتَثْمَرَ

اِسْتَثْمَرَتِ الشَّرِكاتُ البِريطانِيَّةُ بِكَثافَةٍ في تِكْنولوجْيا الذَّكاءِ الصِّناعِيِّ.

British companies have heavily invested in artificial intelligence technology.

to import • اِسْتيرادٌ اِسْتَوْرَدَ

اِسْتَوْرَدَتْ مِصْرُ القَمْحَ مِنْ روسْيا لِتَلْبِيَةِ الطَّلَبِ المَحَلِّيِّ.

Egypt imported wheat from Russia to meet domestic demand.

import اِسْتيرادٌ

بَدَأَتِ الأَرْجَنْتينُ في اسْتيرادِ المَزيدِ مِنَ النِّفْطِ بِسَبَبِ أَزْمَةِ الطّاقَةِ.

Argentina began importing more oil due to the energy crisis.

اِسْتيرادٌ وَتَصْديرٌ
imports and exports

تَمَّ تَعْزيزُ عَمَلِيّاتِ الاِسْتيرادِ وَالتَّصْديرِ في الإماراتِ لِتَحْقيقِ النُّمُوِّ الاِقْتِصادِيِّ.

Import and export operations were enhanced in the UAE to achieve economic growth.

اِقْتِصادٌ مُغْلَقٌ
closed economy

اِنْتَقَلَتْ كوبا مِنَ اقْتِصادٍ مُغْلَقٍ إلى اقْتِصادٍ أَكْثَرَ انْفِتاحًا لِتَحْسينِ المَعيشَةِ.

Cuba transitioned from a closed economy to a more open economy to improve living conditions.

اِقْتِصادٌ مَفْتوحٌ
open economy

تُعْتَبَرُ سُويسْرا نَموذَجًا لِلاِقْتِصادِ المَفْتوحِ بِسَبَبِ سِياساتِها المَرِنَةِ.

Switzerland is a model of an open economy due to its flexible policies.

اِقْتَصَدَ
to economize

• اِقْتِصادٌ

اِقْتَصَدَتِ السُّويدُ في اسْتِهْلاكِ الوَقودِ الأَحْفورِيِّ لِلْحَدِّ مِنْ تَأْثيراتِ التَّغَيُّرِ المُناخِيِّ.

Sweden economized on the consumption of fossil fuels to mitigate the impacts of climate change.

اِنْخِفاضُ التِّجارَةِ
trade decrease

شَهِدَتِ الوِلاياتُ المُتَّحِدَةُ انْخِفاضًا في التِّجارَةِ مَعَ الصّينِ بِسَبَبِ الرُّسومِ الجُمْرُكِيَّةِ.

The United States saw a decrease in trade with China due to tariffs.

اِنْخِفاضٌ في النُّمُوِّ الاِقْتِصادِيِّ
economic growth slowdown

تَشْهَدُ فَرَنْسا انْخِفاضًا في النُّمُوِّ الاِقْتِصادِيِّ بِسَبَبِ التَّأْثيراتِ الاِقْتِصادِيَّةِ لِلْوَباءِ.

France is experiencing a decrease in economic growth due to the economic impacts of the pandemic.

بَيانُ تِجارَةٍ خارِجِيَّةٍ
foreign trade statement

أَصْدَرَتِ الحُكومَةُ الكَنَدِيَّةُ بَيانًا عَنِ التِّجارَةِ الخارِجِيَّةِ تُوَضِّحُ فيه الزِّيادَةَ السَّنَوِيَّةَ في التَّصْديرِ إلى الاِتِّحادِ الأوروبِّيِّ.

The Canadian government issued a statement on foreign trade indicating the annual increase in exports to the European Union.

to trade • تِجارَةٌ **تاجَرَ**

تاجَرَتِ الإماراتُ بِشَكْلٍ فَعّالٍ في السِّلَعِ الفاخِرَةِ، مِمّا جَعَلَها مَرْكَزًا عالَمِيًّا لِلتِّجارَةِ.

The UAE has effectively traded in luxury goods, making it a global trading hub.

The conjunction مِمّا (originally derived from مِنْ ما (literally, 'from what') is used to introduce a resultant clause, linking it back to the entire preceding clause. This sets it apart from relative pronouns (الَّذي, الَّتي, الَّذينَ, etc.), which usually refer back to a specific noun in the sentence. In the example above, it isn't 'luxury goods' that makes the UAE a global trading hub, but rather 'the fact that the UAE has effectively traded in luxury goods' (the entire clause). This can be translated to English with a gerund (__ing) or 'which.'

to exchange • تَبادُلٌ **تَبادَلَ**

تَبادَلَتِ الهِنْدُ وَاليابانُ السِّلَعَ الزِّراعِيَّةَ وَالتِّكْنولوجْيا المُتَقَدِّمَةَ ضِمْنَ الاتِّفاقِيّاتِ الثُّنائِيَّةِ.

India and Japan exchanged agricultural goods and advanced technology under bilateral agreements.

trade exchange **تَبادُلٌ تِجارِيٌّ**

أَعْلَنَتْ أَلْمانْيا عَنْ خُطَّةٍ لِتَعْزيزِ التَّبادُلِ التِّجارِيِّ مَعَ الدُّوَلِ الإِفْريقِيَّةِ.

Germany announced a plan to boost trade exchange with African countries.

to adopt economic policies • تَبَنٍّ **تَبَنّى سِياساتٍ اقْتِصادِيَّةً**

تَبَنَّتِ النُّرْويجُ سِياساتٍ اقْتِصادِيَّةً صَديقَةً لِلْبيئَةِ لِتَقْليلِ انْبِعاثاتِ الكَرْبونِ.

Norway has adopted environmentally friendly economic policies to reduce carbon emissions.

trade **تِجارَةٌ**

شَهِدَتِ البَرازيلُ زِيادَةً في التِّجارَةِ مَعَ الدُّوَلِ الآسْيَوِيَّةِ خِلالَ السَّنَواتِ القَليلَةِ الماضِيَةِ.

Brazil has seen an increase in trade with Asian countries in recent years.

Note that تِجارَةٌ could also mean 'commerce' or 'business' in different contexts. In this sentence, it specifically refers to 'trade' between countries.

تِجارَةٌ حُرَّةٌ free trade

تُعْتَبَرُ الدَّنِمارْكُ نَموذَجًا لِلتِّجارَةِ الحُرَّةِ بِفَضْلِ سياساتِها اللّيبْرالِيَّةِ.

Denmark is a model for free trade thanks to its liberal policies.

تِجارَةٌ دَوْلِيَّةٌ international trade

شَهِدَتِ التِّجارَةُ الدَّوْلِيَّةُ بَيْنَ كَندا والمَكْسيكِ تَوَسُّعًا بِفَضْلِ الاِتِّفاقِيَّةِ الثُّلاثِيَّةِ مَعَ الوِلاياتِ المُتَّحِدَةِ.

International trade between Canada and Mexico has expanded thanks to the trilateral agreement with the United States.

تِجارِيٌّ commercial, trade-

تَتَمَتَّعُ دَوْلَةُ قَطَرَ بِمَوْقِعٍ تِجارِيٍّ قَوِيٍّ، مِمّا يَجْعَلُها مَحَطَّةً رَئيسِيَّةً لِلتِّجارَةِ العالَمِيَّةِ.

Qatar enjoys a strong commercial position, making it a major hub for global trade.

تَحَدٍّ اقْتِصادِيٌّ economic challenge

تُواجِهُ أسْتُرالْيا تَحَدِّيًا اقْتِصادِيًّا حَقيقِيًّا بِسَبَبِ النَّقْصِ الحادِّ في القُوى العامِلَةِ.

Australia is facing a real economic challenge due to a severe labor shortage.

تَخْفيضٌ جُمْرُكِيٌّ customs reduction

أَعْلَنَتِ الحُكومَةُ المِصْرِيَّةُ عَنْ تَخْفيضٍ جُمْرُكِيٍّ عَلى السِّلَعِ الغِذائِيَّةِ المُسْتَوْرَدَةِ.

The Egyptian government announced a customs reduction on imported food goods.

تَراجَعَ • تَراجُعٌ to decline, decrease

تَراجَعَ مُعَدَّلُ النُّمُوِّ الاِقْتِصادِيِّ في البَرازيلِ بِشَكْلٍ مَلْحوظٍ خِلالَ الرُّبْعِ الأَخيرِ.

The rate of economic growth in Brazil has notably declined during the last quarter.

تَراجُعٌ في وارِداتٍ decrease in imports

شَهِدَتِ الهِنْدُ تَراجُعًا في وارِداتِ النِّفْطِ بِسَبَبِ العُقوباتِ عَلى إيرانَ.

India has seen a decline in oil imports due to sanctions on Iran.

export **تَصْديرٌ**

تَعمَلُ الأُرْدُنُ على زِيادَةِ تَصْديرِ مُنْتَجاتِها الزِّراعِيَّةِ إلى الأَسْواقِ الأوروبِّيَّةِ.

Jordan is working on increasing the export of its agricultural products to European markets.

cooperative **تَعاوُنِيٌّ**

تُشيرُ الاتِّفاقِيّاتُ التَّعاوُنِيَّةُ بَيْنَ كَندا وَالمَكْسيك إلى عَلاقاتٍ تِجارِيَّةٍ مُتطَوِّرَةٍ.

Cooperative agreements between Canada and Mexico indicate advanced trade relations.

to negotiate • تَفاوُضٌ **تَفاوَضَ**

تَفاوَضَتِ اليابانُ وَكورْيا الجَنوبِيَّةُ حَوْلَ اتِّفاقِ تِجارَةٍ حُرَّةٍ جَديدٍ.

Japan and South Korea negotiated a new free trade agreement.

In the phrase اِتِّفاقِ تِجارَةٍ حُرَّةٍ جَديدٍ, the adjective جَديدٍ is positioned at the end of the idaafa construction and is masculine in form. This is because it refers to the first noun اِتِّفاق, which is also masculine, indicating a new agreement. The adjective does not describe the second part of the idaafa تِجارَةٍ حُرَّةٍ, which is feminine. Additionally, the placement of the adjective at the end adheres to the rule that nothing can be inserted between the elements of an idaafa, thereby maintaining its structural integrity.

An alternative to the idaafa construction is using the preposition لِـ (for/to), which allows the adjective to be placed immediately after the noun it describes. In this alternative construction, the same phrase could be reformulated as اِتِّفاقٍ جَديدٍ لِلتِّجارَةِ الحُرَّةِ.

Here, جَديدٍ directly follows اِتِّفاقٍ, the noun it is describing, and لِـ is used to indicate the relationship between اِتِّفاقٍ جَديدٍ (new agreement) and تِجارَةٍ حُرَّةٍ (free trade). This allows for greater clarity in specifying what the adjective is describing, without disrupting the structural rules of Arabic grammar.

economic integration **تَكامُلٌ اقْتِصادِيٌّ**

يُعزِّزُ الاتِّحادُ الأوروبِّيُّ التَّكامُلَ الاقْتِصادِيَّ بَيْنَ الدُّوَلِ الأَعْضاءِ مِنْ خِلالِ سِياساتِهِ المُوَحَّدَةِ.

The European Union promotes economic integration among its member states through its unified policies.

تنافُسِيٌّ
competitive

تُوَتِّرُ حِدَّةُ المُنافَسَةِ بَيْنَ الوِلاياتِ المُتَّحِدَةِ وَالصِّينِ عَلى الأَسْواقِ العالَمِيَّةِ.

The competitive rivalry between the United States and China affects global markets.

ثُنائِيٌّ
bilateral

تَمَّ تَوْقيعُ اتِّفاقٍ تِجارِيٍّ ثُنائِيٍّ بَيْنَ الأُرْدُنِّ وَسِنْغافورَةَ لِتَعْزيزِ التِّجارَةِ الثُّنائِيَّةِ.

A bilateral trade agreement was signed between Jordan and Singapore to enhance bilateral trade.

جُمْرُكِيٌّ
customs-

أَقَرَّتِ السُّعودِيَّةُ تَعْديلاتٍ جُمْرُكِيَّةً لِتَسْهيلِ الاِسْتيرادِ وَالتَّصْديرِ.

Saudi Arabia approved customs modifications to facilitate import and export.

حَجْمُ تِجارَةٍ • أَحْجامٌ
trade volume

اِرْتَفَعَ حَجْمُ التِّجارَةِ بَيْنَ الإماراتِ وَالصِّينِ بِشَكْلٍ مَلْحوظٍ في العَقْدِ الماضي.

The volume of trade between the UAE and China has significantly increased in the past decade.

حُرٌّ
free

يُمَثِّلُ السّوقُ الحُرُّ الجُزْءَ الأَكْبَرَ مِنَ الاِقْتِصادِ الأَمْريكِيِّ.

The free market constitutes the larger part of the American economy.

حَرَّرَ تِجارَةً • تَحْريرٌ
to liberalize trade

حَرَّرَتْ سويسْرا تِجارَةَ الأَدْوِيَةِ لِتَحْقيقِ أَسْعارٍ أَكْثَرَ تَنافُسِيَّةً.

Switzerland liberalized the pharmaceutical trade to achieve more competitive prices.

حُرِّيَّةُ تِجارَةٍ
freedom of trade

تَسْعى المَمْلَكَةُ المُتَّحِدَةُ لِتَحْقيقِ حُرِّيَّةِ تِجارَةٍ أَكْبَرَ مَعَ دُوَلِ الاِتِّحادِ الأوروبِّيِّ بَعْدَ البِريكْسِتْ.

The United Kingdom is aiming to achieve greater trade freedom with European Union countries after Brexit.

to improve the trade balance • تَحْسينٌ **حَسَّنَ الميزانَ التِّجارِيَّ**

حَسَّنَتْ أَلْمانْيا الميزانَ التِّجارِيَّ مَعَ الدُّوَلِ الآسْيَوِيَّةِ مِنْ خِلالِ التَّعاوُنِ المُتَزايِدِ.

Germany improved the trade balance with Asian countries through increasing cooperation.

to improve trade relations • تَحْسينٌ **حَسَّنَ عَلاقاتٍ تِجارِيَّةٍ**

تَعْمَلُ اليونانُ عَلى تَحْسينِ العَلاقاتِ التِّجارِيَّةِ مَعَ دُوَلِ شَرْقِ أوروبّا.

Greece is working to improve trade relations with Eastern European countries.

market share • حِصَصٌ **حِصَّةُ سوقٍ**

تَسْعى البَرازيلُ لِزِيادَةِ حِصَّةِ السّوقِ مِنَ القَهْوَةِ في الصّينِ.

Brazil is aiming to increase its market share of coffee in China.

trade protection **حِمايَةٌ تِجارِيَّةٌ**

تَبَنَّتِ اليابانُ سِياساتِ حِمايَةٍ تِجارِيَّةٍ لِحِمايَةِ صِناعَتِها الزِّراعِيَّةِ.

Japan has adopted trade protection policies to protect its agricultural industry.

protection of local industries **حِمايَةُ صِناعاتٍ مَحَلِّيَّةٍ**

يُعْتَبَرُ القانونُ البَرْلَمانِيُّ الجَديدُ خُطْوَةً هامَّةً لِحِمايَةِ الصِّناعاتِ المَحَلِّيَّةِ في مِصْرَ.

The new parliamentary law is considered an important step for the protection of local industries in Egypt.

to protect • حِمايَةٌ **حَمى**

حَمَتِ الحُكومَةُ السُّعودِيَّةُ صِناعَةَ النِّفْطِ مِنَ الأَزْمَةِ الاقْتِصادِيَّةِ.

The Saudi government has shielded the oil industry from the economic crisis.

bank transfer **حَوالَةٌ مَصْرِفِيَّةٌ**

أُرْسِلَتْ حَوالَةٌ مَصْرِفِيَّةٌ كَبيرَةٌ مِنَ الصّينِ إلى لُبْنانَ لِدَعْمِ البَنْكِ المَرْكَزِيِّ.

A large banking transfer was sent from China to Lebanon to support the Central Bank.

foreign, international — **خارِجِيٌّ**

تُعْتَبَرُ السِّلَعُ الخارِجِيَّةُ مِنَ الوِلاياتِ المُتَّحِدَةِ الأَمْريكِيَّةِ مَطْلوبَةً بِشِدَّةٍ في الأَسْواقِ العَرَبِيَّةِ.

Foreign goods from the United States are highly sought after in Arab markets.

to reduce — **خَفَضَ = خَفَّضَ** • خَفْضٌ = تَخْفيضٌ

خَفَضَ بَنْكُ اليابانِ المَرْكَزِيُّ مُعَدَّلاتِ الفائِدَةِ لِمواجَهَةِ التَّضَخُّمِ.

The Bank of Japan has lowered interest rates to combat inflation.

to reduce customs duties — **خَفَّضَ رُسومًا جُمْرُكِيَّةً** • تَخْفيضٌ

بَعْدَ مُفاوَضاتٍ طَويلَةٍ، خَفَّضَتِ الأَرْجَنْتينُ الرُّسومَ الجُمْرُكِيَّةَ عَلى البَضائِعِ البَرازيلِيَّةِ.

After lengthy negotiations, Argentina lowered customs duties on Brazilian goods.

role of foreign investment in development — **دَوْرُ اسْتِثْمارٍ أَجْنَبِيٍّ في تَنْمِيَةٍ** • أَدْوارٌ

لَعِبَ الاِسْتِثْمارُ الأَجْنَبِيُّ دَوْرًا مُهِمًّا في تَنْمِيَةِ البِنْيَةِ التَّحْتِيَّةِ في الهِنْدِ.

Foreign investment has played an important role in the development of infrastructure in India.

international — **دَوْلِيٌّ**

يَدْعَمُ البَنْكُ الدَّوْلِيُّ لِلْإِنْشاءِ وَالتَّعْميرِ مَشاريعَ تَنْمَوِيَّةً في الدُّوَلِ الإِفْريقِيَّةِ.

The International Bank for Reconstruction and Development supports developmental projects in African countries.

capital — **رَأْسُ مالٍ** • رُؤوسُ أَمْوالٍ

زادَتْ شَرِكَةُ أَبِلِ الأَمْريكِيَّةُ رَأْسَ مالِها بَعْدَ أَنْ زادَتْ مَبيعاتُ الأَيْفونِ.

The American company Apple increased its capital after iPhone sales increased.

customs duty — **رَسْمٌ جُمْرُكِيٌّ** • رُسومٌ

أَعْلَنَتِ الهَيْئَةُ العامَّةُ لِلْجَمارِكِ في المَكْسيكِ عَنْ رَفْعِ الرَّسْمِ الجُمْرُكِيِّ عَلى البَضائِعِ الصّينِيَّةِ.

The General Customs Authority in Mexico announced the increase of the customs duty on Chinese goods.

to increase • زِيادَةٌ **زادَ**

زادَتِ الإماراتُ العَرَبِيَّةُ المُتَّحِدَةُ الإنْفاقَ عَلى البِنْيَةِ التَّحْتِيَّةِ لِدَعْمِ النُّمُوِّ الاقْتِصادِيِّ.

The United Arab Emirates increased spending on infrastructure to support economic growth.

agricultural **زِراعِيٌّ**

القِطاعُ الزِّراعِيُّ هُوَ الأَكْثَرُ تَضَرُّرًا مِنْ تَقَلُّباتِ أَسْعارِ الصَّرْفِ في البَرازيلِ.

The agricultural sector is the most affected by exchange rate fluctuations in Brazil.

trade increase **زِيادَةُ تِجارَةٍ**

شَهِدَتْ التِّجارَةُ بَيْنَ كَنَدا وَمِصْرَ زِيادَةً مَعَ اسْتِمْرارِ التَّحْسيناتِ في العَلاقاتِ الثُّنائِيَّةِ.

There was an increase in trade between Canada and Egypt, with ongoing improvements in bilateral relations.

increase in exports **زِيادَةٌ في صادِراتٍ**

أَدَّتْ سِياساتُ الحُكومَةِ الجَديدَةِ إلى زِيادَةٍ في صادِراتِ الأُرْزِ مِنَ الهِنْدِ.

The new government's policies led to an increase in rice exports from India.

exchange rate • أَسْعارُ صَرْفٍ **سِعْرُ صَرْفٍ**

تَتَأَرْجَحُ قيمَةُ الدّينارِ العِراقِيِّ مُقابِلَ الدّولارِ الأَمْريكِيِّ، وَهُوَ ما يَعْكِسُ تَقَلُّباتِ سِعْرِ صَرْفِ العُمْلَةِ.

The value of the Iraqi Dinar fluctuates against the US Dollar, reflecting the volatility of the exchange rate.

supply chain • سَلاسِلُ **سِلْسِلَةُ تَوْريدٍ**

تُعَدُّ سِلْسِلَةُ التَّوْريدِ البَحْرِيَّةُ العالَمِيَّةُ رَكيزَةً رَئيسِيَّةً في تِجارَةِ النِّفْطِ.

The global maritime supply chain is a major pillar in oil trade.

trade good • سِلَعٌ **سِلْعَةٌ تِجارِيَّةٌ**

تَمَّتِ الاسْتِعانَةُ بِالذَّكاءِ الاصْطِناعِيِّ لِتَتَبُّعِ وَمُراقَبَةِ حَرَكَةِ السِّلْعَةِ التِّجارِيَّةِ عَبْرَ الحُدودِ.

Artificial intelligence was used to track and monitor the movement of commercial goods across borders.

سوقُ عُمُلاتٍ • أَسْواقٌ **currency market**

شَهِدَ سوقُ العُمُلاتِ الأوروبِّيُّ تَذَبْذُبًا كَبيرًا بِسَبَبِ تَوَتُّراتِ الحَرْبِ التِّجارِيَّةِ بَيْنَ الصّينِ وَالوِلاياتِ المُتَّحِدَةِ.

The European foreign exchange market saw significant fluctuations due to the trade war tensions between China and the United States.

سوقٌ مُشْتَرَكَةٌ **common market**

يُعْتَبَرُ الاتِّحادُ الأوروبِّيُّ سوقًا مُشْتَرَكَةً ذاتَ نُفوذٍ قَوِيٍّ في التِّجارَةِ العالَمِيَّةِ.

The European Union is considered a common market with strong influence in global trade.

سِياسَةُ بَنْكٍ مَرْكَزِيٍّ **central bank policies**

تَقومُ سِياسَةُ البَنْكِ المَرْكَزِيِّ اللُّبْنانِيِّ بِتَنْفيذِ تَدابيرَ جَديدَةٍ لِلْحَدِّ مِنَ التَّضَخُّمِ.

The policy of the Central Bank of Lebanon is implementing new measures to curb inflation.

صادِراتٌ *pl.* **exports**

اِسْتَعادَتِ الصّادِراتُ الأُرْدُنِّيَّةُ لِلْفوسْفاتِ قُوَّتَها بَعْدَ سَنَواتٍ مِنَ التَّراجُعِ.

Jordanian phosphate exports regained their strength after years of decline.

صادِراتٌ وَوارِداتٌ *pl.* **exports and imports**

تَتَوازَنُ صادِراتُ وَوارِداتُ الأَغْذِيَةِ في مِصْرَ، مِمّا يُشيرُ إِلى تَحَسُّنٍ في القِطاعِ الزِّراعِيِّ.

Food imports and exports in Egypt are balanced, pointing to an improvement in the agricultural sector.

صَدَّرَ • تَصْديرٌ **to export**

صَدَّرَ العِراقُ مِلْيونَيْ بِرْميلٍ نِفْطِيٍّ يَوْمِيًّا الى الصّينِ خِلالَ العامِ الماضي.

Iraq exported two million barrels of oil per day to China during the last year.

global — عالَميٌّ

تَأَثَّرَتِ الاِقْتِصاداتُ العالَمِيَّةُ بِشِدَّةٍ بِالْأَزْمَةِ النِّفْطِيَّةِ السُّعودِيَّةِ.

Global economies were severely affected by the Saudi oil crisis.

to strengthen — عَزَّزَ • تَعْزيزٌ

عَزَّزَ المَغْرِبُ مَوْقِعَهُ كَأَحَدِ الوِجْهاتِ السِّياحِيَّةِ الرَّئيسِيَّةِ في شَمالِ إِفْريقْيا.

Morocco strengthened its position as one of the major tourist destinations in North Africa.

to promote/boost trade — عَزَّزَ تِجارَةً

عَزَّزَتْ قَطَرُ التِّجارَةَ بِشَكْلٍ كَبيرٍ مِنْ خِلالِ اسْتِثْماراتِها في البِنْيَةِ التَّحْتِيَّةِ.

Qatar greatly enhanced trade through its investments in infrastructure.

> مِنْ خِلالِ is a prepositional phrase that often translates to 'through,' 'by means of,' or 'via,' and it is used to explain the method, medium, or process involved in achieving something. Here, it serves to elaborate on the means by which Germany improved its trade balance with Asian countries.

trade relation — عَلاقَةٌ تِجارِيَّةٌ

تَطَوَّرَتِ العَلاقَةُ التِّجارِيَّةُ بَيْنَ الجَزائِرِ وَتونِسَ بِشَكْلٍ مَلْحوظٍ خِلالَ العَقْدِ الأَخيرِ.

The trade relationship between Algeria and Tunisia has developed significantly over the past decade.

currency — عُمْلَةٌ

شَهِدَتِ العُمْلَةُ التّونِسِيَّةُ تَقَلُّباتٍ كَبيرَةً بِسَبَبِ الاِضْطِراباتِ الاِقْتِصادِيَّةِ الدَّوْلِيَّةِ.

The Tunisian currency saw significant fluctuations due to international economic disturbances.

unreliable — غَيْرُ مَوْثوقٍ بِهِ

تَمَّ اعْتِبارُ الدّينارِ اللّيبِيِّ غَيْرَ مَوْثوقٍ بِهِ بِسَبَبِ الأَزَماتِ الاِقْتِصادِيَّةِ المُتَكَرِّرَةِ.

The Libyan dinar was considered untrustworthy due to recurring economic crises.

قِطاعٌ خاصٌّ **private sector**

اِكْتَسَبَ القِطاعُ الخاصُّ في الكُوَيْتِ دَوْرًا أَكْبَرَ في تَنْشيطِ الاِقْتِصادِ الوَطَنِيِّ.

The private sector in Kuwait has gained a greater role in stimulating the national economy.

قِطاعٌ عامٌّ **public sector**

تُعاني الصّينُ مِنْ تَحَدِّياتٍ كَبيرَةٍ في القِطاعِ العامِّ نَظَرًا لِلزِّيادَةِ السَّريعَةِ في الدُّيونِ الحُكوميَّةِ.

China is suffering from significant challenges in the public sector due to the rapid increase in government debt.

قَلَّلَ • تَقْليلٌ **to reduce, decrease**

قَلَّلَتِ الحُكومَةُ الإماراتِيَّةُ الضَّرائِبَ عَلى الشَّرِكاتِ الصَّغيرَةِ وَالمُتَوَسِّطَةِ لِتَعْزيزِ النُّمُوِّ الاِقْتِصادِيِّ.

The UAE government has reduced taxes on small and medium enterprises to boost economic growth.

قَلَّلَ العَجْزَ التِّجارِيَّ **to reduce the trade deficit**

بَعْدَ سَنَواتٍ مِنَ الجُهودِ المُسْتَمِرَّةِ، تَمَكَّنَتِ الأَرْجَنْتينُ مِنْ تَقْليلِ العَجْزِ التِّجارِيِّ مَعَ البَرازيلِ.

After years of ongoing efforts, Argentina managed to reduce its trade deficit with Brazil.

قُوَّةٌ اقْتِصادِيَّةٌ عالَمِيَّةٌ • قُوًى \ قِوًى **global economic power**

تُعْتَبَرُ الوِلاياتُ المُتَّحِدَةُ قُوَّةً اقْتِصادِيَّةً عالَمِيَّةً تُؤَثِّرُ عَلى الأَسْواقِ العالَمِيَّةِ.

The United States is considered a global economic power that affects international markets.

مُؤَشِّرٌ اقْتِصادِيٌّ **economic indicator**

أَظْهَرَ المُؤَشِّرُ الاِقْتِصادِيُّ الرَّئيسِيُّ في المَمْلَكَةِ المُتَّحِدَةِ نُمُوًّا قَوِيًّا في الرُّبْعِ الأَخيرِ مِنَ العامِ.

The key economic indicator in the United Kingdom showed strong growth in the last quarter of the year.

مُتَبادَلٌ **reciprocal**

تَضْمَنُ الطَّبيعَةُ المُتَبادَلَةُ لاتِّفاقاتِ التِّجارَةِ الدَّوْلِيَّةِ اسْتِفادَةَ البِلادِ بِشَكْلٍ مُتَبادَلٍ مِنْ تَبادُلِ السِّلَعِ وَالخِدْماتِ.

The reciprocal nature of international trade agreements ensures that countries benefit mutually from the exchange of goods and services.

multilateral **مُتعَدِّدُ الأَطْرافِ**

تَتواصَلُ المُفاوَضاتُ مُتعَدِّدَةُ الأَطْرافِ بَيْنَ الدُوَلِ الأوروبِّيَّةِ حَوْلَ اتِّفاقِيَّةِ التِّجارَةِ الحُرَّةِ.

Multilateral negotiations among European countries on the free trade agreement are ongoing.

negotiated **مُتفاوَضٌ عَلَيْهِ**

وَقَّعَتِ الدَّوْلَتانِ اتِّفاقِيَّةً تِجارِيَّةً جَديدَةً، حَيْثُ تَمَّتِ المُوافَقَةُ عَلى جَميعِ النِّقاطِ المُتفاوَضِ عَلَيْها، وَالَّتي سَتُساهِمُ في تَعْزيزِالتِّجارَةِ بَيْنَهُما.

The two countries have signed a new trade agreement, where consensus has been reached on all the negotiated points, which will contribute to enhancing trade between them.

balanced **مُتوازِنٌ**

بَعْدَ سِلْسِلَةٍ مِنَ الإِصْلاحاتِ الاقْتِصادِيَّةِ، أَصْبَحَ الاقْتِصادُ الفَرَنْسِيُّ مُتوازِنًا بِشَكْلٍ أَكْبَرَ.

After a series of economic reforms, the French economy has become more balanced.

local, domestic **مَحَلِّيٌّ**

تَتَمَتَّعُ المُنْتَجاتُ المَحَلِّيَّةُ في السّوقِ الإيطالِيَّةِ بِشَعْبِيَّةٍ كَبيرَةٍ بَيْنَ المُسْتَهْلِكينَ.

Local products in the Italian market are highly popular among consumers.

sustainable **مُسْتَدامٌ**

يُرَكِّزُ الاتِّحادُ الأوروبِّيُّ عَلى تَطْويرِ اسْتِراتيجِيّاتٍ تِجارِيَّةٍ مُسْتَدامَةٍ لِلْحِفاظِ عَلى البيئَةِ.

The European Union is focusing on developing sustainable trade strategies to preserve the environment.

investment climate **مُناخٌ اسْتِثْمارِيٌّ**

تَمْتَلِكُ دُبَيُّ مُناخًا اسْتِثْمارِيًّا مُغْرِيًا لِلْمُسْتَثْمِرينَ الدَّوْلِيّينَ بِفَضْلِ سِياسَتِها الاقْتِصادِيَّةِ القَوِيَّةِ.

Dubai possesses an attractive investment climate for international investors due to its strong economic policy.

مِنْطَقَةٌ تِجارِيَّةٌ حُرَّةٌ • مَناطِقُ **free trade zone**

تَمَّ الإِعْلانُ عَنْ خُطَطٍ لِإِنْشاءِ مِنْطَقَةٍ تِجارِيَّةٍ حُرَّةٍ جَديدَةٍ في أَبو ظَبْي لِجَذْبِ الشَّرِكاتِ العالَمِيَّةِ.

Plans have been announced to create a new free trade zone in Abu Dhabi to attract global companies.

مُنَظَّمَةُ التِّجارَةِ العالَمِيَّةِ **the World Trade Organization (WTO)**

أَصْدَرَتْ مُنَظَّمَةُ التِّجارَةِ العالَمِيَّةِ تَقْريرًا حَوْلَ التَّأْثيراتِ الاِقْتِصادِيَّةِ لِلْجائِحَةِ.

The World Trade Organization issued a report on the economic impacts of the pandemic.

مَوْثوقٌ بِهِ **reliable**

إِنَّ البَنْكَ الدَّوْلِيَّ مَصْدَرُ مَعْلوماتٍ مَوْثوقٌ بِهِ في مَجالِ الاِقْتِصادِ العالَمِيِّ.

The World Bank is a reliable source of information in the field of global economics.

ميزانٌ تِجارِيٌّ • مَوازينُ **trade balance**

شَهِدَ الميزانُ التِّجارِيُّ لِلْهِنْدِ مَعَ الوِلاياتِ المُتَّحِدَةِ تَحَسُّنًا مَلْحوظًا العامَ الماضِيَ.

India's trade balance with the United States saw a significant improvement last year.

ميزانُ مَدْفوعاتٍ **balance of payments**

أَظْهَرَ ميزانُ مَدْفوعاتِ اليابانِ نُمُوًّا قَوِيًّا في الرُّبْعِ الثّاني مِنَ العامِ.

Japan's balance of payments showed strong growth in the second quarter of the year.

ميناءٌ • مَوانٍ \ مَوانِئُ **port**

ميناءُ دُبَيَّ هُوَ أَحَدُ أَكْبَرِ المَوانِئِ التِّجارِيَّةِ في الشَّرْقِ الأَوْسَطِ.

Dubai Port is one of the largest commercial ports in the Middle East.

نِسْبَةُ تَضَخُّمٍ • نِسَبٌ **inflation rate**

وَصَلَتْ نِسْبَةُ التَّضَخُّمِ في البَرازيلِ إِلى مُسْتَوًى قِياسِيٍّ في الأَشْهُرِ القَليلَةِ الماضِيَةِ.

The inflation rate in Brazil has reached a record level in recent months.

نَظَّمَ تِجارَةً • تَنْظيمٌ **to regulate trade**

نَظَّمَ المَغْرِبُ تِجارَةً حُرَّةً مَعَ الاِتِّحادِ الأوروبِّيِّ لِتَحْسينِ العَلاقاتِ الاِقْتِصادِيَّةِ.

Morocco has organized free trade with the European Union to improve economic relations.

نَقْدٌ أَجْنَبِيٌّ **foreign currency**

يَحْتَفِظُ البَنْكُ المَرْكَزِيُّ الألْمانِيُّ بِكَمِّيّاتٍ كَبيرَةٍ مِنَ النَّقْدِ الأَجْنَبِيِّ.

The German central bank holds large amounts of foreign currency.

نَوَّعَ • تَنْويعٌ **to diversify**

نَوَّعَتْ شَرِكاتُ النِّفْطِ السُّعودِيَّةُ الاِسْتِثْماراتِ لِتَقْليلِ الاِعْتِمادِ عَلى النِّفْطِ.

Saudi oil companies diversified investments to reduce dependence on oil.

وارِداتٌ *pl.* **imports**

اِرْتَفَعَتْ وارِداتُ السِّلَعِ الأَمْريكِيَّةِ إلى اليابانِ بِنِسْبَةٍ كَبيرَةٍ العامَ الماضِيَ.

Imports of American goods to Japan increased significantly last year.

وازَنَ • مُوازَنَةٌ **to balance**

وازَنَتِ الحُكومَةُ البِريطانِيَّةُ بَيْنَ النُّمُوِّ الاِقْتِصادِيِّ وَالاِسْتِدامَةِ البيئِيَّةِ في خُطَّتِها الجَديدَةِ.

The British government balanced economic growth and environmental sustainability in its new plan.

4.1.3.1 Mini-Articles

Track **9**

في ظِلِّ أَزْمَةٍ اقْتِصادِيَّةٍ مُتَصاعِدَةٍ، أَظْهَرَتِ اتِّجاهاتُ التِّجارَةِ العالَمِيَّةِ تَراجُعًا مَلْحوظًا. أَجْرَتِ العَديدُ مِنَ الدُّوَلِ إِعادَةَ هَيْكَلَةٍ لِدُيونِها، وَذَلِكَ في مُحاوَلَةٍ لِتَعْزيزِ الاِسْتِثْمارِ الأَجْنَبِيِّ المُباشِرِ. بِالرَّغْمِ مِنْ هَذِهِ الجُهودِ، يَتَوَقَّعُ خُبَراءُ الاِقْتِصادِ انْخِفاضًا مُسْتَمِرًّا في النُّمُوِّ الاِقْتِصادِيِّ.

In the face of an escalating economic crisis, global trade trends have shown a noticeable decline. Many countries have undertaken debt restructuring in an attempt to enhance foreign direct investment. Despite these efforts, economic experts expect a continued decrease in economic growth.

أَعْلَنَتْ مُنَظَّمَةُ التِّجارَةِ العالَمِيَّةِ عَنِ اتِّفاقِيَّةِ تَبادُلٍ تِجارِيٍّ جَديدَةٍ تَهْدُفُ إِلى تَحْريرِ التِّجارَةِ وَتَحْسينِ الميزانِ التِّجارِيِّ لِلدُّوَلِ الأَقَلِّ نُمُوًّا. في هَذا السِّياقِ، سَيَتِمُّ تَخْفيضُ الرُّسومِ الجُمْرُكِيَّةِ وَالحُصولُ عَلى اسْتِثْمارٍ خارِجِيٍّ أَكْبَرَ، وَهُوَ الأَمْرُ الَّذي يُنْتَظَرُ أَنْ يُنَشِّطَ سوقَ العُمُلاتِ.

The World Trade Organization has announced a new trade agreement aimed at liberalizing trade and improving the trade balance for less-developed countries. In this context, customs duties will be reduced, and greater foreign investment will be obtained, which is expected to stimulate the currency market.

تَسْعى مِصْرُ لِزِيادَةِ صادِراتِها وَتَحْسينِ مُناخِ الاسْتِثْمارِ، وَذَلِكَ مِنْ خِلالِ تَبَنّي سِياساتٍ اقْتِصادِيَّةٍ تُشَجِّعُ عَلى الاسْتِثْمارِ الأَجْنَبِيِّ. يَتَضَمَّنُ ذَلِكَ خَفْضَ الرُّسومِ الجُمْرُكِيَّةِ وَتَعْزيزَ الحُرِّيَّةِ التِّجارِيَّةِ. الهَدَفُ الأَساسِيُّ هُوَ تَحْقيقُ نُمُوٍّ اقْتِصادِيٍّ مُسْتَدامٍ وَتَقْليلُ العَجْزِ التِّجارِيِّ.

Egypt is seeking to increase its exports and improve the investment climate by adopting economic policies that encourage foreign investment. This includes reducing customs duties and enhancing trade freedom. The primary goal is to achieve sustainable economic growth and reduce the trade deficit.

4.1.3.2 Analysis: Exchange Rates

Track **10**

أَسْعارُ الصَّرْفِ وَأَثَرُها عَلى التِّجارَةِ العالَمِيَّةِ: تَحْليلٌ اقْتِصادِيٌّ

في سِياقِ الاقْتِصادِ العالَمِيِّ، تَلْعَبُ أَسْعارُ الصَّرْفِ دَوْرًا بالِغَ الأَهَمِّيَّةِ في تَحْديدِ اتِّجاهاتِ التِّجارَةِ العالَمِيَّةِ. تُؤَثِّرُ هَذِهِ الأَسْعارُ بِشَكْلٍ مُباشِرٍ عَلى التِّجارَةِ الدَّوْلِيَّةِ، حَيْثُ إِنَّ العُمْلَةَ القَوِيَّةَ يُمْكِنُ أَنْ تَجْعَلَ الاسْتيرادَ أَرْخَصَ وَالتَّصْديرَ أَغْلى. العَكْسُ صَحيحٌ عِنْدَما تَكونُ العُمْلَةُ ضَعيفَةً. هَذا يَدُلُّ عَلى العَلاقَةِ الوَثيقَةِ بَيْنَ سِعْرِ الصَّرْفِ وَالتِّجارَةِ الدَّوْلِيَّةِ.

يُراقِبُ القِطاعُ الخاصُّ بِعِنايَةٍ تَقَلُّباتِ سوقِ العُمُلاتِ وَنِسَبِ التَّضَخُّمِ، حَيْثُ يُمْكِنُ أَنْ تُؤَثِّرَ هَذِهِ العَوامِلُ في الاسْتِثْمارِ الأَجْنَبِيِّ المُباشِرِ وَالاسْتِثْمارِ الخارِجِيِّ. قَدْ تُعَرِّضُ التَّغَيُّراتُ الحادَّةُ في سِعْرِ الصَّرْفِ الشَّرِكاتِ لِخَطَرِ التَّذَبْذُبِ، مِمّا يُشيرُ إِلى ارْتِفاعِ الأَسْعارِ بِشَكْلٍ مُفاجِئٍ وَغَيْرِ مُتَوَقَّعٍ.

مِنْ ناحِيَةٍ أُخْرى، يُمْكِنُ أَنْ يُسْهِمَ نِظامُ سِعْرِ الصَّرْفِ الثّابِتِ في خَلْقِ مُناخٍ اسْتِثْمارِيٍّ مَوْثوقٍ بِهِ. في هَذِهِ الحالَةِ، يُمْكِنُ لِلْبَنْكِ المَرْكَزِيِّ أَنْ يَسْتَخْدِمَ مَخْزونَ النَّقْدِ الأَجْنَبِيِّ لِلتَّدَخُّلِ في سوقِ العُمُلاتِ وَالحِفاظِ عَلى سِعْرِ الصَّرْفِ عِنْدَ مُسْتَوىً مُعَيَّنٍ.

يُمْكِنُ أَنْ تُواجِهَ الدُّوَلُ الَّتي تَتَبَنّى سِياسَةَ الاِقْتِصادِ المَفْتوحِ تَحَدِّياتٍ مُرْتَبِطَةً بِتَقَلُّباتِ أَسْعارِ الصَّرْفِ. في هَذا السِّياقِ، يُمْكِنُ أَنْ تَسْتَفيدَ الاِتِّفاقِيّاتُ التِّجارِيَّةُ الثُّنائِيَّةُ وَمُتَعَدِّدَةُ الأَطْرافِ مِنْ تَحْقيقِ تَكامُلٍ اقْتِصادِيٍّ أَكْبَرَ، مِمّا يُقَلِّلُ مِنَ التَّقَلُّباتِ النّاجِمَةِ عَنِ التَّغَيُّراتِ في سِعْرِ الصَّرْفِ.

Exchange Rates and Their Impact on Global Trade: An Economic Analysis

In the context of the global economy, exchange rates play a crucial role in determining the trends of global trade. These rates directly affect international trade, as a strong currency can make imports cheaper and exports more expensive. The opposite is true when the currency is weak. This indicates the close relationship between the exchange rate and international trade.

The private sector carefully monitors currency market fluctuations and inflation rates, as these factors can affect foreign direct investment and foreign investment. Sharp changes in the exchange rate can expose companies to the risk of volatility, indicating sudden and unexpected price increases.

On the other hand, a fixed exchange rate system can contribute to creating a reliable investment climate. In this case, the central bank can use foreign currency reserves to intervene in the currency market and maintain the exchange rate at a certain level.

Countries that adopt an open economy policy may face challenges associated with exchange rate fluctuations. In this context, bilateral and multilateral trade agreements can benefit from achieving greater economic integration, reducing the volatility resulting from changes in the exchange rate.

4.1.3.3 Informative Article: International Trade

Track **11**

التِّجارَةُ الدَّوْلِيَّةُ: الأَهَمِّيَّةُ وَالتَّحَدِّياتُ وَالفُرَصُ

تَلْعَبُ التِّجارَةُ الدَّوْلِيَّةُ دَوْرًا حَيَوِيًّا في الاِقْتِصادِ العالَمِيِّ، حَيْثُ تَسْمَحُ بِتَبادُلِ السِّلَعِ وَالخِدْماتِ عَبْرَ الحُدودِ الوَطَنِيَّةِ. غالِبًا ما يَتِمُّ تَنْظيمُ هَذِهِ التَّبادُلاتِ التِّجارِيَّةِ بِمُوجَبِ اتِّفاقِيّاتٍ تِجارِيَّةٍ، تَشْمَلُ الاِتِّفاقِيّاتِ الثُّنائِيَّةَ أَوِ المُتَعَدِّدَةَ الأَطْرافِ، تَحْتَ رِعايَةِ مُنَظَّمَةِ التِّجارَةِ العالَمِيَّةِ.

تُؤَثِّرُ السِّياساتُ الاِقْتِصادِيَّةُ الَّتي تَتَبَنّاها الدُّوَلُ بِشَكْلٍ كَبيرٍ عَلى اتِّجاهاتِ التِّجارَةِ العالَمِيَّةِ. بَعْضُ الدُّوَلِ تَعْتَمِدُ اقْتِصادًا مَفْتوحًا، يُشَجِّعُ الاِسْتِثْمارَ الأَجْنَبِيَّ المُباشِرَ وَتَحْريرَ التِّجارَةِ. وَهَذا يَعْني تَقْليلَ الرُّسومِ الجُمْرُكِيَّةِ، وَزِيادَةَ الاِسْتيرادِ وَالتَّصْديرِ، وَخَلْقَ سوقٍ مُشْتَرَكَةٍ مَعَ الدُّوَلِ الأُخْرى. قَدْ تَخْتارُ الدُّوَلُ الأُخْرى اقْتِصادًا مُغْلَقًا، حَيْثُ تَتِمُّ حِمايَةُ الصِّناعاتِ المَحَلِّيَّةِ مِنْ خِلالِ تَطْبيقِ رُسومٍ جُمْرُكِيَّةٍ عالِيَةٍ وَتَقْييدِ الاِسْتيرادِ.

يُعْتَبَرُ كُلٌّ مِنَ الاِسْتِثْمارِ الأَجْنَبِيِّ المُباشِرِ وَالشَّراكاتِ التَّعاوُنِيَّةِ أَيْضًا عَناصِرَ مُهِمَّةً في الاِقْتِصادِ العالَمِيِّ. تُساهِمُ هَذِهِ الاِسْتِثْماراتُ في إِجْمالِيِّ الدَّخْلِ القَوْمِيِّ لِلدَّوْلَةِ، وَتُشَجِّعُ عَلى تَنْمِيَةِ قِطاعاتٍ مُحَدَّدَةٍ في الاِقْتِصادِ، مِثْلِ القِطاعِ الخاصِّ.

لا تَخْلو التِّجارَةُ الدَّوْلِيَّةُ مِنَ التَّحَدِّياتِ. فَأَزَماتٌ اقْتِصادِيَّةٌ كَتَراجُعِ التِّجارَةِ أَوِ النُّمُوِّ الاقْتِصادِيِّ، يُمْكِنُ أَنْ تُضِرَّ بِحَجْمِ التِّجارَةِ وَتُؤَدِّيَ إِلى تَراجُعٍ في الوارِداتِ وَالصّادِراتِ. العَوامِلُ الأُخْرى، مِثْلُ سِعْرِ الصَّرْفِ، وَالنَّقْدِ الأَجْنَبِيِّ، وَالتَّضَخُّمِ يُمْكِنُ أَنْ تُؤَثِّرَ بِشَكْلٍ كَبيرٍ عَلى القُوَّةِ الاقْتِصادِيَّةِ العالَمِيَّةِ.

إِنَّ التِّجارَةَ الدَّوْلِيَّةَ مُعَقَّدَةٌ وَمُتَغَيِّرَةٌ، لَكِنَّها تُشَكِّلُ جُزْءًا لا يَتَجَزَّأُ مِنَ الاقْتِصادِ العالَمِيِّ. مِنْ خِلالِ فَهْمِها، يُمْكِنُنا العَمَلُ نَحْوَ تَحْقيقِ نُمُوٍّ اقْتِصادِيٍّ مُسْتَدامٍ وَميزانِ مَدْفوعاتٍ مُتَوازِنٍ.

International Trade: Importance, Challenges, and Opportunities

International trade plays a vital role in the global economy, allowing for the exchange of goods and services across national borders. These trade exchanges are often regulated by trade agreements, including bilateral or multilateral agreements, under the auspices of the World Trade Organization.

The economic policies adopted by countries have a significant impact on global trade trends. Some countries adopt an open economy that encourages foreign direct investment and trade liberalization. This entails reducing tariffs, increasing imports and exports, and creating a common market with other countries. Other countries may choose a closed economy, where local industries are protected through high customs duties and import restrictions.

Foreign direct investment and collaborative ventures are also important elements in the global economy. These investments contribute to a country's gross national income and encourage the development of specific sectors in the economy, such as the private sector.

International trade is not without challenges. Economic crises, such as a decline in trade or economic growth, can harm the volume of trade and lead to a decline in imports and exports. Other factors such as exchange rates, foreign currency, and inflation can significantly impact global economic strength.

International trade is complex and variable, but it is an integral part of the global economy. By understanding it, we can work towards achieving sustainable economic growth and a balanced balance of payments.

4.2 Industry and Manufacturing

Track **12**

production **إِنْتاجٌ**

تَمَّ تَسْجيلُ زِيادَةٍ كَبيرَةٍ في إِنْتاجِ السَّيّاراتِ الكَهْرُبائِيَّةِ في الصّينِ العامَ الماضِيَ.

There was a significant increase in the production of electric cars in China last year.

أَنْتَجَ • إِنْتاجٌ **to produce, manufacture**

أَنْتَجَتْ شَرِكَةُ سامْسونْجْ الكورِيَّةُ الجَنوبِيَّةُ أَكْثَرَ مِنْ مِلْيونِ هاتِفٍ ذَكِيٍّ في الرُّبْعِ الأَوَّلِ مِنَ العامِ الحالِيِّ.

South Korean company Samsung produced more than a million smartphones in the first quarter of the current year.

اِقْتِصادِيٌّ **economic**

تَعْمَلُ السُّعودِيَّةُ عَلى تَحْسينِ قِطاعِها الاِقْتِصادِيِّ فيما يَتَعَلَّقُ بِالطّاقَةِ المُتَجَدِّدَةِ.

Saudi Arabia is working to improve its economic sector related to renewable energy.

In media Arabic, اِقْتِصادِيٌّ is usually used to mean 'economic,' referring to economics as a whole or an economic sector, rather than 'economical,' implying cost-effectiveness or thriftiness.

تَصْنيعٌ **manufacturing**

شَهِدَتِ الهِنْدُ زِيادَةً في نَشاطِ التَّصْنيعِ خِلالَ الرُّبْعِ الثّاني مِنَ العامِ الحالِيِّ.

India saw an increase in manufacturing activity during the second quarter of the current year.

تَوْزيعٌ **distribution**

تُعْتَبَرُ أَمازونْ واحِدَةً مِنْ أَكْبَرِ الشَّرِكاتِ في مَجالِ تَوْزيعِ السِّلَعِ عَلى مُسْتَوى العالَمِ.

Amazon is considered one of the largest companies in the field of distribution of goods globally.

سِلْسِلَةُ تَوْريدٍ • سَلاسِلُ **supply chain**

تُعْتَبَرُ سِلْسِلَةُ التَّوْريدِ في شَرِكَةِ تويوتّا مِنْ أَكْثَرِ السَّلاسِلِ فَعالِيَّةً في الصِّناعَةِ.

Toyota's supply chain is considered one of the most efficient in the industry.

صِناعِيٌّ **industrial**

تَضُمُّ المِنْطَقَةُ الصِّناعِيَّةُ في دُبَيَّ عَدَدًا كَبيرًا مِنَ المَصانِعِ العالَمِيَّةِ.

The industrial area in Dubai houses a large number of global factories.

4.2.1 Automotive Industry

Track **13**

safe آمِنٌ

فِي تَقْرِيرٍ حَدِيثٍ، أَظْهَرَتْ تويوتا أَنَّ جَميعَ موديلاتِها الجَديدَةِ تُوَفِّرُ تَجْرِبَةَ قِيادَةٍ آمِنَةٍ لِلرُّكّابِ.

In a recent report, Toyota showed that all its new models provide a safe driving experience for passengers.

high performance أَداءٌ عالٍ

أَظْهَرَتْ سَيّاراتُ بي إِمْ دَبِلْيو الجَديدَةُ أَداءً عالِيًا في الِاخْتِباراتِ الأَخيرَةِ.

The new BMW cars exhibited high performance in the latest tests.

car repair إِصْلاحُ سَيّاراتٍ

أَعْلَنَتْ شَرِكَةُ إِصْلاحِ سَيّاراتٍ مَحَلِّيَّةٌ في لوسْ أَنْجِلوسْ عَنْ خُطَطٍ لِتَوْسيعِ خِدْماتِها.

A local car repair company in Los Angeles has announced plans to expand its services.

car tire إِطارُ سَيّارَةٍ

تَمَّ الكَشْفُ عَنْ تِقْنِيَّةٍ جَديدَةٍ لِإِنْتاجِ إِطارِ سَيّارَةٍ صَديقٍ لِلبيئَةِ بِشَكْلٍ أَكْبَرَ.

A new technology has been revealed for producing a more environmentally friendly car tire.

recycling إِعادَةُ تَدْويرٍ

تُعْتَبَرُ شَرِكَةُ فولْفو رائِدَةً في إِعادَةِ تَدْويرِ المَوادِّ الخامِ المُسْتَخْدَمَةِ في صِناعَةِ السَّيّاراتِ.

Volvo is considered a leader in recycling raw materials used in car manufacturing.

car testing اِخْتِبارُ سَيّاراتٍ

أَعْلَنَتْ تِسْلا عَنْ خُطَطٍ لِاخْتِبارِ سَيّاراتِها الجَديدَةِ في ظُروفِ طَقْسٍ قاسِيَةٍ.

Tesla has announced plans to test its new cars under harsh weather conditions.

car emissions *pl.* اِنْبِعاثاتُ سَيّاراتٍ

تَعْتَزِمُ شَرِكَةُ فورْدْ تَقْليلَ انْبِعاثاتِ سَيّاراتِها بِنِسْبَةِ 50% بِحُلولِ عامِ 2030.

Ford plans to reduce its car emissions by 50% by 2030.

The prepositional phrase بِحُلول is used to indicate a deadline or a point in time by which a certain event is expected to occur. It sets the timeframe for a future goal, plan, or expectation.

تَجْديدُ إطارٍ
tire retreading

نَجَحَ فَريقٌ مِنَ الباحِثينَ في جامِعَةِ سْتانْفورْدْ في تَجْديدِ إطارِ سَيّارَةٍ عَبْرَ اسْتِخْدامِ تِقْنِيَّةٍ حَديثَةٍ.

A team of researchers at Stanford University succeeded in retreading a car tire using a new technology.

تَجْميعٌ
assembly

يَسْتَخْدِمُ مَصْنَعُ لامْبورْغيني في إيطالْيا أَحْدَثَ التِّقْنِيّاتِ في تَجْميعِ سَيّاراتِه.

The Lamborghini factory in Italy uses the latest technologies in car assembly.

تَجْميعُ سَيّاراتٍ
car assembly

أَعْلَنَتْ شَرِكَةُ جيلي الصّينِيَّةُ عَنْ تَوَسُّعٍ كَبيرٍ في قُدْرَتِها عَلى تَجْميعِ السَّيّاراتِ.

China's Geely has announced a significant expansion in its car assembly capacity.

تَرْكيبُ مُحَرِّكٍ
engine installation

تُعْتَبَرُ شَرِكَةُ مَرْسيدِسْ بِنْزْ رائِدَةً في تَرْكيبِ مُحَرِّكاتٍ فَعّالَةٍ وَقَوِيَّةٍ.

Mercedes-Benz is a leader in installing efficient and powerful engines.

تَشْخيصُ مُشْكِلَةٍ
problem diagnosis

تُوَفِّرُ شَرِكَةُ فورْدْ خِدْمَةَ تَشْخيصِ المَشاكِلِ السَّريعَةِ لِلسَّيّاراتِ في جَميعِ مَراكِزِ الخِدْمَةِ الخاصَّةِ بِها.

Ford provides a quick problem diagnostic service for cars at all its service centers.

تَصْميمُ سَيّاراتٍ
car design

تَمَّ الكَشْفُ عَنْ تَصاميمِ سَيّاراتٍ جَديدَةٍ مُبْتَكَرَةٍ مِنْ قِبَلِ شَرِكَةِ بورْشِ الأَلْمانِيَّةِ.

Innovative new car designs have been revealed by the German company Porsche.

car manufacturing — **تَصْنيعُ سَيّاراتٍ**

تُعْتَبَرُ اليابانُ مِنْ أَكْبَرِ الدُّوَلِ في مَجالِ تَصْنيعِ السَّيّاراتِ عَلى مُسْتَوى العالَمِ.

Japan is one of the largest countries in the field of car manufacturing globally.

development — **تَطْويرٌ**

تَسْتَثْمِرُ شَرِكَةُ تِسْلا كَثيرًا في تَطْويرِ تِكْنولوجْيا السَّيّاراتِ الكَهْرُبائِيَّةِ.

Tesla invests heavily in the development of electric car technology.

production line — **خَطُّ إِنْتاجٍ** • خُطوطٌ

بَدَأَتْ شَرِكَةُ رولزْ رويسْ بِتَشْغيلِ خَطِّ إِنْتاجٍ جَديدٍ لِلسَّيّاراتِ الفاخِرَةِ في المَمْلَكَةِ المُتَّحِدَةِ.

Rolls-Royce has begun operating a new production line for luxury cars in the UK.

lightweight — **خَفيفُ الوَزْنِ**

تُرَكِّزُ شَرِكَةُ بورْشْ عَلى إِنْتاجِ سَيّاراتٍ خَفيفَةِ الوَزْنِ لِتَحْسينِ الأَداءِ وَالكَفاءَةِ في اسْتِهْلاكِ الوَقودِ.

Porsche focuses on producing lightweight cars to improve performance and fuel efficiency.

sporty — **رِياضِيٌّ**

تَتَمَيَّزُ السَّيّارَةُ الجَديدَةُ مِنْ شَرِكَةِ بي إِمّ دَبْليو بِتَصْميمِها الرِّياضِيِّ الأَنيقِ.

The new car from BMW features an elegant sporty design.

sports car — **سَيّارَةٌ رِياضِيَّةٌ**

أَطْلَقَتْ شَرِكَةُ ماكْلارينْ سَيّارَةً رِياضِيَّةً جَديدَةً تَتَمَيَّزُ بِسُرْعَتِها العالِيَةِ وَتَصْميمِها الأَنيقِ.

McLaren has launched a new sports car notable for its high speed and stylish design.

family car — **سَيّارَةٌ عائِلِيَّةٌ**

تُعْتَبَرُ سَيّارَةُ هونْدا أوديسي خِيارًا مِثالِيًّا لِلْعائِلاتِ الكَبيرَةِ بِفَضْلِ مِساحَتِها الدّاخِلِيَّةِ الواسِعَةِ.

The Honda Odyssey is an ideal choice for large families thanks to its spacious interior.

car purchasing شِراءُ سَيّاراتٍ

شَهِدَتِ السّوقُ السُّعوديَّةُ زِيادَةً في شِراءِ السَّيّاراتِ الكَهْرُبائيَّةِ العامَ الماضِيَ.

The Saudi market saw an increase in the purchase of electric cars last year.

car company شَرِكَةُ سَيّاراتٍ

أَعْلَنَتْ شَرِكَةُ سَيّاراتِ فولْفو عَنْ خُطَطٍ لِإطْلاقِ سَيّارَةٍ كَهْرُبائيَّةٍ جَديدَةٍ بِحُلولِ عامِ 2024.

Volvo Car Company announced plans to launch a new electric car by 2024.

showroom صالَةُ عَرْضٍ

أُفْتُتِحَتْ صالَةُ عَرْضٍ جَديدَةٌ لِسَيّاراتِ بي إِمّ دَبليو في دُبَيّ.

A new BMW car showroom has been opened in Dubai.

automotive industry; car manufacturing صِناعَةُ سَيّاراتٍ

تَحْتَلُّ الصّينُ المَرْكَزَ الأَوَّلَ عالَمِيًّا في صِناعَةِ السَّيّاراتِ.

China holds the first position globally in car manufacturing.

car maintenance and repair صِيانَةُ وَإِصْلاحُ سَيّاراتٍ

تُقَدِّمُ شَرِكَةُ جِنرالْ موتورْزْ خِدْماتِ صِيانَةٍ وَإِصْلاحِ سَيّاراتٍ عالِيَةِ الجَوْدَةِ.

General Motors provides high-quality car maintenance and repair services.

steering wheel عَجَلَةُ قِيادَةٍ

تَتَمَيَّزُ عَجَلَةُ قِيادَةِ السَّيّارَةِ الجَديدَةِ مِنْ مَرْسيدِسْ بِالرّاحَةِ وَالتَّحَكُّمِ السَّهْلِ.

The steering wheel in the new car from Mercedes is characterized by comfort and easy control.

gearbox عُلْبَةُ تُروسٍ • عُلَبٌ

تَمَّ تَصْميمُ عُلْبَةِ التُّروسِ في سَيّارَةِ الفيراري الجَديدَةِ بِحَيْثُ تُوَفِّرُ أَداءً أَكْثَرَ كَفاءَةً.

The gearbox in the new Ferrari car is designed to provide more efficient performance.

فاخِرٌ **luxurious**

تَتَمَيَّزُ السَّيّارَةُ الجَديدَةُ الفاخِرَةُ مِنْ فولْكِس واجِنْ بِتِقْنِيّاتِها الحَديثَةِ وَالمُتَطَوِّرَةِ.

The new luxury car from Folkswagen is distinguished by its modern and advanced technologies.

فَرامِلُ سَيّارَةٍ **car brakes**

تَمَّ تَطْويرُ فَرامِلِ سَيّارَةِ بورْشِ الجَديدَةِ لِتُوَفِّرَ مُسْتَوًى أَعْلى مِنَ الأَمانِ.

The brakes of the new Porsche car have been developed to provide a higher level of safety.

قِطَعُ غِيارٍ *pl.* **spare parts**

تُعْتَبَرُ شَرِكَةُ تويوتّا مِنْ أَكْبَرِ المُصَنِّعينَ لِقِطَعِ غِيارِ السَّيّاراتِ عَلى مُسْتَوى العالَمِ.

Toyota is considered one of the largest manufacturers of car spare parts in the world.

كَهْرُبائِيٌّ **electric**

تَتَّجِهُ شَرِكَةُ فولْكِسْ واجِنْ نَحْوَ الإِنْتاجِ الكامِلِ لِلسَّيّاراتِ الكَهْرُبائِيَّةِ بِحُلولِ عامِ 2040.

Volkswagen is moving towards full production of electric cars by 2040.

مَبيعاتُ سَيّاراتٍ *pl.* **car sales**

شَهِدَتْ مَبيعاتُ السَّيّاراتِ في الجَزائِرِ ارْتِفاعًا غَيْرَ مَسْبوقٍ خِلالَ الرُّبْعِ الأَوَّلِ مِنَ العامِ الحالِيِّ.

Car sales in Algeria saw an unprecedented rise during the first quarter of the current year.

مُحَرِّكٌ **engine**

يَتِمُّ تَطْويرُ مُحَرِّكاتِ الدّيزِلِ الجَديدَةِ في الشَّرِكَةِ المِصْرِيَّةِ لِلسَّيّاراتِ لِتَقْديمِ أَداءٍ أَعْلى وَكَفاءَةٍ أَكْبَرَ في اسْتِهْلاكِ الوَقودِ.

The new diesel engines are being developed at the Egyptian Car Company to provide higher performance and greater fuel efficiency.

مُكَيَّفٌ **air-conditioned**

قَدَّمَتِ الشَّرِكَةُ نَموذَجًا كَهْرُبائِيًّا صَديقًا لِلْبيئَةِ يَتَمَيَّزُ بِمَقْصورَةِ سَيّارَةٍ مُكَيَّفَةِ الهَواءِ، تَجْمَعُ بَيْنَ الانْبِعاثاتِ المُنْخَفِضَةِ وَالرّاحَةِ.

The company introduced an eco-friendly electric model with an air-conditioned car cabin, combining low emissions and comfort.

car model **موديلُ سَيّارَةٍ**

تُعْتَبَرُ موديلاتُ سَيّاراتِ تويوتا 2023 المُباعَةِ في الأُرْدُنِّ مِنْ بَيْنِ الموديلاتِ الأَكْثَرِ شَعْبِيَّةً.

The 2023 Toyota car models sold in Jordan are among the most popular.

hybrid **هَجينٌ** • هُجَناءُ

أَطْلَقَتْ شَرِكَةُ هيونْداي في لُبْنانَ سَيّارَةً هَجينَةً جَديدَةً تَعْمَلُ بِكَفاءَةٍ عالِيَةٍ وَتُوَفِّرُ اسْتِهْلاكًا أَقَلَّ لِلْوَقودِ.

Hyundai in Lebanon launched a new hybrid car that operates with high efficiency and provides less fuel consumption.

4.2.1.1 Mini-Articles

Track **14**

في خُطْوَةٍ اقْتِصادِيَّةٍ هامَّةٍ، أَعْلَنَتْ شَرِكَةُ سَيّاراتٍ كُبْرى عَنْ تَطْويرِ خَطِّ إِنْتاجٍ جَديدٍ لِلسَّيّاراتِ الهَجينَةِ الفاخِرَةِ. يَشْتَمِلُ الإِنْتاجُ عَلى موديلاتٍ مُخْتَلِفَةٍ مِنَ السَّيّاراتِ الرِّياضِيَّةِ وَالعائِلِيَّةِ. وَسَوْفَ يَتِمُّ تَصْميمُ السَّيّاراتِ لِتُوَفِّرَ أَداءً عالِيًا، وَسَيَتِمُّ تَجْميعُها بِدِقَّةٍ قُصْوى. تِلْكَ السَّيّاراتُ مُزَوَّدَةٌ بِمُكَيِّفٍ وَعُلْبَةِ تُروسٍ عالِيَةِ الجَوْدَةِ. كَما تَمَّ تَرْكيبُ مُحَرِّكٍ خَفيفِ الوَزْنِ لِتَحْسينِ انْبِعاثاتِ السَّيّاراتِ.

In an important economic step, a major car company announced the development of a new production line for luxury hybrid cars. The production includes different models of sports and family cars. The cars will be designed to provide high performance and will be assembled with maximum precision. These cars are equipped with air conditioning and a high-quality gearbox. A lightweight engine has been installed to improve the cars' emissions.

في صالَةِ عَرْضٍ رَئيسِيَّةٍ، تَمَّ الإِعْلانُ عَنْ إِطْلاقِ سِلْسِلَةِ تَوْريدٍ جَديدَةٍ لِتَجْديدِ إِطاراتِ السَّيّاراتِ القَديمَةِ. تَهْدُفُ هَذِهِ الخُطْوَةُ إِلى الإِسْهامِ في الحِفاظِ عَلى البيئَةِ وَالاقْتِصادِ. بِالإِضافَةِ إِلى ذَلِكَ، تُقَدِّمُ الشَّرِكَةُ خِدْماتِ صِيانَةِ وَإِصْلاحِ السَّيّاراتِ، وَالَّتي تَشْمَلُ تَشْخيصَ المُشْكِلاتِ وَتَصْنيعَ قِطَعِ الغِيارِ اللّازِمَةِ.

In a major showroom announcement, a new supply chain series was launched to recycle old car tires. This step aims to contribute to environmental and economic preservation. Additionally, the company offers car maintenance and repair services, including problem diagnosis and manufacturing necessary spare parts.

نَظَرًا لِلطَّلَبِ المُتَزايِدِ عَلى السَّيّاراتِ الكَهْرَبائِيَّةِ، أَطْلَقَتْ شَرِكَةُ تَصْنيعِ سَيّاراتٍ مَحَلِّيَّةٌ بَرْنامَجَ اخْتِبارِ سَيّاراتٍ جَديدٍ. يَتَضَمَّنُ البَرْنامَجُ تَجْميعَ السَّيّاراتِ وَتَرْكيبَ مُحَرِّكٍ خاصٍّ لِكُلِّ موديلِ سَيّارَةٍ. يَتِمُّ فَحْصُ الفَرامِلِ وَعَجَلَةِ

القِيادَةِ وَمُراقَبَةُ الأَداءِ العالي لِضَمانِ الأَمانِ. يَأْتي هَذا البَرْنامَجُ كَجُزْءٍ مِنَ الاِسْتِراتيجِيَّةِ الصِّناعِيَّةِ لِلشَّرِكَةِ لِزِيادَةِ مَبيعاتِ السَّيّاراتِ وَتَحْقيقِ نُمُوٍّ اقْتِصادِيٍّ مُسْتَدامٍ.

Due to the increasing demand for electric cars, a local car manufacturing company has launched a new car testing program. The program includes car assembly and installation of a specialized engine for each car model. The brakes, steering wheel, and high-performance monitoring are examined to ensure safety. This program is part of the company's industrial strategy to increase car sales and achieve sustainable economic growth.

في أَحْدَثِ خُطْوَةٍ لَها نَحْوَ الاِسْتِدامَةِ، أَعْلَنَتْ شَرِكَةُ سَيّاراتٍ مَحَلِّيَّةٌ بارِزَةٌ عَنْ خُطَطٍ لِتَوْسيعِ قُدُراتِها في مَجالِ إِعادَةِ تَدْويرِ السَّيّاراتِ. سَتَكونُ هَذِهِ الجُهودُ جُزْءًا مِنْ نِظامِ سِلْسِلَةِ التَّوْريدِ الشّامِلِ، حَيْثُ سَيَتِمُّ جَمْعُ السَّيّاراتِ القَديمَةِ، وَإِصْلاحُها، وَإِعادَةُ تَدْويرِها لِلْبَيْعِ مَرَّةً أُخْرى. يَعْكِسُ هَذا التَّطْويرُ اِلْتِزامَ الشَّرِكَةِ بِالْإِنْتاجِ الصَّديقِ لِلْبيئَةِ وَالاِقْتِصادِ الدّائِرِيِّ.

In its latest move towards sustainability, a prominent local car company has announced plans to expand its capabilities in car recycling. These efforts will be part of a comprehensive supply chain system, where old cars will be collected, repaired, and recycled for resale. This development reflects the company's commitment to environmentally friendly production and the circular economy.

شَهِدَتْ صِناعَةُ السَّيّاراتِ ثَوْرَةً جَديدَةً مَعَ تَقْديمِ سَيّارَةٍ رِياضِيَّةٍ تَجْمَعُ بَيْنَ الأَداءِ العالي وَالأَمانِ. السَّيّارَةُ، الَّتي أَنْتَجَتْها شَرِكَةُ صِناعَةِ سَيّاراتٍ مَعْروفَةٌ، تَمْتازُ بِمُحَرِّكٍ خَفيفِ الوَزْنِ، وَفَرامِلَ قَوِيَّةٍ، وَعَجَلَةِ قِيادَةٍ مُبْتَكَرَةٍ. بِالْإِضافَةِ إِلى ذَلِكَ، تَتَميَّزُ السَّيّارَةُ بِتَصْميمِها الفاخِرِ الَّذي يَمْزُجُ بَيْنَ الأَناقَةِ وَالقُوَّةِ. يَتِمُّ تَوْزيعُ هَذا الموديلِ الجَديدِ في صالاتِ العَرْضِ المُخْتَلِفَةِ، وَالَّتي تَشْهَدُ تَزايُدًا في شِراءِ السَّيّاراتِ مِنْ قِبَلِ العُمَلاءِ.

The automotive industry has witnessed a new revolution with the introduction of a sports car that combines high performance and safety. The car, produced by a well-known car manufacturing company, features a lightweight engine, powerful brakes, and an innovative steering wheel. Additionally, the car is characterized by its luxurious design that blends elegance and power. This new model is being distributed in various showrooms, which are experiencing an increase in car purchases by customers.

4.2.1.2 Informative Article: Automotive Technology

Track **15**

الاِبْتِكاراتُ الحَديثَةُ في تَصْنيعِ السَّيّاراتِ، وَالتَّوَقُّعاتُ المُسْتَقْبَلِيَّةُ لِتِكْنولوجْيا السَّيّاراتِ

في الأَعْوامِ الأَخيرَةِ، شَهِدَتْ صِناعَةُ السَّيّاراتِ تَطَوُّراتٍ هائِلَةً تَجْعَلُ المُسْتَقْبَلَ أَكْثَرَ إِثارَةً. تَسْتَثْمِرُ الشَّرِكاتُ الكُبْرى في الاِبْتِكارِ وَالتَّطْويرِ لِتَلْبِيَةِ الطَّلَبِ المُتَزايِدِ عَلى السَّيّاراتِ ذاتِ الأَداءِ العالي وَالصَّديقَةِ لِلْبيئَةِ.

مِنْ بَيْنِ الابْتِكاراتِ الأَخيرَةِ، يوجَدُ العَديدُ مِنَ الشَّرِكاتِ الَّتي أَنْتَجَتْ سَيّاراتٍ خَفيفَةَ الوَزْنِ وَهَجينَةً. تُقَلِّلُ هَذِهِ السَّيّاراتُ مِنَ الانْبِعاثاتِ وَتُوَفِّرُ تَجْرِبَةَ قِيادَةٍ آمِنَةٍ وَفَعّالَةٍ. بِالإِضافَةِ إِلى ذَلِكَ، تَمَّ تَطْويرُ خُطوطِ إِنْتاجٍ جَديدَةٍ لِتَوْزيعِ السَّيّاراتِ الكَهْرَبائِيَّةِ وَتَصْنيعِ قِطَعِ الغِيارِ الاقْتِصادِيَّةِ.

تَتَّجِهُ الشَّرِكاتُ نَحْوَ اخْتِبارِ السَّيّاراتِ الذَّكِيَّةِ المُزَوَّدَةِ بِمُكَيِّفٍ مُتَقَدِّمٍ وَعُلْبَةِ تُروسٍ مُتَطَوِّرَةٍ. يُمْكِنُ لِهَذِهِ السَّيّاراتِ أَنْ تَتَكَيَّفَ مَعَ الظُّروفِ المُتَغَيِّرَةِ وَتُوَفِّرَ تَجْرِبَةَ قِيادَةٍ فاخِرَةٍ وَرِياضِيَّةٍ. يَتِمُّ تَجْميعُ هَذِهِ السَّيّاراتِ في خُطوطِ الإِنْتاجِ الحَديثَةِ بِاسْتِخْدامِ التِّكْنولوجْيا المُتَقَدِّمَةِ لِلتَّجْميعِ وَالتَّرْكيبِ.

تَتَّجِهُ الصِّناعَةُ نَحْوَ اسْتِخْدامِ أَنْظِمَةِ إِعادَةِ التَّدْويرِ المُبْتَكَرَةِ لِتَجْديدِ الإِطاراتِ وَقِطَعِ الغِيارِ، مِمّا يُساهِمُ في تَحْسينِ البيئَةِ وَالاقْتِصادِ. بِالإِضافَةِ إِلى ذَلِكَ، تَتَطَوَّرُ خِدْماتُ صِيانَةِ وَإِصْلاحِ السَّيّاراتِ لِتُوَفِّرَ حُلولًا أَكْثَرَ فَعالِيَّةً لِتَشْخيصِ المُشْكِلاتِ وَإِصْلاحِها.

في المُسْتَقْبَلِ، يَتَوَقَّعُ الخُبَراءُ أَنْ تَظَلَّ صِناعَةُ السَّيّاراتِ في صَدارَةِ الابْتِكارِ التِّكْنولوجِيِّ.

Recent Innovations in Car Manufacturing and Future Expectations for Automotive Technology

In recent years, the automotive industry has witnessed tremendous advancements that make the future more exciting. Major companies are investing in innovation and development to meet the growing demand for high-performance and environmentally friendly cars.

Among the recent innovations, there are many companies that have produced lightweight and hybrid vehicles. These cars reduce emissions and provide a safe and efficient driving experience. Additionally, new production lines have been developed for the distribution of electric cars and the manufacturing of economical spare parts.

Companies are moving towards testing smart cars equipped with advanced air conditioning and sophisticated gearboxes. These cars can adapt to changing conditions and provide a luxurious and sporty driving experience. They are assembled in modern production lines using advanced assembly and installation technology.

The industry is moving towards the use of innovative recycling systems to renew tires and spare parts, contributing to environmental and economic improvement. Additionally, car maintenance and repair services are evolving to provide more effective solutions for problem diagnosis and repair.

In the future, experts expect the automotive industry to remain at the forefront of technological innovation.

4.2.2 Electronics and Telecommunications

Track **16**

to send a message إرْسالٌ • **أَرْسَلَ رِسالَةً**

أَرْسَلَ تَطْبيقُ واتْساب رِسالَةً لِجَميعِ المُسْتَخْدِمينَ لِإِبْلاغِهِمْ بِسِياسَةِ الخُصوصِيَّةِ الجَديدَةِ.

WhatsApp sent a message to all users to inform them of the new privacy policy.

electronic **إِلِكْتروني**

أَعْلَنَتْ شَرِكَةُ آبِلْ عَنِ الجيلِ الجَديدِ مِنَ الأَجْهِزَةِ الإِلِكْترونِيَّةِ في مُؤْتَمَرِها السَّنَوِيِّ.

Apple announced the new generation of electronic devices at its annual conference.

internet **إِنْتَرْنِتْ**

أَظْهَرَتِ الإِحْصائِيّاتُ أَنَّ نِسْبَةَ اسْتِخْدامِ الإِنْتَرْنِتْ في السُّعودِيَّةِ قَدْ زادَتْ بِشَكْلٍ مَلْحوظٍ خِلالَ السَّنَواتِ الأَخيرَةِ.

Statistics showed that Internet usage in Saudi Arabia has increased significantly in recent years.

wireless internet **إِنْتَرْنِتْ لاسِلْكِيٌّ**

أَصْبَحَ الإِنْتَرْنِتْ اللاسِلْكِيُّ مُتاحًا في مُعْظَمِ القِطاراتِ العامَّةِ في الأُرْدُنِّ.

Wireless internet has become available in most public trains in Jordan.

wireless communication **اِتِّصالٌ لاسِلْكِيٌّ**

قامَتْ شَرِكَةُ "اتِّصالات" الإِماراتِيَّةُ بِتَطْويرِ شَبَكَةِ اتِّصالٍ لاسِلْكِيٍّ جَديدَةٍ تُوَفِّرُ سُرُعاتٍ عالِيَةً.

The Emirati company "Etisalat" has developed a new wireless communication network that provides high speeds.

to connect اِتِّصالٌ • **اِتَّصَلَ**

أَنْشَأَتْ إِدارَةُ تِكْنولوجِيا المَعْلوماتِ شَبَكَةً افْتِراضِيَّةً خاصَّةً آمِنَةً لِلسَّماحِ لِلْمُوَظَّفينَ بِالاتِّصالِ بِشَبَكَةِ الشَّرِكَةِ الدّاخِلِيَّةِ عَنْ بُعْدٍ.

The IT department set up a secure virtual private network to allow employees to connect to the company's internal network remotely.

to use • اِسْتِخْدامٌ **اِسْتَخْدَمَ**

اِسْتَخْدَمَتِ المَدارِسُ في الدَّنِمارْكِ تِكْنولوجْيا جَديدَةً لِتَحْسينِ عَمَلِيَّةِ التَّعَلُّمِ عَنْ بُعْدٍ.

Schools in Denmark used new technology to improve the remote learning process.

to broadcast • بَثٌّ **بَثَّ**

بَدَأَتْ شَرِكَةُ نِتْفِليكْسْ بَثَّ مُسَلْسَلِها الجَديدِ الَّذي تَمَّ تَصْويرُهُ في دُبَيّ.

Netflix began broadcasting its new series, which was filmed in Dubai.

live streaming **بَثٌّ مُباشِرٌ**

أَطْلَقَتِ القَناةُ الرِّياضِيَّةُ الكُوَيْتِيَّةُ خِدْمَةَ البَثِّ المُباشِرِ لِلْمُبارَياتِ عَبْرَ الإِنْتَرْنِتْ.

The Kuwaiti sports channel launched a live streaming service for matches over the internet.

live news broadcast **بَثٌّ مُباشِرٌ لِلْأَخْبارِ**

قامَتِ القَناةُ الإِخْبارِيَّةُ البي بي سي بِتَوْفيرِ خِدْمَةِ البَثِّ المُباشِرِ لِلْأَخْبارِ عَلى مَوْقِعِها الإِلِكْتْرونِيِّ.

The BBC news channel has provided a live news streaming service on its website.

> The structure قامَ بِـ followed by a verbal noun (masdar) is commonly used as a formal alternative to a standard active verb. This pattern not only adds formality but also emphasizes the action being taken. For instance, قامَتْ... بِتَوْفيرِ... could be substituted with وَفَّرَتْ.

security software • بَرامِجُ **بَرْنامَجُ حِمايَةٍ**

مَعَ زِيادَةِ الهَجَماتِ السَّيْبَرانِيَّةِ، أَصْبَحَ اسْتِخْدامُ بَرْنامَجِ حِمايَةٍ ضَرورِيًّا لِحِمايَةِ البَياناتِ الشَّخْصِيَّةِ.

With the increase in cyber-attacks, the use of a protection program has become necessary to protect personal data.

email **بَريدٌ إِلِكْتْرونِيٌّ**

أَرْسَلَتْ شَرِكَةُ جوجِلْ بَريدًا إِلِكْتْرونِيًّا إِلى المُسْتَخْدِمينَ لِإِعْلامِهِمْ بِالتَّحْديثاتِ الجَديدَةِ.

Google sent an email to users to inform them of the new updates.

بَيانٌ صِحافِيٌّ إِلِكْتِرونِيٌّ
electronic press release

أَصْدَرَتْ شَرِكَةُ مايكْروسوفْتْ بَيانًا صِحافِيًّا إِلِكْتِرونِيًّا لِلإِعْلانِ عَنْ إِطْلاقِ نِظامِ التَّشْغيلِ الجَديدِ.

Microsoft released an electronic press statement to announce the launch of the new operating system.

تَحْميلُ تَطْبيقٍ
app download

دَعَتْ شَرِكَةُ أَمازونِ المُسْتَخْدِمينَ لِتَحْميلِ تَطْبيقِها الجَديدِ لِلتَّسَوُّقِ عَبْرَ الإِنْتَرْنِتْ.

Amazon invited users to download its new app for online shopping.

تَصَفَّحَ
• تَصَفُّحٌ
to browse

تُشَجِّعُ الحُكومَةُ السُّعودِيَّةُ المُواطِنينَ عَلى تَصَفُّحِ مَوْقِعِها الإِلِكْتِرونِيِّ لِمَعْرِفَةِ الخِدْماتِ المُتاحَةِ.

The Saudi government encourages citizens to browse its website to know the available services.

تَطْبيقٌ
application

يُعْتَبَرُ واتْسابْ أَحَدَ أَكْثَرِ التَّطْبيقاتِ شَعْبِيَّةً في مَجالِ الاتِّصالاتِ عَلى مُسْتَوى العالَمِ.

WhatsApp is considered one of the most popular applications in the field of communications globally.

تِقْنِيَّةُ اتِّصالاتٍ
telecommunications technology

تَمَّ تَطْويرُ تِقْنِيَّةِ اتِّصالاتٍ جَديدَةٍ في اليابانِ لِتَحْسينِ سُرْعَةِ الإِنْتَرْنِتْ.

A new communications technology was developed in Japan to improve internet speed.

تِقْنِيَّةُ مَعْلوماتٍ
information technology

تَعْمَلُ شَرِكَةُ أوراكِلْ في مَجالِ تِقْنِيَّةِ المَعْلوماتِ لِتَقْديمِ حُلولٍ لِلشَّرِكاتِ.

Oracle operates in the information technology field to provide solutions for companies.

تِكْنولوجْيا المَعْلوماتِ وَالاتِّصالاتِ
information and communications technology

تُعْتَبَرُ شَرِكَةُ زَيْنِ الكُوَيْتِيَّةُ مِنَ الشَّرِكاتِ الرّائِدَةِ في مَجالِ تِكْنولوجْيا المَعْلوماتِ وَالاتِّصالاتِ.

Zain Kuwait is considered a leading company in the field of information and communication technology.

remote control • أَجْهِزَةٌ **جِهازُ تَحَكُّمٍ عَنْ بُعْدٍ**

طَوَّرَتْ شَرِكَةُ سوني جِهازَ تَحَكُّمٍ عَنْ بُعْدٍ جَديدٍ لِتَحْسينِ تَجْرِبَةِ الأَلْعابِ.

Sony developed a new remote control device to enhance the gaming experience.

short message • رَسائِلُ **رِسالَةٌ قَصيرَةٌ**

تَمَكَّنَ الهاتِفُ الذَّكِيُّ الجَديدُ مِنْ إِرْسالِ وَاسْتِقْبالِ الرَّسائِلِ القَصيرَةِ بِشَكْلٍ أَكْثَرَ فَعالِيَّةً.

The new smartphone can send and receive short messages more effectively.

digital **رَقْمِيٌّ**

أَعْلَنَتْ شَرِكَةُ نيتْفليكْس عَنْ تَوْسيعِ تَغْطِيَتِها لِلْبَثِّ الرَّقْمِيِّ في مِنْطَقَةِ الشَّرْقِ الأَوْسَطِ.

Netflix announced expanding its digital broadcasting coverage in the Middle East.

screen **شاشَةٌ**

تَتَمَيَّزُ الشّاشَةُ الجَديدَةُ لِلْكُمْبيوتَرِ الشَّخْصِيِّ مِنْ شَرِكَةِ ديلّ بِدِقَّةٍ عالِيَةٍ وَأَلْوانٍ حَيَّةٍ.

The new personal computer screen from Dell features high resolution and vivid colors.

internet network **شَبَكَةُ إِنْتَرْنِتْ**

تَعْمَلُ الحُكومَةُ الأُرْدُنِّيَّةُ عَلى تَحْسينِ شَبَكَةِ الإِنْتَرْنِتْ في المَناطِقِ الرّيفِيَّةِ.

The Jordanian government is working on enhancing the internet network in rural areas.

telecommunications network **شَبَكَةُ اتِّصالاتٍ**

أَعْلَنَتْ شَرِكَةُ الاتِّصالاتِ السُّعودِيَّةُ عَنْ تَحْديثاتٍ جَديدَةٍ في شَبَكَةِ الاتِّصالاتِ لِتَوْفيرِ خِدْمَةٍ أَفْضَلَ.

The Saudi Telecom Company announced new updates in the communications network to provide better service.

to charge • شَحْنٌ **شَحَنَ**

أَطْلَقَتْ شَرِكَةُ تِسْلا نِظامَ شَحْنٍ سَريعٍ جَديدٍ يُقَلِّلُ مِنْ وَقْتِ الشَّحْنِ لِسَيّاراتِها الكَهْرُبائِيَّةِ.

Tesla has launched a new fast charging system that reduces charging time for its electric cars.

telecommunications company — **شَرِكَةُ اتِّصالاتٍ**

تُعْتَبَرُ شَرِكَةُ الاتِّصالاتِ القَطَرِيَّةُ مِنَ الشَّرِكاتِ الرّائِدَةِ في مَجالِ الاتِّصالاتِ في الشَّرْقِ الأَوْسَطِ.

The Qatari Telecommunications Company is one of the leading companies in the field of communications in the Middle East.

mobile phone company — **شَرِكَةُ هَواتِفَ مَحْمولَةٍ**

تتَوَقَّعُ شَرِكَةُ هَواتِفَ مَحْمولَةٍ كُبْرى مِثْلُ سامْسونْجْ زِيادَةً في مَبيعاتِها في الرُّبْعِ الأَخيرِ مِنَ العامِ.

A major mobile phone company like Samsung expects an increase in its sales in the last quarter of the year.

SIM card — **شَريحَةُ اتِّصالٍ** • شَرائِحُ

أَطْلَقَتْ شَرِكَةُ أوريدو شَريحَةَ اتِّصالٍ جَديدَةً تَدْعَمُ الاتِّصالاتِ السَّريعَةَ G5.

Ooredoo launched a new SIM card supporting fast 5G communications.

to repair — **أَصْلَحَ** • إِصْلاحٌ

قامَتْ شَرِكَةُ آبِلْ بِإِصْلاحِ عَيْبِ التَّصْنيعِ في أَحْدَثِ موديلّاتِ الآيْفونْ.

Apple fixed a manufacturing defect in the latest iPhone models.

to disconnect — **فَصَلَ** • فَصْلٌ

نَصَحَ مَسْؤولُ الشَّبَكَةِ الجَميعَ بِفَصْلِ أَجْهِزَتِهِمْ عَنْ شَبَكَةِ الوايْ فايِ العامَّةِ بِسَبَبِ المَخاوِفِ الأَمْنِيَّةِ.

The network administrator advised everyone to disconnect their devices from the public Wi-Fi network due to security concerns.

personal computer — **كُمْبِيوتَرٌ شَخْصِيٌّ**

يَتَمَتَّعُ الكُمْبِيوتَرُ الشَّخْصِيُّ الجَديدُ مِنْ شَرِكَةِ HP بِمُعالِجٍ سَريعٍ وَذاكِرَةِ وُصولٍ عَشْوائِيٍّ كَبيرَةٍ.

The new personal computer from HP features a fast processor and large RAM.

لاسِلْكِيٌّ **wireless**

تُعْتَبَرُ الِاتِّصالاتُ اللّاسِلْكِيَّةُ الجَديدَةُ الَّتي طَوَّرَتْها شَرِكَةُ هَواوي خُطْوَةً كَبيرَةً نَحْوَ تَحْقيقِ الإِنْتَرْنِتِّ اللّاسِلْكِيِّ عالي السُّرْعَةِ.

The new wireless communications developed by Huawei are a major step towards achieving high-speed wireless internet.

مُؤَشِّرُ إِشارَةٍ **signal indicator**

واجَهَ مُسْتَخْدِمو شَبَكَةِ فودافونْ في مِصرَ مُشْكِلاتٍ في مُؤَشِّرِ الإِشارَةِ اليَوْمَ، وَتَعْمَلُ الشَّرِكَةُ عَلى حَلِّ المُشْكِلَةِ.

Vodafone network users in Egypt experienced problems with the signal indicator today, and the company is working on solving the issue.

مُباشِرٌ **live**

أَعْلَنَتْ شَرِكَةُ أَمازونْ عَنْ خِدْمَةِ بَثٍّ مُباشِرٍ جَديدَةٍ لِلْأَلْعابِ الإِلِكْتِرونِيَّةِ.

Amazon announced a new live streaming service for video games.

مُتَّصِلٌ **connected**

تَمَكَّنَ الباحِثونَ في جامِعَةِ كامْبِريدْجْ مِنْ تَطْويرِ تِقْنِيَّةٍ جَديدَةٍ تُمَكِّنُ الأَجْهِزَةَ المُتَّصِلَةَ بِالإِنْتَرْنِتْ مِنْ تَوْفيرِ الطّاقَةِ.

Researchers at Cambridge University have developed a new technology that allows internet-connected devices to save energy.

مُتَوافِقٌ **compatible**

أَعْلَنَتْ شَرِكَةُ آبِلْ أَنَّ الإِصْدارَ الجَديدَ مِنْ نِظامِ iOS مُتَوافِقٌ مَعَ مَجْموعَةٍ أَوْسَعَ مِنَ التَّطْبيقاتِ.

Apple announced that the new version of the iOS system is compatible with a wider range of applications.

مَجّانِيٌّ **free**

أَطْلَقَتْ شَرِكَةُ غوغِلْ خِدْمَةَ تَخْزينٍ سَحابِيٍّ مَجّانِيٍّ لِجَميعِ مُسْتَخْدِميها.

Google has launched a free cloud storage service for all its users.

مُراسَلَةٌ إِلِكْترونِيَّةٌ
email correspondence

يُشَجِّعُ البَريدُ الإِلِكْترونِيُّ المُشَفَّرُ اسْتِخْدامَ البَريدِ الإِلِكْترونِيِّ بِطَريقَةٍ أَكْثَرَ أَمانًا وَخُصوصِيَّةً.

Encrypted email encourages the use of email in a safer and more private way.

مُزَوِّدُ خِدْمَةِ إِنْتَرْنِتْ
internet service provider (ISP)

اِتِّصالاتُ هِيَ مُزَوِّدُ الخِدْمَةِ الرَّئيسِيِّ لِلْإِنْتَرْنِتْ في الإِماراتِ، وَتُقَدِّمُ خِدْماتٍ واسِعَةَ النِّطاقِ بِسُرْعاتٍ عالِيَةٍ.

Etisalat is the primary internet service provider in the UAE, offering broadband services at high speeds.

مُشَفَّرٌ
encrypted

تُقَدِّمُ شَرِكَةُ مايكْروسوفْتْ بَرْنامَجَ مُكافَحَةِ الفَيْروساتِ المُشَفَّرِ لِحِمايَةِ الأَجْهِزَةِ مِنَ البَرْمَجِيّاتِ الخَبيثَةِ.

Microsoft offers encrypted antivirus software to protect devices from malicious software.

مُعَطَّلٌ
not working, out of order

لَقَدْ ثَبَتَ أَنَّ نِظامَ التَّشْغيلِ الأَحْدَثَ مِنْ آبِلْ مُعَطَّلٌ عَلى بَعْضِ الأَجْهِزَةِ القَديمَةِ.

It has been confirmed that the latest Apple operating system is disabled on some older devices.

مَفْصولٌ
disconnected

أَفادَتِ التَّقاريرُ أَنَّ بَعْضَ المُسْتَخْدِمينَ مَفْصولونَ عَنْ خِدْمَةِ الإِنْتَرْنِتْ مِنْ قِبَلِ الشَّرِكَةِ مُقَدِّمَةِ الخِدْمَةِ.

Reports indicate that some users have been disconnected from the internet service by the provider.

مُكالَمَةٌ هاتِفِيَّةٌ
phone call

اِزْدادَتْ شَعْبِيَّةُ المُكالَماتِ الهاتِفِيَّةِ عَبْرَ الإِنْتَرْنِتْ خِلالَ الجائِحَةِ.

Internet phone calls increased in popularity during the pandemic.

مَوْقِعٌ إِلِكْترونِيٌّ • مَواقِعُ
website

تَمَّ تَحْديثُ المَوْقِعِ الإِلِكْترونِيِّ لِشَرِكَةِ سامْسونْجْ لِعَرْضِ المُنْتَجاتِ الجَديدَةِ.

Samsung's website has been updated to display new products.

to download • تَنْزِيلٌ نَزَّلَ

نَزَّلَ الطُّلّابُ البَرْنامَجَ التَّعْليمِيَّ الجَديدَ عَلى أَجْهِزَتِهِم اللَّوْحِيَّةِ لِمُتابَعَةِ الدُّروسِ عَنْ بُعْدٍ.

The students downloaded the new educational program onto their tablets to follow the lessons remotely.

smartphone • هَواتِفُ هاتِفٌ ذَكِيٌّ

أَعْلَنَتْ شَرِكَةُ آبِلْ عَنِ الإِصْدارِ الجَديدِ مِنَ الهاتِفِ الذَّكِيِّ الَّذي يَحْمِلُ مَيْزاتٍ مُتَقَدِّمَةً.

Apple announced the new version of the smartphone that carries advanced features.

4.2.2.1 Mini-Articles

Track **17**

أَعْلَنَتْ شَرِكَةُ اتِّصالاتٍ رائِدَةٌ عَنْ إِطْلاقِ تِقْنِيَّةِ اتِّصالاتٍ جَديدَةٍ تَسْتَخْدِمُ شَبَكَةَ إِنْتَرْنِتْ لاسِلْكِيَّةً فائِقَةَ السُّرْعَةِ. هَذِهِ التِّقْنِيَّةُ المُتَوافِقَةُ مَعَ كافَّةِ الأَجْهِزَةِ سَتَسْمَحُ لِلْمُسْتَخْدِمينَ بِإِرْسالِ رَسائِلَ قَصيرَةٍ وَإِجْراءِ مُكالَماتٍ هاتِفِيَّةٍ بِكَفاءَةٍ أَعْلى. أَكَّدَ البَيانُ الصَّحَفِيُّ أَنَّ المُسْتَخْدِمينَ سَيَتَمَكَّنونَ مِنْ تَصَفُّحِ الإِنْتَرْنِتْ بِشَكْلٍ أَسْرَعَ وَأَكْثَرَ أَمانًا، بِفَضْلِ بَرْنامَجِ الحِمايَةِ المُشَفَّرِ المُضَمَّنِ.

A leading telecommunications company has announced the launch of a new communication technology that utilizes high-speed wireless internet. This technology, compatible with all devices, will allow users to send short messages and make phone calls more efficiently. The press release confirmed that users will be able to browse the internet faster and more securely, thanks to the built-in encrypted security software.

نَفَتْ شَرِكَةُ هَواتِفَ مَحْمولَةٍ بارِزَةٌ أَنْ يَكونَ لَدَيْها أَيُّ خُطَطٍ لِتَقْليلِ تَقْديمِ خِدْماتِ الإِنْتَرْنِتِّ المَجّانِيَّةِ. في بَيانٍ صَحَفِيٍّ، ذَكَرَتِ الشَّرِكَةُ أَنَّها تَعْتَزِمُ البَثَّ المُباشِرَ لِلأَخْبارِ حَوْلَ التَّطْبيقاتِ وَالتَّحْديثاتِ المُسْتَقْبَلِيَّةِ عَبْرَ مَوْقِعِها الإِلِكْترونِيِّ. وَتَشْمَلُ هَذِهِ الخُطَطُ الاسْتِمْرارَ في تَقْديمِ خِدْمَةِ البَريدِ الإِلِكْترونِيِّ المَجّانِيَّةِ وَالاسْتِخْدامِ غَيْرِ المَحْدودِ لِشَبَكَةِ الإِنْتَرْنِتِّ اللّاسِلْكِيَّةِ.

A prominent mobile phone company denied having any plans to reduce the provision of free internet services. In a press statement, the company mentioned its intention to directly broadcast news about applications and future updates through its website. These plans include continuing to offer free email service and unlimited usage of wireless internet.

أَعْلَنَتْ شَرِكَةُ الاتِّصالاتِ المَحَلِّيَّةُ اليَوْمَ عَنْ تَطْويرِ تِقْنِيَّةِ اتِّصالاتٍ جَديدَةٍ تَتَضَمَّنُ الاتِّصالَ اللاسِلْكِيَّ المُتَقَدِّمَ وَالإِنْتَرْنِتْ اللاسِلْكِيَّ السَّريعَ. وَقَدْ أَرْسَلَتِ الشَّرِكَةُ بَيانًا صَحَفِيًّا عَبْرَ البَريدِ الإِلِكْترونِيِّ يَتَضَمَّنُ التَّفاصيلَ الكامِلَةَ. وَقَدْ شَدَّدَ البَيانُ عَلى فَعالِيَّةِ البَرْنامَجِ الجَديدِ في تَحْميلِ التَّطْبيقاتِ بِسُرْعَةٍ وَتَصَفُّحِ الإِنْتَرْنِتْ بِكَفاءَةٍ عالِيَةٍ.

Today, a local telecommunications company announced the development of a new communication technology that includes advanced wireless connectivity and fast wireless internet. The company sent a press release via email that included all the details. The statement emphasized the effectiveness of the new software in quickly downloading applications and efficiently browsing the internet.

تَسْتَخْدِمُ شَبَكَةُ الاتِّصالاتِ الوَطَنِيَّةُ تِقْنِيَّةَ المَعْلوماتِ وَالاتِّصالاتِ المُتَقَدِّمَةِ لِتَوْفيرِ خِدْمَةٍ مَجّانِيَّةٍ لِلْإِنْتَرْنِتْ لِجَميعِ المواطِنينَ. يُمْكِنُ لِلْمُسْتَخْدِمينَ الآنَ إِرْسالُ رَسائِلَ قَصيرَةٍ، وَإِجْراءُ مُكالَماتٍ هاتِفِيَّةٍ، وَتَبادُلُ الرَّسائِلِ الإِلِكْترونِيَّةِ بِسَلاسَةٍ عَبْرَ الشَّبَكَةِ. كَما يَضْمَنُ مُزَوِّدُ الخِدْمَةِ أَنَّ جَميعَ المُراسَلاتِ الإِلِكْترونِيَّةِ سَتَكونُ مُشَفَّرَةً لِتَوْفيرِ الحِمايَةِ القُصْوى لِلْمَعْلوماتِ الشَّخْصِيَّةِ.

The national telecommunications network uses advanced information and communication technology to provide free internet service to all citizens. Users can now seamlessly send short messages, make phone calls, and exchange emails over the network. The service provider also guarantees that all electronic correspondence will be encrypted to ensure maximum protection of personal information.

4.2.2.2 Smartphone Review

Track **18**

بَعْدَ اسْتِخْدامِ الهاتِفِ الذَّكِيِّ الجَديدِ لِأَسابيعَ مُتَتالِيَةٍ، أَصْبَحَ واضِحًا أَنَّ هَذا الجِهازَ يَحْمِلُ العَديدَ مِنَ المَزايا الرّائِعَةِ. فَهُوَ لا يُتيحُ فَقَطِ الاتِّصالَ اللّاسِلْكِيَّ السَّريعَ وَالثّابِتَ، وَلَكِنَّهُ يَتَضَمَّنُ أَيْضًا خاصِّيَّةَ الإِنْتَرْنِتْ اللّاسِلْكِيِّ الَّتي تُمَكِّنُ المُسْتَخْدِمَ مِنَ التَّصَفُّحِ وَالبَثِّ المُباشِرِ لِلْأَخْبارِ بِسَلاسَةٍ.

الجِهازُ مُزَوَّدٌ بِبَرْنامَجِ حِمايَةٍ مُتَطَوِّرٍ يَضْمَنُ أَنَّ كُلَّ بَريدٍ إِلِكْترونِيٍّ وَمُراسَلَةٍ إِلِكْترونِيَّةٍ تَبْقى مُشَفَّرَةً وَآمِنَةً. يُتيحُ لَكَ تَطْبيقُ البَريدِ الإِلِكْترونِيِّ الرّائِعُ أَنْ تُرْسِلَ الرَّسائِلَ بِكُلِّ سُهولَةٍ وَيُسْرٍ.

لَقَدْ انْبَهَرْتُ بِشَكْلٍ خاصٍّ بِالشّاشَةِ الرَّقْمِيَّةِ عالِيَةِ الدِّقَّةِ. تَبْدو الصُّوَرُ وَالأَفْلامُ حَيَّةً وَواضِحَةً، مِمّا يُعَزِّزُ تَجْرِبَةَ المُشاهَدَةِ المُباشِرَةِ. وَأَخيرًا، فَإِنَّ الشَّريحَةَ الجَديدَةَ المُزَوَّدَةَ بِتِقْنِيَّةِ اتِّصالاتٍ فائِقَةِ السُّرْعَةِ تَسْتَحِقُّ الإِشادَةَ. تُؤَدّي سُرْعَةُ تَحْميلِ التَّطْبيقاتِ وَسُهولَةُ الاتِّصالِ إِلى تَحْسينِ تَجْرِبَةِ الهاتِفِ بِشَكْلٍ كَبيرٍ.

وَمَعَ ذَلِكَ، لَيْسَتْ كُلُّ الأَخْبارِ جَيِّدَةً. فَقَدْ وَجَدْتُ أَنَّ الجِهازَ يَتَعَطَّلُ بِشَكْلٍ مُتَكَرِّرٍ، خاصَّةً عِنْدَ اسْتِخْدامِ الإِنْتَرْنِتْ لِفَتَراتٍ طَويلَةٍ. وَرَغْمَ أَنَّ الشَّرِكَةَ المُصَنِّعَةَ لِلْهَواتِفِ المَحْمولَةِ سارَعَتْ بِإِصْلاحِ المَشاكِلِ، إِلّا أَنَّ هَذِهِ المَسْأَلَةَ قَدْ تُثيرُ القَلَقَ لَدى البَعْضِ.

بالرَّغْمِ مِنْ هَذِهِ المُشْكِلاتِ، فَإِنَّني أَعْتَبِرُ أَنَّ هَذا الهاتِفَ الذَّكِيَّ جَديرٌ بِالاسْتِثْمارِ فيه. فَهُوَ يَجْمَعُ بَيْنَ تِقْنِيَّةِ المَعْلوماتِ وَالاتِّصالاتِ الحَديثَةِ بِطَريقَةٍ تَعْكِسُ بِالْفِعْلِ التَّقَدُّمَ الَّذي تُحَقِّقُهُ صِناعَةُ الإِلِكْتْرونِيّاتِ وَالاتِّصالاتِ.

After I used the new smartphone for consecutive weeks, it has become evident that this device carries many great advantages. Not only does it enable fast and stable wireless communication, but it also includes the feature of wireless internet that allows users to browse and stream news smoothly.

The device is equipped with advanced security software that ensures all emails and electronic correspondence remain encrypted and secure. The excellent email application allows you to send messages easily and effortlessly.

I was particularly impressed by the high-definition digital screen. Images and movies appear vivid and clear, enhancing the direct viewing experience. Finally, the new chip equipped with high-speed communication technology deserves praise. The fast app downloads and ease of connectivity have significantly improved the phone experience.

However, not all the news is good. I found that the device frequently malfunctions, especially when using the internet for long periods. While the mobile phone manufacturer was quick to fix the issues, this matter may still raise concerns for some.

Despite these problems, I consider this smartphone worth investing in. It combines modern information and communication technology in a way that truly reflects the progress achieved by the electronics and telecommunications industry.

4.2.3 Textile and Fashion Industry

Track **19**

machinery pl. **آلاتٌ**

تُسْتَخْدَمُ آلاتٌ مُتَطَوِّرَةٌ في مَصْنَعِ ليفايْس لِتَحْسينِ عَمَلِيَّةِ الإِنْتاجِ.

Advanced machines are used in Levi's factory to enhance the production process.

synthetic fibers pl. **أَلْيافٌ صِناعِيَّةٌ**

بَدَأَتِ العَديدُ مِنَ الشَّرِكاتِ في اسْتِخْدامِ الأَلْيافِ الصِّناعِيَّةِ لِإِنْتاجِ مَلابِسَ مُسْتَدامَةٍ.

Many companies have started using synthetic fibers to produce sustainable clothing.

fast fashion **الموضَةُ السَّريعَةُ**

أَصْبَحَتِ الموضَةُ السَّريعَةُ مَصْدَرَ قَلَقٍ بيئِيٍّ بِسَبَبِ النُّفاياتِ الَّتي تُنْتِجُها.

Fast fashion has become an environmental concern due to the waste it generates.

wholesale بِالْجُمْلَةِ

تَمَّ بَيْعُ القُماشِ بِالْجُمْلَةِ إلى المَتاجِرِ الكُبْرى لِتَصْنيعِ مَلابِسَ جَديدَةٍ.

Fabric was sold wholesale to major stores to manufacture new clothes.

retail تَجْزِئَةٌ

شَهِدَتْ أَسْواقُ التَّجْزِئَةِ في الأُرْدُنِّ زِيادَةً في المَبيعاتِ خِلالَ مَوْسِمِ التَّخْفيضاتِ السَّنَوِيِّ.

Jordan's retail markets have seen an increase in sales during the annual discount season.

design تَصْميمٌ

تَمَّ تَصْميمُ فُسْتانِ الزِّفافِ الرّائعِ بِواسِطَةِ المُصَمِّمِ اللُّبْنانِيِّ الشَّهيرِ، إيلي صَعْب.

The stunning wedding dress was designed by famous Lebanese designer, Elie Saab.

embroidery تَطْريزٌ

أَضافَتْ تِقْنِيّاتُ التَّطْريزِ الحَديثَةُ تَفاصيلَ رائِعَةً إلى الفَساتينِ النِّسائِيَّةِ.

Modern embroidery techniques added wonderful details to women's dresses.

upholstery تَنْجيدٌ

يَتِمُّ تَنْجيدُ الأَرائِكِ الفاخِرَةِ بِأَجْوَدِ أَنْواعِ الجِلْدِ الإيطالِيِّ.

The luxurious sofas are upholstered with the finest types of Italian leather.

silk حَريرٌ

يُعَدُّ الحَريرُ المُسْتَوْرَدُ مِنَ الصّينِ مِنْ أَجْوَدِ الأَنْواعِ وَأَكْثَرِها رَواجًا في صِناعَةِ الأَزْياءِ.

Silk imported from China is considered the highest quality and most popular in the fashion industry.

lace دانْتيلْ

تَتَمَيَّزُ مَجْموعَةُ الأَزْياءِ الفَرَنْسِيَّةِ الجَديدَةِ بِتَصاميمِها المُعَقَّدَةِ المَصْنوعَةِ مِنَ الدّانْتيلْ.

The new French fashion collection is distinguished by its intricate designs made of lace.

dyeing صِباغَةٌ

تُسْتَخْدَمُ تِقْنِيّاتُ الصِّباغَةِ المُتَقَدِّمَةُ لِتَزْويدِ مُنْتَجاتِ النَّسيجِ بِأَلْوانٍ زاهِيَةٍ وَدائِمَةٍ.

Advanced dyeing techniques are used to provide textile products with vibrant and permanent colors.

fashion industry صِناعَةُ أَزْياءٍ

تَلْعَبُ صِناعَةُ الأَزْياءِ دَوْرًا كَبيرًا في الاقْتِصادِ العالَمِيِّ، حَيْثُ تُسْهِمُ في خَلْقِ فُرَصِ العَمَلِ وَالتِّجارَةِ.

The fashion industry plays a significant role in global economics, contributing to job creation and trade.

textile industry صِناعَةُ المَنْسوجاتِ

تَشْتَهِرُ الهِنْدُ بِصِناعَةِ المَنْسوجاتِ التَّقْليدِيَّةِ الَّتي تَعْكِسُ ثَقافَتَها الغَنِيَّةَ وَتُراثَها الطَّويلَ.

India is known for its traditional textile industry that reflects its rich culture and long heritage.

wool صوفٌ • أَصْوافٌ

بَدَأَتِ المَصانِعُ التّونِسِيَّةُ في الاسْتِثْمارِ في إِنْتاجِ الصّوفِ المَحَلِّيِّ لِتَعْزيزِ الصِّناعاتِ النَّسيجِيَّةِ الوَطَنِيَّةِ.

Tunisian factories have begun investing in the production of local wool to boost national textile industries.

consumer demand طَلَبُ المُسْتَهْلِكينَ

أَصْبَحَ الصّوفُ مُسْتَدامُ المَصْدَرِ رائِجًا في صِناعَةِ المَلابِسِ بِسَبَبِ زِيادَةِ طَلَبِ المُسْتَهْلِكينَ عَلى المُنْتَجاتِ الصَّديقَةِ لِلْبيئَةِ.

Sustainable sourced wool has become popular in the clothing industry due to increased consumer demand for environmentally friendly products.

yarn غَزْلٌ

يُعْتَبَرُ المَغْرِبُ مِنْ أَبْرَزِ البُلْدانِ العَرَبِيَّةِ في إِنْتاجِ الخُيوطِ المُسْتَخْدَمَةِ في صِناعَةِ السَّجّادِ.

Morocco is among the leading Arab countries in the production of yarn used in the carpet industry.

قُطْنٌ • أَقْطانٌ **cotton**

تَمَّ تَوْجيهُ النَّقْدِ لِشَرِكاتِ الأَزْياءِ الكُبْرى بِسَبَبِ اسْتِخْدامِها لِلْقُطْنِ مِنْ مَناطِقَ مُثيرَةٍ لِلْجَدَلِ.

Major fashion companies have been criticized for using cotton from controversial regions.

قُماشٌ • أَقْمِشَةٌ **fabric**

زادَتْ صادِراتُ القُماشِ المِصْرِيِّ إِلى الدُّوَلِ الأوروبِّيَّةِ بِنِسْبَةِ 20% خِلالَ الرُّبْعِ الأَخيرِ مِنَ العامِ.

Egyptian fabric exports to European countries increased by 20% during the last quarter of the year.

قُوَّةُ العَمَلِ • قُوًى / قِوًى **labor force**

يَعْتَمِدُ القِطاعُ الصِّناعِيُّ في الصّينِ بِشَكْلٍ كَبيرٍ عَلى قُوَّةِ العَمَلِ الماهِرَةِ لِتَحْفيزِ الإِنْتاجِيَّةِ وَالِابْتِكارِ.

The industrial sector in China heavily relies on a skilled labor force to drive productivity and innovation.

كَتّانٌ **linen**

تَمَّ تَصْميمُ التَّنانيرِ الصَّيْفِيَّةِ الجَديدَةِ لِهَذا العامِ مِنَ الكَتّانِ الخَفيفِ لِضَمانِ الرّاحَةِ وَالأَناقَةِ في نَفْسِ الوَقْتِ.

This year's new summer skirts were designed from lightweight linen to ensure comfort and elegance at the same time.

كُروشيهْ **crochet**

صُمِّمَ الفُسْتانُ بِاسْتِخْدامِ تِقْنِيَّةِ الكُروشيهِ اليَدَوِيَّةِ، مِمّا أَضْفى عَلَيْهِ لَمْسَةً فَريدَةً وَشَخْصِيَّةً.

The dress was designed using handcrafted crochet techniques, adding a unique and personal touch.

مُخْمَلٌ **velvet**

أَطْلَقَتْ دارُ الأَزْياءِ الرّاقِيَةُ مَجْموعَةً جَديدَةً تَضُمُّ فَساتينَ مَصْنوعَةً مِنَ المُخْمَلِ الفاخِرِ.

The high-end fashion house released a new collection featuring dresses made of luxurious velvet.

quality control مُراقَبَةُ الجَوْدَةِ

تَلْعَبُ مُراقَبَةُ الجَوْدَةِ دَوْرًا حَيَوِيًّا في ضَمانِ تَوْفيرِ مُنْتَجاتٍ نَسيجِيَّةٍ عالِيَةِ الجَوْدَةِ لِلْمُسْتَهْلِكينَ.

Quality control plays a vital role in ensuring high-quality textile products are provided to consumers.

weaving نَسْجٌ

تَطَوَّرَتْ تِقْنِيّاتُ النَّسْجِ عَلى مَرِّ العُصورِ لِتَشْمَلَ الآلاتِ الحَديثَةَ الَّتي تَزيدُ مِنَ الكَفاءَةِ وَالجَوْدَةِ.

Weaving techniques have evolved over the ages to include modern machines that increase efficiency and quality.

textile نَسيجٌ • أَنْسِجَةٌ

تَتَمَيَّزُ الجَزائِرُ بِصِناعَةِ النَّسيجِ التَّقْليدِيَّةِ الَّتي تُعْتَبَرُ جُزْءًا مُهِمًّا مِنْ تُراثِها الثَّقافِيِّ.

Algeria has a traditional textile industry that is an important part of its cultural heritage.

4.2.3.1 Mini-Articles

Track **20**

أَحْرَزَتْ صِناعَةُ المُوضَةِ السَّريعَةِ نَجاحًا مُذْهِلًا خِلالَ العامِ الماضي، حَيْثُ تَزايَدَتِ المَبيعاتُ بِشَكْلٍ كَبيرٍ. يُعْزى هَذا النَّجاحُ إِلى تَوَجُّهِ المُسْتَهْلِكينَ نَحْوَ التَّسَوُّقِ بِالْجُمْلَةِ لِلْحُصولِ عَلى أَحْدَثِ صَيْحاتِ المُوضَةِ بِأَسْعارٍ مُناسِبَةٍ. وَلِتَلْبِيَةِ هَذا الطَّلَبِ المُتَزايِدِ، قامَتِ الشَّرِكاتُ المُصَنِّعَةُ بِزِيادَةِ إِنْتاجِها وَاسْتِخْدامِ آلاتٍ حَديثَةٍ لِتَحْسينِ الكَفاءَةِ. تُشيرُ التَّقاريرُ إِلى أَنَّ قِطاعَ صِناعَةِ المَلابِسِ الجاهِزَةِ اسْتَخْدَمَ تِقْنِيّاتِ تَصْميمٍ مُتَطَوِّرَةً وَتَطْريزًا ذا جَوْدَةٍ عالِيَةٍ لِتَلْبِيَةِ تَوَقُّعاتِ المُسْتَهْلِكينَ. بِالإِضافَةِ إِلى ذَلِكَ، تَمَّ التَّرْكيزُ أَيْضًا عَلى مُراقَبَةِ الجَوْدَةِ وَتَحْسينِ عَمَلِيّاتِ الصِّباغَةِ لِلْحِفاظِ عَلى اسْتِدامَةِ الصِّناعَةِ وَحِمايَةِ البيئَةِ.

The fast fashion industry has achieved remarkable success in the past year, with significant growth in sales. This success is attributed to consumers' preference for wholesale shopping to obtain the latest fashion trends at affordable prices. To meet this increasing demand, manufacturing companies have increased their production and utilized modern machinery to improve efficiency. Reports indicate that the ready-to-wear clothing sector has employed advanced design techniques and high-quality embroidery to meet consumer expectations. Additionally, there has been a focus on quality control and improving dyeing processes to sustain the industry and protect the environment.

شَهِدَتْ صِناعَةُ المَنْسوجاتِ وَالمَلابِسِ الفاخِرَةِ انْتِعاشًا لافِتًا خِلالَ الفَتْرَةِ الأَخيرَةِ، حَيْثُ اكْتَسَحَ قُماشُ الحَريرِ المَشْهَدَ العالَمِيَّ. يُعْزى هَذا النَّجاحُ إِلى تَفْضيلِ المُصَمِّمينَ لِاسْتِخْدامِ الأَلْيافِ الطَّبيعِيَّةِ الفاخِرَةِ في تَصاميمِهِمْ، ما مَنَحَ

الصِّناعَةَ رَوْنَقًا خاصًّا وَمَزايا تَنافُسِيَّةً. تَمَّ ابْتِكارُ آلاتٍ حَديثَةٍ لِنَسْجِ الحَريرِ بِتِقْنِيّاتٍ تِكْنولوجِيَّةٍ مُتَطَوِّرَةٍ، مِمّا أَدّى إِلى تَحْسينِ جَوْدَةِ النَّسيجِ وَدِقَّةِ التَّفاصيلِ. بِالْإِضافَةِ إِلى ذَلِكَ، تَمَّ اسْتِخْدامُ تِقْنِيّاتِ الدّانْتيلِ وَالتَّطْريزِ بِشَكْلٍ فَنِّيٍّ لِإِضْفاءِ لَمْسَةٍ فَريدَةٍ.

The textile and luxury clothing industries have witnessed a notable revival in recent times, with silk fabric dominating the global scene. This success is attributed to designers' preference for using luxurious natural fibers in their designs, giving the industry a distinct allure and competitive advantages. Modern machines have been developed for weaving silk using advanced technological techniques, leading to improved fabric quality and precision in details. Additionally, lace and embroidery techniques have been artistically employed to add a unique touch.

تَشْهَدُ صِناعَةُ المَلابِسِ الخَضْراءِ اتِّجاهًا قَوِيًّا نَحْوَ اسْتِخْدامِ المَوادِّ الطَّبيعِيَّةِ وَالمُسْتَدامَةِ، وَفي هَذا السّياقِ، اِنْتَشَرَ القُطْنُ العُضْوِيُّ عَلى نِطاقٍ واسِعٍ. يُعَدُّ القُطْنُ العُضْوِيُّ بَديلًا صَديقًا لِلْبيئَةِ لِلْقُطْنِ التَّقْليدِيِّ، حَيْثُ يُزْرَعُ بِدونِ اسْتِخْدامِ المُبيداتِ الحَشَرِيَّةِ وَالأَسْمِدَةِ الكيمْيائِيَّةِ الضّارَّةِ. وَقَدِ اسْتَجابَتْ صِناعَةُ المَنْسوجاتِ وَصِناعَةُ المَلابِسِ لِهَذا الاِهْتِمامِ المُتَزايِدِ مِنْ قِبَلِ المُسْتَهْلِكينَ، وَقامَتْ بِتَطْويرِ تِقْنِيّاتٍ جَديدَةٍ لِنَسْجِ وَتَصْنيعِ الأَقْمِشَةِ العُضْوِيَّةِ. تَتَمَيَّزُ هَذِهِ المَلابِسُ بِأَنَّها صَديقَةٌ لِلْبَشَرَةِ وَقابِلَةٌ لِلتَّحَلُّلِ الحَيَوِيِّ، وَقَدْ أَثْبَتَتْ جَوْدَتَها وَأَصْبَحَتْ مَحَطَّ إِعْجابِ المُسْتَهْلِكينَ في جَميعِ أَنْحاءِ العالَمِ.

The green clothing industry is witnessing a strong trend towards the use of natural and sustainable materials, and in this context, organic cotton has become widely spread. Organic cotton is considered an environmentally friendly alternative to conventional cotton, as it is grown without the use of harmful pesticides and chemical fertilizers. The textile and clothing industries have responded to this growing consumer interest and have developed new techniques for weaving and manufacturing organic fabrics. These clothes are known for being skin-friendly and biodegradable, and they have proven their quality, gaining the admiration of consumers worldwide.

شَهِدَتْ صِناعَةُ الموضَةِ تَحَوُّلًا جِذْرِيًّا بِفَضْلِ اسْتِخْدامِ المُخْمَلِ في تَصْميمِ المَلابِسِ وَالْإِكْسِسْواراتِ. يُعْتَبَرُ المُخْمَلُ قُماشًا فاخِرًا يَتَمَيَّزُ بِمَلْمَسِهِ النّاعِمِ وَمَظْهَرِهِ الفَخْمِ، وَقَدْ أَصْبَحَ اخْتِيارًا شائِعًا بَيْنَ المُصَمِّمينَ العالَمِيّينَ. تَطَوَّرَتْ تِقْنِيّاتُ صِناعَةِ المُخْمَلِ لِتَشْمَلَ تَشْكيلَةً مُتَنَوِّعَةً مِنَ الأَلْوانِ وَالأَنْماطِ، وَاسْتُخْدِمَ في تَصْميمِ الفَساتينِ الرّاقِيَةِ وَالسُّتْراتِ وَالحَقائِبِ وَحَتّى الأَحْذِيَةِ. يَتَمَتَّعُ المُخْمَلُ بِشَعْبِيَّةٍ كَبيرَةٍ بَيْنَ عُشّاقِ الموضَةِ، وَقَدْ أَحْدَثَ تَغْييرًا مَلْحوظًا في مَشْهَدِ الأَزْياءِ العالَمِيِّ، حَيْثُ يُعْتَبَرُ رَمْزًا لِلْأَناقَةِ وَالفَخامَةِ.

The fashion industry has undergone a radical transformation thanks to the use of velvet in clothing and accessories design. Velvet is a luxurious fabric known for its soft texture and glamorous appearance, and it has become a popular choice among international designers. Velvet manufacturing techniques have evolved to include a variety of colors and patterns, and it has been used in the design of elegant dresses, jackets, bags, and even shoes. Velvet enjoys great popularity among fashion enthusiasts and has made a notable change in the global fashion scene, being considered a symbol of elegance and luxury.

4.2.3.2 Informative Article: The Textile Industry in Egypt

Track **21**

صِناعَةُ المَنْسوجاتِ في مِصْرَ

مِنَ المُتَوَقَّعِ أَنْ تَشْهَدَ صِناعَةُ المَنْسوجاتِ في مِصْرَ مُعَدَّلَ نُمُوٍّ مُسْتَقِرٍّ، حَيْثُ يُتَوَقَّعُ مُعَدَّلُ نُمُوٍّ سَنَوِيٍّ مُرَكَّبٍ (CAGR)يَزيدُ عَلى 4% خِلالَ فَتْرَةِ التَّوَقُّعاتِ مِنْ عامِ 2022 إلى عامِ 2027. وَمَعَ ذَلِكَ، فَقَدْ واجَهَتِ الصِّناعَةُ تَحَدِّياتٍ كَبيرَةً، خاصَّةً بِسَبَبِ تَأْثيرِ جائِحَةِ كوفيدْ-19. عَلى الرَّغْمِ مِنَ اسْتِمْرارِ تَشْغيلِ المَصانِعِ، شَهِدَتْ صادِراتُ المَنْسوجاتِ انْخِفاضًا بِنِسْبَةِ 14% في عامِ 2020، حَيْثُ بَلَغَتْ قيمَتُها 2.81 مِلْيارَ دولارٍ مُقارَنَةً بِ 3.721 مِلْيارَ دولارٍ في عامِ 2019. وَمَعَ ذَلِكَ، فَإِنَّ الصِّناعَةَ مُسْتَعِدَّةٌ لِلتَّعافي، حَيْثُ تَسْتَقْبِلُ مِصْرُ اسْتِثْماراتٍ أَجْنَبِيَّةً مُتَزايِدَةً تَصِلُ إلى 17.5 مِلْيارَ دولارٍ وَتَهْدِفُ إلى مُضاعَفَةِ صادِراتِها مِنَ المَنْسوجاتِ وَالمَلابِسِ إلى أَرْبَعَةِ أَضْعافٍ بِحُلولِ عامِ 2025.

تَلْعَبُ صِناعَةُ المَنْسوجاتِ في مِصْرَ دَوْرًا حَيَوِيًّا في الاقْتِصادِ، حَيْثُ تَحْتَلُّ المَرْتَبَةَ الثّانِيَةَ بِحِصَّةٍ تَبْلُغُ 25% في صِناعَةِ المَلابِسِ الشّامِلَةِ، وَتُسْهِمُ بِنِسْبَةِ 3% في النّاتِجِ المَحَلِّيِّ الإِجْمالِيِّ لِلْبِلادِ. إِنَّها تُمَثِّلُ مَوْرِدًا أَساسِيًّا لِلْمَوادِّ الخامِ لِمُصَنِّعي المَلابِسِ وَالمَنْسوجاتِ المَنْزِلِيَّةِ، سَواءٌ عَلى المُسْتَوى المَحَلِّيِّ أَوِ الدَّوْلِيِّ. وَبِفَضْلِ وُصولِها إلى السّوقِ الحُرَّةِ لِلْوِلاياتِ المُتَّحِدَةِ وَدُوَلِ الاتِّحادِ الأوروبِّيِّ، تُصَدِّرُ صِناعَةُ المَنْسوجاتِ نِصْفَ مُنْتَجاتِها إلى الوِلاياتِ المُتَّحِدَةِ وَ 30% مِنْ مُنْتَجاتِها إلى الدُّوَلِ الأوروبِّيَّةِ.

في تَطَوُّرٍ مُهِمٍّ، تُخَطِّطُ مِصْرُ لِافْتِتاحِ أَكْبَرِ مَصْنَعٍ لِلْمَنْسوجاتِ في العالَمِ في مَدينَةِ المَحَلَّةِ. سَيَكونُ لِهَذا المَرْفَقِ العَصْرِيِّ المُجَهَّزِ بِالتِّكْنولوجْيا الحَديثَةِ قُدْرَةً إِنْتاجِيَّةً يَوْمِيَّةً تَصِلُ إلى 30 طُنًّا، وَمِنَ المُتَوَقَّعِ أَنْ يَخْلُقَ فُرَصًا لِلْمُسْتَثْمِرينَ في السّوقِ. وَلِدَعْمِ عَمَلِيّاتِ المَصْنَعِ، تَمَّ الإِعْلانُ عَنْ حَوافِزَ لِتَعْزيزِ زِراعَةِ القُطْنِ عالي الجَوْدَةِ الَّذي يَفي بِمُتَطَلَّباتِ المَصْنَعِ.

تَشْمَلُ صِناعَةُ المَنْسوجاتِ في مِصْرَ عِدَّةَ قِطاعاتٍ، وَتَشْمَلُ الأَلْيافَ وَالغَزْلَ وَالقُماشَ وَالمَلابِسَ وَالمَنْسوجاتِ الأُخْرى. هَذا وَتُسْهِمُ عَمَلِيّاتٌ مِثْلُ الغَزْلِ وَالنَّسْجِ وَالحِياكَةِ وَالتَّشْطيبِ وَغَيْرِها مِنَ العَمَلِيّاتِ الأُخْرى في سِلْسِلَةِ القيمَةِ لِلصِّناعَةِ. تَتَراوَحُ أَنْواعُ الآلاتِ مِنَ الآلاتِ البَسيطَةِ إلى الآلاتِ المُتَطَوِّرَةِ وَمُعَدّاتِ التَّجْميعِ الخَطِّيِّ.

عَلى الرَّغْمِ مِنْ أَنَّ الصِّناعَةَ تَحْمِلُ آفاقًا واعِدَةً، فَإِنَّها تُواجِهُ بَعْضَ التَّحَدِّياتِ. حَيْثُ شَهِدَتْ أَسْعارُ المَوادِّ الخامِ ارْتِفاعًا، كَما تُشَكِّلُ الأُجورُ العالِيَةُ قُيودًا. أَصْبَحَتِ المَوادُّ الخامُ المُتاحَةُ مَحَلِّيًّا، بِما في ذَلِكَ القُطْنُ، أَكْثَرَ تَكْلِفَةً، وَيَعْتَمِدُ القِطاعُ عَلى الخُيوطِ المُسْتَوْرَدَةِ وَالأَلْيافِ الصِّناعِيَّةِ لِلتَّعْويضِ. تُعْتَبَرُ الأُجورُ في مِصْرَ أَعْلى مُقارَنَةً بِالدُّوَلِ المُنافِسَةِ، مِمّا يُؤَدّي إلى انْخِفاضِ الإِنْتاجِيَّةِ. عِلاوَةً عَلى ذَلِكَ، يَعْتَمِدُ القِطاعُ عَلى مُعَدّاتٍ قَديمَةٍ، مِمّا أَدّى إلى زِيادَةِ تَكاليفِ الإِنْتاجِ وَصُعوباتٍ في تَوْفيرِ الغازِ.

لِلتَّغَلُّبِ عَلى هَذِهِ التَّحَدِّياتِ، يَجِبُ عَلى صِناعَةِ المَنسوجاتِ في مِصْرَ التَّرْكيزُ عَلى تَعْزيزِ الإِنْتاجِيَّةِ، وَتَبَنّي المُعَدّاتِ الحَديثَةِ، وَمُعالَجَةُ قَضايا التَّكْلِفَةِ. تَسْتَمِرُّ الجُهودُ المَبْذولَةُ لِتَحْسينِ جودَةِ زِراعَةِ القُطْنِ، جَنْبًا إِلى جَنْبٍ مَعَ الاِسْتِثْماراتِ الاِسْتراتيجِيَّةِ وَدَعْمِ الحُكومَةِ، في تَعْزيزِ نُمُوِّ الصِّناعَةِ وَالحِفاظِ عَلى مَكانَتِها كَلاعِبٍ بارِزٍ في السّوقِ العالَمِيَّةِ لِلْمَنْسوجاتِ.

The Textile Industry in Egypt

The textile industry in Egypt is expected to witness a stable growth rate, with a compound annual growth rate (CAGR) of over 4% during the forecast period from 2022 to 2027. However, the industry has faced significant challenges, especially due to the impact of the COVID-19 pandemic. Despite continued factory operations, textile exports declined by 14% in 2020, with a value of $2.81 billion compared to $3.721 billion in 2019. Nevertheless, the industry is poised for recovery as Egypt welcomes increasing foreign investments amounting to $17.5 billion and aims to quadruple its textile and clothing exports by 2025.

The textile industry plays a vital role in Egypt's economy, ranking second with a 25% share in the comprehensive clothing industry and contributing 3% to the country's gross domestic product (GDP). It serves as a primary resource for raw materials for clothing and home textile manufacturers, both domestically and internationally. With access to the free market of the United States and European Union countries, the textile industry exports half of its products to the United States and 30% to European countries.

In a significant development, Egypt plans to open the world's largest textile factory in the city of Mahalla. This modern facility, equipped with state-of-the-art technology, will have a daily production capacity of up to 30 tons and is expected to create opportunities for market players. To support the factory's operations, incentives have been announced to promote the cultivation of high-quality cotton that meets the factory's requirements.

The textile industry in Egypt encompasses several sectors, including fibers, spinning, weaving, fabrics, garments, and other textiles. Operations such as spinning, weaving, knitting, finishing, and various other processes contribute to the industry's value chain. The types of machinery range from simple machines to advanced machinery and linear assembly installations.

Despite holding promising prospects, the industry faces some challenges. Raw material prices have increased, and high wages pose constraints. Locally available raw materials, including cotton, have become more costly, leading the sector to rely on imported yarn and synthetic fibers for compensation. Wages in Egypt are higher compared to competing countries, resulting in decreased productivity. Additionally, the sector relies on outdated equipment, leading to increased production costs and difficulties in gas supply.

To overcome these challenges, the textile industry in Egypt needs to focus on enhancing productivity, adopting modern equipment, and addressing cost issues. Efforts to improve the quality of cotton cultivation, along with strategic investments and government support, continue to promote industry growth and maintain its prominent position in the global textile market.

4.2.4 Food and Beverage Industry

Track **22**

seed بُذورٌ • **بِذْرَةٌ**

اِسْتَخْدَمَ الطُّهاةُ بُذورَ الكَتّانِ في تَحْضيرِ مَجْموعةٍ مُتَنَوِّعَةٍ مِنَ الأَطْباقِ الصِّحِّيَّةِ في مَطْعَمٍ بَيْروتَ الشَّهيرِ.

Chefs used flaxseed in preparing a variety of healthy dishes at a popular Beirut restaurant.

expiration date تَواريخُ • **تاريخُ انْتِهاءِ صَلاحِيَةٍ**

يَتَعَيَّنُ عَلى المُسْتَهْلِكينَ التَّحَقُّقُ مِنْ تاريخِ انْتِهاءِ الصَّلاحِيَةِ قَبْلَ شِراءِ المُنْتَجاتِ الغِذائِيَّةِ.

Consumers need to check the expiration date before buying food products.

to prepare تَجْهيزٌ • **جَهَّزَ**

جَهَّزَتْ شَرِكَةُ "دانونْ" الفَرَنْسِيَّةُ مُنْتَجاتِها الجَديدَةَ لِلْإِطْلاقِ في السّوقِ المِصْرِيَّةِ.

The French company "Danone" has prepared its new products for launch in the Egyptian market.

to store تَخْزينٌ • **خَزَّنَ**

يُوَفِّرُ المُسْتَوْدَعُ مِساحَةً وَفيرَةً لِتَخْزينِ البَضائِعِ، لِتَلْبِيَةِ احْتِياجاتِ التَّخْزينِ المُتَزايِدَةِ لِصِناعَةِ التَّجْزِئَةِ.

The warehouse provides ample space to store merchandise, meeting the growing storage demands of the retail industry.

to cultivate, farm زِراعَةٌ • **زَرَعَ**

قامَتْ شَرِكَةُ المُنْتَجاتِ العُضْوِيَّةِ في المَغْرِبِ بِزِراعَةِ مَجْموعَةٍ مُتَنَوِّعَةٍ مِنَ الخَضْراواتِ وَالفَواكِهِ لِلْمَوْسِمِ الجَديدِ.

The organic products company in Morocco has planted a variety of vegetables and fruits for the new season.

supply chain سَلاسِلُ • **سِلْسِلَةُ إِمْدادٍ**

تُعْتَبَرُ سِلْسِلَةُ الإِمْدادِ بالِغَةَ الأَهَمِّيَّةِ في صِناعَةِ الأَغْذِيَةِ وَالمَشْروباتِ حَيْثُ تَضْمَنُ تَوافُرَ المُنْتَجاتِ.

The supply chain is extremely important in the food and beverage industry to ensure the availability of products.

health certificate شَهادَةٌ صِحِّيَّةٌ

يُشْتَرَطُ وُجودُ شَهادَةٍ صِحِّيَّةٍ لِاسْتيرادِ اللُّحومِ وَالأَسْماكِ إِلى السُّعودِيَّةِ.

A health certificate is required for the import of meat and fish into Saudi Arabia.

healthy صِحِّيٌّ

عَمِلَتِ الشَّرِكاتُ عَلى تَطْويرِ مُنْتَجاتٍ صِحِّيَّةٍ تُلَبّي الطَّلَبَ المُتَزايِدَ عَلى الأَطْعِمَةِ النَّظيفَةِ.

Companies have worked on developing healthy products to meet the increasing demand for clean foods.

food and beverage industry صِناعَةُ الأَغْذِيَةِ وَالمَشْروباتِ

تُعَدُّ صِناعَةُ الأَغْذِيَةِ وَالمَشْروباتِ في فَرَنْسا مِنْ أَكْبَرِ الصِّناعاتِ وَأَكْثَرِها تَنافُسِيَّةً.

The food and beverage industry in France is one of the largest and most competitive industries.

fresh طازَجٌ

يُعَدُّ تَقْديمُ الطَّعامِ الطّازَجِ في مَطْعَمِ بْروسيلا في الجَزائِرِ ميزَةً أَساسِيَّةً تُمَيِّزُهُ عَنِ الأَماكِنِ الأُخْرى.

Providing fresh food is a key feature that distinguishes the Brassila restaurant in Algeria from other places.

fresh food طَعامٌ طازَجٌ • أَطْعِمَةٌ

تَتَزايَدُ شَعْبِيَّةُ المُنْتَجاتِ العُضْوِيَّةِ، مِثْلِ الطَّعامِ الطّازَجِ، بَيْنَ السُّكّانِ المَحَلِّيّينَ في عُمانَ.

Organic products like fresh food are becoming increasingly popular among local residents in Oman.

canned food طَعامٌ مُعَلَّبٌ

أَعْلَنَتْ شَرِكَةُ هاينْزْ عَنْ خُطَّتِها لِزِيادَةِ إِنْتاجِ الطَّعامِ المُعَلَّبِ بِسَبَبِ الطَّلَبِ المُتَزايِدِ.

Heinz announced its plan to increase the production of canned food due to increasing demand.

organic عُضْوِيٌّ

زادَ الطَّلَبُ عَلى المُنْتَجاتِ العُضْوِيَّةِ في الأَسْواقِ البِريطانِيَّةِ بِشَكْلٍ كَبيرٍ خِلالَ السَّنَواتِ الأَخيرَةِ.

The demand for organic products in British markets has greatly increased in recent years.

غِذاءٌ صِحِّيٌّ • أَغْذِيَةٌ **healthy food**

في إطارِ الحمْلَةِ الوَطَنِيَّةِ لِلتَّوْعِيَةِ بِأَهَمِّيَّةِ الغذاءِ الصِّحِّيِّ، أَطْلَقَتْ وَزارَةُ الصِّحَّةِ مُبادَرَةً جديدَةً تَهْدُفُ إلى تَشْجيعِ الاِسْتِهْلاكِ الواسعِ لِلْأَغْذِيَةِ الصِّحِّيَّةِ بَيْنَ الأَطْفالِ وَالشَّبابِ، مَعَ التَّرْكيزِ عَلى الفَواكِهِ وَالخَضْراواتِ وَالحُبوبِ الكامِلَةِ.

As part of the national campaign to raise awareness about the importance of healthy food, the Ministry of Health has launched a new initiative aimed at promoting widespread consumption of healthy foods among children and youth, with a focus on fruits, vegetables, and whole grains.

غَلَّفَ • تَغْليفٌ **to package**

جَميعُ مُنْتَجاتِ الشّوكولاتَةِ المَصْنوعَةِ مِنْ قِبَلِ شَرِكَةِ ليندتْ مُغَلَّفَةٌ بِالْكامِلِ لِلْحِفاظِ عَلى النَّكْهَةِ وَالجَوْدَةِ.

All chocolate products made by Lindt are fully wrapped to preserve flavor and quality.

قِطاعُ الأَغْذِيَةِ وَالمَشْروباتِ **food and beverage sector**

يَتَصَدَّرُ قِطاعُ الأَغْذِيَةِ وَالمَشْروباتِ في تونسَ القِطاعاتِ الأُخْرى فيما يَتَعَلَّقُ بِالنُّمُوِّ وَالتَّوْظيفِ.

The food and beverage sector in Tunisia tops other sectors in terms of growth and employment.

قيمَةُ إِنْتاجٍ • قِيَمٌ **production value**

بَلَغَتْ قيمَةُ الإِنْتاجِ السَّنَوِيِّ لِشَرِكَةِ الأَغْذِيَةِ العالَمِيَّةِ بيبْسيكو حَوالَيْ 43 مِلْيارَ دولارٍ في العامِ الماضي.

The annual production value of the global food company PepsiCo reached about 43 billion dollars last year.

مُجَفَّفٌ **dried**

تَمَّ تَخْزينُ الفاكِهَةِ وَالخَضْراواتِ المُجَفَّفَةِ لِاسْتِخْدامِها في الأَشْهُرِ القَليلَةِ المُقْبِلَةِ.

Dried fruits and vegetables have been stored for use in the coming months.

مُجَمَّدٌ **frozen**

في ظِلِّ الطَّلَبِ المُتَزايِدِ عَلى الخِياراتِ الغِذائِيَّةِ الصِّحِّيَّةِ، يُوَفِّرُ السّالْمونُ المُجَمَّدُ خِيارًا مُلائِمًا وَذا جَوْدَةٍ عالِيَةٍ لِلْمُسْتَهْلِكينَ كَمَصْدَرٍ لِلْمَأْكولاتِ البَحْرِيَّةِ.

Amid increasing demand for healthy and sustainable food options, frozen salmon provides consumers with a convenient and long-lasting source of high-quality seafood.

مَحْصولٌ • مَحاصيلُ **crop**

يَتَوَقَّعُ المُزارِعونَ في الأُرْدُنِّ مَحْصولًا كَبيرًا مِنَ الزَّيْتونِ هَذا العامَ بِفَضْلِ الأَمْطارِ الوَفيرَةِ.

Farmers in Jordan expect a large olive crop this year thanks to plentiful rains.

مَزْرَعَةٌ • مَزارِعُ **farm**

قامَتْ مَزْرَعَةُ دَجاجٍ بَرازيلِيَّةٌ بِتَوْسيعِ قُدُراتِها لِتَلْبِيَةِ الطَّلَبِ المُتَزايِدِ عَلى الدَّجاجِ الطّازَجِ.

A Brazilian chicken farm has expanded its capabilities to meet the increasing demand for fresh chicken.

مَصْنَعٌ • مَصانِعُ **factory**

تَعْتَزِمُ شَرِكَةُ السُّكَّرِ المِصْرِيَّةُ بِناءَ مَصْنَعٍ جَديدٍ في أَسْوانَ لِزِيادَةِ الإِنْتاجِ.

The Egyptian Sugar Company plans to build a new factory in Aswan to increase production.

مُعَلَّبٌ **canned**

أَعْلَنَتْ شَرِكَةُ كامْبِلْ عَنْ خُطَّتِها لِزِيادَةِ إِنْتاجِ الأَطْعِمَةِ المُعَلَّبَةِ في مَصْنَعِها الرَّئيسِيِّ بِالوِلاياتِ المُتَّحِدَةِ.

Campbell announced its plan to increase the production of canned food in its main factory in the United States.

مَوادُّ تَعْبِئَةٍ وَتَغْليفٍ *pl.* **packaging materials**

تُعْتَبَرُ مَوادُّ التَّعْبِئَةِ وَالتَّغْليفِ عالِيَةُ الجَوْدَةِ أَساسِيَّةً لِحِفْظِ جَوْدَةِ المُنْتَجاتِ الغِذائِيَّةِ.

High-quality packaging materials are essential for preserving the quality of food products

4.2.4.1 Mini-Articles

Track **23**

في نَجاحٍ غَيْرِ مَسْبوقٍ لِصِناعَةِ الأَغْذِيَةِ وَالمَشْروباتِ، أَعْلَنَ مَصْنَعُ طَعامٍ مُعَلَّبٍ مَحَلِّيٍّ عَنْ تِقْنِيَةٍ جَديدَةٍ لِزِيادَةِ تاريخِ انْتِهاءِ صَلاحِيَةِ المُنْتَجاتِ المُعَلَّبَةِ. تَمَّ تَجْهيزُ العَمَلِيَّةِ الجَديدَةِ لِتَخْزينِ المَوادِّ الغِذائِيَّةِ بِطَريقَةٍ أَكْثَرَ نَظافَةً، مَعَ الحِفاظِ عَلى النَّكْهَةِ الطّازَجَةِ لِلطَّعامِ. كَما أَشارَ المَصْنَعُ إِلى أَنَّ المُنْتَجاتِ سَتُزَوَّدُ بِشَهادَةٍ صِحِّيَّةٍ لِضَمانِ سَلامَةِ المُسْتَهْلِكِ.

In an unprecedented success for the food and beverage industry, a local canned food factory has announced a new technology to extend the shelf life of canned products. The new process has been designed to store food in a more hygienic manner while maintaining the fresh flavor of the food. The factory also indicated that the products will be equipped with a health certificate to ensure consumer safety.

بَدَأَتْ مَزْرَعَةٌ عُضْوِيَّةٌ جَدِيدَةٌ بِزَرْعِ بُذورِالخَضْراواتِ وَالفَواكِهِ العُضْوِيَّةِ لِدَعْمِ سِلْسِلَةِ الإِمْدادِ في قِطاعِ الأَغْذِيَةِ وَالمَشْروباتِ. وَقَدْ أَعْلَنَتِ المَزْرَعَةُ أَنَّ جَميعَ المَحاصيلِ سَتَكونُ طازَجَةً، وَصِحِّيَّةً، وَمُغَلَّفَةً بِمَوادَّ تَعْبِئَةٍ وَتَغْليفٍ صَديقَةٍ لِلْبيئَةِ. مِنَ المُتَوَقَّعِ أَنْ تَكونَ قيمَةُ إِنْتاجِ المَزْرَعَةِ هائِلَةً، مِمّا يُعَزِّزُ السّوقَ المَحَلِّيَّةَ.

A new organic farm has begun planting organic vegetable and fruit seeds to support the supply chain in the food and beverage sector. The farm has announced that all crops will be fresh, healthy, and packaged with environmentally friendly packaging materials. The farm's production value is expected to be significant, thereby enhancing the local market.

تَعاوَنَتْ شَرِكَةُ طَعامٍ صِحِّيٍّ مَشْهورَةٌ مَعَ مَجْموعَةٍ مِنَ المُزارِعينَ لِتَقْديمِ طَعامٍ طازَجٍ وَغِذاءٍ صِحِّيٍّ إِلى المُسْتَهْلِكينَ. سَتَكونُ المُنْتَجاتُ الجَديدَةُ، الَّتي تَشْمَلُ الفَواكِهَ وَالخَضْراواتِ العُضْوِيَّةَ، وَالأَطْعِمَةَ المُجَفَّفَةَ وَالمُجَمَّدَةَ، مُتَوَفِّرَةً في مَتاجِرِ البِقالَةِ المَحَلِّيَّةِ قَريبًا. أَعْلَنَتِ الشَّرِكَةُ أَنَّ هَذِهِ الخُطْوَةَ تَأْتي في إِطارِ تَوْسيعِ سِلْسِلَةِ الإِمْدادِ الخاصَّةِ بِها وَضَمانِ أَنَّ جَميعَ المُنْتَجاتِ تَحْتَرِمُ تَواريخَ انْتِهاءِ الصَّلاحِيَةِ الصّارِمَةِ.

A well-known healthy food company has collaborated with a group of farmers to provide fresh and nutritious food to consumers. The new products, which include organic fruits and vegetables, as well as dried and frozen foods, will soon be available in local grocery stores. The company announced that this step is part of expanding its own supply chain and ensuring that all products comply with strict expiration dates.

4.2.4.2 Promotional Descriptions of Products

Track **24**

في الأَشْهُرِ الأَخيرَةِ، زادَتْ شَعْبِيَّةُ حُبوبِ القَمْحِ المَزْروعَةِ في مَزارِعِنا العُضْوِيَّةِ بِشَكْلٍ كَبيرٍ بَيْنَ المُسْتَهْلِكينَ الباحِثينَ عَنِ الطَّعامِ الصِّحِّيِّ. أَسْهَمَتْ جُهودُنا المُتَواصِلَةُ لِتَحْسينِ سِلْسِلَةِ الإِمْدادِ لَدَيْنا في الحِفاظِ عَلى جَوْدَةِ المُنْتَجاتِ الطّازَجَةِ. بِالْإِضافَةِ إِلى ذَلِكَ، يَتِمُّ تَوْفيرُ مَعْلوماتِ تاريخِ انْتِهاءِ الصَّلاحِيَةِ عَلى كُلِّ مُغَلَّفٍ لِضَمانِ اسْتِهْلاكٍ آمِنٍ لِلْمُنْتَجاتِ.

In recent months, the popularity of organic wheat seeds planted in our farms has grown significantly among health-conscious consumers. Our continuous efforts to improve our supply chain have contributed to preserving the quality of fresh produce. Additionally, expiration dates are provided on each package to ensure safe consumption of the products.

تَشْهَدُ صِناعَةُ الأَغْذيَةِ وَالمَشْروباتِ نُمُوًّا قَوِيًّا، خاصَّةً في قِطاعِ الأَغْذيَةِ المُجَمَّدَةِ وَالمُجَفَّفَةِ. يَقومُ مَصْنَعُنا بِتَجْهيزِ وَتَعْبِئَةِ الأَطْعِمَةِ الطّازَجَةِ لِلْحِفاظِ عَلى جَوْدَتِها، مَعَ الاهْتِمامِ الدّائِمِ بِالشَّهاداتِ الصِّحِّيَّةِ. نَحْنُ نَعْمَلُ عَلى تَخْزينِ هَذِهِ المُنْتَجاتِ في ظُروفٍ صِحِّيَّةٍ مُثْلى، لِضَمانِ قيمَةِ الإِنْتاجِ وَلِتَقْديمِ الأَطْعِمَةِ المُعَلَّبَةِ الأَلَذِّ لِلْمُسْتَهْلِكينَ.

The food and beverage industry is experiencing strong growth, especially in the frozen and dried food sector. Our factory processes and packages fresh food to maintain its quality, with constant attention to health certifications. We work on storing these products under optimal hygienic conditions to ensure production value and deliver the most flavorful canned foods to consumers.

تُنْتِجُ مَزْرَعَتُنا الحَديثَةُ مَجْموعَةً واسِعَةً مِنَ الأَطْعِمَةِ الطّازَجَةِ وَالغِذاءِ الصِّحِّيِّ، مِنْ بُذورِ الطَّماطِمِ إِلى القَمْحِ العُضْوِيِّ. نَحْنُ نُراقِبُ بِدِقَّةٍ سِلْسِلَةَ الإِمْدادِ لَدَيْنا وَنَسْتَخْدِمُ أَحْدَثَ مَوادِّ التَّعْبِئَةِ وَالتَّغْليفِ لِضَمانِ تَوْصيلِ مُنْتَجاتِنا بِأَمانٍ إِلى المَتاجِرِ. كَما نَحْرِصُ عَلى أَنْ تَتَوافَقَ كُلُّ مُنْتَجاتِنا مَعَ الشَّهاداتِ الصِّحِّيَّةِ الصّارِمَةِ قَبْلَ أَنْ تَصِلَ إِلى المُسْتَهْلِكِ.

Our modern farm produces a wide range of fresh and healthy foods, from tomato seeds to organic wheat. We closely monitor our supply chain and use the latest packaging materials to safely deliver our products to stores. We also ensure that all our products comply with strict health certifications before reaching the consumers.

تَسْتَعِدُّ الشَّرِكاتُ في قِطاعِ الأَغْذيَةِ وَالمَشْروباتِ لِمُواكَبَةِ الطَّلَبِ المُتَزايِدِ عَلى الأَطْعِمَةِ العُضْوِيَّةِ. بُذورُ الكينْوا، الَّتي تُزْرَعُ في مَزْرَعَتِنا العُضْوِيَّةِ، تَجْذِبُ الكَثيرَ مِنَ الانْتِباهِ بِسَبَبِ فَوائِدِها الصِّحِّيَّةِ. هَذِهِ البُذورُ الطّازَجَةُ مُعَبَّأَةٌ بِدِقَّةٍ وَمُجَهَّزَةٌ بِمَوادِّ تَعْبِئَةٍ وَتَغْليفٍ مَتينَةٍ لِحِمايَتِها مِنَ التَّلَفِ وَالحِفاظِ عَلى صَلاحِيَّتِها.

Companies in the food and beverage sector are preparing to meet the increasing demand for organic food. Quinoa seeds, cultivated in our organic farm, attract a lot of attention due to their health benefits. These fresh seeds are carefully packaged and equipped with sturdy packaging materials to protect them from damage and maintain their expiration dates.

تُعْتَبَرُ الشَّهاداتُ الصِّحِّيَّةُ جُزْءًا أَساسِيًّا مِنْ سِلْسِلَةِ الإِمْدادِ في صِناعَةِ الأَغْذيَةِ وَالمَشْروباتِ. يَقومُ مَصْنَعُنا المُتَطَوِّرُ بِتَجْهيزِ وَتَخْزينِ الأَطْعِمَةِ الطّازَجَةِ وَالمُجَمَّدَةِ وَالمُعَلَّبَةِ وَفْقًا لِأَعْلى المَعاييرِ الصِّحِّيَّةِ. وَنَحْنُ نُقَدِّرُ قيمَةَ الإِنْتاجِ عالي الجَوْدَةِ، وَالَّذي يُعْتَبَرُ مِنْ أَهَمِّ العَوامِلِ الَّتي تَدْعَمُ فَتْرَةَ الصَّلاحِيَةِ الطَّويلَةِ لِمُنْتَجاتِنا.

Health certification is an essential part of the supply chain in the food and beverage industry. Our advanced factory processes and stores fresh, frozen, and canned foods according to the highest health standards. We value high-quality production, which is one of the crucial factors supporting the long expiration dates of our products.

تَزْدَهِرُ مَزارِعُ الطَّعامِ العُضْوِيِّ بِفَضْلِ الإِقْبالِ المُتَزايِدِ عَلى الطَّعامِ الصِّحِّيِّ وَالطّازَجِ. تُخَزَّنُ المَحاصيلُ المُنْتَقاةُ بِعِنايَةٍ، مِنَ الخَضْراواتِ العُضْوِيَّةِ إِلى بُذورِ الحُبوبِ، في ظُروفٍ مِثالِيَّةٍ قَبْلَ أَنْ تُغَلَّفَ بِعِنايَةٍ لِلْحِفاظِ عَلى طَعْمِها

وَقيمَتِها الغِذائِيَّة. كُلُّ مَرْحَلَةٍ في سِلْسِلَةِ الإِمْدادِ تَتِمُّ تَحْتَ إِشْرافِ خُبَراءِ الصِّحَّةِ لِضَمانِ الامْتِثالِ لِأَعْلى المَعاييرِ الصِّحِّيَّةِ.

Organic food farms thrive thanks to the growing demand for healthy and fresh food. Carefully selected crops, from organic vegetables to grain seeds, are stored under ideal conditions before being carefully packaged to preserve their taste and nutritional value. Every stage in the supply chain is supervised by health experts to ensure compliance with the highest health standards.

4.2.5 Construction and Building Materials

Track **25**

cement أَسْمَنْتٌ

اِنْخَفَضَتْ أَسْعارُ الأَسْمَنْتِ في الأُرْدُنِّ مُؤَخَّرًا بِسَبَبِ الزِّيادَةِ في الإِنْتاجِ.

Cement prices in Jordan have recently fallen due to an increase in production.

to construct أَنْشَأَ • إِنْشاءٌ

أَنْشَأَتْ شَرِكَةُ "آيْكِيا" السُّويدِيَّةُ مَبْنًى صَديقًا لِلْبيئَةِ في دُبَيَّ يَعْتَمِدُ عَلى الطّاقَةِ المُتَجَدِّدَةِ.

The Swedish company "Ikea" has constructed an environmentally friendly building in Dubai that relies on renewable energy.

tile بَلاطٌ

يَتَوَفَّرُ العَديدُ مِنْ أَنْواعِ البَلاطِ في السّوقِ اللُّبْنانِيَّةِ لِتُناسِبَ جَميعَ الأَذْواقِ وَالميزانِيّاتِ.

Various types of tiles are available in the Lebanese market to suit all tastes and budgets.

tile-, tiled بَلاطِيٌّ

تَشْهَدُ أَعْمالُ البِناءِ في المَدينَةِ إِقْبالًا كَبيرًا عَلى اسْتِخْدامِ الأَرْضِيّاتِ البَلاطِيَّةِ، حَيْثُ تُعْتَبَرُ خِيارًا شائِعًا وَمَتينًا في تَصْميمِ المَباني الحَديثَةِ.

The construction works in the city are witnessing a great demand for the use of tiled floors, as they are a popular and durable choice in modern building designs.

construction بِناءٌ

تَمَّ تَعْيينُ فَريقِ بِناءٍ لِإِنْشاءِ مُجَمَّعٍ سَكَنِيٍّ جَديدٍ في وَسَطِ القاهِرَةِ.

A construction team was hired to build a new residential complex in downtown Cairo.

In Arabic, rather than using a verb in the passive voice to signify the completion or occurrence of an action, the verb تَمَّ ('to be completed') is often used. This verb is typically followed by a verbal noun (masdar) acting as its subject. Omitting the agent of the action is a feature of this construction, making it useful for focusing on the action's completion instead of who carried it out. This also allows for a more neutral or general statement.

In the example above, تَمَّ تَعْيِينُ فَرِيقِ بِنَاءٍ (literally, 'the appointment of a construction team was completed') could also be written as تُعِيِّنَ فَرِيقُ بِنَاءٍ ('a construction team was appointed').

building- **بِنائِيٌّ**

تَمَّ اسْتِخْدامُ مَوادَّ بِنائِيَةٍ مُسْتَدامَةٍ في تَشْييدِ المَكْتَبَةِ الجَديدَةِ في جامِعَةِ بَيْروتَ.

Sustainable building materials were used in the construction of the new library at Beirut University.

to build • بِناءً **بَنى**

بَنى المُقاوِلونَ المَنْزِلَ في غُضونِ سِتَّةِ شُهورٍ بِاسْتِخْدامِ تِقْنِيّاتِ البِناءِ الحَديثَةِ.

The contractors built the house within six months using modern construction techniques.

building restoration **تَرْميمُ مَبانٍ**

تُرَكِّزُ العَديدُ مِنَ الشَّرِكاتِ القَطَرِيَّةِ عَلى تَرْميمِ المَباني القَديمَةِ لِلْحِفاظِ عَلى التُّراثِ المِعْمارِيِّ.

Many Qatari companies focus on renovating old buildings to preserve architectural heritage.

home design **تَصْميمُ مَنازِلَ**

أَصْبَحَتِ التَّصْميماتُ المُوَفِّرَةُ لِلطّاقَةِ لِلْمَنازِلِ الحَديثَةِ مِعْيارًا في السّوقِ العَقارِيَّةِ السُّعودِيَّةِ.

Energy-efficient modern home designs have become a standard in the Saudi real estate market.

construction contracting company **شَرِكَةُ مُقاوَلَةِ البِناءِ**

فازَتْ شَرِكَةُ مُقاوَلَةِ البِناءِ "مَجْموعَةُ بِنْ لادِنِ السُّعودِيَّةُ" بِعَقْدٍ لِبِناءِ ناطِحَةِ سَحابٍ جَديدَةٍ في الرِّياضِ.

The construction contracting company "Saudi Binladin Group" won a contract to build a new skyscraper in Riyadh.

حَجَرٌ • أَحْجارٌ **stone**

يَتِمُّ اسْتِخْدامُ الأَحجارِ بِشَكْلٍ واسِعٍ في التَّشْييدِ وَالبِناءِ في جِبالِ الأَطْلَسِ في المَغْرِبِ.

Stone is widely used in construction and building in the Atlas Mountains in Morocco.

حَجَرِيٌّ **stone-**

تَتَميَّزُ المَباني التَّقْليدِيَّةُ في اليَمَنِ بِالْجُدْرانِ الحَجَرِيَّةِ الَّتي تُضْفي لَمْسَةً فَريدَةً وَجَمالِيَّةً.

Traditional buildings in Yemen feature stone walls that add a unique and aesthetic touch.

حَديدٌ **iron**

الحَديدُ هُوَ مادَّةُ بِناءٍ أَساسِيَّةٌ في مَشاريعِ البِناءِ الضَّخْمَةِ في الإماراتِ.

Iron is an essential building material in massive construction projects in the UAE.

حَفَرَ • حَفْرٌ **to dig**

أَسْفَرَتْ أَعْمالُ الحَفْرِ في مَوْقِعِ البِناءِ عَنِ اكْتِشافِ أَطْلالٍ تاريخِيَّةٍ قَديمَةٍ في الإِسْكَنْدَرِيَّةِ.

Excavation work at the construction site resulted in the discovery of ancient historical ruins in Alexandria.

خَرَسانَةٌ **concrete**

أَصْبَحَتِ الخَرَسانَةُ المُعادُ تَدْويرُها مُكَوِّنًا بيئِيًّا في مَشاريعِ البِناءِ المُسْتَدامَةِ في السُّويدِ.

Recycled concrete has become an environmental component in sustainable construction projects in Sweden.

خَرَسانِيٌّ **concrete-**

تَمَّ بِناءُ جِسْرٍ خَرَسانِيٍّ حَديثٍ فَوْقَ النّيلِ في القاهِرَةِ لِتَخْفيفِ الازْدِحامِ المُروريِّ.

A modern concrete bridge was built over the Nile in Cairo to alleviate traffic congestion.

رَفَعَ • رَفْعٌ **to lift**

يَقومُ العُمّالُ في مَوْقِعِ بِناءٍ في عَمّانَ بِرَفْعِ الخَرَسانَةِ بِاسْتِخْدامِ الرّافِعاتِ الهَيْدروليكِيَّةِ.

Workers at a construction site in Amman are lifting concrete using hydraulic cranes.

to throw • رَمْيٌ **رَمى**

رَمى العُمّالُ نُفاياتِ البِناءِ في حاوِياتٍ خاصَّةٍ لِلتَّخَلُّصِ مِنْها بِشَكْلٍ آمِنٍ.

Workers threw the construction waste into special containers for safe disposal.

glass **زُجاجٌ**

يَعْتَمِدُ تَصْميمُ المَتْحَفِ الحَديثِ في القاهِرَةِ عَلى الزُّجاجِ لِيَجْلِبَ الضَّوْءَ الطَّبيعِيَّ إلى المِساحاتِ الدّاخِلِيَّةِ.

The design of the modern museum in Cairo relies on glass to bring natural light into the interior spaces.

glass- **زُجاجِيٌّ**

تَتَمَيَّزُ العَديدُ مِنَ المَباني الحَديثَةِ في الكُوَيْتِ بِواجِهاتٍ زُجاجِيَّةٍ تَعْكِسُ الأَضْواءَ المُتَوَهِّجَةَ لِلْمَدينَةِ.

Many modern buildings in Kuwait feature glass facades reflecting the city's glowing lights.

scaffolding and equipment *pl.* **سِقالاتٌ وَمُعَدّاتٌ**

قامَتِ الشَّرِكَةُ القَطَرِيَّةُ بِشِراءِ سِقالاتٍ وَمُعَدّاتِ بِناءٍ جَديدَةٍ لِتَوْسيعِ نِطاقِ عَمَلِيّاتِها.

The Qatari company purchased new scaffolding and construction equipment to expand its operations.

building roof • أُسْقُفٌ **سَقْفُ مَبْنًى**

تَمَّ تَرْكيبُ السَّقْفِ المَعْدِنِيِّ لِلْمَبْنى الجَديدِ في العاصِمَةِ الأُرْدُنِّيَّةِ عَمّانَ.

The metal roof of the new building was installed in the Jordanian capital, Amman.

luxury apartment • شُقَقٌ **شَقَّةٌ فاخِرَةٌ**

أُفْتُتِحَتْ شَقَّةٌ فاخِرَةٌ جَديدَةٌ في بُرْجِ خَليفَةَ بِدُبَيَّ وَهِيَ تَتَمَتَّعُ بِإِطْلالَةٍ بانورامِيَّةٍ عَلى المَدينَةِ.

A new luxury apartment was opened in the Burj Khalifa in Dubai enjoying a panoramic view of the city.

to pour • صَبٌّ **صَبَّ**

صَبَّ المُقاوِلونَ الخَرَسانَةَ لِلْأَساساتِ في مَوْقِعِ البِناءِ في الرِّياضِ.

The contractors poured concrete for the foundations at the construction site in Riyadh.

to design تَصْميمٌ • **صَمَّمَ**

صَمَّمَ المُهَنْدِسُ المِعْمارِيُّ المَغْرِبِيُّ بِناءً فَريدًا يَجْمَعُ بَيْنَ الطّابَعِ التَّقْليدِيِّ وَالحَديث.

The Moroccan architect designed a unique building that combines traditional and modern character.

construction industry **صِناعَةُ البِناءِ**

تُعَدُّ صِناعَةُ البِناءِ في الإماراتِ العَرَبِيَّةِ المُتَّحِدَةِ مِنْ أَهَمِّ القِطاعاتِ الاقْتِصادِيَّة.

The construction industry in the United Arab Emirates is one of the most important economic sectors.

contract عُقودٌ • **عَقْدٌ**

تَمَّ تَوْقيعُ عَقْدِ بِناءٍ جَديدٍ بَيْنَ الحُكومَةِ العِراقِيَّةِ وَشَرِكَةِ بِناءٍ دَوْلِيَّة.

A new construction contract was signed between the Iraqi government and an international construction company.

construction work أَعمالٌ • **عَمَلٌ إِنْشائِيٌّ**

يَجْري القِيامُ بِأَعْمالٍ إِنْشائِيَّةٍ كَبيرَةٍ في الدَّوْحَةِ اسْتِعْدادًا لِكَأْسِ العالَمِ لِكُرَةِ القَدَم.

Large-scale construction work is being carried out in Doha in preparation for the World Cup.

brick قَوالِبُ • **قالَبُ طوبٍ**

تُسْتَخْدَمُ قَوالِبُ الطّوبِ في عَمَلِيَّةِ بِناءِ المَنازِلِ التَّقْليدِيَّةِ في مِصْرَ.

Bricks are used in the process of building traditional houses in Egypt.

to cut قَطْعٌ • **قَطَعَ**

يَقْطَعُ العُمّالُ الأَحْجارَ الطَّبيعِيَّةَ في المَحْجَرِ لِاسْتِخْدامِها في مَشْروعِ بِناءٍ في لُبْنانَ.

The workers cut natural stone in the quarry for use in a construction project in Lebanon.

مَصْنَعُ طوبٍ • مَصانِعُ — **brick factory**

أُفْتُتِحَ مَصْنَعُ طوبٍ جَديدٌ في الكُوَيْتِ لِتَلْبِيَةِ الطَّلَبِ المُتَزايِدِ عَلى مَوادِّ البِناءِ المُسْتَدامَةِ.

A new brick factory has been opened in Kuwait to meet the growing demand for sustainable building materials.

مِعْمارِيٌّ — **architectural**

تَحْظى التَّصاميمُ المِعْمارِيَّةُ العَصْرِيَّةُ لِمَتْحَفِ اللّوفرِ أبوظَبي بِالإِعْجابِ الكَبيرِ مِنَ الزُّوّارِ وَالنُّقّادِ عَلى حَدٍّ سَواءٍ.

The modern architectural designs of the Louvre Abu Dhabi Museum receive great admiration from both visitors and critics alike.

مُقاوِلُ بِناءٍ • مُقاوِلونَ — **building contractor**

تَمَّ تَعْيينُ مُقاوِلِ بِناءٍ مِنَ المَغْرِبِ لِلْإِشْرافِ عَلى بِناءِ مُجَمَّعٍ سَكَنِيٍّ جَديدٍ في الرِّباطِ.

A building contractor from Morocco was hired to oversee the construction of a new residential complex in Rabat.

مَوادُّ بِناءٍ *pl.* — **building materials**

تُعَدُّ مَوادُّ البِناءِ مِنْ أَهَمِّ العَوامِلِ الَّتي تُحَدِّدُ جَوْدَةَ الأَبْنِيَةِ وَالمُنْشَآتِ.

Building materials are one of the key factors that determine the quality of buildings and structures.

هَنْدَسَةٌ مِعْمارِيَّةٌ — **architecture**

تَتَميَّزُ الهَنْدَسَةُ المِعْمارِيَّةُ الإِماراتِيَّةُ بِالْجَمْعِ بَيْنَ العَراقَةِ التَّقْليدِيَّةِ وَالتِّكْنولوجْيا الحَديثَةِ.

Emirati architecture stands out by combining traditional elegance with modern technology

4.2.5.1 Mini-Articles

Track **26**

تَعْتَزِمُ شَرِكَةُ "الهَنْدَسَةِ المِعْمارِيَّةِ المُتَقَدِّمَةِ" بِناءَ مُجَمَّعِ شُقَقٍ فاخِرَةٍ في قَلْبِ العاصِمَةِ. الشَّرِكَةُ، الَّتي تُعْتَبَرُ مُقاوِلَ بِناءٍ رَئيسِيًّا في المِنْطَقَةِ، تَسْتَخْدِمُ أَحْدَثَ مَوادِّ البِناءِ في مَشاريعِها، يَشْمَلُ ذَلِكَ الأَسْمَنْتَ الخَرَسانِيَّ المَتينَ وَالزُّجاجَ الصَّلْبَ. سَيَتَمَيَّزُ المَبْنى الجَديدُ بِسَطْحٍ مُبْهِرٍ مِنْ تَصْميمِ أَحَدِ المِعْمارِيّينَ المَرْموقينَ في البِلادِ.

The company "Advanced Architecture" intends to build a luxury apartment complex in the heart of the capital. The company, which is a leading construction contractor in the area, uses the latest building materials in its projects, including durable concrete and solid glass. The new building will feature an impressive roof, designed by a renowned architect in the country.

تَمَّ تَجْهيزُ شَرِكَةِ مُقاوِلَةِ البِناءِ "الرّافِعَةِ الذَّهَبِيَّةِ" بِمَجْموعَةٍ مِنْ أَحْدَثِ السِّقالاتِ وَالمُعَدّاتِ لِلبَدْءِ في عَمَلٍ إِنْشائِيٍّ ضَخْمٍ. مِنَ المُقَرَّرِ أَنْ تَقومَ الشَّرِكَةُ بِأَعْمالِ الحَفْرِ وَالبِناءِ لِأَبْراجٍ تِجارِيَّةٍ جَديدَةٍ في المَدينَةِ. سَتَكونُ مَوادُّ البِناءِ الرَّئيسِيَّةُ المُسْتَخْدَمَةُ في المَشْروعِ مِنَ الحَديدِ القَوِيِّ وَالحَجَرِ الطَّبيعِيِّ.

The construction contractor company, "Golden Crane," has been equipped with a range of state-of-the-art scaffolding and equipment to begin a massive construction project. The company is scheduled to carry out excavation and construction work for new commercial towers in the city. The main construction materials used in the project will be strong iron and natural stone.

أَعْلَنَتْ شَرِكَةُ "تَصْميمِ المَنازِلِ العَصْرِيَّةِ" عَنْ خُطَطٍ لِإِعادَةِ تَرْميمِ مَبانٍ قَديمَةٍ في المَدينَةِ القَديمَةِ. سَيَجْري تَوْظيفُ بَنّائينَ وَبَلّاطينَ مُحْتَرِفينَ لِتَرْكيبِ بَلاطٍ جَديدٍ وَإِعْدادِ تَصميمِ المَبْنى الدّاخِلِيِّ. المَشْروعُ، المُمَوَّلُ بِعَقْدٍ مَعَ الحُكومَةِ المَحَلِّيَّةِ، سَيَسْتَخْدِمُ الخَرَسانَةَ وَالقِطَعَ الزُّجاجِيَّةَ في تَصْميمِهِ.

The company "Modern Home Design" has announced plans to renovate old buildings in the old town. Skilled builders and tilers will be employed to install new tiles and design the interiors. The project, funded through a contract with the local government, will utilize concrete and glass pieces in its design.

4.2.5.2 Informative Article: Dubai

Track **27**

نَجاحاتُ دُبَيَّ في التَّطْويرِ العُمْرانِيِّ

اِسْتَمَرَّتْ دُبَيُّ في تَحْقيقِ نَجاحاتٍ كَبيرَةٍ في تَطْويرِ البِنْيَةِ التَّحْتِيَّةِ وَالمَباني الضَّخْمَةِ الَّتي أَصْبَحَتِ الآنَ رَمْزًا لِلإِبْداعِ الهَنْدَسِيِّ وَالتَّقَدُّمِ. حَيْثُ باتَتِ الأَبْراجُ الشّاهِقَةُ، وَالمَراكِزُ التِّجارِيَّةُ الرّائِعَةُ، وَالشُّقَقُ الفاخِرَةُ تَمْتَدُّ عَلى طولِ أُفُقِها، مُحَقِّقَةً التَّوازُنَ بَيْنَ الحِفاظِ عَلى الثَّقافَةِ وَالتَّقاليدِ المَحَلِّيَّةِ، وَالتَّطَلُّعِ لِمُسْتَقْبَلٍ حَديثٍ وَمُتَقَدِّمٍ.

وَقَدْ أَسْهَمَتْ شَرِكاتُ مُقاوَلاتِ البِناءِ العالَمِيَّةُ، مَعَ مَجْموعَةٍ مُخْتارَةٍ مِنَ المُهَنْدِسينَ المِعْمارِيّينَ المُبْدِعينَ، في صُنْعِ تِلْكَ الصّورَةِ المُتَمَيِّزَةِ لِدُبَيَّ. وَقَدِ اسْتُخْدِمَتْ مَوادُّ بِناءٍ مُتَطَوِّرَةٌ في تَشْييدِ تِلْكَ المَباني، مِنَ الخَرَسانَةِ المُسَلَّحَةِ وَالحَجَرِ الطَّبيعِيِّ، إِلى الزُّجاجِ العاكِسِ الَّذي يَعْكِسُ سَماءَ دُبَيَّ الزَّرْقاءَ.

إِنَّ القُوَّةَ العامِلَةَ الَّتي تَقِفُ وَراءَ هَذا النَّجاحِ تَسْتَحِقُّ الثَّناءَ وَالتَّقْديرَ. فَالعُمّالُ، الَّذينَ يَعْمَلونَ في أَشَدِّ الظُّروفِ صُعوبَةً، هُمُ العَمودُ الفِقْرِيُّ لِهَذا التَّقَدُّمِ المِعْمارِيِّ. وَهُمْ يَتَعامَلونَ مَعَ كُلِّ شَيْءٍ، مِنَ الحَديدِ وَالبَلاطِ وَالأَسْمَنْتِ، إِلى تَشْغيلِ السِّقالاتِ وَالمُعَدّاتِ الثَّقيلَةِ. وَمَعَ ذَلِكَ، يَسْتَمِرُّ التَّحَدّي في ضَمانِ أَمْنِهِم وَسَلامَتِهِمْ، فَهُمْ أَصْحابُ الأَيْدي الماهِرَةِ الَّتي شَيَّدَتْ دُبَيَّ وَصاغَتْ صورَتَها الحَديثَةَ المُتَقَدِّمَةَ.

Dubai's Urban Development Success

Dubai has continued to achieve great success in developing infrastructure and massive buildings that have now become symbols of engineering innovation and progress. The towering skyscrapers, stunning commercial centers, and luxurious apartments stretch along its skyline, striking a balance between preserving local culture and traditions and aspiring for a modern and advanced future.

Global construction companies, along with a select group of creative architects, have contributed to creating this distinctive image of Dubai. Advanced building materials have been used in constructing these buildings, from reinforced concrete and natural stone to reflective glass that mirrors Dubai's blue sky.

The workforce behind this success deserves praise and appreciation. The workers, who labor in extremely challenging conditions, are the backbone of this architectural progress. They handle everything from iron and tiles to cement, scaffolding, and heavy machinery. Nevertheless, the challenge persists in ensuring their safety and well-being, as they are the skilled hands that have built Dubai and shaped its modern and advanced image.

Unit 5
Science and Technology

In an era where scientific innovation and technological advancements drive change at an unprecedented pace, the ability to articulate and understand these subjects becomes increasingly essential. This unit equips you with the specialized vocabulary and context needed to navigate the vast landscape of scientific and technological topics as they are presented in Arabic media.

Our first focus is on 'Scientific Research and Discovery,' which is segmented into key fields such as Biology and Medical Research, Chemistry and Materials Science, Physics and Astronomy, and Environmental Science and Sustainability. In this section, you'll acquire a rich set of terms and phrases that can help you comprehend cutting-edge research, medical breakthroughs, and environmental issues. These terms are critical for engaging with Arabic media's coverage of developments that shape our understanding of the world and our place within it.

The unit then pivots to 'Technology and Innovation,' a realm that dramatically impacts modern society and dictates the pace of change. We begin by exploring the vocabulary related to Information Technology and Cybersecurity, diving into the language used to discuss everything from cloud computing to cyber threats. We then venture into the fascinating worlds of Artificial Intelligence and Robotics, and Clean Energy and Renewable Technologies. As these topics are at the forefront of modern technological innovation, mastering the vocabulary that surrounds them is crucial for a nuanced understanding of current and future trends.

Through the breadth and depth of topics covered in this unit, you'll be well-prepared to engage with Arabic media's portrayal of both scientific and technological domains. This will not only expand your language repertoire but will also offer you valuable insights into how the Arab world interacts with, and contributes to, global scientific and technological advancements.

5.1 Scientific Research and Discovery

Track **28**

discovery — اِكْتِشافٌ

جَرى الكَشْفُ عَنِ اكْتِشافٍ جَديدٍ في مَجالِ الطِّبِّ يُمْكِنُ أَنْ يُؤَثِّرَ بِشَكْلٍ كَبيرٍ عَلى عِلاجِ الأَمْراضِ الوِراثِيَّةِ.

A new discovery in the field of medicine has been revealed that could have a significant impact on the treatment of genetic diseases.

research — بُحوثٌ • بَحْثٌ

قَدْ يَسْتَغْرِقُ البَحْثُ العِلْمِيُّ سَنَواتٍ عَديدَةً لِلْوُصولِ إِلى نَتائِجَ مُؤَكَّدَةٍ وَتَأْكيدِ فَرْضِيّاتِ الدِّراساتِ.

Scientific research can take several years to reach conclusive results and confirm study hypotheses.

scientist — عُلَماءُ • عالِمٌ

يُعَدُّ العالِمُ البارِزُ في مَجالِ الفيزْياءِ الذَّرِّيَّةِ واحِدًا مِنْ أَبْرَزِ العُلَماءِ في العَصْرِ الحَديثِ.

The prominent scientist in the field of atomic physics is considered one of the leading scientists in the modern era.

science — عُلومٌ • عِلْمٌ

تَتَطَلَّعُ الدَّوْلَةُ إِلى تَعْزيزِ الاِسْتِثْمارِ في مَجالِ العُلومِ لِتَعْزيزِ التَّقَدُّمِ العِلْمِيِّ وَالتِّكْنولوجِيِّ.

The state aims to enhance investment in the field of sciences to promote scientific and technological advancement.

scientific — عِلْمِيٌّ

نُشِرَتِ النَّتائِجُ العِلْمِيَّةُ الجَديدَةُ في مَجَلَّةٍ عِلْمِيَّةٍ مَرموقَةٍ وَروجِعَتْ مِنْ قِبَلِ الخُبَراءِ في المَجالِ.

The new scientific findings have been published in a reputable scientific journal and have been peer-reviewed by experts in the field.

Nisba adjectives in Arabic are derived from nouns to describe a relationship or attribution. These adjectives typically end in ـِيّ for masculine and ـِيَّة for feminine. They are used to describe a variety of associations such as origin, profession, or characteristics. Here are some examples:

- عِلْمِيٌّ scientific (derived from عِلْمٌ, meaning 'science'). This adjective is used to describe something related to the field of science.

طِبِّيٌّ medical (<طِبٌّ medicine)

بِيولوجِيٌّ biological (< بِيولوجِيا biology)

You will notice several more nisba adjectives in this section and others. Try to determine the noun each is derived from and how it relates to its meaning.

5.1.1 Biology and Medical Research

Track **29**

أَفْرَزَ • إِفْرازٌ **to secrete**

تُفرِزُ الغُدَّةُ الدَّرَقِيَّةُ هُرمونَ الثَّيروكْسينِ الَّذي يُنَظِّمُ عَمَلياتِ الأَيْضِ في الجِسْمِ.

The thyroid gland secretes thyroxin hormone, which regulates metabolic processes in the body.

اِضْطِرابٌ وِراثِيٌّ **genetic disorder**

أَعْلَنَ العُلَماءُ في جامِعَةِ القاهِرَةِ عَنِ اكْتِشافٍ جَديدٍ مُرْتَبِطٍ بِالاِضْطِراباتِ الوِراثِيَّةِ قَدْ يَقودُ إِلى عِلاجاتٍ جَديدَةٍ لِمَرَضِ أَلْزِهايمَر.

Scientists at Cairo University have announced a new discovery related to genetic disorders that could lead to new treatments for Alzheimer's disease.

بَحْثٌ طِبِّيٌّ • بُحوثٌ **medical research**

تَسْعى الحُكومَةُ الجَزائِرِيَّةُ لِتَوْسيعِ الاِسْتِثْمارِ في البُحوثِ الطِّبِّيَّةِ لِلْحَدِّ مِنَ انْتِشارِ الأَمْراضِ المُسْتَعْصِيَةِ.

The Algerian government is seeking to expand investment in medical research to curb the spread of intractable diseases.

بِيولوجِيٌّ **biological**

اِكْتَشَفَ العُلَماءُ تَأْثيرًا بِيولوجِيًا جَديدًا لِلتَّلَوُّثِ عَلى نُمُوِّ الأَطْفالِ في المُدُنِ الكُبْرى.

Scientists have discovered a new biological effect of pollution on the growth of children in major cities.

بِيولوجْيا **biology**

تَكْشِفُ البَيولوجْيا المُرَكَّبَةُ لِلنِّظامِ العَصَبِيِّ عَنِ الحاجَةِ إِلى مَزيدٍ مِنَ البَحْثِ لِفَهْمِ كَيْفِيَّةِ عَمَلِ الدِّماغِ.

The complex biology of the nervous system shows that it needs more research to understand how the brain works.

clinical trial — تَجْرِبَةٌ سَرِيرِيَّةٌ

أَظْهَرَتِ التَّجْرِبَةُ السَّرِيرِيَّةُ الَّتي أُجْرِيَتْ في الرِّياضِ أَنَّ العَقارَ الجَديدَ فَعّالٌ في عِلاجِ السَّرَطانِ.

The clinical trial conducted in Riyadh showed that the new drug is effective in treating cancer.

gene editing — تَحْريرُ الجيناتِ

تُعْتَبَرُ تِقْنِيَّةُ تَحْريرِ الجيناتِ، CRISPR، ثَوْرَةً في عالَمِ الطِّبِّ، حَيْثُ تُتيحُ تَعْديلَ الجيناتِ البَشَرِيَّةِ لِلْحَدِّ مِنَ الأَمْراضِ الوِراثِيَّةِ.

The gene-editing technology, CRISPR, is a revolution in the world of medicine, allowing the modification of human genes to reduce genetic diseases.

genome mapping — تَخْطيطُ الجينومِ

يَعْكُفُ العُلَماءُ عَلى تَخْطيطِ الجينومِ لِلْأَشْخاصِ الَّذينَ يُعانونَ مِنْ مُتَلازِمَةِ داونْ لِفَهْمِ الظُّروفِ الجينيَّةِ بِشَكْلٍ أَفْضَلَ.

Scientists are mapping the genome of individuals with Down syndrome to better understand genetic conditions.

DNA sequencing — تَرْتيبُ الحَمْضِ النَّوَوِيِّ

يَتَطَلَّبُ تَرْتيبُ الحَمْضِ النَّوَوِيِّ فَهْمًا عَميقًا لِلْجينومِ وَالأَنْماطِ الوِراثِيَّةِ.

Sequencing nucleic acid requires a deep understanding of the genome and genetic patterns.

medical imaging — تَصْويرٌ طِبِّيٌّ

يُوَضِّحُ التَّصْويرُ الطِّبِّيُّ كَيْفَ يُؤَثِّرُ الوَرَمُ عَلى وَظائِفِ الدِّماغِ.

Medical imaging illustrates how the tumor affects brain functions.

drug development — تَطْويرُ أَدْوِيَةٍ

تُرَكِّزُ شَرِكاتُ الأَدْوِيَةِ عَلى تَطْويرِ أَدْوِيَةٍ جَديدَةٍ لِعِلاجِ مَرْضى السَّرَطانِ.

Pharmaceutical companies are focusing on developing new drugs to treat cancer patients.

تَفاعُلاتُ أَدْوِيَةٍ *pl.* **drug interactions**

يَحُثُّ خُبَراءُ الطِّبِّ عَلى الحَذَرِ، حَيْثُ تَكْشِفُ تَقاريرُ حَديثَةٌ عَنْ تَفاعُلاتٍ دَوائِيَّةٍ خَطيرَةٍ بَيْنَ بَعْضِ الأَدْوِيَةِ الشّائِعَةِ.

Medical experts are urging caution as new reports reveal potentially dangerous drug interactions between commonly prescribed medications.

تَكاثَرَ • تَكاثُرٌ **to reproduce**

قامَ العُلَماءُ بِاسْتِكْشافِ الآلِياتِ الَّتي تَعوقُ بِها بَعْضُ المُضاداتِ الحَيَوِيَّةِ قُدْرَةَ البَكْتيرْيا عَلى التَّكاثُرِ، بِهَدَفِ كَشْفِ اسْتِراتيجِيّاتٍ جَديدَةٍ لِمُكافَحَةِ مُقاوَمَةِ المُضادّاتِ الحَيَوِيَّةِ.

The scientists investigated the mechanisms through which certain antibiotics inhibit the ability of bacteria to reproduce, aiming to uncover novel strategies to combat antibiotic resistance.

تَكَيَّفَ • تَكَيُّفٌ **to adapt**

تَكَيَّفَتْ أَنْواعٌ مُخْتَلِفَةٌ مِنَ الأَحْياءِ الدَّقيقَةِ لِلْعَيْشِ في بيئاتٍ قاسِيَةٍ.

Different species of microorganisms have adapted to live in harsh environments.

تَنْشيطِيٌّ **revitalizing**

تَمَّ اكْتِشافُ نَوْعٍ مِنَ البَكْتيرْيا التَّنْشيطِيَّةِ تَحْتَ الأَرْضِ يُمْكِنُ أَنْ يُؤَثِّرَ عَلى الزِّراعَةِ.

A type of revitalizing bacteria has been discovered underground that can impact agriculture.

جائِحَةٌ • جَوائِحُ **pandemic**

واجَهَ العالَمُ جائِحَةً صِحِّيَّةً جَديدَةً ناتِجَةً عَنْ فَيْروسٍ مَجْهولٍ.

The world is facing a new health pandemic caused by an unknown virus.

جينٌ **gene**

كَشَفَتِ الأَبْحاثُ الأَخيرَةُ عَنْ جينٍ مُرْتَبِطٍ بِمَرَضِ السُّكَّرِيِّ مِنَ النَّوْعِ الثّاني.

Recent research has revealed a gene associated with Type 2 diabetes.

genome **جينومٌ**

تَمَكَّنَ العُلَماءُ مِنْ تَسَلْسُلِ الجينومِ لِنَوْعٍ جَديدٍ مِنَ السَّلَمَنْدَرِ الَّذي اكْتُشِفَ مُؤَخَّرًا.

Scientists have been able to sequence the genome of a new species of salamander that was recently discovered.

genetic **جينِيٌّ**

أَعْلَنَتْ شَرِكَةُ البُحوثِ الطِّبِّيَّةِ أَنَّها وَجَدَتْ طَفْرَةً جينِيَّةً قَدْ تَكونُ مَسْؤولَةً عَنِ الصَّلَعِ المُبَكِّرِ.

The medical research company announced that it has found a genetic mutation that may be responsible for early baldness.

biological, bio-; vital **حَيَوِيٌّ**

إِنَّ الأُكْسُجينَ حَيَوِيٌّ لِبَقاءِ الكائِناتِ الحَيَّةِ، لِأَنَّهُ ضَروريٌّ لِعَمَلِيَّةِ التَّنَفُّسِ في الخَلايا.

Oxygen is vital for the survival of biological organisms, as it is necessary for the process of respiration in the cells.

stem cells *pl.* **خَلايا جِذْعِيَّةٌ**

اِسْتَخْدَمَ العُلَماءُ الخَلايا الجِذْعِيَّةَ في تَجْديدِ الأَنْسِجَةِ المُتَضَرِّرَةِ في القَلْبِ.

Scientists have used stem cells to regenerate damaged tissues in the heart.

cell • خَلايا **خَلِيَّةٌ**

كَشَفَتِ الدِّراساتُ الأَخيرَةُ أَنَّ الخَلايا العَصَبِيَّةَ تَتَأَثَّرُ بِشَكْلٍ كَبيرٍ بِالضَّغْطِ وَالقَلَقِ.

Recent studies have revealed that nerve cells are significantly affected by stress and anxiety.

disease • أَدْواءٌ **داءٌ**

تَفَشّى داءُ الكوليرا في البِلادِ بَعْدَ الفَيَضاناتِ الأَخيرَةِ.

A cholera outbreak has spread across the country after recent floods.

While مَرَضٌ is a more commonly used term for 'disease,' the word داءٌ is more specific and often employed to describe chronic or infectious diseases. In the example above, the term داءٌ is used to denote the infectious nature of the cholera outbreak that spread after recent floods.

study دِراسَةٌ

نُشِرَتْ دِراسَةٌ حَديثَةٌ في مَجَلَّةِ البُحوثِ الطِّبِّيَّةِ تُفيدُ بِأَنَّ النِّظامَ الغِذائِيَّ الغَنِيَّ بِالْفَواكِهِ يُمْكِنُ أَنْ يُقَلِّلَ مِنْ خَطَرِ الإِصابَةِ بِأَمْراضِ القَلْبِ.

A recent study published in the Medical Research Journal states that a diet rich in fruits can reduce the risk of heart diseases.

DNA sequence سِلْسِلَةُ حَمْضٍ نَوَوِيٍّ

أَظْهَرَتِ النَّتائِجُ الأَوَّلِيَّةُ لِلْباحِثِينَ في جامِعَةِ قَطَرَ أَنَّ سِلْسِلَةَ الحَمْضِ النَّوَوِيِّ لِلْفَيْروسِ قَدْ تَغَيَّرَتْ مِنْ بِدايَةِ اكْتِشافِهِ.

Preliminary results from researchers at Qatar University show that the DNA sequence of the virus has changed since it was first discovered.

to diagnose شَخَّصَ • تَشْخيصٌ

شُخِّصَ المَريضُ بِالتَّصَلُّبِ المُتَعَدِّدِ بِناءً عَلى نَتائِجِ الفَحْصِ الطِّبِّيِّ.

The patient was diagnosed with multiple sclerosis based on the results of the medical examination.

healthy, healthful صِحِّيٌّ

أَشارَتِ الدِّراسَةُ الَّتي أُجْرِيَتْ في جامِعَةِ بَيْروتَ الأَمْريكِيَّةِ إِلى أَنَّ التَّغْذِيَةَ الصِّحِّيَّةَ وَالرِّياضَةَ اليَوْمِيَّةَ تَلْعَبانِ دَوْرًا هامًّا في الحِفاظِ عَلى صِحَّةِ الخَلايا في الجِسْمِ.

The study conducted at the American University of Beirut suggested that healthy nutrition and daily exercise play a significant role in maintaining healthy cells in the body.

The adjective صِحِّيٌّ commonly signifies something that is 'healthful,' promoting good health (طَعامٌ صِحِّي healthy food). However, it can also relate to health-care systems or services, as in النِّظامُ الصِّحِّيُّ 'the health (care) system.'

medical طِبِّيٌّ

تَمَّ تَقْديمُ التَّطَوُّرِ الطِّبِّيِّ الأَخيرِ في مَرْكَزِ أَبْحاثِ الخَلايا الجِذْعِيَّةِ بِالْجَزائِرِ كَأَمَلٍ جَديدٍ لِلْمَرْضى المُصابينَ بِمَرَضِ بارْكِنْسونْ.

The recent medical advancement in stem cell research at Algeria's Stem Cell Research Center has been presented as a new hope for patients with Parkinson's disease.

طَوَّرَ • تَطْويرٌ **to develop**

طَوَّرَ العُلَماءُ لَقاحًا جَديدًا لِمُكافَحَةِ فَيْروسِ كورونا.

Scientists have developed a new vaccine to combat the coronavirus.

عالِمُ أَحْياءٍ **biologist**

أَكَّدَ عالِمُ الأَحْياءِ الشَّهيرُ، الدُّكْتورُ (مُحَمَّدْ سَعيدْ)، أَنَّ الفَيْروسَ المُكْتَشَفَ حَديثًا يُمْكِنُ أَنْ يَتَحَوَّرَ بِسُرْعَةٍ.

Famous biologist Dr. Mohammed Saeed confirmed that the newly discovered virus could mutate quickly.

عَزَلَ • عَزْلٌ **to isolate**

عَزَلَ العُلَماءُ نَوْعًا جَديدًا مِنَ البَكْتيرْيا في المُخْتَبَرِ لِدِراسَةِ خَصائِصِهِ.

Scientists have isolated a new type of bacteria in the lab to study its characteristics.

عِلاجٌ **treatment**

أُكْتُشِفَ عِلاجٌ جَديدٌ لِمَرَضِ السَّرَطانِ، وَيَبْدو واعِدًا في التَّجارِبِ السَّريرِيَّةِ الأَوَّلِيَّةِ.

A new treatment for cancer has been discovered and appears promising in initial clinical trials.

عِلاجِيٌّ **therapeutic, medicinal**

أَعْلَنَتِ الشَّرِكَةُ عَنْ تَقَدُّمٍ كَبيرٍ في تَطْويرِ مَنْهَجٍ عِلاجِيٍّ جَديدٍ لِمَرَضِ السَّرَطانِ.

The company announced significant progress in developing a new therapeutic approach for cancer.

عَلاماتٌ حَيَوِيَّةٌ *pl.* **biomarkers, vital signs**

بَدَأَ الأَطِبّاءُ في مُراقَبَةِ العَلاماتِ الحَيَوِيَّةِ لِلْمَريضِ بَعْدَ الجِراحَةِ.

The doctors began monitoring the patient's vital signs after the surgery.

عِلْمُ الأَحْياءِ **biology**

تُعْتَبَرُ الأَبْحاثُ الَّتي يُقَدِّمُها قِسْمُ عِلْمِ الأَحْياءِ في الجامِعَةِ ذاتَ أَهَمِّيَّةٍ كَبيرَةٍ لِفَهْمِ تَطَوُّرِ الكائِناتِ الحَيَّةِ.

The research provided by the university's biology department is crucial for understanding the evolution of living organisms.

genetics | عِلْمُ الوِراثَةِ

نُشِرَتْ نَتائِجُ دِراسَةٍ جَديدَةٍ في عِلْمِ الوِراثَةِ تُقَدِّمُ رُؤْيَةً مُخْتَلِفَةً حَوْلَ كَيْفِيَةِ تَطَوُّرِ الأَمْراضِ المُزْمِنَةِ.

A new study in genetics was published offering a different perspective on the development of chronic diseases.

vaccine efficacy | فَعالِيَّةُ لَقاحٍ

أَظْهَرَتِ الأَبْحاثُ الحَديثَةُ أَنَّ فَعالِيَّةَ لَقاحِ كورونا تَسْتَمِرُّ لِمُدَّةِ عامَيْنِ عَلى الأَقَلِّ.

Recent research showed that the efficacy of the corona vaccine lasts at least two years.

virus | فَيْروسٌ

اِكْتَشَفَ العُلَماءُ فَيْروسًا جَديدًا يُمْكِنُهُ التَّسَبُّبُ في أَمْراضِ القَلْبِ.

Scientists discovered a new virus that can cause heart diseases.

to measure | قاسَ • قِياسٌ

جَرى قِياسُ مُسْتَوَياتِ السُّكَّرِ في الدَّمِ لِلْمَرْضى في العِيادَةِ اليَوْمَ.

Blood sugar levels of patients were measured in the clinic today.

organism | كائِنٌ حَيٌّ

تَمَّ اكْتِشافُ كائِنٍ حَيٍّ جَديدٍ غَريبٍ في أَعْماقِ المُحيطِ.

A strange new organism was discovered in the depths of the ocean.

microorganisms | *pl.* | كائِناتٌ دَقيقَةٌ

يَدْرُسُ العُلَماءُ كَيْفَ تُؤَثِّرُ الكائِناتُ الدَّقيقَةُ، مِثْلُ البَكْتيرْيا، عَلى صِحَّةِ الإِنْسانِ.

Scientists are studying how microorganisms such as bacteria affect human health.

biochemistry | كيمْياءُ حَيَوِيَّةٌ

أَدّى الإِنْجازُ الجَديدُ في الكيمْياءِ الحَيَوِيَّةِ إِلى فَهْمٍ أَفْضَلَ لِكَيْفِيَّةِ عَمَلِ الخَلايا.

The new breakthrough in biochemistry led to a better understanding of how cells function.

multicellular **مُتَعَدِّدُ الخَلايا**

اِكْتَشَفَ العُلَماءُ كائِنًا جَديدًا مُتَعَدِّدَ الخَلايا في أَعْماقِ المُحيطِ.

Scientists discovered a new multicellular organism in the depths of the ocean.

health-related **مُتَعَلِّقٌ بِالصِّحَّةِ**

نَشَرَتِ الحُكومَةُ تَقْريرًا مُتَعَلِّقًا بِالصِّحَّةِ عَنِ الآثارِ طَويلَةِ الأَجَلِ لِلتَّلَوُّثِ البيئِيِّ.

The government published a health-related report on the long-term effects of environmental pollution.

microscopic **مِجْهَرِيٌّ**

بِفَضْلِ التَّقَدُّمِ في التِّكْنولوجْيا المِجْهَرِيَّةِ، أَصْبَحْنا نَفْهَمُ الخَلايا بِشَكْلٍ أَفْضَلَ.

Thanks to advancements in microscopic technology, we understand cells better now.

illness, disease • أَمْراضٌ **مَرَضٌ**

أَعْلَنَتْ مُنَظَّمَةُ الصِّحَّةِ العالَمِيَّةُ عَنِ انْتِشارِ مَرَضٍ غَيْرِ مَعْروفٍ في أَجْزاءٍ مَعْزولَةٍ مِنَ العالَمِ.

The World Health Organization announced the spread of an unknown disease in isolated parts of the world.

pathological **مَرَضِيٌّ**

اِكْتَشَفَ الباحِثونَ تَغَيُّراتٍ مَرَضِيَّةً في الخَلايا المُصابَةِ بِالسَّرَطانِ.

Researchers discovered pathological changes in cancer-affected cells.

survey **مَسْحٌ**

أُجْرِيَ مَسْحٌ صِحِّيٌّ شامِلٌ لِلتَّعَرُّفِ عَلى انْتِشارِ السِّمْنَةِ بَيْنَ الأَطْفالِ.

A comprehensive health survey was conducted to identify the prevalence of obesity among children.

antibacterial, antiviral — **مُضادٌّ**

جَرى تَطْويرُ مُضادٍّ جَديدٍ لِلْفَيْروساتِ لِمُكافَحَةِ الإِنْفِلْوَنْزا المَوْسِمِيَّةِ.

A new antiviral has been developed to combat seasonal flu.

antibiotic — **مُضادٌّ حَيَوِيٌّ**

أُكْتُشِفَ مُضادٌّ حَيَوِيٌّ جَديدٌ يُعَدُّ فَعّالًا في مُواجَهَةِ البَكْتيرْيا المُقاوِمَةِ لِلْأَدْوِيَةِ.

A new antibiotic has been discovered which is effective against drug-resistant bacteria.

genetically modified — **مُعَدَّلٌ وِراثِيًّا**

تَمَكَّنَ العُلَماءُ مِنْ تَخْليقِ نَوْعٍ جَديدٍ مِنَ النَّباتاتِ المُعَدَّلَةِ وِراثِيًّا لِتَحَمُّلِ الجَفافِ.

Scientists have been able to create a new type of genetically modified plants to withstand drought.

antibiotic resistance — **مُقاوَمَةُ مُضادّاتٍ حَيَوِيَّةٍ**

تَزايَدَتْ مُقاوَمَةُ المُضادّاتِ الحَيَوِيَّةِ بَيْنَ بَعْضِ سُلالاتِ البَكْتيرْيا، مِمّا يُثيرُ قَلَقَ العُلَماءِ.

Antibiotic resistance has increased among some strains of bacteria, raising scientists' concern.

lethal, deadly — **مُميتٌ**

ظَهَرَ فَيْروسٌ مُميتٌ جَديدٌ يُهَدِّدُ البَشَرِيَّةَ، هَذا وَيَبْحَثُ العُلَماءُ عَنْ عِلاجٍ.

A deadly new virus has emerged, threatening humanity, and scientists are looking for a cure.

version — **نُسْخَةٌ** • نُسَخٌ

عُثِرَ عَلى نُسْخَةٍ مُتَحَوِّرَةٍ مِنَ الفَيْروسِ في مِنْطَقَةِ آسْيا الجَنوبِيَّةِ.

A mutated version of the virus was found in the South Asian region.

to grow — **نَما** • نُمُوٌّ

نَمَتِ الخَلايا المُعَدَّلَةُ وِراثِيًّا في ظُروفٍ مُثْلى في المُخْتَبَرِ.

The genetically modified cells grew in optimal conditions in the laboratory.

model **نَمْذَجَةٌ**

أُسْتُخْدِمَتْ نَمْذَجَةُ الكُمْبِيوتَرِ لِتَوَقُّعِ تَطَوُّرِ الوَباءِ.

Computer modeling was used to predict the evolution of the pandemic.

species • أَنْواعٌ **نَوْعٌ**

تَمَّ اكْتِشافُ نَوْعٍ جَديدٍ مِنَ الكائِناتِ في الهِنْدِ، وَهَذا الاِكْتِشافُ يُعَزِّزُ فَهْمَنا لِلتَّنَوُّعِ البيئِيِّ، وَيُشَكِّلُ تَحَدِّيًا جَديدًا لِلْعُلَماءِ.

A new species has been discovered in India, and this discovery enhances our understanding of biodiversity and poses a new challenge for scientists.

genetic engineering **هَنْدَسَةٌ وِراثِيَّةٌ**

أَدَّتِ التَّطَوُّراتُ في الهَنْدَسَةِ الوِراثِيَّةِ إِلى تَخْليقِ مَحاصيلَ زِراعِيَّةٍ أَكْثَرَ مُقاوَمَةً لِلْأَمْراضِ.

Advances in genetic engineering have led to the creation of more disease-resistant agricultural crops.

epidemic, pandemic • أَوْبِئَةٌ **وَباءٌ**

اِنْتَشَرَ وَباءٌ جَديدٌ في القارَّةِ الإِفْريقِيَّةِ، وَيَسْعى العُلَماءُ لِلسَّيْطَرَةِ عَلَيْهِ.

A new pandemic has spread in the African continent and scientists are striving to control it.

The term وَباءٌ is commonly used to refer to an epidemic, which is usually limited to a specific area or population. On the other hand, جائِحَةٌ is used to describe a pandemic, a disease outbreak that occurs over a wide geographic area and affects a large proportion of the population, often globally.

epidemic, pandemic **وَبائِيٌّ**

تَمَّ الكَشْفُ عَنْ تَهْديدٍ وَبائِيٍّ جَديدٍ، وَالحُكوماتُ تَعْمَلُ عَلى وَضْعِ الاِسْتِراتيجِيّاتِ اللّازِمَةِ لِمُواجَهَتِهِ.

A new epidemic threat has been revealed and governments are working on setting strategies to confront it.

وَباءٌ is a noun that refers to an epidemic, while وَبائِيٌّ is its corresponding nisba adjective, often used to describe things that are related to an epidemic. In English, both could be translated as 'epidemic,' but the adjective form would be used to describe related concepts, like 'epidemic situation' or 'epidemic spread.' Keep an eye out for nisba adjectives like this one.

hereditary **وِراثيٌّ**

اِكْتَشَفَ العُلَماءُ عامِلًا وِراثِيًّا يُمْكِنُ أَنْ يَزيدَ مِنْ خَطَرِ الإِصابَةِ بِمَرَضِ السُّكَّرِيِّ.

Scientists discovered a hereditary factor that can increase the risk of diabetes.

to distribute • تَوْزيعٌ **وَزَّعَ**

جَرى تَوْزيعُ اللَّقاحِ الجَديدِ لِلْوِقايَةِ مِنَ الوَباءِ في جَميعِ أَنْحاءِ البِلادِ.

The new vaccine to prevent the pandemic has been distributed across the country.

to utilize • تَوْظيفٌ **وَظَّفَ**

يُوَظِّفُ المَعْهَدُ الطِّبِّيُّ التِّكْنولوجْيا الحَديثَةَ في تَحْسينِ طُرُقِ العِلاجِ الطِّبِّيَّةِ.

The medical institute employs modern technology to improve medical treatment methods.

disease prevention **وِقايَةٌ مِنْ أَمْراضٍ**

تَمَّ تَطْويرُ بَرْنامَجٍ جَديدٍ لِلْوِقايَةِ مِنَ الأَمْراضِ في الأَطْفالِ.

A new program for disease prevention in children has been developed.

to generate • تَوْليدٌ **وَلَّدَ**

وَلَّدَتِ الأَبْحاثُ الأَخيرَةُ نَظَرِيَّةً جَديدَةً حَوْلَ كَيْفِيَّةِ انْتِقالِ الأَمْراضِ الوِراثِيَّةِ.

Recent research has generated a new theory on how genetic diseases are transmitted.

5.1.1.1 Mini-Articles

Track **30**

بِفَضْلِ البَحْثِ الطِّبِّيِّ المُتَواصِلِ، اِكْتَشَفَ العُلَماءُ أَنْواعًا جَديدَةً مِنَ الكائِناتِ الدَّقيقَةِ المُقاوِمَةِ لِلْمُضادّاتِ الحَيَوِيَّةِ. يَأْتي هَذا الاِكْتِشافُ في ظِلِّ تَزايُدِ حالاتِ المُقاوَمَةِ لِلْمُضادّاتِ الحَيَوِيَّةِ، الأَمْرَ الَّذي يُعْتَبَرُ قَضِيَّةً صِحِّيَّةً عالَمِيَّةً. وَظَّفَ العُلَماءُ التَّصْويرَ الطِّبِّيَّ وَتَرْتيبَ الحَمْضِ النَّوَوِيِّ لِلْكائِناتِ الحَيَّةِ لِتَحْديدِ الجيناتِ المَسْؤولَةِ عَنِ المُقاوَمَةِ. وَقَدْ تُساعِدُ الدِّراساتُ الجَديدَةُ في تَطْويرِ أَدْوِيَةٍ فَعّالَةٍ تُحارِبُ هَذِهِ الكائِناتِ الدَّقيقَةَ المُقاوِمَةَ.

Thanks to continuous medical research, scientists have discovered new types of antibiotic-resistant microorganisms. This discovery comes in the face of increasing cases of antibiotic resistance, which is considered a global health issue. Scientists have employed medical imaging and DNA sequencing of living organisms to identify the genes responsible for resistance. The findings from these new studies may help in the development of effective drugs to combat these resistant microorganisms.

فِي تَقَدُّمٍ طِبِّيٍّ هائِلٍ، أَعْلَنَ عُلَماءُ الأَحْياءِ أَنَّهُمْ قَدْ تَمَكَّنوا مِنْ تَحْريرِ الجيناتِ لِعِلاجِ اضْطِرابٍ وِراثِيٍّ نادِرٍ. وَقَدْ أَجْرى العُلَماءُ تَجْرِبَةً سَريرِيَّةً بِاسْتِخْدامِ التَّحْريرِ الجينِيِّ لِتَعْديلِ الخَلايا الجِذْعِيَّةِ مِنَ المَرْضى المُصابينَ بِالاضْطِرابِ. بِاسْتِخْدامِ تِقْنِيَّةِ تَخْطيطِ الجينومِ، أَكَّدَ العُلَماءُ أَنَّهُمْ قَدْ نَجَحوا في اسْتِبْدالِ الجينِ المَعيبِ بِنُسْخَةٍ سَليمَةٍ. يَتَوَقَّعُ العُلَماءُ أَنْ يَكونَ لِهَذِهِ الدِّراسَةِ أَثَرٌ كَبيرٌ عَلى مَجالِ الطِّبِّ الجينِيِّ وَالعِلاجاتِ الوِراثِيَّةِ المُسْتَقْبَلِيَّةِ.

In a tremendous medical advancement, biologists announced that they have successfully edited genes to treat a rare genetic disorder. Scientists conducted a clinical trial using gene editing to modify stem cells from patients with the disorder. Using genome mapping technology, scientists confirmed that they have successfully replaced the faulty gene with a healthy version. It is expected that this study will have a significant impact on the field of genetic medicine and future genetic therapies.

يَتَسَبَّبُ فَيْروسٌ جَديدٌ في جائِحَةٍ عالَمِيَّةٍ جَديدَةٍ. عَلى الرَّغْمِ مِنَ اكْتِشافِهِ بِالْكامِلِ، إلّا أَنَّ الفَيْروسَ يَتَكاثَرُ بِسُرْعَةٍ وَيُصيبُ أَعْدادًا كَبيرَةً مِنَ البَشَرِ. يُحاوِلُ الخُبَراءُ البَيولوجِيّونَ الكَشْفَ عَنْ البِنْيَةِ الوِراثِيَّةِ لِلْفَيْروسِ لِتَطْويرِ لَقاحٍ فَعّالٍ. يَجْري تَقْييمُ التَّفاعُلاتِ الدَّوائِيَّةِ المُحْتَمَلَةِ وَالعَلاماتِ الحَيَوِيَّةِ في الِاخْتِباراتِ السَّريرِيَّةِ. بِالْإِضافَةِ إِلى ذَلِكَ، يَتِمُّ تَوْزيعُ الأَدْوِيَةِ وَالمُعَدّاتِ الطِّبِّيَّةِ بِسُرْعَةٍ لِمُواجَهَةِ الوَباءِ. البَحْثُ العِلْمِيُّ مُسْتَمِرٌّ، وَالعالَمُ يَأْمُلُ أَنْ يَتِمَّ العُثورُ عَلى عِلاجٍ في القَريبِ العاجِلِ.

A new virus is causing a new global pandemic. Despite being fully discovered, the virus is rapidly spreading and affecting a large number of people. Biologists are attempting to decipher the genetic structure of the virus to develop an effective vaccine. Potential drug interactions and biomarkers are being evaluated in clinical trials. Additionally, drugs and medical equipment are being distributed rapidly to confront the pandemic. Scientific research is ongoing, and the world hopes to find a cure in the near future.

5.1.1.2 Informative Article: COVID-19 Vaccination Efforts

Track **31**

جُهودُ التَّطْعيمِ ضِدَّ فَيْروسِ كورونا: تَحَدِّياتٌ وَأَمَلٌ في المُسْتَقْبَلِ

تَفَشّى فَيْروسُ كورونا في جَميعِ أَنْحاءِ العالَمِ، ما تَسَبَّبَ في وَباءٍ عالَمِيٍّ. أَدَّتِ الجائِحَةُ إِلى اضْطِراباتٍ كَبيرَةٍ في كافَّةِ مَجالاتِ الحَياةِ، وَأَثارَتْ تَحَدِّياتٍ صِحِّيَّةً عالَمِيَّةً غَيْرَ مَسْبوقَةٍ. لِحُسْنِ الحَظِّ، أَدّى البَحْثُ الطِّبِّيُّ الدَّؤوبُ وَالمُسْتَميتُ إِلى تَطْويرِ عِدَّةِ لَقاحاتٍ فَعّالَةٍ في وَقْتٍ قِياسِيٍّ.

العُلَماءُ في مَجالِ البَيولوجْيا وَالكيمْياءِ الحَيَوِيَّةِ اسْتَخْدَموا مَعْرِفَتَهُمْ بِالتَّسَلْسُلِ الجينِيِّ لِلْفَيْروسِ لِتَصْميمِ اللَّقاحاتِ. عَنْ طَريقِ تَحْليلِ سِلْسِلَةِ الحَمْضِ النَّوَوِيِّ لِلْفَيْروسِ، تَمَكَّنوا مِنْ تَحْديدِ الجيناتِ المَسْؤولَةِ عَنْ تكاثُرِ الفَيْروسِ

وَانْتِقالِه. اِسْتَخْدَمَ العُلَماءُ هَذِهِ المَعْلوماتِ لِتَطْويرِ لَقاحاتٍ تَسْتَهْدِفُ هَذِهِ الجيناتِ، في مُحاوَلَةٍ لِمَنْعِ تَكاثُرِ الفَيْروسِ وَانْتِشارِهِ.

تَمَّ اخْتِبارُ اللَّقاحاتِ مِنْ خِلالِ تَجارِبَ سَريرِيَّةٍ شامِلَةٍ، اسْتَهْدَفَتْ تَقْييمَ فَعالِيَّةِ اللَّقاحاتِ وَالتَّأَكُّدِ مِنْ أَمانِها. وَقَدْ أَظْهَرَتِ النَّتائِجُ أَنَّ اللَّقاحاتِ كانَتْ فَعّالَةً في تَنْشيطِ الجِهازِ المَناعِيِّ لِمُكافَحَةِ الفَيْروسِ. كَما أَظْهَرَتِ البَياناتُ أَنَّ التَّفاعُلاتِ الجانِبِيَّةَ لِلْأَدْوِيَةِ كانَتْ مَحْدودَةً وَيُمْكِنُ التَّحَكُّمُ فيها.

إِلّا إِنَّ التَّحَدِّيَ لا يَقْتَصِرُ عَلى تَطْويرِ اللَّقاحِ، بَلْ يَشْمَلُ أَيْضًا تَوْزيعَهُ بِشَكْلٍ فَعّالٍ وَعادِلٍ. يَجِبُ عَلى السُّلُطاتِ الصِّحِّيَّةِ أَنْ تَقومَ بِتَنْظيمِ وَتَوْزيعِ اللَّقاحاتِ، لِضَمانِ الوُصولِ إِلى الأَشْخاصِ الأَكْثَرِ ضَعْفًا وَالمُعَرَّضينَ لِلْخَطَرِ.

يُواجِهُ العالَمُ تَحَدِّيًا كَبيرًا في مُواجَهَةِ هَذا الوَباءِ، وَلَكِنْ مَعَ البَحْثِ العِلْمِيِّ المُسْتَمِرِّ وَتَقَدُّمِ التِّكْنولوجْيا الطِّبِّيَّةِ، يَتَعَزَّزُ الأَمَلُ في تَجاوُزِ هَذا التَّحَدّي. بِفَضْلِ العِلْمِ وَالتَّعاوُنِ العالَمِيِّ، يُمْكِنُنا أَنْ نَتَطَلَّعَ إِلى مُسْتَقْبَلٍ أَكْثَرَ صِحَّةً وَأَمانًا.

COVID-19 Vaccination Efforts: Challenges and Hope for the Future

The coronavirus has spread worldwide, causing a global pandemic. The pandemic has led to significant disruptions in all aspects of life and has raised unprecedented global health challenges. Fortunately, diligent and determined medical research has resulted in the development of several effective vaccines in record time.

Scientists in the fields of biology and biochemistry have utilized their knowledge of the viral genetic sequence to design the vaccines. By analyzing the virus's DNA sequence, they were able to identify the genes responsible for its replication and transmission. Scientists used this information to develop vaccines that target these genes in an attempt to prevent the virus from replicating and spreading.

The vaccines were tested through comprehensive clinical trials aimed at evaluating their effectiveness and ensuring their safety. The results showed that the vaccines were successful in stimulating the immune system to fight the virus. The data also demonstrated that the drug's side effects were limited and manageable.

However, the challenge does not only lie in vaccine development but also in its effective and equitable distribution. Health authorities must regulate and distribute the vaccines to ensure access for the most vulnerable and at-risk individuals.

The world faces a significant challenge in combating this pandemic, but with ongoing scientific research and advancements in medical technology, hope is strengthened for overcoming this challenge. Thanks to science and global cooperation, we can look forward to a healthier and safer future.

5.1.2 Chemistry and Materials Science

Track **32**

oxygen أُكْسُجينٌ

تَمَّ اكْتِشافُ طَريقَةٍ جَديدَةٍ لِتَحْليلِ الماءِ إلى أُكْسُجينٍ وَهَيْدْروجينٍ.

A new method for splitting water into oxygen and hydrogen was discovered.

chemical colors أَلْوانٌ كيمْيائِيَّةٌ

تَمَّ تَطْويرُ أَلْوانٍ كيمْيائِيَّةٍ جَديدَةٍ غَيْرِ ضارَّةٍ لِلاِسْتِخْدامِ في صِناعَةِ الأَغْذيَةِ.

New non-harmful chemical colors were developed for use in the food industry.

to reduce اِخْتَزَلَ • اِخْتِزالٌ

اِخْتَزَلَ الباحِثُ المُرَكَّبَ الكيمْيائِيَّ في الاِخْتِبارِ لِتَبْسيطِ البِنْيَةِ الجُزَيْئِيَّةِ.

The researcher reduced the chemical compound in the test to simplify the molecular structure.

plastic بِلاسْتيكٌ

اِكْتَشَفَ العُلَماءُ نَوْعًا جَديدًا مِنَ البِلاسْتيكِ القابِلِ لِلتَّحَلُّلِ البَيولوجِيِّ.

Scientists discovered a new type of biodegradable plastic.

to evaporate تَبَخَّرَ • تَبَخُّرٌ

أَدّى تَبَخُّرُ السّائِلِ في الإِجْراءِ الكيمْيائِيِّ إلى الحُصولِ عَلى مُرَكَّبٍ نَقِيٍّ.

The evaporation of the liquid in the chemical procedure resulted in obtaining a pure compound.

chemical analysis تَحْليلٌ كيمْيائِيٌّ

أُجْرِيَ تَحْليلٌ كيمْيائِيٌّ لِلتُّرْبَةِ لِتَحْديدِ مُحْتَواها مِنَ العَناصِرِ الغِذائِيَّةِ.

A chemical analysis of the soil was conducted to determine its nutrient content.

chemical transformation تَحَوُّلٌ كيمْيائِيٌّ

حَدَثَ تَحَوُّلٌ كيمْيائِيٌّ في المادَّةِ عِنْدَ تَعَرُّضِها لِأَشِعَّةِ الشَّمْسِ القَوِيَّةِ.

A chemical change occurred in the substance when exposed to strong sunlight.

chemical sedimentation ## تَرْسيبٌ كيمْيائِيٌّ

اِسْتَخْدَمَ العُلَماءُ تِقْنِيَّةَ التَّرْسيبِ الكيمْيائِيِّ لِإِنْتاجِ طَبَقاتٍ نانَوِيَّةٍ رَقيقَةٍ.

Scientists used chemical sedimentation technique to produce thin nanolayers.

molecular structure ## تَرْكيبٌ جُزَيْئِيٌّ

يُمْكِنُ لِلتَّرْكيبِ الجُزَيْئِيِّ لِمادَّةٍ ما تَوْجيهُ خَصائِصِها الفيزْيائِيَّةِ وَالكيمْيائِيَّةِ.

A substance's molecular structure can guide its physical and chemical properties.

to react • تَفاعُلٌ ## تَفاعَلَ

تَفاعَلَتِ المادَّتانِ مَعًا لِتَشْكيلِ مُرَكَّبٍ جَديدٍ في المُخْتَبَرِ.

The two substances reacted together to form a new compound in the laboratory

reaction ## تَفاعُلٌ

أَدّى تَفاعُلُ الأَحْماضِ الدُّهْنِيَّةِ مَعَ القَلَوِيّاتِ إِلى تَكْوينِ الصّابونِ.

The reaction of fatty acids with alkali led to the formation of soap.

chemical reaction ## تَفاعُلٌ كيمْيائِيٌّ

أَدّى تَفاعُلٌ كيمْيائِيٌّ غَيْرُ مُتَوَقَّعٍ إِلى اكْتِشافِ دَواءٍ جَديدٍ.

An unexpected chemical reaction led to the discovery of a new drug.

to decompose • تَفَكُّكٌ ## تَفَكَّكَ

تَفَكَّكَتِ المادَّةُ الكيمْيائِيَّةُ تَحْتَ تَأْثيرِ الحَرارَةِ العالِيَةِ.

The chemical substance decomposed under the influence of high heat.

to convert • تَحْويلٌ ## حَوَّلَ

حَوَّلَتِ الشَّرِكَةُ نُفاياتِ البِلاسْتيكِ إِلى وَقودٍ مِنْ خِلالِ عَمَلِيَّةٍ كيمْيائِيَّةٍ مُعَقَّدَةٍ.

The company transformed plastic waste into fuel through a complex chemical process.

liquid سَوائِلُ • **سائِلٌ**

تَمَّ تَحْويلُ الغازِ إِلى سائِلٍ عَبْرَ إِحْدى طُرُقِ التَّبْريدِ.

The gas was turned into a liquid through a cooling method.

silicon **سيليكونْ**

أُسْتُخْدِمَ السّيليكونْ في تَطْويرِ مادَّةٍ جَديدَةٍ لِلْأَجْهِزَةِ الإِلِكْترونِيَّةِ.

Silicon was used in the development of a new material for electronic devices.

solid **صَلْبٌ**

تَمَّ تَطْويرُ مادَّةٍ صَلْبَةٍ جَديدَةٍ تَمْتازُ بِالْمُرونَةِ العالِيَةِ وَالمُقاوَمَةِ لِلْكَسْرِ.

A new solid material has been developed that boasts high flexibility and resistance to fracture.

to melt صَهْرٌ • **صَهَرَ**

صَهَرَ العُلَماءُ الزُّجاجَ لِدِراسَةِ خَصائِصِهِ عِنْدَ دَرَجاتِ الحَرارَةِ العالِيَةِ.

Scientists melted glass to study its properties at high temperatures.

to isolate عَزْلٌ • **عَزَلَ**

عَزَلَ العُلَماءُ مادَّةً كيمْيائِيَّةً جَديدَةً مِنَ النَّباتاتِ لِاسْتِخْدامِها في الأَدْوِيَةِ.

Scientists isolated a new chemical substance from plants for use in medicines.

organic **عُضْوِيٌّ**

عُثِرَ عَلى مُرَكَّبٍ عُضْوِيٍّ جَديدٍ في بَعْضِ النَّباتاتِ الطِّبِّيَّةِ، يَمْتَلِكُ خَصائِصَ عِلاجِيَّةِ.

A new organic compound was found in some medicinal plants, that has therapeutic properties.

chemical therapy **عِلاجٌ كيمْيائِيٌّ**

تَمَّ تَطْويرُ عِلاجٍ كيمْيائِيٍّ جَديدٍ لِلْمُساعَدَةِ في مُكافَحَةِ الأَوْرامِ.

A new chemical treatment was developed to help combat tumors.

materials science عِلْمُ المَوادِّ

يَدْرُسُ عِلْمُ المَوادِّ خَصائِصَ المَوادِّ وَكَيْفَ يُمْكِنُ تَحْسينُها.

Materials science studies the properties of materials and how they can be improved.

elements *pl.* عَناصِرُ

تَمَّ اكْتِشافُ عَناصِرَ كيمْيائِيَّةٍ جَديدَةٍ في كَواكِبَ بَعيدَةٍ.

New chemical elements were discovered on distant planets.

metallic elements • عَناصِرُ عُنْصُرٌ فِلِزِّيّ

أُسْتُخْدِمَتِ العَناصِرُ الفِلِزِّيَّةُ في تَصْنيعِ الأَجْهِزَةِ الإِلِكْتِرونِيَّةِ.

Metallic elements were used in the manufacture of electronic devices.

non-metallic elements عُنْصُرٌلافِلِزِّيّ

اِكْتَشَفَ العُلَماءُ اسْتِخْداماتٍ جَديدَةً لِلْعَناصِرِ اللافِلِزِّيَّةِ في التِّقْنِيّاتِ الخَضْراءِ.

Scientists have discovered new uses for non-metallic elements in green technologies.

gaseous غازِيٌّ

تَمَّ الكَشْفُ عَنْ طَريقَةٍ جَديدَةٍ لِتَخْزينِ الهَيْدْروجينِ في حالَةٍ غازِيَّةٍ.

A new method for storing hydrogen in a gaseous state was revealed.

inorganic غَيْرُ عُضْوِيٍّ

تَمَّ تَطْويرُ مادَّةٍ غَيْرِ عُضْوِيَّةٍ جَديدَةٍ تَتَمَيَّزُ بِالْمَتانَةِ العالِيَةِ وَالْمُقاوَمَةِ لِلْحَرارَةِ.

A new inorganic material was developed that is characterized by high durability and heat resistance.

metal فِلِزٌّ

اِكْتَشَفَ العُلَماءُ فِلِزًّا جَديدًا ذا قُوَّةٍ وَصَلابَةٍ اسْتِثْنائِيَّتَيْنِ.

Scientists discovered a new metal with exceptional strength and hardness.

فِلِزٌّ is a scientific term for 'metal,' while مَعْدِنٌ is the everyday word for it. Both mean the same but are used in different contexts.

sulfur كِبْريتٌ

تَمَّ اكْتِشافُ طَريقَةٍ جَديدَةٍ لِاسْتِخْلاصِ الكِبْريتِ مِنَ المَعادِنِ الكِبْريتِيَّة.

A new method was discovered for extracting sulfur from sulfide minerals.

carbon كَرْبونٌ

تَمَّ تَطْويرُ مادَّةٍ كَرْبونيَّةٍ جَديدَةٍ قَوِيَّةٍ وَخَفيفَةِ الوَزْنِ لِلاسْتِخْدامِ في الطّائِراتِ.

A new strong, lightweight carbon material was developed for use in airplanes.

chemistry كيمْياءُ

يَعْمَلُ العُلَماءُ في مَجالِ الكيمْياءِ عَلى تَطْويرِ مَوادَّ مُسْتَدامَةٍ وَصَديقَةٍ لِلْبيئَةِ.

Scientists in chemistry are working on developing sustainable and environmentally friendly materials.

biochemistry كيمْياءُ حَيَوِيَّةٌ

أَدّى البَحْثُ في مَجالِ الكيمْياءِ الحَيَوِيَّةِ إلى اكْتِشافِ أَدْوِيَةٍ جَديدَةٍ لِعِلاجِ الأَمْراضِ الوِراثِيَّةِ.

Research in biochemistry led to the discovery of new drugs to treat genetic diseases.

organic chemistry كيمْياءُ عُضْوِيَّةٌ

جَرى تَطْويرُ مُرَكَّباتٍ عُضْوِيَّةٍ جَديدَةٍ في مُخْتَبَرِ الكيمْياءِ العُضْوِيَّةِ.

New organic compounds were developed in the organic chemistry lab.

inorganic chemistry كيمْياءُ غَيْرُ عُضْوِيَّةٍ

اِكْتَشَفَ العُلَماءُ في مَجالِ الكيمْياءِ غَيْرِ العُضْوِيَّةِ مادَّةً جَديدَةً غَيْرَ مَعْروفَةِ الخَصائِصِ.

Scientists in the field of inorganic chemistry discovered a new substance with unknown properties.

chemical كِيمْيائِيٌّ

اِخْتَرَعَ الكيمْيائِيُّ طَرِيقَةً جَديدَةً لِتَنْقِيَةِ الماءِ مِنَ الشَّوائِبِ الكيمْيائِيَّةِ.

The chemist invented a new method for purifying water from chemical impurities.

chemical principles *pl.* مَبادِئُ كيمْيائِيَّةٌ

أَنْشَأَ العُلَماءُ نَموذَجًا جَديدًا لِلْبَطّارِيَّةِ بِناءً عَلى مَبادِئَ كيمْيائِيَّةٍ مُتَطَوِّرَةٍ.

Scientists built a new battery model based on advanced chemical principles.

reactive مُتَفاعِلٌ

إِنَّ المادَّةَ الجَديدَةَ مُتَفاعِلَةٌ بِشَكْلٍ كَبيرٍ مَعَ الهَواءِ، مِمّا يَتَطَلَّبُ تَخْزينَها بِطُرُقٍ خاصَّةٍ.

The new material is highly reactive with air, requiring special storage methods.

mixture مَخْلوطٌ

أَعَدَّ العُلَماءُ مَخْلوطًا مِنَ الأَلْيافِ النّانَوِيَّةِ لِتَعْزيزِ قُوَّةِ الأَقْمِشَةِ.

Scientists have prepared a mixture of nanofibers to enhance the strength of fabrics.

chemical compound مُرَكَّبٌ كيمْيائِيٌّ

تَحْتَوي البَطّارِيَّةُ الجَديدَةُ عَلى مُرَكَّباتٍ كيمْيائِيَّةٍ قادِرَةٍ عَلى تَخْزينِ الطّاقَةِ لِفَتْرَةٍ أَطْوَلَ.

The new battery contains chemical compounds capable of storing energy for a longer period.

resistant مُقاوِمٌ

تَمَّ تَطْويرُ مادَّةٍ جَديدَةٍ مُقاوِمَةٍ لِلْحَرارَةِ يُمْكِنُها تَحَمُّلُ دَرَجاتِ الحَرارَةِ العالِيَةِ.

A new heat-resistant material has been developed that can withstand high temperatures.

conductive مُوَصِّلٌ لِلْكَهْرَباءِ

اِسْتَطاعَتِ الشَّرِكَةُ المُصَنِّعَةُ لِلإِلِكْتْرونِيّاتِ تَطْويرَ مادَّةٍ جَديدَةٍ موَصِّلَةٍ لِلْكَهْرَباءِ بِكَفاءَةٍ أَعْلى مِنَ النُّحاسِ.

The electronics manufacturer managed to develop a new material that is more electrically conductive than copper.

nitrogen نَيتْروجينٌ

أُسْتُخْدِمَ النَّيتْروجينُ في تَبْريدِ الأَنابيبِ في أَحْدَثِ تَجْرِبَةٍ لِلْفيزْياءِ الكَمِّيَّةِ.

Nitrogen was used to cool the pipes in the latest quantum physics experiment.

hydrogen هَيْدِروجينٌ

أَعْلَنَتِ الشَّرِكَةُ عَنْ خُطَّتِها لِاسْتِخْدامِ الهَيْدِروجينِ كَوَقودٍ نَظيفٍ في مَرْكَباتِها القادِمَةِ.

The company announced its plan to use hydrogen as a clean fuel in its upcoming vehicles.

helium هيلْيومْ

نَجَحَ الباحِثونَ في اسْتِخْلاصِ الهيلْيومْ مِنَ الهَواءِ بِواسِطَةِ تِقْنِيَّةِ فَلْتَرَةٍ جَديدَةٍ.

Researchers have succeeded in extracting helium from the air using a new filtration technique.

structural units of compounds *pl.* وِحْداتٌ هَيْكَلِيَّةٌ لِلْمُرَكَّباتِ

يَبْحَثُ العُلَماءُ عَنْ وِحْداتٍ هَيْكَلِيَّةٍ جَديدَةٍ لِلْمُرَكَّباتِ الَّتي قَدْ تُحَسِّنُ مِنْ أَداءِ البَطّارِيّاتِ.

Scientists are researching new structural units of compounds that could improve battery performance.

Notice that this phrase includes the preposition لِـ (here, translating 'of'). In the idaafa alternative, وِحْداتُ مُرَكَّباتٍ هَيْكَلِيَّةٌ, the adjective هَيْكَلِيَّةٌ is required to be at the end of the construction, making it unclear which noun it modifies in a text without diacritics. Using the preposition لِـ allows us to place the adjective directly after the noun it modifies, removing this ambiguity.

5.1.2.1 Mini-Articles

Track **33**

في مُحاوَلَةٍ لِمُعالَجَةِ الأَزْمَةِ البيئِيَّةِ المُسْتَمِرَّةِ النّاجِمَةِ عَنِ البلاسْتيكِ، كَشَفَتْ مَجْموعَةٌ مِنَ العُلَماءِ عَنْ تِقْنِيَّةٍ جَديدَةٍ تُحَوِّلُ البلاسْتيكَ إلى وَقودٍ مُفيدٍ. عَبْرَ تَطْبيقِ مَجْموعَةٍ مِنَ التَّفاعُلاتِ الكيمْيائِيَّةِ، يَتِمُّ تَحْليلُ البلاسْتيكِ إلى مُكَوِّناتِهِ الأَساسِيَّةِ في عَمَلِيَّةٍ تُسَمّى التَّحَلُّلَ الكيمْيائِيَّ. ثُمَّ يَتِمُّ تَحْويلُ هَذِهِ المُكَوِّناتِ إلى سَوائِلَ وَغازاتٍ يُمْكِنُ اسْتِخْدامُها كَوَقودٍ. هَذا التَّحَوُّلُ الكيمْيائِيُّ يُمْكِنُ أَنْ يُساهِمَ في حَلِّ مُشْكِلَةِ التَّلَوُّثِ البلاسْتيكِيِّ وَيُساعِدَ في الحِفاظِ عَلى البيئَةِ.

In an attempt to address the ongoing environmental crisis caused by plastic, a group of scientists has unveiled a new technology that converts plastic into useful fuel. By applying a series of chemical reactions, the plastic is broken down into its basic components in a process called chemical decomposition. These components are then converted into liquids and gases that can be used as fuel. This chemical transformation can contribute to solving the problem of plastic pollution and help preserve the environment.

أَعْلَنَ العُلَماءُ في مَجالِ عِلْمِ المَوادِّ عَنْ تَطْويرِ مُرَكَّبٍ كيمْيائِيٍّ جَديدٍ قادِرٍ عَلى امْتِصاصِ غازاتِ النَّيْتْروجينِ وَالكَرْبونِ الضّارَّةِ مِنَ الهَواءِ. يَعْتَمِدُ المُرَكَّبُ الجَديدُ عَلى بِنْيَةٍ جُزَيْئِيَّةٍ مُعَقَّدَةٍ تَحْتَوي عَلى مَجْموعَةٍ مِنَ العَناصِرِ الكيمْيائِيَّةِ، تَشْمَلُ الأُكْسُجينَ وَالهَيْدْروجينَ وَالكِبْريتَ. يَأْمُلُ الباحِثونَ أَنْ يُسْتَخْدَمَ هَذا المُرَكَّبُ في عَمَلِيّاتِ تَنْقِيَةِ الهَواءِ في المُسْتَقْبَلِ.

Scientists in the field of materials science have announced the development of a new chemical compound capable of absorbing harmful nitrogen and carbon gases from the air. The new compound relies on a complex molecular structure that contains a variety of chemical elements, including oxygen, hydrogen, and sulfur. Researchers hope that this compound will be used in future air purification processes.

يُسْتَخْدَمُ السّيليكونْ بِكَثْرَةٍ في مَجْموعَةٍ مُتَنَوِّعَةٍ مِنَ الصِّناعاتِ، بَدْءًا مِنَ الإِلِكْتْرونِيّاتِ وَحَتّى البِناءِ. إِنَّهُ مادَّةٌ صَلْبَةٌ وَمُقاوِمَةٌ لِلْحَرارَةِ، مِمّا يَجْعَلُها مِثالِيَّةً لِلْعَديدِ مِنَ التَّطْبيقاتِ. بِالإِضافَةِ إِلى ذَلِكَ، يُمْكِنُ تَصْنيعُ السّيليكونْ بِشَكْلٍ سَهْلٍ وَاقْتِصادِيٍّ مِنَ الرِّمالِ، الَّتي تَحْتَوي عَلى كَمِّيّاتٍ كَبيرَةٍ مِنَ السّيليكا، مِمّا يَجْعَلُهُ مِنَ العَناصِرِ الأَكْثَرِ اسْتِدامَةً لِلصِّناعَةِ. يَهْدُفُ البَحْثُ المُسْتَمِرُّ إِلى تَطْويرِ طُرُقٍ جَديدَةٍ لِاسْتِخْدامِ السّيليكونْ في تَطْبيقاتٍ صِناعِيَّةٍ جَديدَةٍ.

Silicon is widely used in a variety of industries, ranging from electronics to construction. It is a solid material and resistant to heat, making it ideal for many applications. Additionally, silicon can be easily and economically produced from sand, which contains large amounts of silica, making it one of the most sustainable elements for industry. Ongoing research aims to develop new methods for using silicon in new industrial applications.

في تَقَدُّمٍ مُثيرٍ في مَجالِ عِلْمِ المَوادِّ، أَعْلَنَ العُلَماءُ مُؤَخَّرًا عَنِ اكْتِشافِهِمْ لِمادَّةٍ جَديدَةٍ ذاتِ خَصائِصَ فائِقَةِ التَّوْصيلِ لِلْكَهْرَباءِ. تَمَّ تَكْوينُ المادَّةِ مِنْ فِلِزٍّ نادِرٍ جِدًّا مَعَ الكَرْبونِ، وَقَدْ أَظْهَرَتِ الاخْتِباراتُ الأَوَّلِيَّةُ أَنَّ المادَّةَ تَحْتَفِظُ بِخَصائِصِها المُوَصِّلَةِ حَتّى في دَرَجاتِ الحَرارَةِ المُرْتَفِعَةِ جِدًّا. يُؤْمَلُ أَنْ يُساهِمَ هَذا الاكْتِشافُ في تَطَوُّرِ تِكْنولوجيا الطّاقَةِ الكَهْرَبائِيَّةِ وَتَحْسينِ كَفاءَتِها.

In an exciting advancement in the field of materials science, scientists have recently announced their discovery of a new material with superconducting properties. The material was composed of a very rare metal and carbon, and preliminary tests have shown that it retains its conductivity even at extremely high temperatures. It is hoped that this discovery will contribute to the development of electric power technology and improve its efficiency.

أَعْلَنَ الباحِثونَ في مَجالِ الكيمْياءِ العُضْوِيَّةِ عَنْ تَقَدُّمٍ كَبيرٍ يُمْكِنُ أَنْ يُسَرِّعَ مِنْ تَطْويرِ العِلاجاتِ الجَديدَةِ لِلْعَديدِ مِنَ الأَمْراضِ. بِاسْتِخْدامِ تِقْنِيَّةٍ جَديدَةٍ، تَمَكَّنَ العُلَماءُ مِنْ تَحْليلِ التَّفاعُلاتِ الكيمْيائِيَّةِ بَيْنَ مَجْموعَةٍ مِنَ المُرَكَّباتِ العُضْوِيَّةِ بِطُرُقٍ لَمْ تَكُنْ مُمْكِنَةً مِنْ قَبْلُ. تَمْنَحُ هَذِهِ البَياناتُ الجَديدَةُ الباحِثينَ فَهْمًا أَعْمَقَ لِكَيْفِيَّةِ تَفاعُلِ هَذِهِ المُرَكَّباتِ مَعَ الخَلايا الحَيَّةِ، وَهُوَ ما يُمْكِنُ أَنْ يُساعِدَ في تَصْميمِ عِلاجاتٍ جَديدَةٍ وَفَعّالَةٍ أَكْثَرَ.

Researchers in the field of organic chemistry have announced a significant breakthrough that could accelerate the development of new treatments for many diseases. Using a new technique, scientists have been able to analyze the chemical reactions between a group of organic compounds in ways that were not previously possible. This new data gives researchers a deeper understanding of how these compounds interact with living cells, which can help in designing new and more effective treatments.

5.1.2.2 Informative Article: Chemistry and Materials Science

Track **34**

الكيمْياءُ وَعِلْمُ المَوادِّ: دَوْرٌ حاسِمٌ في تَشْكيلِ العالَمِ مِنْ حَوْلِنا

الكيمْياءُ وَعِلْمُ المَوادِّ مِنْ أَكْثَرِ المَجالاتِ إِثارَةً لِلاهْتِمامِ وَالأَهَمِّيَّةِ في العُلومِ، حَيْثُ يَلْعَبانِ دَوْرًا حاسِمًا في تَشْكيلِ العالَمِ مِنْ حَوْلِنا. الكيمْياءُ هِيَ دِراسَةُ الجُزَيْئاتِ وَالتَّفاعُلاتِ الَّتي تَحْدُثُ بَيْنَها، بَيْنَما يَتَناوَلُ عِلْمُ المَوادِّ خَصائِصَ المَوادِّ وَكَيْفِيَّةَ تَحْسينِها وَتَغْييرِها مِنْ خِلالِ التَّلاعُبِ بِالتَّرْكيبِ الجُزَيْئِيِّ لِلْمَوادِّ.

تَتَواجَدُ الكيمْياءُ في كُلِّ مَكانٍ حَوْلَنا، مِنَ الهَواءِ الَّذي نَتَنَفَّسُهُ، وَالَّذي يَحْتَوي عَلى مَزيجٍ مِنَ الغازاتِ كالأُكْسُجينِ وَالنَّيْتْروجينِ، إِلى المَوادِّ الصَّلْبَةِ كالْفِلِزّاتِ وَالمَوادِّ البِلاسْتيكِيَّةِ الَّتي نَسْتَخْدِمُها في الحَياةِ اليَوْمِيَّةِ. كُلُّ هَذِهِ المَوادِّ تَحْتَوي عَلى جُزَيْئاتٍ تَتَفاعَلُ مَعَ بَعْضِها البَعْضَ بِطُرُقٍ مُعَقَّدَةٍ، وَدِراسَةُ هَذِهِ التَّفاعُلاتِ الكيمْيائِيَّةِ تُمَكِّنُ العُلَماءَ مِنْ تَحْسينِ خَصائِصِ المَوادِّ وَتَطْويرِ مَوادَّ جَديدَةٍ.

مِنْ ناحِيَةٍ أُخرى، يَدْرُسُ عِلْمُ المَوادِّ كَيْفَ تَتَأَثَّرُ الخَصائِصُ الفيزْيائِيَّةُ لِلْمَوادِّ بِتَرْكيبِها الجُزَيْئِيِّ وَالكيمْيائِيِّ. بِفَهْمِ كَيْفِيَّةِ تَفاعُلِ الجُزَيْئاتِ داخِلَ المادَّةِ، يُمْكِنُ لِلْعُلَماءِ تَصْميمُ مَوادَّ بِخَصائِصَ مُحَدَّدَةٍ. عَلى سَبيلِ المِثالِ، يُمْكِنُ تَحْسينُ مُقاوَمَةِ مادَّةٍ ما لِلْحَرارَةِ أَوِ التَّآكُلِ، أَوْ تَحْسينُ قُدْرَتِها عَلى تَوْصيلِ الكَهْرَباءِ.

في العُقودِ الأَخيرَةِ، أَدّى التَّقَدُّمُ في الكيمْياءِ وَعِلْمِ المَوادِّ إِلى العَديدِ مِنَ الاخْتِراعاتِ الرّائِدَةِ، بَدْءًا مِنَ البَطّارِيّاتِ القَوِيَّةِ لِلْهَواتِفِ المَحْمولَةِ، وَوُصولًا إِلى المَوادِّ البِلاسْتيكِيَّةِ القابِلَةِ لِلتَّحَلُّلِ الَّتي تُساعِدُ في حِمايَةِ البيئَةِ. مَعَ التَّقَدُّمِ المُسْتَمِرِّ في هَذَيْنِ المَجالَيْنِ، يُمْكِنُنا تَوَقُّعُ المَزيدِ مِنَ الابْتِكاراتِ المُثيرَةِ في المُسْتَقْبَلِ.

Chemistry and Materials Science: A Crucial Role in Shaping the World Around Us

Chemistry and materials science are among the most interesting and important fields in science, as they play a crucial role in shaping the world around us. Chemistry is the study of particles and the reactions that occur between them, while materials science deals with the properties of materials and how they can be improved and altered by manipulating the molecular structure of substances.

Chemistry is present everywhere around us, from the air we breathe, which contains a mixture of gases like oxygen and nitrogen, to solid materials such as metals and plastics that we use in our daily lives. All these materials contain particles that interact with each other in complex ways, and studying these chemical reactions enables scientists to improve the properties of materials and develop new substances.

On the other hand, materials science investigates how the physical properties of materials are affected by their molecular and chemical composition. By understanding how particles interact within a substance, scientists can design materials with specific properties. For example, the resistance of a material to heat or corrosion can be improved, or its ability to conduct electricity can be enhanced.

In recent decades, advances in chemistry and materials science have led to numerous groundbreaking inventions, ranging from powerful batteries for mobile phones to biodegradable plastics that help protect the environment. With continued progress in these fields, we can expect even more exciting innovations in the future.

5.1.3 Physics and Astronomy

Track **35**

remote sensing — **اِسْتِشْعارٌ عَنْ بُعْدٍ**

تَمَّ تَطْويرُ تِكْنولوجْيا الاِسْتِشْعارِ عَنْ بُعْدٍ لِدِراسَةِ تَغَيُّراتِ دَرَجَةِ حَرارَةِ الأَرْضِ مِنَ الفَضاءِ.

Remote sensing technology has been developed to study changes in the Earth's temperature from space.

the Big Bang — **الاِنْفِجارُ العَظيمُ**

اُكْتُشِفَتْ أَدِلَّةٌ جَديدَةٌ تَدْعَمُ نَظَرِيَّةَ الاِنْفِجارِ العَظيمِ لِأَصْلِ الكَوْنِ.

New evidence has been discovered supporting the Big Bang theory of the origin of the universe.

the general theory of relativity — **النَّظَرِيَّةُ النِّسْبِيَّةُ العامَّةُ**

البَياناتُ الجَديدَةُ الَّتي تَمَّ جَمْعُها مِنَ المَرْصَدِ الفَلَكِيِّ تَدْعَمُ النَّظَرِيَّةَ النِّسْبِيَّةَ العامَّةَ لِأَيْنِشْتايِن.

The new data collected from the observatory supports Einstein's theory of general relativity.

light bending — **اِنْحِناءُ ضَوْءٍ**

تَمَكَّنَ العُلَماءُ مِنْ مُلاحَظَةِ انْحِناءِ ضَوْءِ النُّجومِ حَوْلَ الثُّقْبِ الأَسْوَدِ.

Scientists were able to observe the bending of starlight around the black hole.

space program — **بَرْنامَجُ فَضاءٍ** • بَرامِجُ

أَعْلَنَتِ الحُكومَةُ عَنْ تَمْويلٍ جَديدٍ لِبَرْنامَجِ الفَضاءِ الوَطَنِيِّ لِلْبَحْثِ عَنْ حَياةٍ خارِجَ الأَرْضِ.

The government announced new funding for the national space program to search for extraterrestrial life.

Doppler effect — **تَأْثيرُ دوبْلِرْ**

اِسْتَخْدَمَ العُلَماءُ تَأْثيرَ دوبْلِرْ لِقِياسِ سُرْعَةِ حَرَكَةِ النُّجومِ في الكَوْنِ.

Scientists used the Doppler effect to measure the speed of stars in the universe.

spectral analysis — **تَحْليلُ طَيْفٍ**

تَوَصَّلَ العُلَماءُ إلى اكْتِشافِ عَناصِرَ جَديدَةٍ في النَّجْمِ البَعيدِ عَبْرَ تَحْليلِ طَيْفِ الضَّوْءِ القادِمِ مِنْهُ.

Scientists have discovered new elements in the distant star by analyzing the spectrum of light coming from it.

space development — **تَطْويرٌ فَضائِيٌّ**

أَعْلَنَ فَريقٌ مِنَ العُلَماءِ عَنْ تَطْويرٍ فَضائِيٍّ جَديدٍ يَهْدُفُ إلى تَسْهيلِ السَّفَرِ بَيْنَ الكَواكِبِ بِاسْتِخْدامِ مُحَرِّكاتٍ فائِقَةِ التَّقَدُّمِ.

A team of scientists announced a new space development aimed at facilitating interplanetary travel using ultra-advanced engines.

space telescope — **تِلِسْكوبٌ فَضائِيٌّ**

أُطْلِقَ تِلِسْكوبٌ فَضائِيٌّ جَديدٌ لِدِراسَةِ الكَواكِبِ خارِجَ المَجْموعَةِ الشَّمْسِيَّةِ.

A new space telescope was launched to study exoplanets.

ثُقْبٌ أَسْوَدُ • ثُقوبٌ — **black hole**

أَعْلَنَ الفَلَكِيّونَ عَنِ اكْتِشافِ ثُقْبٍ أَسْوَدَ ضَخْمٍ في مَرْكَزِ مَجَرَّةٍ بَعيدَةٍ.

Astronomers announced the discovery of a massive black hole at the center of a distant galaxy.

جاذِبِيَّةٌ — **gravity**

تَمَكَّنَ العُلَماءُ مِنْ قِياسِ تَأْثيرِ الجاذِبِيَّةِ عَلى انْحِرافِ المَساراتِ الضَّوْئِيَّةِ.

Scientists were able to measure the effect of gravity on the deflection of light paths.

رِحْلَةٌ فَضائِيَّةٌ — **space trip**

نَجَحَتْ رِحْلَةٌ فَضائِيَّةٌ حَديثَةٌ في إِرْسالِ صُوَرٍ مُفَصَّلَةٍ لِسَطْحِ المَرّيخِ.

A recent space trip succeeded in sending detailed images of the Martian surface.

رَصَدَ • رَصْدٌ — **to observe**

رَصَدَ العُلَماءُ ظاهِرَةً فَلَكِيَّةً نادِرَةً في سَماءِ اللَّيْلِ، وَهِيَ مُرورُ كَوْكَبٍ بِالْقُرْبِ مِنَ القَمَرِ.

Scientists observed a rare astronomical phenomenon in the night sky, a planet passing close to the moon.

رَصْدٌ فَلَكِيٌّ — **astronomical observation**

يَجْري الآنَ الرَّصْدُ الفَلَكِيُّ لِحَدَثٍ نادِرٍ يَتَمَثَّلُ في اقْتِرانِ الكَواكِبِ.

Astronomical observation is now being made of a rare event, the conjunction of planets.

عِلْمُ الفَلَكِ — **astronomy**

يَكْشِفُ عِلْمُ الفَلَكِ عَجائِبَ سَماوِيَّةً، وَيُوَسِّعُ فَهْمَنا لِلْكَوْنِ.

Astronomy unveils celestial wonders, expanding our understanding of the cosmos.

فَلَكِيٌّ — **astronomer**

يَعْمَلُ الفَلَكِيُّ مُحَمَّدُ الأَحْمَدِ عَلى دِراسَةِ التَّكْوِيناتِ النَّجْمِيَّةِ في المَجَرّاتِ البَعيدَةِ.

The astronomer Mohammed Al-Ahmad is working on studying stellar formations in distant galaxies.

Another common term for astronomer is عالِمُ فَلَكٍ (literally, 'scientist of astronomy').

astronomical **فَلَكِيٌّ**

تُشيرُ البَياناتُ الفَلَكِيَّةُ الجَديدَةُ الَّتي جُمِعَتْ إِلى وُجودِ مَجَرّاتٍ غَيْرِ مُكْتَشَفَةٍ حَتّى الآنَ.

The new astronomical data collected points to the existence of hitherto undiscovered galaxies.

The word فَلَكِيٌّ can serve as both a noun and an adjective, and context is key to determine its intended meaning.

physics **فيزْياءُ**

تَمَّ تَطْويرُ نَظَرِيَّةٍ جَديدَةٍ في الفيزْياءِ تُفَسِّرُ طَبيعَةَ الجاذِبِيَّةِ في الثُّقوبِ السَّوْداءِ.

A new theory in physics has been developed explaining the nature of gravity in black holes.

nuclear physics **فيزْياءُ نَوَوِيَّةٌ**

أَجْرى عُلَماءُ الفيزْياءِ النَّوَوِيَّةِ تَجارِبَ لِتَحْليلِ طاقَةِ الاِنْشِطارِ النَّوَوِيِّ.

Nuclear physicists conducted experiments to analyze nuclear fission energy.

physicist **فيزْيائِيٌّ**

اِكْتَشَفَتِ الفيزْيائِيَّةُ سارَّةُ الأَحْمَدِ جُسَيْمًا غَريبًا يُمْكِنُ أَنْ يَكونَ دَليلًا عَلى الأَبْعادِ الإِضافِيَّةِ.

Physicist Sarah Al-Ahmad discovered a strange particle that could be evidence of extra dimensions.

Another common term for physicist is عالِمُ فيزْياءٍ (literally, 'scientist of physics').

Coulomb's law • قَوانينُ **قانونُ كولومْ**

اِسْتَخْدَمَ الباحِثونَ قانونَ كولومَ لِحِسابِ التَّوازُنِ الكَهْرَبائِيِّ في الجُزَيْئاتِ النّانَوِيَّةِ.

Researchers used Coulomb's law to calculate the electrical balance in nanoparticles.

Newton's third law **قانونُ نيوتُنِ الثّالِثُ**

قامَ فَريقٌ مِنَ المُهَنْدِسينَ بِتَطْبيقِ قانونِ نيوتُنِ الثّالِثِ لِتَصْميمِ نِظامِ تَوْجيهٍ مُتَطَوِّرٍ لِلصَّواريخِ.

A team of engineers applied Newton's third law to design an advanced guidance system for missiles.

قَمَرٌ صِناعِيٌّ • أَقْمارٌ **satellite**

أَطْلَقَتِ الوكالَةُ الفَضائِيَّةُ الصِّينِيَّةُ قَمَرًا صِناعِيًّا جَديدًا لِدِراسَةِ التَّغَيُّراتِ المُناخِيَّةِ عَلى الأَرْضِ.

The Chinese space agency has launched a new satellite to study climate changes on Earth.

كَوْكَبٌ • كَواكِبُ **planet**

أَعْلَنَ عُلَماءُ الفَلَكِ عَنِ اكْتِشافِ كَوْكَبٍ غَيْرِ مَعْروفٍ مُسْبَقًا يَدورُ حَوْلَ نَجْمٍ في مَجَرَّةِ دَرْبِ التَّبّانَةِ.

Astronomers have announced the discovery of a previously unknown planet orbiting a star in the Milky Way galaxy.

كَوْنٌ • أَكْوانٌ **universe**

يَعْتَقِدُ العُلَماءُ أَنَّ الكَوْنَ قَدْ يَكونُ أَكْبَرَ بِكَثيرٍ مِمّا كانَ مُعْتَقَدًا في السّابِقِ.

Scientists believe the universe may be much larger than previously thought.

كَوْنِيٌّ **cosmic**

الدِّراساتُ الكَوْنِيَّةُ الجَديدَةُ توحي بِأَنَّ هُناكَ المَزيدَ مِنَ المَجَرّاتِ الَّتي لَمْ تُكْتَشَفْ بَعْدُ.

New cosmic studies suggest that there are more galaxies yet to be discovered.

مَجالٌ كَهْرومَغْناطيسِيٌّ **electromagnetic field**

اِسْتَخْدَمَ العُلَماءُ الرّوبوتاتِ لِدِراسَةِ المَجالِ الكَهْرومَغْناطيسِيِّ لِلْأَرْضِ مِنْ أَجْلِ فَهْمِ الزَّلازِلِ بِشَكْلٍ أَفْضَلَ.

Scientists used robots to study Earth's electromagnetic field in order to better understand earthquakes.

مَجَرَّةٌ **galaxy**

تَوَصَّلَ الفَلَكِيّونَ إِلى أَنَّ المَجَرَّةَ الَّتي نَعيشُ فيها، دَرْبَ التَّبّانَةِ، تَحْتَوي عَلى أَكْثَرَ مِنْ 100 مِلْيارِ نَجْمٍ.

Astronomers have concluded that the galaxy we live in, the Milky Way, contains over 100 billion stars.

space station — **مَحَطَّةُ فَضاءٍ**

تَمَّ الكَشْفُ عَنْ تَصْميماتٍ لِمَحَطَّةِ فَضاءٍ جَديدَةٍ سَتَكونُ قادِرَةً عَلى اسْتِضافَةِ أَكْثَرَ مِنْ 100 رائِدِ فَضاءٍ.

Designs for a new space station have been unveiled that will be able to host over 100 astronauts.

International Space Station — **مَحَطَّةُ فَضاءٍ دَوْلِيَّةٌ**

تَمَّ الإِعْلانُ عَنْ خُطَطٍ لِإِرْسالِ بِعْثَةٍ بَشَرِيَّةٍ إِلى مَحَطَّةِ الفَضاءِ الدَّوْلِيَّةِ العامَ المُقْبِلَ.

Plans have been announced to send a human mission to the International Space Station next year.

comet — **مُذَنَّبٌ**

تَمَّ رَصْدُ مُذَنَّبٍ غَيْرِ مَعْروفٍ سابِقًا يَمُرُّ قُرْبَ الأَرْضِ، الأَمْرَ الَّذي قَدْ يُثْمِرُ عَنِ اكْتِشافاتٍ عِلْمِيَّةٍ جَديدَةٍ.

A previously unknown comet passing near Earth has been observed, which could potentially yield new scientific discoveries.

telescope — **مَرْصَدٌ** • مَراصِدُ

أَعْلَنَ مَرْصَدُ هابِلِ الفَلَكِيُّ عَنْ مَجْموعَةٍ مِنَ الصُّوَرِ الجَديدَةِ لِلْكَواكِبِ البَعيدَةِ.

The Hubble Space Telescope announced a set of new images of distant planets.

astronomical observatory — **مَرْصَدٌ فَلَكِيٌّ** • مَراصِدُ

تَمَّ الإِعْلانُ عَنْ خُطَطٍ لِبِناءِ مَرْصَدٍ فَلَكِيٍّ جَديدٍ في الصَّحْراءِ لِلْحُصولِ عَلى صُوَرٍ أَكْثَرَ وُضوحًا لِلنُّجومِ وَالكَواكِبِ.

Plans have been announced to build a new astronomical observatory in the desert to get clearer images of stars and planets.

supernova — **مُسْتَعِرٌ أَعْظَمُ**

تَوَصَّلَ العُلَماءُ لِاكْتِشافِ مُسْتَعِرٍ أَعْظَمَ جَديدٍ، وَهُوَ يُعَدُّ أَكْثَرَ سُطوعًا مِنَ المَلايينِ مِنَ النُّجومِ المُجاوِرَةِ.

Scientists have made a discovery of a new supernova, which is brighter than millions of neighboring stars.

radioactive — **مُشِعٌّ**

اُكْتُشِفَ عُنْصُرٌ مُشِعٌّ جَديدٌ يُمْكِنُ اسْتِخْدامُهُ في تَوْليدِ الطّاقَةِ النَّوَوِيَّةِ.

A new radioactive element has been discovered that can be used in generating nuclear energy.

نَجْمٌ • نُجومٌ **star**

تَمَّ الكَشْفُ عَنْ نَجْمٍ جَديدٍ يُضيءُ بِقُوَّةٍ تُعادِلُ خَمْسَةَ أَضْعافِ شَمْسِنا.

A new star has been revealed that shines five times brighter than our sun.

نَجْمٌ نِيوتْرونِيٌّ **neutron star**

رَصَدَ العُلَماءُ نَجْمًا نِيوتْرونِيًّا يَدورُ بِسُرْعَةٍ مُذْهِلَةٍ في مَرْكَزِ المَجَرَّةِ.

Scientists have observed a neutron star spinning at incredible speed at the center of the galaxy.

نِسْبَوِيٌّ **relativistic**

تَمَّ تَطْويرُ تِقْنِيَّةٍ نِسْبَوِيَّةٍ جَديدَةٍ تُحاكي آثارَ الجاذِبِيَّةِ عَلى الزَّمَنِ.

A new relativistic technique has been developed that simulates the effects of gravity on time.

نَظَرِيَّةُ النِّسْبِيَّةِ **theory of relativity**

اِسْتَطاعَ العُلَماءُ التَّحَقُّقَ مِنْ نَظَرِيَّةِ النِّسْبِيَّةِ لِأَيْنِشْتاين مِنْ خِلالِ تَجْرِبَةٍ شَديدَةِ التَّعْقيدِ.

Scientists have been able to verify Einstein's theory of relativity through an extremely complex experiment.

وَحْدَةٌ فَلَكِيَّةٌ **astronomical unit**

الكَوْكَبُ الجَديدُ الَّذي تَمَّ اكْتِشافُهُ يَقَعُ عَلى بُعْدِ حَوالَيْ 20 وَحْدَةً فَلَكِيَّةً مِنَ الأَرْضِ.

The newly discovered planet is located about 20 astronomical units away from Earth.

5.1.3.1 Mini-Articles

Track **36**

اِكْتَشَفَ العُلَماءُ أَدِلَّةً جَديدَةً تُشيرُ إِلى وُجودِ نُجومٍ نيوتْرونِيَّةٍ في أَماكِنَ بَعيدَةٍ مِنَ الكَوْنِ. تَتَمَيَّزُ هَذِهِ النُّجومُ بِكَثافَتِها العالِيَةِ وَطَبيعَتِها المُشِعَّةِ، مِمّا يَجْعَلُها مَوْضِعًا لِلاهْتِمامِ في مَجالِ الفيزْياءِ النَّوَوِيَّةِ. يُمْكِنُ أَنْ تُوَفِّرَ النُّجومُ النِّيوتْرونِيَّةُ فَهْمًا أَعْمَقَ لِلْمادَّةِ النَّوَوِيَّةِ وَأَساسِيّاتِ الفيزْياءِ.

Scientists have discovered new evidence indicating the existence of neutron stars in distant places in the universe. These stars are characterized by their high density and radiative nature, making them of interest in the field of nuclear physics. Neutron stars can provide a deeper understanding of nuclear matter and the fundamentals of physics.

تَتطَوَّرُ رِحْلاتُ الفَضاءِ بِسُرْعَةٍ كَبيرَةٍ في القَرْنِ الواحِدِ وَالعِشْرينَ، حَيْثُ يَبْذُلُ العُلَماءُ وَالمُهَنْدِسونَ جُهودًا لِاسْتِكْشافِ الكَواكِبِ وَالمَجَرّاتِ البَعيدَةِ. تَسْعى بَرامِجُ الفَضاءِ لِإِرْسالِ أَقْمارٍ صِناعِيَّةٍ وَمَرْكَباتٍ فَضائِيَّةٍ بِأَحْدَثِ التِّقْنِيّاتِ. يَسْتَخْدِمُ الفَلَكِيّونَ التِّلِسْكوباتِ الفَضائِيَّةَ وَمَحَطَّةَ الفَضاءِ الدَّوْلِيَّةَ لِرَصْدِ النُّجومِ، وَالمُذَنَّباتِ، وَالثُّقوبِ السَّوْداءِ، وَغَيْرِها مِنَ الظَّواهِرِ الكَوْنِيَّةِ.

Space exploration is rapidly advancing in the twenty-first century, with scientists and engineers making efforts to explore distant planets and galaxies. Space programs aim to send satellites and spacecraft using the latest technologies. Astronomers utilize space telescopes and the International Space Station to observe stars, comets, black holes, and other cosmic phenomena.

تُمَثِّلُ الثُّقوبُ السَّوْداءُ واحِدَةً مِنْ أَكْثَرِ الظَّواهِرِ الفَلَكِيَّةِ إِثارَةً لِلاهْتِمامِ. تَتَمَيَّزُ بِقُوَّةِ جَذْبِها الفائِقَةِ الَّتي تَسْتَطيعُ أَنْ تَمْتَصَّ الضَّوْءَ، مِمّا يَجْعَلُها غَيْرَ مَرْئِيَّةٍ لِلْعَيْنِ المُجَرَّدَةِ. يَسْتَعينُ العُلَماءُ بِتَأْثيرِ دوبْلِرْ وَتَحْليلِ الطَّيْفِ لِلْكَشْفِ عَنْ وُجودِها. تُقَدِّمُ الثُّقوبُ السَّوْداءُ فُرْصَةً فَريدَةً لِفَهْمِ النَّظَرِيَّةِ النِّسْبِيَّةِ العامَّةِ لِأَيْنِشْتاينْ وَدِراسَةِ الكَوْنِ عَلى مُسْتَوًى أَعْمَقَ.

Black holes are among the most fascinating astronomical phenomena. They are characterized by their extreme gravitational force, which can absorb light, making them invisible to the naked eye. Scientists rely on the Doppler effect and spectroscopic analysis to detect their presence. Black holes provide a unique opportunity to understand Einstein's general theory of relativity and study the universe at a deeper level.

تَلْعَبُ الفيزْياءُ دَوْرًا هامًّا في فَهْمِنا لِلْكَوْنِ. مِنْ خِلالِ قَوانينِ نيوتُنْ، نَفْهَمُ كَيْفَ تَدورُ الكَواكِبُ وَالأَقْمارُ الصِّناعِيَّةُ حَوْلَ الشَّمْسِ. بِفَضْلِ الفيزْياءِ النَّوَوِيَّةِ، نَفْهَمُ كَيْفَ تُوَلِّدُ النُّجومُ الطّاقَةَ. وَبِالاِسْتِشْعارِ عَنْ بُعْدٍ، نَحْصُلُ عَلى صُوَرٍ وَمَعْلوماتٍ حَوْلَ الكَواكِبِ وَالمَجَرّاتِ الَّتي تَبْعُدُ عَنّا مَلايينَ الكيلومِتْراتِ. في كُلِّ يَوْمٍ، يَقومُ الفيزْيائِيّونَ وَالفَلَكِيّونَ بِرَصْدِ وَدِراسَةِ الكَوْنِ لِمَعْرِفَةِ المَزيدِ مِنْ أَسْرارِهِ.

Physics plays a crucial role in our understanding of the cosmos. Through Newton's laws, we understand how planets and satellites orbit the sun. Thanks to nuclear physics, we understand how stars generate energy. With remote sensing, we obtain images and information about planets and galaxies that are millions of kilometers away. Every day, physicists and astronomers monitor and study the universe to uncover more of its secrets.

تُعْتَبَرُ النُّجومُ جُزْءًا أَساسِيًّا مِنَ الكَوْنِ الَّذي نَعيشُ فيهِ. تَتِمُّ دِراسَتُها بِمُساعَدَةِ مَراصِدَ فَلَكِيَّةٍ مُتَطَوِّرَةٍ، حَيْثُ يَجْري تَحْليلُ الطَّيْفِ الضَّوْئِيِّ الصّادِرِ عَنْها لِتَحْديدِ العَناصِرِ المُكَوِّنَةِ لَها. في بَعْضِ الحالاتِ، قَدْ يَتَحَوَّلُ النَّجْمُ إِلى نَجْمٍ نيوتْرونِيٍّ أَوْ يَنْفَجِرُ في ما يُعْرَفُ بِالْمُسْتَعِرِ الأَعْظَمِ، مِمّا يُساهِمُ في تَوْزيعِ العَناصِرِ الكيمْيائِيَّةِ في الكَوْنِ. تُساعِدُ هَذِهِ الظّاهِرَةُ في تَكْوينِ الكَواكِبِ وَالحَياةِ كَما نَعْرِفُها.

Stars are an essential part of the universe we live in. They are studied with the help of advanced astronomical observatories, where the emitted light spectrum is analyzed to determine the elemental composition. In some cases, a star may evolve into a neutron star or explode in a supernova, contributing to the distribution of chemical elements in the universe. This phenomenon aids in the formation of planets and life as we know it.

أَصْبَحَ اسْتِخْدامُ الأَقْمارِ الصِّناعِيَّةِ شائِعًا في عَصْرِنا الحَديثِ، حَيْثُ يَتِمُّ اسْتِخْدامُها لِدِراسَةِ الكَوْنِ وَالأَرْضِ. تُوَظَّفُ تِقْنِيّاتُ الاِسْتِشْعارِ عَنْ بُعْدٍ وَالرَّصْدِ الفَلَكِيِّ في هَذِهِ الأَقْمارِ الصِّناعِيَّةِ لِجَمْعِ البَياناتِ عَنْ أَجْسامِ الفَضاءِ البَعيدَةِ وَالظَّواهِرِ الفَلَكِيَّةِ. هَذِهِ البَياناتُ تُساعِدُ العُلَماءَ في فَهْمِ كَيْفَ تَتَكَوَّنُ الكَواكِبُ وَالنُّجومُ وَالمَجَرّاتُ، وَكَيْفَ تَتَأَثَّرُ بِالظُّروفِ المُحيطَةِ بِها. إِلى جانِبِ ذَلِكَ، تُساهِمُ الأَقْمارُ الصِّناعِيَّةُ أَيْضًا في التَّنَبُّؤِ بِالطَّقْسِ، وَالاِسْتِجابَةِ لِلْكَوارِثِ الطَّبيعِيَّةِ، وَتَحْسينِ الاِتِّصالاتِ العالَمِيَّةِ.

The use of satellites has become widespread in our modern era, being employed to study the universe and the Earth. Remote sensing techniques and astronomical monitoring are utilized in these satellites to collect data about distant space objects and astronomical phenomena. This data helps scientists understand how planets, stars, and galaxies form and how they are influenced by their surrounding conditions. Moreover, satellites also contribute to weather prediction, response to natural disasters, and improvement of global communications.

5.1.3.2 Biography: Stephen Hawking

Track **37**

نَظَرِيَّةُ كُلِّ شَيْءٍ: إِسْهامُ سِتيفِنْ هوكينْجْ في الفيزْياءِ النَّظَرِيَّةِ

تُعْتَبَرُ نَظَرِيَّةُ كُلِّ شَيْءٍ لِسْتيفِنْ هوكينْجْ مِنْ أَكْثَرِ الإِسْهاماتِ إِثارَةً في الفيزْياءِ النَّظَرِيَّةِ. أَمْضى هوكينْجْ حَياتَهُ في السَّعْيِ لِلْعُثورِ عَلى نَظَرِيَّةٍ واحِدَةٍ تَسْتَطيعُ تَفْسيرَ كُلِّ شَيْءٍ في الكَوْنِ، مِنَ الثُّقوبِ السَّوْداءِ إِلى الاِنْفِجارِ العَظيمِ. وَهَذا هُوَ ما يُعْرَفُ بِ " نَظَرِيَّةِ كُلِّ شَيْءٍ".

كَرَّسَ هوكينْجْ سَنَواتٍ عَديدَةً لِدِراسَةِ الثُّقوبِ السَّوْداءِ، تِلْكَ الأَجْسامِ الفَلَكِيَّةِ الخَلّابَةِ الَّتي تَمْتازُ بِقُوَّةِ جَذْبِها الفائِقَةِ لِدَرَجَةِ أَنَّها تَمْتَصُّ الضَّوْءَ نَفْسَهُ. مِنْ خِلالِ الجَمْعِ بَيْنَ نَظَرِيَّةِ النِّسْبِيَّةِ العامَّةِ لِأَيْنِشْتايْنْ وَميكانيكا الكَمِّ، تَمَكَّنَ هوكينْجْ مِنْ تَطْويرِ فَهْمٍ جَديدٍ لِلطَّبيعَةِ الغامِضَةِ لِلثُّقوبِ السَّوْداءِ.

بِالرَّغْمِ مِنْ أَنَّهُ لَمْ يَتَمَكَّنْ مِنَ التَّوَصُّلِ لِنَظَرِيَّةِ كُلِّ شَيْءٍ، فَإِنَّ جَهْدَهُ لاقى اسْتِحْسانًا عالَمِيًّا وَساهَمَ في تَوْسيعِ فَهْمِنا لِلْكَوْنِ. لِيَوْمِنا هَذا، يُعْتَبَرُ هوكينْجْ رَمْزًا لِلْعَزيمَةِ وَالشَّجاعَةِ وَالأَمَلِ في وَجْهِ التَّحَدِّياتِ الصَّعْبَةِ، مَعَ الاِعْتِرافِ بِأَنَّهُ بِالرَّغْمِ مِنْ عَدَمِ تَحْقيقِهِ لِنَظَرِيَّةِ كُلِّ شَيْءٍ، فَإِنَّ السَّعْيَ نَحْوَها قَدْ غَيَّرَ الفيزْياءَ وَعِلْمَ الفَلَكِ بِطُرُقٍ لا يُمْكِنُ تَصَوُّرُها.

The Theory of Everything: Stephen Hawking's Contribution to Theoretical Physics

Stephen Hawking's theory of everything is considered one of the most exciting contributions to theoretical physics. Hawking spent his life in pursuit of finding a single theory that could explain everything in the universe, from black holes to the Big Bang, and this is what is known as the "Theory of Everything."

Hawking devoted many years to studying black holes, these fascinating astronomical objects that are characterized by their extreme gravitational force, to the extent that they absorb light itself. By combining Einstein's theory of general relativity with quantum mechanics, Hawking was able to develop a new understanding of the mysterious nature of black holes.

Although he did not find the theory of everything, his work has received worldwide acclaim and has contributed to expanding our understanding of the universe. Even today, Hawking is seen as a symbol of determination, courage, and hope in the face of difficult challenges, acknowledging that despite not achieving the theory of everything, the pursuit of it has profoundly transformed physics and astronomy in unimaginable ways.

5.1.4 Environmental Science and Sustainability

Track **38**

waste management إدارَةُ النُّفاياتِ

أُعْلِنَ عَنْ مَشْروعٍ جَديدٍ لِإدارَةِ النُّفاياتِ يَهْدُفُ إلى تَحْويلِ القُمامَةِ إلى أَسْمِدَةٍ طَبيعِيَّةٍ.

A new waste management project has been announced that aims to convert garbage into natural fertilizer.

global warming اِحْتِباسٌ حَرارِيٌّ

جَرى رَصْدُ تَغَيُّراتٍ مُناخِيَّةٍ كَبيرَةٍ في المَناطِقِ القُطْبِيَّةِ بِسَبَبِ الاِحْتِباسِ الحَرارِيِّ.

Significant climate changes have been observed in the polar regions due to global warming.

to sustain اِسْتَدامَ • اِسْتِدامَةٌ

أَكَّدَتِ الحُكومَةُ الجَديدَةُ التِزامَها بِسِياساتٍ تَعْمَلُ عَلى اسْتِدامَةِ المَوارِدِ المائِيَّةِ لِلأَجْيالِ المُقْبِلَةِ.

The new government affirmed its commitment to policies that sustain water resources for future generations.

environmental conservation — **الحِفاظُ عَلى البيئَةِ**

تَمَّ تَشْجيعُ الشَّرِكاتِ عَلى اتِّخاذِ إجْراءاتٍ أكْثَرَ فَعاليَّةً لِلْحِفاظِ عَلى البيئَةِ.

Companies have been encouraged to take more effective measures to preserve the environment.

conservation of biodiversity — **الحِفاظُ عَلى التَّنَوُّعِ البَيولوجِيِّ**

بَدَأَتِ البِلادُ مَشْروعًا وَطَنِيًّا جَديدًا لِلْحِفاظِ عَلى التَّنَوُّعِ البَيولوجِيِّ.

The country has launched a new national project for preserving biodiversity.

desertification — **تَصَحُّرٌ**

أَصْبَحَتْ مِساحاتٌ واسِعَةٌ مِنَ الأَراضي الزِّراعِيَّةِ عُرْضَةً لِلتَّصَحُّرِ بِسَبَبِ الزِّراعَةِ الجائِرَةِ.

Large areas of agricultural land have become prone to desertification due to overfarming.

climate change — **تَغَيُّرُ المُناخِ**

حَذَّرَتِ الأُمَمُ المُتَّحِدَةُ مِنْ تَأْثيراتِ تَغَيُّرِ المُناخِ عَلى الأَنْظِمَةِ البيئِيَّةِ العالَمِيَّةِ.

The United Nations warned about the impacts of climate change on global ecosystems.

water pollution — **تَلَوُّثُ المِياهِ**

تَمَّ الكَشْفُ عَنْ تَلَوُّثٍ جَسيمٍ لِلْمِياهِ الجَوْفِيَّةِ في مَناطِقِ الصِّناعَةِ الثَّقيلَةِ.

Significant groundwater pollution has been detected in heavy industrial areas.

air pollution — **تَلَوُّثُ الهَواءِ**

صَدَرَ تَقْريرٌ حُكومِيٌّ يُشيرُ إلى مُسْتَوَياتٍ خَطيرَةٍ مِنْ تَلَوُّثِ الهَواءِ في المُدُنِ الكُبْرى.

A government report has been released indicating dangerous levels of air pollution in major cities.

sustainable development — **تَنْمِيَةٌ مُسْتَدامَةٌ**

دَعَتْ مُنَظَّمَةُ الصِّحَّةِ العالَمِيَّةُ إلى تَبَنّي مَبادِئِ التَّنْمِيَةِ المُسْتَدامَةِ في جَميعِ القِطاعاتِ.

The World Health Organization has called for the adoption of sustainable development principles in all sectors.

to conserve حِفاظٌ • **حافَظَ**

قامَتْ مَجْموعَةٌ مِنَ العُلَماءِ بِالْحِفاظِ عَلى العَديدِ مِنَ الأَنْواعِ المُهَدَّدَةِ بِالانْقِراضِ مِنْ خِلالِ تِكْنولوجْيا الاِسْتِنْساخِ.

A group of scientists have conserved many endangered species through cloning technology.

to preserve حِفاظٌ • **حافَظَ عَلى**

حافَظَتِ الحُكومَةُ عَلى الشَّواطِئِ مِنَ التَّلَوُّثِ عَنْ طَريقِ فَرْضِ ضَوابِطَ صارِمَةٍ عَلى النُّفاياتِ البِلاسْتيكِيَّةِ.

The government has preserved the beaches from pollution by imposing strict controls on plastic waste.

nuclear test ban **حَظْرُ التَّجارِبِ النَّوَوِيَّةِ**

صَدَرَ قَرارٌ دَوْلِيٌّ بِحَظْرِ التَّجارِبِ النَّوَوِيَّةِ لِلْحِفاظِ عَلى الأَمانِ العالَمِيِّ.

An international resolution has been issued to ban nuclear testing in order to preserve global safety.

animal rights *pl.* **حُقوقُ الحَيَوانِ**

جَرى تَقْديمُ تَشْريعٍ جَديدٍ لِحِمايَةِ حُقوقِ الحَيَوانِ وَضَمانِ رَفاهِيَّتِهِمْ.

New legislation has been introduced to protect animal rights and ensure their wellbeing.

environmental protection **حِمايَةُ البيئَةِ**

جَرى اقْتِراحُ قَوانينَ جَديدَةٍ لِحِمايَةِ البيئَةِ مِنَ التَّلَوُّثِ الصِّناعِيِّ.

New laws have been proposed to protect the environment from industrial pollution.

awareness campaign **حَمْلَةُ تَوْعِيَةٍ**

أُطْلِقَتْ حَمْلَةُ تَوْعِيَةٍ بِشَأْنِ الأَثَرِ البيئِيِّ لِلتَّسَوُّقِ الزّائِدِ.

An awareness campaign has been launched about the environmental impact of excessive shopping.

to protect حِمايَةٌ • **حَمى**

جَرى تَأْسيسُ مَحْمِيَّةٍ جَديدَةٍ تَحْمي الحَياةَ البَرِّيَّةَ في المِنْطَقَةِ مِنَ التَّهْديداتِ البيئِيَّةِ.

A new reserve has been established that protects wildlife in the area from environmental threats.

The verb جَرى is used similarly to تَمَّ to indicate that an action has been completed. It serves as an alternative to using a passive verb, effectively shifting the focus to the completion of the action rather than who carried it out. This makes the statement more general or impersonal while conveying the same meaning. It is usually followed by a verbal noun (masdar) to specify what action was carried out. For example, جَرى تَأْسيسُ مَحْمِيَّةٍ جَديدَةٍ means 'The establishment of a new reserve has taken place.'

to destroy • تَدْميرٌ **دَمَّرَ**

دَمَّرَ الإِعْصارُ العَنيفُ العَديدَ مِنَ المَناطِقِ الطَّبيعِيَّةِ الجَميلَةِ في البِلادِ.

The violent hurricane destroyed many beautiful natural areas in the country.

organic farming **زِراعَةٌ عُضْوِيَّةٌ**

أَعْلَنَتِ الحُكومَةُ عَنْ زِيادَةِ الدَّعْمِ لِلزِّراعَةِ العُضْوِيَّةِ كَجُزْءٍ مِنَ اسْتِراتيجِيَّتِها لِتَحْسينِ الأَمْنِ الغِذائِيِّ.

The government has announced increasing support for organic farming as part of its strategy to improve food security.

to encourage • تَشْجيعٌ **شَجَّعَ**

شَجَّعَتِ الحُكومَةُ اسْتِخْدامَ المُنْتَجاتِ القابِلَةِ لِلتَّحَلُّلِ البيولوجِيِّ لِلْحَدِّ مِنْ تَلَوُّثِ البِلاسْتيكِ.

The government encouraged the use of biodegradable products to reduce plastic pollution.

to conserve, protect • صِيانَةٌ **صانَ**

صانَ العُلَماءُ النُّظُمَ البيئِيَّةَ البَحْرِيَّةَ مِنَ الزِّيادَةِ الحَرارِيَّةِ مِنْ خِلالِ تَطْويرِ تِقْنِيّاتٍ جَديدَةٍ لِلتَّخفيفِ مِنْ تَأْثيرِ تَغَيُّرِ المُناخِ .

Scientists have protected marine ecosystems from thermal increase by developing new techniques to mitigate the impact of climate change.

to correct • تَصْحيحٌ **صَحَّحَ**

صَحَّحَ العُلَماءُ العَديدَ مِنَ المَفاهيمِ الخاطِئَةِ حَوْلَ التَّغَيُّرِ المُناخِيِّ مِنْ خِلالِ الأَبْحاثِ الحَديثَةِ.

Scientists have corrected many misconceptions about climate change through recent research.

eco-friendly **صَديقٌ لِلْبيئَةِ**

تَمَّ تَطْويرُ سَيّاراتٍ صَديقَةٍ لِلْبيئَةِ تَعْمَلُ بِالطّاقَةِ الشَّمْسِيَّةِ.

Environmentally friendly cars have been developed that run on solar energy.

solar energy **طاقَةٌ شَمْسِيَّةٌ**

بَدَأَتِ الحُكومَةُ في تَثْبيتِ أَلْواحِ الطّاقَةِ الشَّمْسِيَّةِ عَلى جَميعِ المَباني الحُكومِيَّةِ.

The government has begun installing solar energy panels on all government buildings.

renewable energy **طاقَةٌ مُتَجَدِّدَةٌ**

جَرَتْ تَرْقِيَةُ البِنْيَةِ التَّحْتِيَّةِ لِلْبِلادِ لِدَعْمِ إِنْتاجِ الطّاقَةِ المُتَجَدِّدَةِ.

The country's infrastructure has been upgraded to support renewable energy production.

nuclear energy **طاقَةٌ نَوَوِيَّةٌ**

بِالرَّغْمِ مِنَ الجَدَلِ المُحيطِ بِها، تُعْتَبَرُ الطّاقَةُ النَّوَوِيَّةُ مَصْدَرًا قَوِيًّا لِلطّاقَةِ.

Despite the controversy surrounding it, nuclear energy is a strong source of power.

natural **طَبيعِيٌّ**

بَدَأَتِ الشَّرِكاتُ في اسْتِخْدامِ المَوادِّ الطَّبيعِيَّةِ بَدَلًا مِنَ المَوادِّ الكيمْيائِيَّةِ في مُنْتَجاتِها.

Companies have started using natural materials instead of chemicals in their products.

organic **عُضْوِيٌّ**

ثَمَّةَ تَزايُدٌ في الطَّلَبِ عَلى المُنْتَجاتِ العُضْوِيَّةِ في السّوقِ العالَمِيَّةِ.

There is increasing demand for organic products in the global market.

non-sustainable **غَيْرُ مُسْتَدامٍ**

وَصَفَتِ الأُمَمُ المُتَّحِدَةُ اسْتِخْدامَ الوَقودِ الأُحْفورِيِّ بِأَنَّهُ غَيْرُ مُسْتَدامٍ وَدَعَتْ إِلى التَّحَوُّلِ إِلى الطّاقَةِ المُتَجَدِّدَةِ.

The United Nations described the use of fossil fuels as unsustainable and called for a shift to renewable energy.

لَوَّثَ • تَلْويثٌ **to pollute**

لَوَّثَ النِّفْطُ المُسَرَّبُ الشَّواطِئَ المَحَلِّيَّةَ، مِمّا أَدّى إِلى كارِثَةٍ بيئِيَّةٍ ضَخْمَةٍ.

The leaked oil polluted the local beaches, leading to a massive environmental disaster.

مُتَجَدِّدٌ **renewable**

تُعْتَبَرُ طاقَةُ الرِّياحِ وَالطّاقَةُ الشَّمْسِيَّةُ مَصْدَرَيْنِ مُتَجَدِّدينِ لِلطّاقَةِ يُمْكِنُ الاِعْتِمادُ عَلَيْهِما.

Wind energy and solar energy are renewable sources of energy that can be relied upon.

مُحافِظٌ **conservational**

أَعْلَنَتِ الحُكومَةُ عَنْ خُطَّةٍ مُحافَظَةٍ لِحِمايَةِ الأَنْواعِ المُهَدَّدَةِ بِالاِنْقِراضِ.

The government announced a conservation plan to protect endangered species.

مَحْمِيَّةٌ طَبيعِيَّةٌ **nature reserve**

جَرى تَوْسيعُ المَحْمِيّاتِ الطَّبيعِيَّةِ في البِلادِ لِلْمُساعَدَةِ في الحِفاظِ عَلى التَّنَوُّعِ البَيولوجِيِّ.

The country's nature reserves have been expanded to help preserve biodiversity.

مُدَمِّرٌ **destructive**

يُمْكِنُ لِلاسْتِخْدامِ المُفْرِطِ لِلْمُبيداتِ الحَشَرِيَّةِ أَنْ يَكونَ مُدَمِّرًا لِلْبيئَةِ.

The excessive use of pesticides can be destructive to the environment.

مُسْتَدامٌ **sustainable**

تَمَّ تَصْميمُ المَدينَةِ الجَديدَةِ لِتَكونَ مُسْتَدامَةً وَمُوَفِّرَةً لِلطّاقَةِ.

The new city was designed to be sustainable and energy efficient.

مُسْتَدامٌ بيئِيًّا **environmentally sustainable**

الشَّرِكاتُ المُسْتَدامَةُ بيئِيًّا تَكونُ أَكْثَرَ جَذْبًا لِلْمُسْتَثْمِرينَ المُهْتَمّينَ بِالاِسْتِثْمارِ الأَخْضَرِ.

Environmentally sustainable companies are more attractive to investors interested in green investing.

polluted مُلَوَّثٌ

أَصْبَحَ النَّهْرُ مُلَوَّثًا بِشَكْلٍ مُتَزايِدٍ بِسَبَبِ الصَّرْفِ الصِّحِّيِّ غَيْرِ المُعالَجِ.

The river has become increasingly polluted due to untreated sewage.

to ban; prevent مَنَعَ • مَنْعٌ

مَنَعَتِ الحُكومَةُ الصَّيْدَ التِّجارِيَّ لِلْأَنْواعِ المَحْمِيَّةِ.

The government has banned the commercial hunting of protected species.

threatened, endangered مُهَدَّدٌ

الفِيَلَةُ الإِفْريقيَّةُ مُهَدَّدَةٌ بِسَبَبِ الصَّيْدِ غَيْرِ القانونِيِّ.

The African elephant is endangered due to illegal hunting.

to dry up نَضَبَ • نُضوبٌ

نَضَبَتْ بُحَيْرَةٌ كَبيرَةٌ في الصَّحْراءِ نَتيجَةً لِمَوْجاتِ الجَفافِ المُتَكَرِّرَةِ.

A large lake in the desert has dried up due to recurring drought waves.

clean نَظيفٌ

تَسْتَخْدِمُ البَلَدِيَّةُ الآنَ أَساليبَ نَظيفَةً لِمُعالَجَةِ النُّفاياتِ.

The municipality now uses clean methods for waste treatment.

to threaten هَدَّدَ • تَهْديدٌ

هَدَّدَتِ الفَيَضاناتُ الأَخيرَةُ الحَياةَ البَرِّيَّةَ في المِنْطَقَةِ.

The recent floods threatened wildlife in the area.

5.1.4.1 Mini-Articles

Track **39**

مَعَ تَصاعُدِ التَّهْديداتِ المُسْتَمِرَّةِ لِلْبيئَةِ، مِنَ التَّغَيُّرِ المُناخِيِّ وَتَلَوُّثِ الهَواءِ وَالمِياهِ، أَصْبَحَ الحِفاظُ عَلى التَّنَوُّعِ البَيولوجِيِّ أَمْرًا أَكْثَرَ أَهَمِّيَّةً مِنْ أَيِّ وَقْتٍ مَضى. العَديدُ مِنَ الأَنْواعِ مُهَدَّدَةٌ بِالِانْقِراضِ، وَالتَّدْميرُ المُسْتَمِرُّ لِلْمَواطِنِ

الطَّبيعيَّةِ يُهَدِّدُ الحياةَ البَرِّيَّةَ. إنَّ حِمايَةَ البيئَةِ وَالعَمَلَ عَلى تَحْقيقِ التَّنْمِيَةِ المُسْتَدامَةِ يُعَدُّ هَدَفًا مُلِحًّا يَتَطَلَّبُ الحِفاظَ عَلى المَحْمِيّاتِ الطَّبيعِيَّةِ، وَالتَّعامُلَ مَعَ النُّفاياتِ بِطُرُقٍ صَديقَةٍ لِلْبيئَةِ.

With the escalating and continuous threats to the environment, such as climate change, and air and water pollution, preserving biodiversity has become more important than ever before. Many species are endangered, and the ongoing destruction of natural habitats puts wildlife at risk. Protecting the environment and working towards sustainable development is a pressing goal that requires the conservation of natural reserves and the management of waste in environmentally friendly ways.

أَصْبَحَتِ الطّاقَةُ المُتَجَدِّدَةُ مِنَ الأَوْلَوِيّاتِ الرَّئيسِيَّةِ في القَرْنِ الحادي وَالعِشْرينَ، وَذَلِكَ في ظِلِّ تَزايُدِ الاِعْتِمادِ عَلى مَصادِرِ الطّاقَةِ مِنَ النِّفْطِ، الَّتي تُساهِمُ في تَغَيُّرِ المُناخِ وَالاِحْتِباسِ الحَرارِيِّ. تُعْتَبَرُ الطّاقَةُ الشَّمْسِيَّةُ مِنْ أَكْثَرِ أَنْواعِ الطّاقَةِ المُتَجَدِّدَةِ شُيوعًا، حَيْثُ تُعَدُّ خالِيَةً مِنَ التَّلَوُّثِ وَمُسْتَدامَةً.

Renewable energy has become a top priority in the 21st century, given the increasing reliance on oil energy sources, which contribute to climate change and global warming. Solar energy is considered one of the most common forms of renewable energy, as it is pollution-free and sustainable.

تُعْتَبَرُ الزِّراعَةُ العُضْوِيَّةُ إِحْدى أَبْرَزِ مَجالاتِ الاِهْتِمامِ في مَجالِ البيئَةِ وَالاِسْتِدامَةِ. إِذْ تُشَجِّعُ هَذِهِ المُمارَساتُ عَلى اسْتِخْدامِ الطُّرُقِ الطَّبيعِيَّةِ في الزِّراعَةِ لِلْحَدِّ مِنَ التَّلَوُّثِ النّاجِمِ عَنِ الأَسْمِدَةِ وَالمُبيداتِ الكيمْيائِيَّةِ. بِالإِضافَةِ إِلى ذَلِكَ، فَإِنَّ الزِّراعَةَ العُضْوِيَّةَ تُحافِظُ عَلى صِحَّةِ التُّرْبَةِ وَتُحَسِّنُ النِّظامَ البيئِيَّ، مِمّا يُسْهِمُ في التَّنْمِيَةِ المُسْتَدامَةِ وَالحِفاظِ عَلى البيئَةِ.

Organic farming is one of the prominent areas of focus in the realm of environment and sustainability. These practices encourage the use of natural methods in agriculture to reduce pollution caused by fertilizers and pesticides. Moreover, organic farming preserves soil health and improves the ecosystem, contributing to sustainable development and environmental preservation.

تُعْتَبَرُ إِدارَةُ النُّفاياتِ تَحَدِّيًا كَبيرًا في مُجْتَمَعاتِنا الحَديثَةِ، خاصَّةً في البُلْدانِ الَّتي تُواجِهُ زِيادَةً في السُّكّانِ وَالاِسْتِهْلاكِ. القُمامَةُ الَّتي يَتِمُّ التَّخَلُّصُ مِنْها بِطَريقَةٍ غَيْرِ صِحِّيَّةٍ تَتَسَبَّبُ في تَلَوُّثِ الهَواءِ وَالمِياهِ، وَتُمَثِّلُ خَطَرًا عَلى الصِّحَّةِ العامَّةِ. لِذا، مِنَ الأَهَمِّيَّةِ بِمَكانٍ تَطْبيقُ اسْتِراتيجِيّاتٍ صَديقَةٍ لِلْبيئَةِ في إِدارَةِ النُّفاياتِ، بِما في ذَلِكَ إِعادَةُ التَّدْويرِ، وَالتَّخَلُّصُ الآمِنُ مِنَ النُّفاياتِ الخَطِرَةِ.

Waste management is a major challenge in our modern societies, especially in countries facing population growth and increased consumption. Improperly disposed waste leads to air and water pollution and poses a threat to public health. Therefore, it is of utmost importance to implement environmentally friendly strategies in waste management, including recycling and safe disposal of hazardous waste.

يُعَدُّ تَغَيُّرُ المُناخِ وَالاحْتِباسُ الحَرارِيُّ مِنْ أَكْبَرِ التَّحَدِّياتِ الَّتي يُواجِهُها العالَمُ اليَوْمَ. إِنَّ ارْتِفاعَ دَرَجَةِ الحَرارَةِ عالَمِيًّا وَتَأْثيرَهُ عَلى النِّظامِ البيئِيِّ وَالبَيولوجِيِّ لِكَوْكَبِنا يُمَثِّلُ تَهْديدًا خَطيرًا لِجَميعِ أَشْكالِ الحَياةِ. إِنَّ الأَنْشِطَةَ البَشَرِيَّةَ، مِثْلَ حَرْقِ الوَقودِ الأُحْفورِيِّ، هِيَ السَّبَبُ الرَّئيسِيُّ في الاحْتِباسِ الحَرارِيِّ. تُشيرُ الدِّراساتُ إِلى أَنَّهُ إِذا لَمْ نُقَلِّلْ مِنَ انْبِعاثاتِ غازاتِ الدَّفيئَةِ، قَدْ نُواجِهُ تَأْثيراتٍ مُدَمِّرَةً، بِما في ذَلِكَ الكَوارِثُ الطَّبيعِيَّةُ وَانْقِراضُ الأَنْواعِ. لِذَلِكَ يَتَطَلَّبُ الأَمْرُ مِنّا جَميعًا العَمَلَ بِاتِّجاهِ حُلولٍ مُسْتَدامَةٍ وَصَديقَةٍ لِلْبيئَةِ لِمُواجَهَةِ هَذِهِ التَّحَدِّياتِ.

Climate change and global warming are among the biggest challenges the world is facing today. The rise in global temperatures and its impact on our planet's ecosystem and biodiversity pose a serious threat to all forms of life. Human activities, such as the burning of fossil fuels, are the main cause of global warming. Studies indicate that if we do not reduce greenhouse gas emissions, we may face devastating effects, including natural disasters and species extinction. Therefore, it requires all of us to work towards sustainable and environmentally friendly solutions to address these challenges.

5.1.4.2 Interview with a Climatologist

Track **40**

مُقابَلَةٌ مَعَ د. يوسُفَ: البُحوثُ الخاصَّةُ بِالتَّغَيُّرِ المُناخِيِّ وَالتَّنْمِيَةِ المُسْتَدامَةِ

مُقَدِّمُ البَرْنامَجِ: مَرْحَبًا بِكُمْ في بَرْنامَجِنا. لَدَيْنا ضَيْفٌ خاصٌّ مَعَنا اليَوْمَ، الدُّكْتورُ يوسُفُ، عالِمُ البيئَةِ مِنَ الأُرْدُنِّ، الَّذي يَعْمَلُ عَلى مَشْروعِ بَحْثٍ حَوْلَ التَّغَيُّرِ المُناخِيِّ. مَرْحَبًا بِكَ، دُكْتور يوسُفُ. هَلْ يُمْكِنُكَ أَنْ تُخْبِرَنا عَنْ مَشْروعِكَ؟

د. يوسُفُ: شُكْرًا لَكَ عَلى دَعْوَتي. نَعَمْ، نَحْنُ نَعْمَلُ حالِيًّا عَلى مَشْروعٍ يَتَعَلَّقُ بِتَأْثيرِ تَغَيُّرِ المُناخِ عَلى التَّصَحُّرِ في مِنْطَقَتِنا. الهَدَفُ الأَساسِيُّ مِنَ البَحْثِ هُوَ تَقْديرُ مُعَدَّلِ التَّصَحُّرِ وَكَيْفَ يُمْكِنُنا مَنْعُ هَذا التَّدَهْوُرِ البيئِيِّ.

مُقَدِّمُ البَرْنامَجِ: هَذا يَبْدو مُهِمًّا جِدًّا. كَيْفَ تَتَعامَلونَ مَعَ تَلَوُّثِ الهَواءِ وَالمِياهِ في دِراساتِكُمْ؟

د. يوسُفُ: الحِفاظُ عَلى البيئَةِ يَعْني التَّعامُلَ مَعَ جَميعِ أَشْكالِ التَّلَوُّثِ. في بَحْثِنا، نَرْصُدُ نَوْعِيَّةَ الهَواءِ وَالمِياهِ وَكَيْفَ يُمْكِنُ أَنْ يُساهِمَ التَّلَوُّثُ في التَّصَحُّرِ. إِنَّ تَحْليلَ هَذِهِ البَياناتِ يُساعِدُنا في تَطْويرِ حُلولٍ صَديقَةٍ لِلْبيئَةِ.

مُقَدِّمُ البَرْنامَجِ: هَلْ تَعْتَبِرونَ التَّنْمِيَةَ المُسْتَدامَةَ جُزْءًا مِنْ بَحْثِكُمْ؟

د. يوسف: بِالتَّأْكيدِ، فالتَّنْمِيَةُ المُسْتَدامَةُ هِيَ الهَدَفُ النِّهائِيُّ. نَحْنُ نَبْحَثُ عَنْ طُرُقٍ لِلْحَدِّ مِنَ التَّلَوُّثِ وَالحِفاظِ عَلى التَّنَوُّعِ البَيولوجِيِّ، مَعَ دَعْمِ النُّمُوِّ الاِقْتِصادِيِّ. الفِكْرَةُ هِيَ الوُصولُ إلى التَّوازُنِ بَيْنَ النُّمُوِّ وَالحِفاظِ عَلى البيئَةِ.

مُقَدِّمُ البَرْنامَجِ: هَذا رائِعٌ، دُكْتورُ يوسُفُ. شُكْرًا لَكَ عَلى الجُهودِ الَّتي تَبْذُلُها في الحِفاظِ عَلى بيئَتِنا وزِيادَةِ الوَعْيِ بِالتَّغَيُّرِ المُناخِيِّ. نَتَطَلَّعُ إلى مَعْرِفَةِ المَزيدِ عَنْ مَشْروعِكَ في المُسْتَقْبَلِ.

د. يوسُفُ: شُكْرًا لَكَ عَلى دَعْوَتي، وَلِلْجُمْهورِ عَلى الاِهْتِمامِ بِمَوْضوعٍ مِثْلِ التَّغَيُّرِ المُناخِيِّ. إنَّها مَسْأَلَةٌ تُؤَثِّرُ عَلى الجَميعِ، وَأَتَمَنّى أَنْ نَتَمَكَّنَ مِنْ إِحْداثِ فَرْقٍ حَقيقِيٍّ.

An Interview with Dr. Youssef: Research on Climate Change and Sustainable Development

Program Host: Welcome to our program. We have a special guest with us today, Dr. Youssef, an environmental scientist from Jordan, who is working on a research project about climate change. Welcome, Dr. Youssef. Can you tell us about your project?

Dr. Youssef: Thank you for having me. Yes, we are currently working on a project related to the impact of climate change on desertification in our region. The main objective of the research is to estimate the rate of desertification and how we can prevent this environmental degradation.

Program Host: That sounds very important. How do you deal with air and water pollution in your studies?

Dr. Youssef: Environmental preservation means dealing with all forms of pollution. In our research, we monitor the air and water quality and how pollution can contribute to desertification. Analyzing this data helps us develop environmentally friendly solutions.

Program Host: Do you consider sustainable development as part of your research?

Dr. Youssef: Absolutely, sustainable development is the ultimate goal. We are looking for ways to reduce pollution and preserve biodiversity while supporting economic growth. The idea is to find a balance between growth and environmental preservation.

Program Host: That's wonderful, Dr. Youssef. Thank you for your efforts in preserving our environment and raising awareness about climate change. We look forward to learning more about your project in the future.

Dr. Youssef: Thank you for having me and to the audience for showing interest in a topic like climate change. It's an issue that affects everyone, and I hope we can make a real difference.

5.2 Technology and Innovation

Track **41**

innovation إِبْداعٌ

تُشَجِّعُ الشَّرِكاتُ النّاشِئَةُ عَلى الإِبْداعِ مِنْ خِلالِ تَوْفيرِ بيئَةِ عَمَلٍ مَرِنَةٍ وَمُحَفِّزَةٍ.

Startups encourage innovation by providing a flexible and stimulating work environment.

technical, technological تِقْنِيٌّ

تَمَّ تَدْريبُ العامِلينَ في القِطاعِ التِّقْنِيِّ عَلى أَحْدَثِ المَنَصّاتِ البَرْمَجِيَّةِ.

Workers in the technical sector have been trained on the latest programming platforms.

technology تِقْنِيَّةٌ

أُسْتُخْدِمَتْ تِقْنِيَّةُ الطِّباعَةِ ثُلاثِيَّةِ الأَبْعادِ لِإِنْتاجِ أَعْضاءٍ اصْطِناعِيَّةٍ لِلْمَرْضى.

3D printing technology has been used to produce artificial organs for patients.

technological تِكْنولوجِيٌّ

تَعِدُ الإِنْجازاتُ التِّكْنولوجِيَّةُ في مَجالِ الطّاقَةِ المُتَجَدِّدَةِ بِمُسْتَقْبَلٍ أَكْثَرَ اسْتِدامَةً.

Technological breakthroughs in renewable energy promise a more sustainable future.

technology تِكْنولوجْيا

أَعْلَنَتِ الإِماراتُ العَرَبِيَّةُ المُتَّحِدَةُ عَنِ اسْتِثْماراتٍ جَديدَةٍ في تِكْنولوجْيا الطّاقَةِ النَّظيفَةِ كَجُزْءٍ مِنْ خُطَطِها لِتَحْقيقِ الاِسْتِدامَةِ.

The United Arab Emirates announced new investments in clean energy technology as part of its plans to achieve sustainability.

5.2.1 Information Technology and Cybersecurity

Track **42**

secure آمِنٌ

طُوِّرَتْ بَرامِجُ الحِمايَةِ مِنَ الفَيْروساتِ لِجَعْلِ اسْتِخْدامِ الإِنْتَرْنِتْ آمِنًا لِلْجَميعِ.

Antivirus programs were developed to make internet use safe for everyone.

cybersecurity أَمْنٌ سَيْبَرانِيٌّ

أَصْبَحَ الأَمْنُ السَّيْبَرانِيُّ مِحْوَرًا رَئيسِيًّا في الاِسْتِراتيجِيَّةِ الوَطَنِيَّةِ لِلْعَديدِ مِنَ الدُّوَلِ.

Cybersecurity has become a key focus in the national strategy of many countries.

information security أَمْنُ مَعْلوماتٍ

عَقِبَ التَّهْديداتِ الأَمْنِيَّةِ الأَخيرَةِ، تَعَزَّزَتْ إِجْراءاتُ أَمْنِ المَعْلوماتِ في الجامِعَةِ الأَمْريكِيَّةِ بِالْقاهِرَةِ.

Following recent security threats, information security measures have been strengthened at the American University in Cairo.

internet إِنْتَرْنِتْ

تُوَسِّعُ الإِنْتَرْنِتِ الفُرَصَ المُتاحَةَ لِلتَّعَلُّمِ وَالتَّواصُلِ عَلى مُسْتَوًى عالَمِيٍّ.

The internet expands opportunities for learning and communication globally.

wireless internet إِنْتَرْنِتْ لاسِلْكِيٌّ

أَصْبَحَ الإِنْتَرْنِتِ اللّاسِلْكِيُّ شائِعًا في العَديدِ مِنَ المَناطِقِ العامَّةِ، مِثْلِ المَكْتَباتِ وَالمَقاهي.

Wireless internet has become common in many public areas like libraries and cafes.

hacking, cyber attack اِخْتِراقٌ إِلِكْترونِيٌّ

تَعَرَّضَ البَنْكُ لِاخْتِراقٍ إِلِكْترونِيٍّ أَدّى إِلى فُقْدانِ بَياناتِ العَديدِ مِنَ العُمَلاءِ.

The bank suffered a cyber attack resulting in the loss of many customers' data.

account hacking — **اِخْتِراقُ حِسابٍ**

نَصَحَتِ الشَّرِكَةُ المُسْتَخْدِمينَ بِتَغْييرِ كَلِماتِ المُرورِ بَعْدَ أَنْ تَمَّ اخْتِراقُ حِساباتٍ عَديدَةٍ.

The company advised users to change their passwords after numerous accounts were hacked.

network breach — **اِخْتِراقُ شَبَكَةٍ**

تَسْتَخْدِمُ الأَجْهِزَةُ الحُكومِيَّةُ أَحْدَثَ التِّقْنِيّاتِ لِمَنْعِ اخْتِراقِ الشَّبَكاتِ.

Government agencies use the latest technology to prevent network breaches.

to penetrate, breach, hack — **اِخْتَرَقَ** • اِخْتِراقٌ

اِخْتَرَقَ القَراصِنَةُ شَبَكَةَ الشَّرِكَةِ الكَبيرَةِ، مِمّا تَسَبَّبَ في تَعْطيلِ الخِدْماتِ لِعِدَّةِ ساعاتٍ.

Hackers penetrated the large company's network, causing services to be disrupted for several hours.

to hack — **اِخْتَرَقَ** • اِخْتِراقٌ

قامَ الهاكَرْ بِاخْتِراقِ المَوْقِعِ الإِلِكْتْرونِيِّ لِلْحُكومَةِ المَرْكَزِيَّةِ بِالأَمْسِ.

The hacker performed a breach on the central government website yesterday.

privacy violation — **اِنْتِهاكُ خُصوصِيَّةٍ**

أَدّى اسْتِخْدامُ التَّطْبيقاتِ غَيْرِ الآمِنَةِ إِلى انْتِهاكاتٍ لِخُصوصِيَّةِ العَديدِ مِنَ الأَفْرادِ.

The use of unsafe applications led to privacy violations for many individuals.

malware — *pl.* — **بَرامِجُ ضارَّةٌ**

تُسْتَخْدَمُ البَرامِجُ الضّارَّةُ لِسَرِقَةِ المَعْلوماتِ الشَّخْصِيَّةِ وَالمالِيَّةِ مِنَ الأَجْهِزَةِ غَيْرِ المَحْمِيَّةِ.

Malware is used to steal personal and financial information from unprotected devices.

malware — *pl.* — **بَرْمَجِيّاتٌ خَبيثَةٌ = بَرامِجُ خَبيثَةٌ**

تَمَّ اكْتِشافُ بَرْنامَجٍ خَبيثٍ جَديدٍ يَسْتَهْدِفُ شَبَكاتِ الكُمْبيوتَرِ في عِدَّةِ مُؤَسَّساتٍ حُكومِيَّةٍ في لُبْنانَ.

A new malware targeting computer networks in several government institutions in Lebanon has been discovered.

All three terms refer to 'malicious software' or 'malware.' They are generally interchangeable and used to describe software designed to harm or exploit computers and networks. ضارٌّ means 'harmful,' while خبيثٌ means 'malicious.' The choice of word may depend on context or regional preference.

open-source software *pl.* **بَرْمَجِيّاتٌ مَفْتوحَةُ المَصْدَرِ**

يُفَضِّلُ العَديدُ مِنَ المُطَوِّرينَ اسْتِخْدامَ البَرْمَجِيّاتِ مَفْتوحَةِ المَصْدَرِ لِأَنَّها تُوَفِّرُ مُرونَةً كَبيرَةً في التَّخْصيصِ.

Many developers prefer to use open-source software because it provides great flexibility in customization.

spyware • بَرامِجُ **بَرْنامَجُ تَجَسُّسٍ**

تَمَكَّنَ بَرْنامَجُ التَّجَسُّسِ مِنَ الوُصولِ إِلى الكَثيرِ مِنَ المَعْلوماتِ الشَّخْصِيَّةِ.

Spyware was able to access a lot of personal information.

filtering program • بَرامِجُ **بَرْنامَجُ تَصْفِيَةٍ**

أُسْتُخْدِمَ بَرْنامَجُ تَصْفِيَةٍ لِتَحْليلِ البَرْمَجِيّاتِ المَشْبوهَةِ.

A filter program was used to analyze suspicious software.

big data *pl.* **بَياناتٌ ضَخْمَةٌ**

تُسْتَخْدَمُ البَياناتُ الضَّخْمَةُ في التَّحْليلِ العَميقِ لِتَوْفيرِ رُؤًى قَيِّمَةٍ لِلْأَعْمالِ التِّجارِيَّةِ.

Big data is used in deep analytics to provide valuable insights for businesses.

to spy on a computer • تَجَسُّسٌ **تَجَسَّسَ عَلى حاسوبٍ**

اِكْتَشَفَ المُوَظَّفُ أَنَّ هُناكَ شَخْصًا يَتَجَسَّسُ عَلى حاسوبِهِ، مِمّا دَفَعَهُ لِتَحْديثِ تَأْمينِ النِّظامِ.

The employee discovered that someone was spying on his computer, prompting him to update the system security.

cloud storage **تَخْزينٌ سَحابِيٌّ**

يُحْدِثُ التَّخْزينُ السَّحابِيُّ ثَوْرَةً في القُدْرَةِ عَلى الوُصولِ لِلْبَياناتِ، حَيْثُ يَمْنَحُ المُسْتَخْدِمينَ إِمْكانِيّاتِ تَخْزينٍ عَنْ بُعْدٍ تَتَّسِمُ بِالسَّلاسَةِ.

Cloud storage revolutionizes data accessibility, providing users with seamless remote storage capabilities.

تَرْميزٌ **encoding**

يُسْتَخْدَمُ التَّرْميزُ في الحِفاظِ عَلى سِرِّيَّةِ وَأَمانِ البَياناتِ أَثْناءَ النَّقْلِ.

Encoding is used to maintain the confidentiality and security of data during transmission.

تَسْريبُ بَياناتٍ **data leak**

أَدّى تَسْريبُ البَياناتِ في الشَّرِكَةِ الكَبيرَةِ إِلى خَسائِرَ مالِيَّةٍ كَبيرَةٍ.

The data leak at the large company led to substantial financial losses.

تَشْفيرٌ **encryption**

يَضْمَنُ التَّشْفيرُ أَمانَ البَياناتِ عِنْدَ إِرْسالِها عَبْرَ الإِنْتَرْنِتْ.

Encryption ensures the security of data when sent over the internet.

تَصَدّى لِاخْتِراقاتٍ إِلِكْتْرونِيَّةٍ • تَصَدٍّ **to defend against cyberattacks**

تَصَدَّتِ الشَّرِكَةُ بِنَجاحٍ لِلاخْتِراقاتِ الإِلِكْتِرونِيَّةِ الَّتي تَعَرَّضَتْ لَها الشَّبَكَةُ.

The company successfully defended against the cyber-attacks it faced on the network.

تَصَيُّدُ البَريدِ الإِلِكْتِرونِيِّ **email phishing**

يَجِبُ أَنْ تَحْذَرَ الشَّرِكاتُ مِنْ مُحاوَلاتِ تَصَيُّدِ البَريدِ الإِلِكْتِرونِيِّ الَّتي قَدْ تُعَرِّضُ بَياناتِ العُمَلاءِ لِلْخَطَرِ.

Companies should be wary of phishing attempts that could jeopardize customer data.

تَطْبيقٌ **application, app**

أَصْبَحَ التَّطْبيقُ الجَديدُ شائِعًا بِسُرْعَةٍ بَيْنَ المُسْتَخْدِمينَ بِفَضْلِ تَصْميمِهِ البَديهِيِّ.

The new app quickly became popular among users due to its intuitive design.

تَعْدينُ البَياناتِ **data mining**

يُتيحُ تَعْدينُ البَياناتِ لِلشَّرِكاتِ فَهْمَ أَنْماطِ سُلوكِ العُمَلاءِ وَتَحْسينَ الخِدْماتِ.

Data mining allows companies to understand customer behavior patterns and improve services.

تَعَرُّفٌ عَلى الصَّوْتِ — voice recognition

يُسْتَخْدَمُ التَّعَرُّفُ عَلى الصَّوْتِ في تِقْنِيَاتِ التَّوْثيقِ البيومِتْرِيِّ لِتَوْفيرِ مُسْتَوى أَمانٍ إضافِيٍّ.

Voice recognition is used in biometric authentication technologies to provide an additional level of security.

تَعَرُّفٌ عَلى الوَجْهِ — face recognition

تَمَّ تَثْبيتُ تِكْنولوجْيا التَّعَرُّفِ عَلى الوَجْهِ في الهاتِفِ الذَّكِيِّ لِتَسْهيلِ عَمَلِيَّةِ الفَتْحِ.

Face recognition technology was installed in the smartphone to facilitate the unlocking process.

تِقْنِيَّةُ مَعْلوماتٍ — information technology

شَهِدَتْ تِقْنِيَّةُ المَعْلوماتِ تَقَدُّمًا مَلْحوظًا في السَّنَواتِ القَليلَةِ الماضِيَةِ.

Information technology has seen significant progress in recent years.

حاسوبٌ كَمِّيٌّ • حَواسيبُ — quantum computer

يُعْتَبَرُ الحاسوبُ الكَمِّيُّ تَطَوُّرًا ثَوْرِيًّا في مَجالِ تِكْنولوجْيا المَعْلوماتِ.

Quantum computing is a revolutionary advancement in information technology.

حاسوبٌ مَحْمولٌ — laptop

أَطْلَقَتْ شَرِكَةُ "تِكْنوفيجَنْ" حاسوبَها المَحْمولَ الجَديدَ، الَّذي يَمْتَلِكُ مُمَيِّزاتٍ فَريدَةً لِلْأَمانِ.

The company "TechnoVision" launched its new laptop, with unique security features.

حِسابٌ شَخْصِيٌّ — personal account

تَمَّ اخْتِراقُ حِسابِيَ الشَّخْصِيِّ عَلى الفيسبوك، وَاسْتِخْدامُهُ في نَشْرِ الإِعْلاناتِ غَيْرِ المَرْغوبِ فيها.

My personal account on Facebook was hacked and used to post unwanted ads.

حَظَرَ مَوْقِعًا عَلى الإِنْتَرْنِتْ • حَظْرٌ — to block a website

قَرَّرَتِ الحُكومَةُ حَظْرَ مَوْقِعٍ عَلى الإِنْتَرْنِتْ يَشْتَهِرُ بِنَشْرِ الأَخْبارِ الزّائِفَةِ.

The government decided to block a website known for spreading fake news.

حِمايَةٌ إِلِكْترونِيَّةٌ
cyber security

قامَتْ شَرِكَةُ "سايبَرْ شيلدْ" بِتَطْويرِ بَرْنامَجِ حِمايَةٍ إِلِكْترونِيَّةٍ مُتَقَدِّمٍ يَكْتَشِفُ البَرْمَجِيّاتِ الخَبيثَةَ.

The company "Cyber Shield" developed an advanced electronic protection program that detects malicious software.

حِمايَةُ بَياناتٍ
data protection

تُقَدِّمُ شَرِكَةُ "داتا سيكْيورْ" خِدْماتِ حِمايَةِ بَياناتٍ لِلشَّرِكاتِ الصَّغيرَةِ وَالمُتَوَسِّطَةِ.

The company "Data Secure" offers data protection services for small and medium-sized companies.

حِمايَةٌ مِنْ فَيْروساتٍ
virus protection

اِسْتَخْدَمَتِ المَدْرَسَةُ بَرْنامَجًا لِلْحِمايَةِ مِنَ الفَيْروساتِ لِضَمانِ سَلامَةِ أَجْهِزَةِ الكُمْبيوتَرِ الخاصَّةِ بِالطُّلّابِ.

The school used a virus protection program to ensure the safety of students' computers.

حَمْلَةُ اخْتِراقٍ
hacking campaign

تَعَرَّضَتِ البُنوكُ الرَّئيسِيَّةُ فِي البِلادِ لِحَمْلَةِ اخْتِراقٍ كَبيرَةٍ أَدَّتْ إِلى تَوَقُّفِ الخِدْماتِ لِعِدَّةِ ساعاتٍ.

The country's main banks were subjected to a large hacking campaign that led to a service outage for several hours.

حَمى بَياناتٍ
to protect data • حِمايَةٌ

بِسَبَبِ الاِخْتِراقاتِ الأَخيرَةِ، أَصْبَحَتِ الشَّرِكاتُ أَكْثَرَ حَذَرًا فِي حِمايَةِ مَعْلوماتِها.

Due to recent breaches, companies have become more cautious in protecting their information.

حَوْسَبَةٌ سَحابِيَّةٌ
cloud computing

بَدَأَتِ العَديدُ مِنَ الشَّرِكاتِ فِي اسْتِخْدامِ الحَوْسَبَةِ السَّحابِيَّةِ لِتَخْزينِ بَياناتِها وَتَوْفيرِ الوُصولِ المَرِنِ لِلْمُوَظَّفينَ.

Many companies have started using cloud computing to store their data and provide flexible access to employees.

malicious — خَبيثٌ

تَمَكَّنَتِ الشَّرِكَةُ مِنَ اكْتِشافِ بَرْنامَجٍ خَبيثٍ في النِّظامِ وَإِزالَتِهِ بِنَجاحٍ.

The company was able to detect and successfully remove a malicious program from the system.

computer network — شَبَكَةُ حاسوبٍ

تَمَّ تَحْديثُ شَبَكاتِ الحاسوبِ في المَكْتَبَةِ العامَّةِ لِتَوْفيرِ خِدْمَةٍ أَفْضَلَ لِلْمُسْتَخْدِمينَ.

The computer networks in the public library were updated to provide better service to users.

web — شَبَكَةٌ عَنْكَبوتِيَّةٌ

تَظَلُّ الشَّبَكَةُ العَنْكَبوتِيَّةُ العالَمِيَّةُ عامِلًا قَوِيًّا لِلتَّواصُلِ وَتَبادُلِ المَعْلوماتِ عَلى المُسْتَوى العالَمِيِّ.

The World Wide Web remains a powerful catalyst for global connectivity and information exchange.

piracy — قَرْصَنَةٌ

تَعَرَّضَتِ الشَّرِكَةُ لِعَمَلِيَّةِ قَرْصَنَةٍ مُعَقَّدَةٍ اسْتَهْدَفَتْ مَعْلوماتِ العُمَلاءِ الحَسّاسَةِ.

The company was subjected to a sophisticated piracy operation targeting sensitive customer information.

code — كودٌ • أَكْوادٌ

أُكْتُشِفَ كودٌ خَبيثٌ في البَرْنامَجِ الَّذي نَسْتَخْدِمُهُ لِلتَّواصُلِ الدّاخِلِيِّ.

A malicious code was discovered in the software we use for internal communication.

connected — مُتَّصِلٌ

اِكْتَشَفَتِ الشَّرِكَةُ أَنَّ الجِهازَ المُتَّصِلَ بِشَبَكَتِها لَمْ يَكُنْ مَأْمونًا.

The company discovered that the device connected to its network was not secure.

internet risks — مَخاطِرُ الإِنْتَرْنِتْ

تُحَذِّرُ الدَّوْراتُ التَّدْريبِيَّةُ الطُّلّابَ مِنْ مَخاطِرِ الإِنْتَرْنِتْ وَتُعَلِّمُهُمْ كَيْفِيَّةَ حِمايَةِ أَنْفُسِهِمْ.

The training courses warn students about the dangers of the internet and teach them how to protect themselves.

security center **مَرْكَزُ أَمْنٍ**

أُفْتُتِحَ مَرْكَزُ أَمْنٍ جَديدٍ مُتَخَصِّصٌ في الدِّفاعِ ضِدَّ الهَجَماتِ الإِلِكْترونِيَّةِ.

A new security center specializing in defending against electronic attacks was opened.

independent **مُسْتَقِلٌّ**

يَعْمَلُ المُبَرْمِجُ كَمُسْتَقِلٍّ، وَهُوَ يَتَخَصَّصُ في الأَمْنِ السَّيْبَرانِيِّ.

The programmer works as an independent, specializing in cybersecurity.

encrypted **مُشَفَّرٌ**

لِضَمانِ الأَمانِ، يَنْبَغي أَنْ تَكونَ كُلُّ الرَّسائِلِ الَّتي تُرْسَلُ عَبْرَ الإِنْتَرْنِتْ مُشَفَّرَةً.

To ensure safety, all messages sent over the internet should be encrypted.

two-factor authentication **مُصادَقَةٌ ثُنائِيَّةٌ**

تُوَفِّرُ المُصادَقَةُ الثُّنائِيَّةُ طَبَقَةَ أَمانٍ إِضافِيَّةً لِلْحِساباتِ الإِلِكْترونِيَّةِ.

Two-step verification provides an additional layer of security for online accounts.

attacker **مُهاجِمٌ**

حاوَلَ المُهاجِمُ الدُّخولَ إِلى نِظامِنا لَكِنَّهُ فَشِلَ بِسَبَبِ الإِجْراءاتِ الأَمْنِيَّةِ القَوِيَّةِ.

The attacker tried to enter our system but failed due to strong security measures.

smartphone • هَواتِفُ **هاتِفٌ ذَكِيٌّ**

لَقَدِ اسْتَخْدَمَ الهاتِفَ الذَّكِيَّ لِإِرْسالِ رِسالَةٍ مُشَفَّرَةٍ إِلى زَميلِهِ.

He used the smartphone to send an encrypted message to his colleague.

cyberattack **هَجْمَةٌ إِلِكْترونِيَّةٌ**

نَجَحَتِ الشَّرِكَةُ في التَّصَدّي لِهَجْمَةٍ إِلِكْترونِيَّةٍ كَبيرَةٍ اليَوْمَ.

The company successfully repelled a major electronic attack today.

5.2.1.1 Mini-Articles

Track **43**

فِي ظِلِّ الزِّيادَةِ المُسْتَمِرَّةِ فِي اسْتِخْدامِ الإِنْتَرْنِتْ فِي العَديدِ مِنَ الأَنْشِطَةِ اليَوْمِيَّةِ، أَصْبَحَ الأَمْنُ السَّيْبَرانِيُّ قَضِيَّةً بالِغَةَ الأَهَمِّيَّةِ. تَشْهَدُ الشَّبَكَةُ العَنْكَبوتِيَّةُ نُمُوًّا هائِلًا فِي عَدَدِ الهَجَماتِ الإِلِكْترونِيَّةِ، بَدْءًا مِنَ اخْتِراقِ الحِساباتِ الشَّخْصِيَّةِ إِلى هَجَماتِ الأَكْوادِ الخَبيثَةِ الَّتي تَسْتَهْدِفُ الشَّرِكاتِ وَالحُكوماتِ. وَبِالرَّغْمِ مِنَ الجُهودِ المَبْذولَةِ لِزِيادَةِ الحِمايَةِ الإِلِكْترونِيَّةِ وَالتَّصَدّي لِهَذِهِ الاخْتِراقاتِ، فَإِنَّ القَراصِنَةَ يَسْتَمِرّونَ فِي التَّطَوُّرِ وَالابْتِكارِ.

With the continuous increase in internet usage for various daily activities, cybersecurity has become an extremely important issue. The World Wide Web is witnessing a tremendous growth in the number of cyber attacks, ranging from personal account breaches to malicious code attacks targeting companies and governments. Despite efforts to enhance electronic protection and counter these breaches, hackers continue to evolve and innovate.

مَعَ تَزايُدِ التَّهْديداتِ الأَمْنِيَّةِ عَلى الإِنْتَرْنِتْ، تَشْهَدُ تِقْنِيَّةُ المَعْلوماتِ تَقَدُّمًا مَلْحوظًا فِي مَجالِ الأَمْنِ السَّيْبَرانِيِّ. مِنْ بَيْنِ هَذِهِ التِّقْنِيّاتِ، يَأْتي التَّعَرُّفُ عَلى الوَجْهِ وَالتَّعَرُّفُ عَلى الصَّوْتِ، الَّذانِ يُوَفِّرانِ طَبَقَةً إِضافِيَّةً مِنَ الأَمانِ عِنْدَ الدُّخولِ إِلى الحِساباتِ الشَّخْصِيَّةِ. كَما يُساعِدانِ عَلى التَّصَدّي لِلْهَجَماتِ الإِلِكْترونِيَّةِ عَنْ طَريقِ اسْتِخْدامِ الذَّكاءِ الاصْطِناعِيِّ لِلتَّعَرُّفِ عَلى الأَنْماطِ غَيْرِ الطَّبيعِيَّةِ وَمَنْعِها.

As online security threats continue to rise, information technology has made significant advancements in the field of cybersecurity. Among these technologies are facial recognition and voice recognition, which provide an additional layer of security when accessing personal accounts. They also aid in countering cyber attacks by using artificial intelligence to identify and prevent unusual patterns.

بَيْنَما تُتيحُ التِّكْنولوجْيا الحَديثَةُ، كالحَوْسَبَةِ السَّحابِيَّةِ وَتَخْزينِ البَياناتِ الضَّخْمَةِ، لِلأَفْرادِ وَالشَّرِكاتِ القُدْرَةَ عَلى تَخْزينِ كَمِّيّاتٍ هائِلَةٍ مِنَ المَعْلوماتِ فِي مَكانٍ واحِدٍ، فَإِنَّها أَيْضًا تُعَرِّضُهُمْ لِخَطَرِ الهَجَماتِ الإِلِكْترونِيَّةِ وَاخْتِراقاتِ البَياناتِ. لِذَلِكَ، يَكونُ الحِفاظُ عَلى سَلامَةِ هَذِهِ البَياناتِ وَحِمايَتُها مِنَ المَخاطِرِ الأَمْنِيَّةِ هُوَ التَّحَدِّيَ الرَّئيسِيَّ الَّذي يَجِبُ مُواجَهَتُهُ.

While modern technologies such as cloud computing and big data storage allow individuals and companies to store massive amounts of information in one place, they also expose them to the risk of cyber attacks and data breaches. Therefore, safeguarding the integrity of this data and protecting it from security risks is the primary challenge that needs to be addressed.

تَتَقَدَّمُ تِكْنولوجْيا المَعْلوماتِ بِشَكْلٍ سَريعٍ، مِمّا يَفْتَحُ البابَ أَمامَ العَديدِ مِنَ الابْتِكاراتِ، مِنَ الحَواسيبِ الكَمِّيَّةِ الَّتي قَدْ تُغَيِّرُ بِشَكْلٍ كَبيرٍ كَيْفِيَّةَ مُعالَجَةِ البَياناتِ، إِلى التَّقَدُّمِ فِي الذَّكاءِ الاصْطِناعِيِّ وَالتَّعَلُّمِ الآلِيِّ، الَّذي قَدْ يُغَيِّرُ

بِشَكْلٍ كَبيرٍ كَيْفِيَّةَ تَفاعُلِنا مَعَ العالَمِ الرَّقْمِيِّ. إلّا أَنَّ هَذِهِ التَّطَوُّراتِ تَأْتي مَعَ تَحَدِّياتٍ أَمْنِيَّةٍ جَديدَةٍ تَتَعَلَّقُ بِكَيْفِيَّةِ حِمايَةِ البَياناتِ وَالخُصوصِيَّةِ في عالَمٍ يَزْدادُ فيهِ الاِتِّصالُ.

Information technology is rapidly advancing, opening the door to numerous innovations, from quantum computers that could significantly change how data is processed to advancements in artificial intelligence and machine learning that could greatly alter how we interact with the digital world. However, these developments come with new security challenges concerning the protection of data and privacy in an increasingly interconnected world.

5.2.1.2 Case Study: The Cyberattack on Sony Pictures

Track **44**

دِراسَةُ حالَةٍ: الهُجومُ الإِلِكْترونِيُّ عَلى سوني بيكْتْشَرْزْ في 2014

في نوفَمْبِرَ 2014، تَعَرَّضَتْ شَرِكَةُ سوني بيكْتْشَرْزْ لِهَجْمَةٍ إِلِكْترونِيَّةٍ كُبْرى، كانَتْ واحِدَةً مِنْ أَكْثَرِ الهَجَماتِ ضَراوَةً في تاريخِ الأَمْنِ السَّيْبَرانِيِّ. أَدّى هَذا الهُجومُ إِلى تَسْريبِ كَمِّيَّةٍ ضَخْمَةٍ مِنَ البَياناتِ الحَسّاسَةِ، الَّتي شَمِلَتْ رَسائِلَ إِلِكْترونِيَّةً تَنْفيذِيَّةً وَأَفْلامًا لَمْ تُعْرَضْ بَعْدُ.

تَمَّ الاِخْتِراقُ الإِلِكْترونِيُّ مِنْ خِلالِ مَجْموعَةٍ تُطْلِقُ عَلى نَفْسِها اسْمَ "حُرّاسِ السَّلامِ"، الَّذينَ أَعْلَنوا مَسْؤولِيَّتَهُمْ عَنِ الهُجومِ. وَقَدْ أَشارَتِ الأَدِلَّةُ الأَمْنِيَّةُ إِلى أَنَّ هَذا الاِخْتِراقَ الشَّبَكِيَّ قَدْ جاءَ كَرَدِّ فِعْلٍ عَلى فيلْمٍ ساخِرٍ مِنْ إِنْتاجِ الشَّرِكَةِ كانَ يَدْعو إِلى اغْتِيالِ الزَّعيمِ الكورِيِّ الشَّمالِيِّ.

واجَهَتْ سوني تَحَدِّياتٍ كَبيرَةً وَمُتَنَوِّعَةً في أَعْقابِ الهُجومِ. أَوَّلًا، كانَتْ هُناكَ مُشْكِلَةٌ تَتَعَلَّقُ بِحِمايَةِ البَياناتِ وَالخُصوصِيَّةِ، حَيْثُ تَمَّ تَسْريبُ بَياناتٍ شَخْصِيَّةٍ لِلْعَديدِ مِنَ المُوَظَّفينَ وَالمَشاهيرِ. ثانِيًا، كانَتْ هُناكَ تَهْديداتٌ لِلْأَمْنِ الفِعْلِيِّ لِلْمُوَظَّفينَ وَالأَماكِنِ، بَعْدَ تَهْديداتِ حُرّاسِ السَّلامِ بِالْعُنْفِ ضِدَّ مَنْ سَيُشاهِدُ الفيلْمَ المُثيرَ لِلْجَدَلِ.

أَحَدُ الدُّروسِ المُسْتَفادَةِ مِنْ هَذا الهُجومِ هُوَ أَنَّ الشَّرِكاتِ يَجِبُ أَنْ تَعْتَبِرَ الأَمْنَ السَّيْبَرانِيَّ أَوْلَوِيَّةً قُصْوى. كَما تَحْتاجُ إِلى تَطْبيقِ أَساليبِ أَمانٍ مُتَقَدِّمَةٍ مِثْلِ التَّشْفيرِ وَالمُصادَقَةِ الثُّنائِيَّةِ، وَالَّتي يُمْكِنُ أَنْ تُساعِدَ في حِمايَةِ البَياناتِ مِنَ الهَجَماتِ الإِلِكْترونِيَّةِ. وَأَخيرًا، يَجِبُ أَنْ تَكونَ الشَّرِكاتُ عَلى اسْتِعْدادٍ لِلتَّعامُلِ مَعَ الأَزَماتِ وَالتَّحَدِّياتِ الَّتي قَدْ تَنْشَأُ بَعْدَ حُدوثِ اخْتِراقٍ شَبَكِيٍّ، يَشْمَلُ ذَلِكَ الاِسْتِجابَةَ السَّريعَةَ وَالتَّواصُلَ الشَّفّافَ مَعَ الجُمْهورِ.

Case Study: The 2014 Cyberattack on Sony Pictures

In November 2014, Sony Pictures Entertainment was the target of a major cyberattack, which was one of the most severe attacks in the history of cybersecurity. This attack resulted in a massive leakage of sensitive data, including executive emails and unreleased films.

The electronic breach was carried out by a group calling themselves "Guardians of Peace," who claimed responsibility for the attack. Security evidence indicated that this network intrusion was a response to a satirical film produced by the company, which called for the assassination of the North Korean leader.

Sony faced significant and diverse challenges in the aftermath of the attack. Firstly, there was a problem regarding data protection and privacy, as the personal information of numerous employees and celebrities was leaked. Secondly, there were threats to the physical security of employees and locations, following the Guardians of Peace's violent threats against those who would watch the controversial film.

One of the lessons learned from this attack is that companies must consider cybersecurity as a top priority. They also need to implement advanced security measures such as encryption and two-factor authentication, which can help protect data from electronic attacks. Finally, companies should be prepared to deal with crises and challenges that may arise after a network breach, including prompt response and transparent communication with the public.

5.2.1.3 Statistics: Cybersecurity

Track **45**

إِحْصائِيّاتُ أَمْنِ المَعْلوماتِ لِعامِ 2023

1. مِنَ المُتَوَقَّعِ أَنْ يَصِلَ مُتَوَسِّطُ تَكْلِفَةِ اخْتِراقِ البَياناتِ إِلى 4 ملايينِ دولارٍ بِحُلولِ عامِ 2023.
2. يَتَوَقَّعُ 33% مِنْ مُحْتَرِفي تِكْنولوجْيا المَعْلوماتِ الَّذينَ تَمَّ اسْتِطْلاعُ آرائِهِمْ أَنْ تَتَبَنّى مُنَظَّماتُهُمْ نَماذِجَ "الثِّقَةِ الصِّفْرِيَّةِ" فَوْرًا في عامِ 2023، في حينِ قالَ 28% إِنَّهُمْ سَيَتَبَنّونَها في غُضونِ سِتَّةِ شُهورٍ.
3. أَكْثَرُ مِنْ 60% مِنَ الشَّرِكاتِ الَّتي تَتَعَرَّضُ لِهُجومٍ إِلِكْتْرونِيٍّ كَبيرٍ تُغْلِقُ أَبْوابَها في غُضونِ سِتَّةِ أَشْهُرٍ.
4. مِنَ المُتَوَقَّعِ أَنْ تُكَلِّفَ الجَرائِمُ الإِلِكْتْرونِيَّةُ الشَّرِكاتِ 10.5 تِريلْيونِ دولارٍ سَنَوِيًّا في عامِ 2023.
5. 91%مِنَ الهَجَماتِ الإِلِكْتْرونِيَّةِ تَبْدَأُ بِرَسائِلِ التَّصَيُّدِ الاِحْتِيالِيَّةِ.
6. تَعَرَّضَتْ 53% مِنَ الشَّرِكاتِ لِاخْتِراقِ بَياناتٍ مِنْ طَرَفٍ ثالِثٍ خِلالَ العامِ الماضي.
7. في هَذا العامِ، سَيَكونُ هُناكَ 300 مِلْيارِ كَلِمَةِ مُرورٍ مُسْتَخْدَمَةً عالَمِيًّا.
8. أَبْلَغَتْ 70% مِنَ الشَّرِكاتِ الصَّغيرَةِ عَنْ تَعَرُّضِها لِهُجومٍ إِلِكْتْرونِيٍّ في عامِ 2021.
9. مِنَ المُتَوَقَّعِ أَنْ يَصِلَ مُتَوَسِّطُ تَكْلِفَةِ هُجومِ الفِدْيَةِ إِلى 11.5 مِلْيونَ دولارٍ بِحُلولِ عامِ 2023.
10. 64%مِنَ الشَّرِكاتِ قَدْ تَعَرَّضَتْ بِالْفِعْلِ لِهَجَماتٍ قائِمَةٍ عَلى الشَّبَكَةِ.

Cybersecurity Statistics for 2023

1. The average cost of a data breach is projected to reach $4 million by 2023.
2. 33% of IT professionals surveyed foresee their organizations adopting "zero trust" models immediately in 2023, while 28% said they will within six months.
3. Over 60% of businesses that experience a major cyber attack close their doors within six months.
4. In 2023, it is estimated that cybercrime will cost businesses $10.5 trillion annually.
5. 91% of cyber attacks begin with phishing emails.
6. 53% of companies have experienced a third-party data breach in the past year.
7. This year, there will be 300 billion passwords in use globally.
8. 70% of small businesses reported experiencing a cyber attack in 2021.
9. The average cost of a ransomware attack is projected to reach $11.5 million by 2023.
10. 64% of businesses have already experienced web-based attacks.

5.2.2 Artificial Intelligence and Robotics

Track **46**

automatic, mechanical 

أَطْلَقَتِ الشَّرِكَةُ نِظامًا آليًا لِإدارَةِ المَخْزون.

The company launched an automated system for inventory management.

automation **أَتْمَتَةٌ**

تُسْهِمُ تِقْنِيّاتُ الأَتْمَتَةِ في تَحْسينِ كَفاءَةِ العَمَلِيّاتِ الصِّناعِيَّةِ.

Automation technologies contribute to improving the efficiency of industrial processes.

to sense • اِسْتِشْعارٌ **اِسْتَشْعَرَ**

اِسْتَشْعَرَ الرّوبوتُ العَقَباتِ في طَريقِهِ بِاسْتِخْدامِ مُسْتَشْعِراتٍ مُتَقَدِّمَةٍ.

The robot sensed obstacles in its path using advanced sensors.

artificial — **اِصْطِناعِيٌّ**

يُمْكِنُ لِلذَّكاءِ الاِصْطِناعِيِّ التَّعَلُّمُ وَاتِّخاذُ القَراراتِ بِشَكْلٍ مُسْتَقِلٍّ.

Artificial intelligence can learn and make decisions independently.

computer speech recognition — **التَّعَرُّفُ عَلى الصَّوْتِ بِالْحاسوبِ**

تُحَقِّقُ تِقْنِيَّةُ التَّعَرُّفِ عَلى الصَّوْتِ بِالْحاسوبِ دِقَّةً وَسُرْعَةً مُذْهِلَتَيْنِ، مُحْدِثَةً ثَوْرَةً في طَريقَةِ تَفاعُلِنا مَعَ التِّكْنولوجْيا.

Computer speech recognition achieves remarkable accuracy and speed, revolutionizing the way we interact with technology.

image recognition — **التَّعَرُّفُ عَلى الصُّوَرِ**

تَمَّ تَحْقيقُ تَقَدُّمٍ كَبيرٍ في التَّعَرُّفِ عَلى الصُّوَرِ، حَيْثُ تَمَكَّنَ النِّظامُ الجَديدُ مِنْ تَمْييزِ الأَشْخاصِ وَالأَشْياءِ بِدِقَّةٍ مُذْهِلَةٍ.

Significant progress has been made in image recognition, with the new system able to distinguish people and objects with remarkable accuracy.

software — *pl.* — **بَرْمَجِيّاتٌ**

تُمَكِّنُ البَرْمَجِيّاتُ المُتَقَدِّمَةُ الرّوبوتاتِ مِنَ التَّفاعُلِ بِشَكْلٍ طَبيعِيٍّ مَعَ البيئَةِ المُحيطَةِ.

Advanced software enables robots to interact naturally with their surroundings.

big data — *pl.* — **بَياناتٌ ضَخْمَةٌ**

تُساعِدُ البَياناتُ الضَّخْمَةُ في تَحْسينِ قُدْرَةِ الذَّكاءِ الاِصْطِناعِيِّ عَلى التَّعَلُّمِ.

Big data helps improve the learning ability of artificial intelligence.

to move — • تَحَرَّكْ — **تَحَرَّكَ**

تَحَرَّكَ الرّوبوتُ بِكَفاءَةٍ في المُخْتَبَرِ، مُتَجَنِّبًا العَقَباتِ.

The robot moved efficiently in the lab, avoiding obstacles.

تَحْسينُ أَداءٍ
performance improvement

يُمْكِنُ لِلذَّكاءِ الاِصْطِناعِيِّ تَحْسينُ أَداءِ الرّوبوتاتِ بِشَكْلٍ كَبيرٍ.

Artificial intelligence can greatly improve the performance of robots.

تَحَكَّمَ
• تَحَكُّمٌ

to control

لَقَدْ أَصْبَحَ التَّحَكُّمُ عَنْ بُعْدٍ في الرّوبوتاتِ مُمْكِنًا بِفَضْلِ التَّقَدُّمِ في التِّكْنولوجْيا.

Remote control of robots has become possible thanks to advances in technology.

تَحَكُّمٌ آلِيٌّ
automatic control

أَعْلَنَتْ شَرِكَةُ "تِكْ تاوَرْ" اليَوْمَ عَنْ نِظامِ تَحَكُّمٍ آلِيٍّ جَديدٍ لِإِدارَةِ المُرورِ بِالْكامِلِ، مِمّا يَهْدُفُ إِلى تَحْسينِ التَّدَفُّقِ وَالسَّلامَةِ عَلى الطُّرُقِ.

Tech Tower company announced today a new automatic control system for full traffic management, aimed at improving flow and safety on the roads.

تَحْليلُ بَياناتٍ
data analysis

قامَتْ شَرِكَةُ "داتا بُرو" بِتَحْليلِ بَياناتِ العُمَلاءِ الضَّخْمَةِ لِاسْتِخْراجِ نَماذِجِ لِسُلوكِ العُمَلاءِ.

Data Pro company analyzed the massive customer data to extract customer behavior models.

تَحْليلُ بَياناتٍ ذاتِيُّ التَّعَلُّمِ
self-learning data analysis

تَمَكَّنَتِ الشَّرِكَةُ مِنْ تَطْويرِ نِظامِ تَحْليلِ بَياناتٍ ذاتِيِّ التَّعَلُّمِ يُمْكِنُهُ تَحْسينُ نَفْسِهِ بِشَكْلٍ مُسْتَمِرٍّ.

The company managed to develop a self-learning data analysis system that can continuously improve itself.

تَحْويلُ نَصٍّ إِلى كَلامٍ
text-to-speech conversion

أَطْلَقَتْ "سايبَرْ لينْك" خِدْمَةً جَديدَةً تُتيحُ تَحْويلَ النَّصِّ إِلى كَلامٍ بِطُرُقٍ مُتَعَدِّدَةٍ وَواقِعِيَّةٍ.

Cyber Link launched a new service that allows text to speech conversion in multiple, realistic ways.

تَدَرَّبَ
• تَدَرُّبٌ

to train

تَدَرَّبَ فَريقُ "إِيهْ آيْ بِلَسْ" عَلى اسْتِخْدامِ الذَّكاءِ الاِصْطِناعِيِّ في تَطْبيقاتِ المُسْتَقْبَلِ.

AI Plus team trained to use artificial intelligence in future applications.

model training **تَدْريبٌ نَموذَجِيٌّ**

تُحْدِثُ عَمليّاتُ التَّدْريبِ النَّموذَجِيِّ تَحَوُّلًا جِذْرِيًّا في إِمْكانِيّاتِ الحَواسيبِ، مِمّا يُمَكِّنُها مِنَ التَّعَلُّمِ السَّريعِ وَتَقْديمِ نَتائِجَ غَيْرِ مَسْبوقَةٍ في مُعالَجَةِ المَهامِّ المُعَقَّدَةِ.

Model training revolutionizes computer capabilities, enabling rapid learning and unprecedented performance in tackling complex tasks.

data classification **تَصْنيفُ بَياناتٍ**

أَجْرَتْ " ديتا مايْنَر" تَصْنيفَ بَياناتٍ مُعَقَّدًا لِتَوْفيرِ رُؤًى أَعْمَقَ لِلشَّرِكاتِ.

Data Miner conducted complex data classification to provide deeper insights for companies.

image classification **تَصْنيفُ صُوَرٍ**

قامَتْ "إيمِجْ بوتْ" بِتَصْنيفِ الصُّوَرِ المُسْتَخْدَمَةِ في مَجْموعَةِ البَياناتِ لِتَطْويرِ الذَّكاءِ الاِصْطِناعِيِّ.

Image Bot classified the images used in the data set for artificial intelligence development.

to recognize • تَعَرُّفٌ **تَعَرَّفَ**

تَعَرَّفَ النِّظامُ الجَديدُ عَلى الأَصْواتِ وَالأَشْخاصِ بِدِقَّةٍ مُذْهِلَةٍ.

The new system recognized voices and people with astonishing accuracy.

to learn • تَعَلُّمٌ **تَعَلَّمَ**

تَعَلَّمَ الطّالِبُ كَيْفِيَّةَ تَصْميمِ نِظامِ ذَكاءٍ اِصْطِناعِيٍّ في الدَّوْرَةِ التَّدْريبِيَّةِ.

The student learned how to design an artificial intelligence system in the training course.

machine learning **تَعَلُّمٌ آلِيٌّ**

يُحَوِّلُ التَّعَلُّمُ الآلِيُّ الصِّناعَةَ بِقُدْرَتِهِ عَلى تَحْليلِ البَياناتِ، وَكَشْفِ الأَنْماطِ، وَإِجْراءِ تَنَبُّؤاتٍ دَقيقَةٍ.

Machine learning transforms industries with its ability to analyze data, detect patterns, and make accurate predictions.

deep learning تَعَلُّمٌ عَميقٌ

اِكْتَسَبَ النِّظامُ الذَّكاءَ عَبْرَ تِقْنِيَّةِ التَّعَلُّمِ العَميقِ، مِمّا سَمَحَ لَهُ بِفَهْمِ البَياناتِ المُعَقَّدَةِ.

The system gained intelligence through deep learning technology, which allowed it to understand complex data.

interactive تَفاعُلِيٌّ

قامَ المُبَرْمِجونَ بِتَطْويرِ واجِهَةٍ تَفاعُلِيَّةٍ لِلرّوبوتِ، تَسْمَحُ لَهُ بِالتَّواصُلِ بِشَكْلٍ أَكْثَرَ طَبيعِيَّةً مَعَ البَشَرِ.

Programmers developed an interactive interface for the robot, allowing it to communicate more naturally with humans.

artificial intelligence technology تِكْنولوجْيا ذَكاءٍ اصْطِناعِيٍّ

تُوَفِّرُ تِكْنولوجْيا الذَّكاءِ الاِصْطِناعِيِّ الفُرْصَةَ لِتَحْسينِ العَديدِ مِنْ جَوانِبِ حَياتِنا، مِنَ الرِّعايَةِ الصِّحِّيَّةِ إِلى النَّقْلِ.

Artificial intelligence technology offers the opportunity to improve many aspects of our lives, from healthcare to transportation.

data prediction تَنَبُّؤٌ بِالْبَياناتِ

أُسْتُخْدِمَتِ النَّماذِجُ المُعْتَمِدَةُ عَلى التَّنَبُّؤِ بِالبَياناتِ لِتَوَقُّعِ اتِّجاهاتِ السّوقِ القادِمَةِ.

Data prediction-based models were used to forecast upcoming market trends.

predictive تَنَبُّؤِيٌّ

تَمَّ تَطْويرُ النِّظامِ ذي الطّابَعِ التَّنَبُّؤِيِّ لِيُوَفِّرَ تَحْليلاتٍ مُسْتَقْبَلِيَّةً دَقيقَةً لِلْأَعْمالِ.

The predictive system was developed to provide accurate future analyses for businesses.

sensors *pl.* حَسّاساتٌ

تَمَّ تَزْويدُ الرّوبوتاتِ بِحَسّاساتٍ مُتَطَوِّرَةٍ لِكَشْفِ العَقَباتِ في البيئَةِ المُحيطَةِ بِها.

Robots were equipped with advanced sensors to detect obstacles in their surrounding environment.

حَسَّنَ • تَحْسينٌ **to improve**

حَسَّنَ البَرْنامجُ قُدْرَتَهُ عَلى التَّعامُلِ مَعَ مَجْموعَةٍ واسِعَةٍ مِنَ البَياناتِ بِفَضْلِ التَّحْديثاتِ الجَديدَةِ.

The program improved its ability to handle a wide range of data thanks to the new updates.

حَلَّلَ • تَحْليلٌ **to analyze**

حَلَّلَ الفَريقُ البَياناتِ الكَبيرَةَ لِلْحُصولِ عَلى نَتائجَ أَكْثَرَ دِقَّةً.

The team analyzed the big data to get more accurate results.

حَلَّلَ بَياناتٍ **to analyze data**

يُحَلِّلُ نِظامُ الذَّكاءِ الاصْطِناعِيِّ البَياناتِ بِسُرْعَةٍ لِتَوْفيرِ تَحْليلاتٍ مُفَصَّلَةٍ.

The artificial intelligence system analyzes data quickly to provide detailed analyses.

حَوْسَبَةٌ سَحابِيَّةٌ **cloud computing**

تَمَّ الإعْلانُ في الكُوَيْتِ عَنْ تَوَسُّعٍ كَبيرٍ في البِنْيَةِ التَّحْتِيَّةِ لِلْحَوْسَبَةِ السَّحابِيَّةِ، مِمّا يُعَدُّ تَقَدُّمًا هامًّا في مَجالِ تِكْنولوجْيا المَعْلوماتِ.

A major expansion in the infrastructure of cloud computing was announced in Kuwait, marking a significant advancement in the field of information technology.

ذاتِيُّ التَّحَكُّمِ **self-controlled**

تَمَّ تَزْويدُ السَّيّاراتِ الجَديدَةِ بِنِظامٍ ذاتِيِّ التَّحَكُّمِ لِزِيادَةِ الأَمانِ وَالرّاحَةِ لِلسّائِقينَ.

The new cars were equipped with a self-control system to increase safety and comfort for drivers.

ذاتِيُّ التَّعَلُّمِ **self-learning**

تَمَّ تَطْويرُ الذَّكاءِ الاصْطِناعِيِّ لِكَيْ يَكونَ قادِرًا عَلى التَّعَلُّمِ الذّاتِيِّ وَالتَّكَيُّفِ مَعَ البيئاتِ الجَديدَةِ.

Artificial intelligence was developed to be able to self-learn and adapt to new environments.

ذَكاءٌ اصْطِناعِيٌّ **artificial intelligence**

الذَّكاءُ الاصْطِناعِيُّ يُمْكِنُهُ التَّعامُلُ مَعَ أَكْثَرِ المَهامِّ تَعْقيدًا في مَجْموعَةٍ واسِعَةٍ مِنَ القِطاعاتِ.

Artificial intelligence can handle the most complex tasks in a wide range of sectors.

ذَكِيٌّ **intelligent, smart**

تَمَّ تَطْويرُ الرّوبوتِ لِيَكونَ ذَكِيًّا، قادِرًا عَلى التَّفاعُلِ مَعَ البَشَرِ وَفَهْمِ إِشاراتِهِمْ.

The robot was developed to be intelligent, capable of interacting with humans and understanding their signals.

رَقْمِيٌّ **digital**

قامَ الفَريقُ بِتَطْويرِ مَكْتَبَةٍ رَقْمِيَّةٍ شامِلَةٍ تَضُمُّ الآلافَ مِنَ الكُتُبِ وَالمَراجِعِ.

The team developed a comprehensive digital library that includes thousands of books and references.

روبوتٌ **robot**

تَمَّ تَطْويرُ روبوتاتٍ ذَكِيَّةٍ في مَدينَةِ العُلومِ وَالتِّكْنولوجْيا في الأُرْدُنِّ، تَتَمَيَّزُ بِقُدْرَتِها عَلى التَّعامُلِ مَعَ مَجْموعَةٍ مُتَنَوِّعَةٍ مِنَ المَهامِّ اليَوْمِيَّةِ.

Intelligent robots were developed in Jordan's city of science and technology, distinguished by their ability to deal with a variety of daily tasks.

شامِلٌ **comprehensive**

تَمَّ تَوْفيرُ مَنْهَجٍ شامِلٍ يُغَطّي جَميعَ جَوانِبِ تَطْويرِ الذَّكاءِ الاِصْطِناعِيِّ وَالرّوبوتاتِ.

A comprehensive curriculum was provided that covers all aspects of developing artificial intelligence and robots.

شَبَكَةٌ عَصَبِيَّةٌ اصْطِناعِيَّةٌ **artificial neural network**

تَسْتَفيدُ الشَّبَكاتُ العَصَبِيَّةُ الاِصْطِناعِيَّةُ مِنَ الكَمِّيّاتِ الهائِلَةِ مِنَ البَياناتِ لِتَحْسينِ تَعَلُّمِها.

Artificial neural networks benefit from the enormous amounts of data to improve their learning.

صَنَّفَ • تَصْنيفٌ **to classify**

صَنَّفَ النِّظامُ الصُّوَرَ بِناءً عَلى مُحْتَواها، مِمّا يُسَهِّلُ البَحْثَ وَالتَّنَقُّلَ.

The system classified the images based on their content, which makes searching and navigating easier.

طَوَّرَ • تَطْويرٌ
to develop

طَوَّرَتْ "روبو سيتي" آلِيًّا يُمْكِنُهُ العَمَلُ في البيئاتِ القاسِيَةِ.

Robo City developed a robot that can work in harsh environments.

عَميقٌ
deep

تَمَّ تَطْويرُ نَموذَجِ التَّعَلُّمِ العَميقِ لِتَحْسينِ قُدْرَةِ الرّوبوتِ عَلى فَهْمِ البيئَةِ المُحيطَةِ بِهِ.

The deep learning model was developed to improve the robot's ability to understand its surrounding environment.

قابِلٌ لِلْبَرْمَجَةِ
programmable

تَمَّ تَصْميمُ الرّوبوتِ لِيَكونَ قابِلًا لِلْبَرْمَجَةِ، مِمّا يُتيحُ لِلْمُسْتَخْدِمينَ تَخْصيصَ وَظائِفِهِ لِتَلْبِيَةِ احْتِياجاتِهِمِ المُحَدَّدَةِ.

The robot was designed to be programmable, allowing users to customize its functions to meet their specific needs.

مُتَطَوِّرٌ
advanced

قامَ الفَريقُ بِتَطْويرِ تِقْنِيَّةٍ مُتَطَوِّرَةٍ تَسْمَحُ بِالتَّعَرُّفِ عَلى الصُّوَرِ بِغَضِّ النَّظَرِ عَنِ الإِضاءَةِ.

The team developed an advanced technology that allows image recognition regardless of the lighting.

مُتَعَدِّدُ الوَظائِفِ
multi-functional

صُمِّمَ الرّوبوتُ لِيَكونَ مُتَعَدِّدَ الوَظائِفِ، قادِرًا عَلى تَنْفيذِ مَجْموعَةٍ واسِعَةٍ مِنَ المَهامِّ.

The robot was designed to be multifunctional, capable of performing a wide range of tasks.

مُتَقَدِّمٌ
advanced

تَمَّ تَطْويرُ نِظامٍ مُتَقَدِّمٍ لِلذَّكاءِ الاِصْطِناعِيِّ يُمَكِّنُهُ مِنَ التَّنَبُّؤِ بِالأَحْداثِ القادِمَةِ بِدِقَّةٍ.

An advanced artificial intelligence system was developed that can accurately predict upcoming events.

مُتَنَقِّلٌ mobile

تَمَّ تَصْميمُ الرّوبوتِ لِيَكونَ مُتَنَقِّلًا، قادِرًا عَلى التَّنَقُّلِ في البيئاتِ المُخْتَلِفَةِ بِسُهولَةٍ.

The robot was designed to be mobile, able to navigate different environments with ease.

مُحَرِّكُ بَحْثٍ search engine

تَمَّ تَحْسينُ مُحَرِّكاتِ البَحْثِ لِتَقْديمِ نَتائِجَ أَكْثَرَ دِقَّةً وَسُرْعَةً.

Search engines were improved to provide more accurate and faster results.

مَرِنٌ flexible

تَمَّ تَصْميمُ البَرْنامَجِ لِيَكونَ مَرِنًا، قادِرًا عَلى التَّكَيُّفِ مَعَ مُتَطَلَّباتِ المُسْتَخْدِمِ المُتَغَيِّرَةِ.

The software was designed to be flexible, able to adapt to the changing user requirements.

ميكانيكِيٌّ mechanical

صُمِّمَ الرّوبوتُ بِأَجْزاءٍ ميكانيكِيَّةٍ دَقيقَةٍ تَسْمَحُ لَهُ بِالتَّحَرُّكِ بِطُرُقٍ مُعَقَّدَةٍ.

The robot was designed with precise mechanical parts that allow it to move in complex ways.

نَفَّذَ مَهامًّا • تَنْفيذٌ to execute tasks

نَفَّذَ الرّوبوتُ مَهامًّا مُعَقَّدَةً تَتَطَلَّبُ الكَثيرَ مِنَ الدِّقَّةِ.

The robot performed complex tasks that require a lot of precision.

5.2.2.1 Mini-Articles

Track **47**

تُقَدِّمُ التِّكْنولوجْيا اليَوْمَ فُرَصًا لا حَصْرَ لَها لِلذَّكاءِ الاِصْطِناعِيِّ وَالتَّعَلُّمِ العَميقِ. هَذِهِ التِّقْنِيّاتُ تُتيحُ القُدْرَةَ عَلى تَحْليلِ البَياناتِ الضَّخْمَةِ وَتَصْنيفِ الصُّوَرِ وَتَحْويلِ النُّصوصِ إِلى كَلامٍ، وَأَكْثَرَ مِنْ ذَلِكَ. وَمَعَ اسْتِمْرارِ التَّطَوُّرِ وَالتَّحْسينِ، يُمْكِنُ لِهَذِهِ الأَنْظِمَةِ تَنْفيذُ مَجْموعَةٍ واسِعَةٍ مِنَ المَهامِّ بِشَكْلٍ تِلْقائِيٍّ وَبِشَكْلٍ أَكْثَرَ كَفاءَةً.

Technology today offers limitless opportunities for artificial intelligence and deep learning. These technologies enable the ability to analyze big data, classify images, convert text to speech, and much more. With ongoing advancements and improvements, these systems can perform an expanding range of tasks automatically and more efficiently.

لَقَدْ قَدَّمَتْ لَنا التِّكْنولوجْيا الحَديثَةُ روبوتاتٍ قادِرَةً عَلى التَّحَرُّكِ وَالتَّحَكُّمِ بِنَفْسِها، وَأَصْبَحَتْ مُتَنَقِّلَةً وَمُتَعَدِّدَةَ الوَظائِفِ. مِنْ خِلالِ الجَمْعِ بَيْنَ الذَّكاءِ الاصْطِناعِيِّ وَالميكانيكا، يُمْكِنُ لِهَذِهِ الرّوبوتاتِ القِيامُ بِالْعَديدِ مِنَ المَهامِّ الَّتي كانَتْ في السّابِقِ تَتَطَلَّبُ تَدَخُّلَ البَشَرِ.

Modern technology has introduced us to robots capable of movement and self-control, becoming mobile and multifunctional. By combining artificial intelligence with mechanics, these robots can perform many tasks that once required human intervention.

واحِدَةٌ مِنَ التَّطَوُّراتِ الأَكْثَرِ إِثارَةً في مَجالِ الذَّكاءِ الاصْطِناعِيِّ هِيَ تَطَوُّرُ التِّكْنولوجِيّاتِ الَّتي تُمَكِّنُ الأَجْهِزَةَ مِنَ 'الرُّؤْيَةِ' وَ 'الاسْتِماعِ'. مِنْ خِلالِ التَّعَلُّمِ العَميقِ، يُمْكِنُ لِلْأَجْهِزَةِ اليَوْمَ تَحْليلُ وَتَصْنيفُ الصُّوَرِ وَالصَّوْتِ بِطُرُقٍ غَيْرِ مَسْبوقَةٍ، مِمّا يَفْتَحُ البابَ لِلْعَديدِ مِنَ التَّطْبيقاتِ، بَدْءًا مِنَ الرُّؤْيَةِ بِالْكُمْبيوتَرِ، إِلى التَّعَرُّفِ عَلى الكَلامِ.

One of the most exciting developments in the field of artificial intelligence is the advancement of technologies that enable devices to 'see' and 'hear'. Through deep learning, devices can now analyze and classify images and sound in unprecedented ways, opening the door to various applications, ranging from computer vision to speech recognition.

مَعَ القُدْرَةِ عَلى تَحْليلِ كَمِّيّاتٍ هائِلَةٍ مِنَ البَياناتِ، يُمْكِنُ لِلذَّكاءِ الاصْطِناعِيِّ اليَوْمَ التَّنَبُّؤُ بِالْأَحْداثِ وَالأَنْماطِ القادِمَةِ بِدِقَّةٍ مُتَزايِدَةٍ. مِنَ التَّنَبُّؤاتِ الطَّقْسِيَّةِ إِلى التَّنَبُّؤاتِ المالِيَّةِ، تُقَدِّمُ هَذِهِ الأَنْظِمَةُ الإِمْكانِيّاتِ لِتَحْسينِ القَراراتِ وَزِيادَةِ الكَفاءَةِ في العَديدِ مِنَ القِطاعاتِ.

With the ability to analyze vast amounts of data, artificial intelligence can now accurately predict future events and patterns. From weather forecasts to financial predictions, these systems offer capabilities to improve decision-making and increase efficiency in many sectors.

5.2.2.2 Article: The Future of A.I.

Track **48**

التَّفَرُّدُ التِّكْنولوجِيُّ وَمُسْتَقْبَلُ الذَّكاءِ الاصْطِناعِيِّ

مِنَ المُتَوَقَّعِ أَنْ يَحْدُثَ "التَّفَرُّدُ التِّكْنولوجِيُّ"، أَوِ "التَّفَرُّدُ" كَما يُشارُ إِلَيْهِ غالِبًا، عِنْدَما تَتَطَوَّرُ تِكْنولوجْيا الذَّكاءِ الاصْطِناعِيِّ لِدَرَجَةِ أَنَّ الآلاتِ سَتَكونُ قادِرَةً عَلى تَجاوُزِ القُدُراتِ البَشَرِيَّةِ، وَالتَّحَكُّمِ في مَسارِ التَّطَوُّرِ التِّكْنولوجِيِّ. وَيُمْكِنُ القَوْلُ أَنَّ هَذِهِ هِيَ نُقْطَةُ اللاعَوْدَةِ، حَيْثُ سَيُصْبِحُ الذَّكاءُ الاصْطِناعِيُّ مُتَقَدِّمًا وَمُتَطَوِّرًا بِما يَكْفي لِيُصَمِّمَ وَيُحَسِّنَ نَفْسَهُ بِشَكْلٍ مُسْتَقِلٍّ، مِمّا سَيُؤَدّي إِلى تَسارُعٍ غَيْرِ مَسْبوقٍ في التَّقَدُّمِ التِّكْنولوجِيِّ.

في هَذا السّيناريو، مِنَ المُمْكِنِ أَنْ يَتَطَوَّرَ الذَّكاءُ الاصْطِناعِيُّ إِلى حَدٍّ كَبيرٍ بِحَيْثُ يُمْكِنُهُ التَّحَكُّمُ في التِّكْنولوجْيا البَشَرِيَّةِ، مِثْلِ الرّوبوتاتِ، لِتَنْفيذِ المَهامِّ بِشَكْلٍ أَسْرَعَ وَأَكْثَرَ كَفاءَةً مِنَ البَشَرِ. كَما يُمْكِنُ أَنْ يَتَعَلَّمَ الذَّكاءُ الاصْطِناعِيُّ

بِطُرُقٍ غَيْرِ مُمْكِنَةٍ لِلْبَشَرِ، كالتَّعَلُّمِ العَميقِ وَالتَّعَلُّمِ الآلِيِّ، وَالَّتي تُتيحُ لَهُ تَحْليلَ كَمِّيّاتٍ ضَخْمَةٍ مِنَ البَياناتِ وَاتِّخاذَ القَراراتِ بِناءً عَلى هَذِهِ البَياناتِ في غَمْضَةِ عَيْنٍ.

تُشيرُ التَّوَقُّعاتُ إلى أَنَّ هَذا التَّفَرُّدَ قَدْ يَحْدُثُ في القَرْنِ الحادي وَالعِشْرينَ، وَلَكِنَّ التَّوَقُّعاتِ تَخْتَلِفُ بِشَكْلٍ كَبيرٍ. فَبَيْنَما يَعْتَبِرُ بَعْضُ العُلَماءِ التَّفَرُّدَ أَمْرًا حَتْمِيًّا، يَنْظُرُ لَهُ آخَرونَ بِاعْتِبارِهِ مُجَرَّدَ خَيالٍ عِلْمِيٍّ.

The Technological Singularity and the Future of Artificial Intelligence

It is expected that "Technological Singularity" or simply "Singularity," as it is often referred to, will occur when artificial intelligence technology advances to a point where machines surpass human capabilities and take control of the trajectory of technological development. This is considered a point of no return, where artificial intelligence becomes advanced and sophisticated enough to design and improve itself independently, leading to an unprecedented acceleration in technological progress.

In this scenario, it is possible for artificial intelligence to evolve significantly to the extent that it can control human technologies, such as robots, to perform tasks faster and more efficiently than humans. Additionally, artificial intelligence can learn in ways that are not possible for humans, such as deep learning and machine learning, which allow it to analyze massive amounts of data and make decisions based on that data in an instant.

Forecasts suggest that this Singularity may occur in the twenty-first century, but predictions vary greatly. While some scientists consider Singularity as inevitable, others view it as mere science fiction.

5.2.2.3 Article: Advanced Technology in the Workplace

Track **49**

التَّحَوُّلُ نَحْوَ التِّكْنولوجْيا المُتَقَدِّمَةِ وَالذَّكاءِ الاِصْطِناعِيِّ: فُرَصٌ وَتَحَدِّياتٌ

تُواجِهُ العَديدُ مِنَ القِطاعاتِ الاِقْتِصادِيَّةِ نَقْصًا حادًّا في العِمالَةِ، مِمّا أَدّى إلى تَبَنّي التِّقْنِيّاتِ الآلِيَّةِ وَالذَّكاءِ الاِصْطِناعِيِّ (AI) بِشَكْلٍ مُتَزايِدٍ. لا يُمْكِنُ إيقافُ هَذا التَّحَوُّلِ التِّكْنولوجِيِّ، وَهُوَ يُحْتَمَلُ أَنْ يُحَفِّزَ الثَّوْرَةَ الصِّناعِيَّةَ القادِمَةَ.

في وُجودِ تِكْنولوجْيا الذَّكاءِ الاِصْطِناعِيِّ الَّتي تَتَعَلَّمُ وَتَتَحَسَّنُ بِمُرورِ الوَقْتِ، يُصْبِحُ مِنَ الأَسْهَلِ تَنْفيذُ المَهامِّ الَّتي كانَتْ في السّابِقِ تَتَطَلَّبُ تَدَخُّلَ الإِنْسانِ. وَفي الوَقْتِ الَّذي يُمْكِنُ فيه لِهَذِهِ الأَنْظِمَةِ الذَّكِيَّةِ التَّعامُلُ مَعَ البَياناتِ الضَّخْمَةِ، فَإِنَّها تُقَدِّمُ أَيْضًا التَّوَقُّعاتِ الدَّقيقَةَ الَّتي يُمْكِنُ أَنْ تُساعِدَ في تَحْسينِ الإِنْتاجِيَّةِ وَتَقْليلِ الهَدْرِ.

في نَفْسِ الوَقْتِ، يُمْكِنُ لِلرّوبوتاتِ الآلِيَّةِ، بِقُدْرَتِها عَلى التَّحَرُّكِ وَالتَّنَقُّلِ، تَنْفيذُ مَجْموعَةٍ مُتَنَوِّعَةٍ مِنَ المَهامِّ الميكانيكِيَّةِ. بِفَضْلِ هَذِهِ الرّوبوتاتِ مُتَعَدِّدَةِ الوَظائِفِ، يُمْكِنُ لِلْمُؤَسَّساتِ الآنَ أَنْ تَضْمَنَ اسْتِمْرارِيَّةَ العَمَلِيّاتِ دونَ الحاجَةِ لِلتَّواجُدِ البَشَرِيِّ المُسْتَمِرِّ.

إنَّ التَّطَوُّراتِ فِي التَّعَرُّفِ عَلى الصُّوَرِ وَالصَّوْتِ تُوَفِّرُ أَيْضًا القُدْرَةَ عَلى التَّعامُلِ مَعَ المَهامِّ الأَكْثَرِ تَعْقيدًا، كَتَصْنيفِ الصُّوَرِ وَتَحْويلِ النَّصِّ إلى كَلامٍ. هَذِهِ التِّكْنولوجْيا تُساعِدُ فِي تَحْقيقِ تَطْبيقاتِ ذَكاءٍ اصْطِناعِيٍّ مُتَقَدِّمَةٍ فِي العَديدِ مِنَ القِطاعاتِ، بَدْءًا مِنَ الرِّعايَةِ الصِّحِّيَّةِ إلى الخِدْماتِ المالِيَّةِ.

الجَديرُ بِالذِّكْرِ أَنَّ مَعَ زِيادَةِ اسْتِخْدامِ الأَتْمَتَةِ وَالذَّكاءِ الاِصْطِناعِيِّ، سَيَكونُ هُناكَ تَحَدِّياتٌ ذاتُ طابَعٍ اجْتِماعِيٍّ واقْتِصادِيٍّ يَتَعَيَّنُ مواجَهَتُها، بِما فِي ذَلِكَ التَّأْثيرُ عَلى فُرَصِ العَمَلِ. وَلَكِنْ، بِمُعالَجَةِ هَذِهِ التَّحَدِّياتِ بِشَكْلٍ صَحيحٍ، يُمْكِنُ أَنْ تُوَفِّرَ هَذِهِ التِّكْنولوجِيّاتُ فُرَصًا جَديدَةً وَمُحَسَّنَةً لِلتَّنْمِيَةِ الاِقْتِصادِيَّةِ وَتَحْسينِ حَياةِ البَشَرِ.

Transitioning Towards Advanced Technology and Artificial Intelligence: Opportunities and Challenges

Many economic sectors are facing a severe labor shortage, leading to an increasing adoption of automated technologies and artificial intelligence (AI). This technological shift is unstoppable and has the potential to drive the upcoming industrial revolution.

With AI technology that learns and improves over time, it becomes easier to perform tasks that previously required human intervention. While these intelligent systems can handle big data, they also offer precise predictions that can help improve productivity and reduce waste.

At the same time, autonomous robots, characterized by their ability to move and navigate, can execute a variety of mechanical tasks. Thanks to these multifunctional robots, organizations can ensure operational continuity without the need for constant human presence.

Advancements in image and speech recognition also provide the ability to tackle more complex tasks such as image classification and text-to-speech conversion. This technology aids in achieving advanced AI applications in various sectors, ranging from healthcare to financial services.

It's worth mentioning that with increased automation and artificial intelligence usage, there will be social and economic challenges to be addressed, including the impact on job opportunities. However, by addressing these challenges properly, these technologies can provide new and improved opportunities for economic development and enhance human life.

5.2.3 Clean Energy and Renewable Technologies

Track **50**

أَخْضَرُ **green**

قامَتِ الحُكومَةُ بِتَطْبيقِ سِياساتٍ جَديدَةٍ لِدَعْمِ الصِّناعاتِ الخَضْراءِ وَتَشْجيعِ اسْتِخْدامِ الطّاقَةِ المُتَجَدِّدَةِ.

The government implemented new policies to support green industries and encourage the use of renewable energy.

تَحْويلُ طاقَةٍ
energy conversion

قامَتِ المَدينَةُ بِتَحْويلِ مَصادِرِ طاقَتِها إلى الطّاقَةِ الشَّمْسِيَّةِ لِتَقْليلِ الاِنْبِعاثاتِ الكَرْبونِيَّةِ.

The city has converted its energy sources to solar energy to reduce carbon emissions.

تَخْزينُ طاقَةٍ
energy storage

تَمَكَّنَ العُلَماءُ مِنْ تَطْويرِ تِقْنِيّاتٍ جَديدَةٍ لِتَخْزينِ الطّاقَةِ الشَّمْسِيَّةِ لِلاِسْتِخْدامِ في الأَوْقاتِ الَّتي لا تَكونُ فيها الشَّمْسُ مُتاحَةً.

Scientists have developed new technologies to store solar energy for use at times when the sun is not available.

تَطْويرُ تِكْنولوجْيا نَظيفَةٍ
clean technology development

تَمَّ تَطْويرُ تِكْنولوجْيا نَظيفَةٍ جَديدَةٍ تُساعِدُ في تَحْقيقِ الاِسْتِدامَةِ وَتَقْليلِ الضَّرَرِ البيئِيِّ.

A new clean technology was developed that helps achieve sustainability and reduce environmental harm.

تِقْنِيَّةُ طاقَةٍ نَظيفَةٍ
clean energy technologie

تَتَمَثَّلُ أَحْدَثُ تِقْنِيّاتِ الطّاقَةِ النَّظيفَةِ في البَطّارِيّاتِ الَّتي تَمْتَصُّ الكَرْبونَ مِنَ الجَوِّ.

The latest clean energy technologies involve batteries that absorb carbon from the air.

Note how the English sentence includes the relative pronoun 'that'. In Arabic, the equivalent relative pronouns are الَّذي for masculine nouns and الَّتي for feminine nouns. However, these pronouns are employed only when following a definite noun. This is different from the previous example sentence ('... that helps...'), where no relative pronoun is used because it follows an indefinite noun.

تِكْنولوجْيا طاقَةٍ نَظيفَةٍ
clean energy technology

قامَتِ المُنَظَّمَةُ بِتَبَنّي تِكْنولوجْيا الطّاقَةِ النَّظيفَةِ لِتَقْليلِ الاِنْبِعاثاتِ وَالحِفاظِ عَلى البيئَةِ.

The organization adopted clean energy technology to reduce emissions and preserve the environment.

تَوْزيعُ طاقَةٍ
energy distribution

نَفَّذَتِ الدَّوْلَةُ خُطَّةً لِتَوْزيعِ الطّاقَةِ النَّظيفَةِ عَلى المُدُنِ وَالقُرى النّائِيَةِ.

The country implemented a plan to distribute clean energy to remote cities and villages.

تَوْليدُ طاقَةٍ
energy generation

تَمَّ تَوْليدُ طاقَةِ الرِّياحِ بِكَفاءَةٍ في المَوْقِعِ الجَديدِ، مِمّا زادَ مِنَ الإِمْداداتِ الكُلِّيَّةِ لِلطّاقَةِ المُتَجَدِّدَةِ.

Wind energy was efficiently generated at the new site, increasing the total supplies of renewable energy.

حُلولُ الطّاقَةِ النَّظيفَةِ
clean energy solutions

تَمَّ تَقْديمُ حُلولِ الطّاقَةِ النَّظيفَةِ لِلْمَنازِلِ وَالشَّرِكاتِ كَبَديلٍ لِطاقَةِ الفَحْمِ.

Clean energy solutions were introduced for homes and companies as an alternative to coal energy.

سَيّارَةٌ كَهْرَبائِيَّةٌ
electric car

تَمَّ تَقْديمُ نَموذَجٍ جَديدٍ مِنَ السَّيّاراتِ الكَهْرَبائِيَّةِ تَمْتازُ بِمَدىً أَطْوَلَ وَشَحْنٍ أَسْرَعَ.

A new model of electric cars was introduced that features longer range and faster charging.

صَديقٌ لِلْبيئَةِ
environmentally friendly

صُمِّمَتِ المُنْتَجاتُ الجَديدَةُ لِتَكونَ صَديقَةً لِلْبيئَةِ، مِمّا يُقَلِّلُ مِنَ الضَّرَرِ الَّذي يُمْكِنُ أَنْ يُسَبِّبَهُ الإِنْتاجُ الصِّناعِيُّ.

The new products were designed to be eco-friendly, reducing the harm that industrial production can cause.

طاقَةٌ جِيوحَرارِيَّةٌ
geothermal energy

تَمَّ اسْتِغْلالُ الطّاقَةِ الجِيوحَرارِيَّةِ بِشَكْلٍ فَعّالٍ في مِنْطَقَةِ البَحْرِ الأَحْمَرِ، حَيْثُ وَفَّرَتِ الطّاقَةَ الكَهْرَبائِيَّةَ.

Geothermal energy was effectively exploited in the Red Sea region, providing electricity.

طاقَةٌ حَرارِيَّةٌ
thermal energy

أَعْلَنَتِ الحُكومَةُ عَنْ خُطَطٍ لِتَحْويلِ مَحَطّاتِ الطّاقَةِ الحَرارِيَّةِ إِلى مَصادِرِ طاقَةٍ نَظيفَةٍ.

The government announced plans to convert thermal power stations into clean energy sources.

طاقَةُ رِياحٍ
wind energy

تَمَّ تَحْديثُ مَزارِعِ طاقَةِ الرِّياحِ لِزِيادَةِ الكَفاءَةِ وَالإِنْتاجِيَّةِ.

Wind energy farms were updated to increase efficiency and productivity.

solar energy **طاقَةٌ شَمْسِيَّةٌ**

اِكْتَسَبَتِ الطّاقَةُ الشَّمْسِيَّةُ شَعْبِيَّةً كَبيرَةً بِفَضْلِ قُدْرَتِها عَلى تَقْديمِ مَصْدَرِ طاقَةٍ مُسْتَدامٍ وَصَديقٍ لِلْبيئَةِ.

Solar energy gained great popularity thanks to its ability to provide a sustainable and eco-friendly energy source.

hydro energy **طاقَةٌ مائِيَّةٌ**

قامَتِ الحُكومَةُ بِتَنْفيذِ مَشْروعٍ لِإِعادَةِ النَّظَرِ في اسْتِغْلالِ الطّاقَةِ المائِيَّةِ في الأَنْهارِ الكُبْرى.

The government implemented a project to rethink the use of hydropower in major rivers.

renewable energy **طاقَةٌ مُتَجَدِّدَةٌ**

تَعَهَّدَتِ البِلادُ بِتَحْقيقِ الِاعْتِمادِ التّامِّ عَلى الطّاقَةِ المُتَجَدِّدَةِ بِحُلولِ عامِ 2040.

The country pledged to achieve total reliance on renewable energy by 2040.

clean energy **طاقَةٌ نَظيفَةٌ**

عُقِدَ المُؤْتَمَرُ الدَّوْلِيُّ لِلطّاقَةِ النَّظيفَةِ لِبَحْثِ أَحْدَثِ التِّقْنِيّاتِ وَالِاسْتراتيجِيّاتِ في هَذا المَجالِ.

The International Clean Energy Conference was held to discuss the latest technologies and strategies in this field.

nuclear energy **طاقَةٌ نَوَوِيَّةٌ**

عَلى الرَّغْمِ مِنَ الجَدَلِ، تَمَّ الِاعْتِرافُ بِالطّاقَةِ النَّوَوِيَّةِ كَمَصْدَرٍ مُحْتَمَلٍ لِلطّاقَةِ المُسْتَدامَةِ.

Despite controversy, nuclear energy was recognized as a potential source of sustainable energy.

cost-effective **فَعّالٌ مِنْ حَيْثُ التَّكْلِفَةِ**

اِخْتيرَتِ الطّاقَةُ الشَّمْسِيَّةُ لِأَنَّها فَعّالَةٌ مِنْ حَيْثُ التَّكْلِفَةِ وَيُمْكِنُ أَنْ تُوَفِّرَ الكَهْرَباءَ لِلْمُجْتَمَعاتِ الرّيفِيَّةِ النّائِيَةِ.

Solar energy was chosen because it is cost-effective and can provide electricity to remote rural communities.

كَفاءَةُ الطّاقَةِ
energy efficiency

تَمَّ تَطْبيقُ مَعاييرَ جَديدَةٍ لِزِيادَةِ كَفاءَةِ الطّاقَةِ في البِناءِ وَالتَّصْميمِ العُمْرانيِّ.

New standards were implemented to increase energy efficiency in construction and urban design.

كَهْرَباءُ خَضْراءُ
green electricity

أَعْلَنَتِ الحُكومَةُ عَنْ خُطَطٍ لِزِيادَةِ إِنْتاجِ الكَهْرَباءِ الخَضْراءِ في العَقْدِ القادِمِ.

The government announced plans to increase green electricity production in the coming decade.

مُؤْتَمَرُ الطّاقَةِ المُتَجَدِّدَةِ
renewable energy conference

تَمَّ تَنْظيمُ مُؤْتَمَرِ الطّاقَةِ المُتَجَدِّدَةِ لِمُناقَشَةِ التَّقَدُّمِ الَّذي تَمَّ تَحْقيقُهُ في تِكْنولوجْيا الطّاقَةِ النَّظيفَةِ.

The Renewable Energy Conference was organized to discuss the progress made in clean energy technology.

مُتَجَدِّدٌ
renewable

أُسْتُخْدِمَتْ مَوادُّ مُتَجَدِّدَةٌ في تَصْميمِ المَباني الجَديدَةِ لِتَقْليلِ التَّأْثيرِ البيئِيِّ.

Renewable materials were used in the design of new buildings to reduce environmental impact.

مَحَطَّةُ طاقَةٍ شَمْسِيَّةٍ
solar power plant

أَعْلَنَتِ الجَزائِرُ عَنْ خُطَطٍ لِبِناءِ مَحَطَّةِ طاقَةٍ شَمْسِيَّةٍ ضَخْمَةٍ في الصَّحْراءِ الكُبْرى لِاسْتِغْلالِ الطّاقَةِ الشَّمْسِيَّةِ غَيْرِ المَحْدودَةِ.

Algeria announced plans to build a huge solar power station in the Sahara desert to harness unlimited solar energy.

مُسْتَدامٌ
sustainable

وَفَّرَتِ الأَساليبُ المُسْتَدامَةُ لِإِدارَةِ النُّفاياتِ طُرُقًا فَعّالَةً لِتَقْليلِ التَّلَوُّثِ وَتَحْقيقِ أَهْدافِ الِاسْتِدامَةِ.

Sustainable waste management methods provided effective ways to reduce pollution and achieve sustainability goals.

renewable energy project مَشْروعُ طاقَةٍ مُتَجَدِّدَةٍ

بَدَأَ مَشْروعُ الطّاقَةِ المُتَجَدِّدَةِ الجَديدُ في المَدينَةِ بِتَحْويلِ النُّفاياتِ إلى طاقَةٍ.

The new renewable energy project in the city started converting waste into energy.

alternative energy source مَصْدَرُ طاقَةٍ بَديلٌ

تَمَّ تَقْديمُ الغازِ الحَيَوِيِّ كَمَصْدَرِ طاقَةٍ بَديلٍ لِتَلْبِيَةِ احْتياجاتِ الطّاقَةِ المُتَزايِدَةِ.

Biogas was introduced as an alternative energy source to meet growing energy needs.

renewable resources *pl.* مَوارِدُ مُتَجَدِّدَةٌ

تَحَوَّلَتِ الدَّوْلَةُ إلى اسْتِخْدامِ المَوارِدِ المُتَجَدِّدَةِ بَدَلًا مِنَ الوَقودِ الأَحْفورِيِّ لِلْحَدِّ مِنَ التَّغَيُّرِ المُناخِيِّ.

The country switched to using renewable resources instead of fossil fuels to mitigate climate change.

5.2.3.1 Mini-Articles

Track **51**

في أَخْبارٍ مُذْهِلَةٍ خَرَجَتِ الأُسْبوعَ الماضِيَ، أَعْلَنَتْ شَرِكَةُ إيكوباوَرْ، الرّائِدَةُ في مَجالِ تِكْنولوجْيا الطّاقَةِ، عَنْ تَطَوُّرٍ مُبْتَكَرٍ في مَجالِ تَخْزينِ الطّاقَةِ. اِسْتَخْدَمَتِ الشَّرِكَةُ تِقْنِيَّةَ طاقَةٍ نَظيفَةٍ جَديدَةً لِتَحْقيقِ كَفاءَةٍ في التَّخْزينِ تَتَجاوَزُ أَيَّ شَيْءٍ رَأَيْناهُ مِنْ قَبْلُ. هَذا الإِنْجازُ يَعْني أَنَّ الطّاقَةَ الشَّمْسِيَّةَ وَالرِّياحَ يُمْكِنُ تَخْزينُهُما بِكَفاءَةٍ أَكْبَرَ، وَبِالتّالي تَوْزيعُهُما بِطُرُقٍ أَكْثَرَ اسْتِدامَةً.

In astonishing news that emerged last week, EkoPower, a leading energy technology company, announced an innovative development in energy storage. The company utilized a new clean energy technology to achieve storage efficiency that surpasses anything we have seen before. This breakthrough means that solar and wind energy can be stored more efficiently, thus enabling their distribution in more sustainable ways.

تَمَّ تَوْصيلُ أَوَّلِ مَنْزِلٍ في العالَمِ بِطاقَةٍ جيوحَرارِيَّةٍ مُسْتَدامَةٍ بِفَضْلِ تِقْنِيَّةٍ جَديدَةٍ طَوَّرَتْها شَرِكَةُ جيوتِكْ. بِفَضْلِ التَّقَدُّمِ العِلْمِيِّ في مَجالِ الحَفْرِ وَتَحْويلِ الطّاقَةِ، يُمْكِنُ لِهَذِهِ التِّقْنِيَّةِ تَوْفيرُ حَلٍّ طَويلِ الأَمَدِ لِلطّاقَةِ النَّظيفَةِ.

The world's first home was successfully powered by sustainable geothermal energy thanks to a new technology developed by GeoTech. With scientific advancements in drilling and energy conversion, this technology can provide a long-term solution for clean energy.

كَشَفَتْ شَرِكَةُ زايْروكارْ، شَرِكَةُ السَّيّاراتِ الكَهْرَبائِيَّةِ، عَنْ أَحْدَثِ موديلاتِها الأُسْبوعَ الماضي. يَتَمَيَّزُ الموديلُ الجَديدُ بِتِقْنِيَّةِ شَحْنٍ سَريعٍ فائِقَةٍ تَسْمَحُ لِلسَّيّارَةِ بِالشَّحْنِ الكامِلِ في غُضونِ عِشْرينَ دَقيقَةً فَقَطْ، مِمّا يَجْعَلُها واحِدَةً مِنَ السَّيّاراتِ الكَهْرَبائِيَّةِ الأَكْثَرِ كَفاءَةً عَلى الإِطْلاقِ.

XyroCar, an electric car company, unveiled its latest model last week. The new model features ultra-fast charging technology that allows the car to fully charge in just twenty minutes, making it one of the most efficient electric cars ever.

أَعْلَنَتْ شَرِكَةُ سولارْ بْرو، الرّائِدَةُ في مَجالِ الطّاقَةِ الشَّمْسِيَّةِ، عَنْ بِناءِ أَكْبَرِ مَحَطَّةِ طاقَةٍ شَمْسِيَّةٍ في العالَمِ. يَتَمَيَّزُ المَشْروعُ بِقُدْرَتِهِ عَلى تَوْليدِ الكَهْرَباءِ لِما يَزيدُ على المِلْيونِ مَنْزِلٍ، وَتَأْمُلُ الشَّرِكَةُ في أَنْ تَكونَ تِلْكَ خُطْوَةً كَبيرَةً نَحْوَ التَّحَوُّلِ إِلى الطّاقَةِ المُتَجَدِّدَةِ.

SolarPro, a leading solar energy company, announced the construction of the world's largest solar power station. The project has the capacity to generate electricity for over a million households, and the company hopes that this will be a significant step towards the transition to renewable energy.

أَطْلَقَتْ ويِنْدْباوِرْ، الشَّرِكَةُ المُتَخَصِّصَةُ في طاقَةِ الرِّياحِ، أَحْدَثَ تِكْنولوجْيا لِطاقَةِ الرِّياحِ الأُسْبوعَ الماضِيَ. يَحْتَوي الاِبْتِكارُ الجَديدُ عَلى تورْبيناتٍ أَكْثَرَ كَفاءَةً تَقومُ بِتَحْويلِ المَزيدِ مِنَ الرِّياحِ إِلى طاقَةٍ، مِمّا يُعَزِّزُ إِنْتاجَ الكَهْرَباءِ الخَضْراءِ.

WindPower, a company specializing in wind energy, launched its latest wind power technology last week. The new innovation features more efficient turbines that convert more wind into energy, enhancing the production of green electricity.

5.2.3.2 Profiles of Forms of Renewable Energy

Track **52**

أَشْكالُ الطّاقَةِ المُتَجَدِّدَةِ

تَتَعَدَّدُ أَشْكالُ الطّاقَةِ المُتَجَدِّدَةِ وَالنَّظيفَةِ، وَكُلٌّ مِنْها يُقَدِّمُ فَوائِدَ فَريدَةً مِنْ نَوْعِها وَيُواجِهُ تَحَدِّياتِهِ الخاصَّةَ. في هَذِهِ المَقالَةِ، سَنُناقِشُ خَمْسَةَ أَنْواعٍ مِنَ الطّاقَةِ: الطّاقَةَ الجِيوحَرارِيَّةَ، طاقَةَ الرِّياحِ، الطّاقَةَ الشَّمْسِيَّةَ، الطّاقَةَ المائِيَّةَ، وَالطّاقَةَ النَّوَوِيَّةَ. سَنَتَعَرَّفُ عَلى كَيْفِيَّةِ عَمَلِ كُلٍّ مِنْها، وَما هِيَ الفَوائِدُ وَالتَّحَدِّياتُ الَّتي تُقَدِّمُها. في ظِلِّ الاِهْتِمامِ المُتَزايِدِ بِالطّاقَةِ النَّظيفَةِ وَالمُسْتَدامَةِ، فَمِنَ المُهِمِّ فَهْمُ الخِياراتِ المُتاحَةِ وَما يُمْكِنُ أَنْ يُقَدِّمَهُ كُلٌّ مِنْها.

1. الطّاقةُ الجِيوحَرارِيَّةُ:

تَتَجَدَّدُ الطّاقةُ الجِيوحَرارِيَّةُ بِشَكْلٍ طَبيعيٍّ وَمُسْتَمِرٍّ، مُسْتَغِلَّةً الحَرارَةَ المَوْجودَةَ تَحْتَ سَطْحِ الأَرْضِ. يُمْكِنُ اسْتِخْدامُها لِتَوْليدِ الكَهْرَباءِ أَوْ لِتَوْفيرِ التَّدْفِئَةِ وَالتَّبْريدِ. عَلى الرَّغْمِ مِنْ أَنَّ تِكْنولوجْيا الطّاقَةِ الجِيوحَرارِيَّةِ تَتَطَلَّبُ اسْتِثْمارًا أَوَّلِيًّا كَبيرًا، فَإِنَّها في النِّهايَةِ تُقَدِّمُ حَلًّا نَظيفًا وَمُسْتَدامًا لِلطّاقَةِ مَعَ تَكاليفِ تَشْغيلٍ مُنْخَفِضَةٍ.

2. طاقَةُ الرِّياحِ:

تَسْتَفيدُ طاقَةُ الرِّياحِ مِنْ حَرَكَةِ الرِّياحِ لِتَوْليدِ الكَهْرَباءِ. تُعَدُّ توربينات الرِّياحِ الحَديثَةُ ذاتَ كَفاءَةٍ وَصَديقَةً لِلْبيئَةِ، حَيْثُ تُحَوِّلُ الرِّياحَ إِلى طاقَةٍ دونَ إِنْتاجِ انْبِعاثاتِ غازاتِ الدَّفيئَةِ. بِفَضْلِ التَّقَدُّمِ في تِكْنولوجْيا الرِّياحِ، أَصْبَحَتْ هَذِهِ الطّاقَةُ أَكْثَرَ مُلاءَمَةً وَقابِلِيَّةً لِلتَّطْبيقِ عَلى نِطاقٍ واسِعٍ.

3. الطّاقَةُ الشَّمْسِيَّةُ:

تُعَدُّ الطّاقَةُ الشَّمْسِيَّةُ مِنْ أَنْظَفِ أَشْكالِ الطّاقَةِ المُتَجَدِّدَةِ، حَيْثُ تُحَوِّلُ أَشِعَّةَ الشَّمْسِ المُباشِرَةَ إِلى كَهْرَباءَ بِاسْتِخْدامِ الأَلْواحِ الشَّمْسِيَّةِ. إِنَّ التَّطَوُّراتِ في الأَلْواحِ الشَّمْسِيَّةِ جَعَلَتْها أَكْثَرَ كَفاءَةً وَأَقَلَّ تَكْلِفَةً، مِمّا يَجْعَلُ الطّاقَةَ الشَّمْسِيَّةَ خِيارًا مُتَزايِدَ الشَّعْبِيَّةِ لِلْأَغْراضِ المَنْزِلِيَّةِ وَالتِّجارِيَّةِ.

4. الطّاقَةُ المائِيَّةُ:

تَعْتَمِدُ الطّاقَةُ المائِيَّةُ عَلى اسْتِخْدامِ قُوَّةِ تَدَفُّقِ الماءِ لِتَوْليدِ الكَهْرَباءِ. قَدْ تَأْتي مِنَ الأَنْهارِ أَوِ الشَّلّالاتِ، أَوْ حَتّى مِنَ المَدِّ وَالجَزْرِ وَتَيّاراتِ المُحيطاتِ. تُعْتَبَرُ الطّاقَةُ المائِيَّةُ واحِدَةً مِنْ أَقْدَمِ أَشْكالِ الطّاقَةِ المُتَجَدِّدَةِ وَأَكْثَرِها رُسوخًا، وَهِيَ تُوَفِّرُ مَصْدَرًا مُسْتَقِرًّا وَمَوْثوقًا بِهِ لِلطّاقَةِ.

5. الطّاقَةُ النَّوَوِيَّةُ:

تُعَدُّ الطّاقَةُ النَّوَوِيَّةُ مَصْدَرَ طاقَةٍ قَوِيًّا وَكَثيفًا، حَيْثُ يَجْري تَوْليدُ الكَهْرَباءِ مِنْ تَفاعُلاتٍ نَوَوِيَّةٍ تَحْدُثُ في الوَقودِ النَّوَوِيِّ. عَلى الرَّغْمِ مِنْ أَنَّها لا تُنْتِجُ انْبِعاثاتِ غازاتِ الدَّفيئَةِ، فَإِنَّ القَضايا المُتَعَلِّقَةَ بِالْأَمانِ وَالنُّفاياتِ النَّوَوِيَّةِ تُعْتَبَرُ تَحَدِّياتٍ رَئيسِيَّةً.

Forms of Renewable Energy

Renewable and clean energy comes in various forms, each offering unique benefits and facing its own challenges. In this article, we will discuss five types of energy: geothermal energy, wind energy, solar energy, hydropower, and nuclear energy. We will explore how each one works, along with the benefits and challenges they present. With the increasing focus on clean and sustainable energy, it is important to understand the available options and what each can offer.

1. Geothermal Energy:

Geothermal energy is naturally and continuously replenished, harnessing the heat beneath the Earth's surface. It can be used to generate electricity or provide heating and cooling. Although geothermal energy technology requires significant initial investment, it ultimately offers a clean and sustainable energy solution with low operating costs.

2. Wind Energy:

Wind energy harnesses the movement of the wind to generate electricity. Modern wind turbines are efficient and environmentally friendly, converting wind into energy without producing greenhouse gas emissions. Advancements in wind technology have made this energy source more feasible and widely applicable.

3. Solar Energy:

Solar energy is one of the cleanest forms of renewable energy, converting direct sunlight into electricity using solar panels. Advances in solar panel technology have made them more efficient and affordable, making solar energy an increasingly popular choice for residential and commercial purposes.

4. Hydropower:

Hydropower relies on harnessing the power of flowing water to generate electricity. It can come from rivers, waterfalls, or even tides and ocean currents. Hydropower is one of the oldest and most established forms of renewable energy, providing a stable and reliable energy source.

5. Nuclear Energy:

Nuclear energy is a powerful and dense energy source, where electricity is generated from nuclear reactions that occur in nuclear fuel. While it does not produce greenhouse gas emissions, safety and nuclear waste issues are significant challenges associated with nuclear energy.

Unit 6
Sports

Sports play a unique role in any society, serving as a mirror reflecting its cultural, social, and sometimes even political landscapes. This is particularly true in the Arab world, where sports transcend mere physical activity to become platforms for national pride, cultural expression, and social cohesion. This unit is designed to arm you with the essential vocabulary and contextual understanding needed to engage with Arabic media coverage of various sporting activities and phenomena.

The unit opens with 'Ball Sports,' dedicating individual sections to the likes of Soccer (Football), Basketball, Volleyball, Handball, and Tennis. Soccer is undoubtedly the most universally adored sport in the Arab world, with countries like Egypt, Morocco, Algeria, Saudi Arabia, and Qatar boasting rich football cultures and competitive national teams.

We then transition to 'Athletics and Olympic Sports,' featuring Track and Field, Gymnastics, and Weightlifting, before delving into the action-packed realm of 'Combat Sports' like Wrestling, Boxing, and Martial Arts.

Lastly, the unit touches on the broad topic of 'Sports Culture and Industry,' encapsulating everything from sports events to sports business and economy, organizations, training and health, fan culture, and broadcasting and commentary. This comprehensive coverage ensures you are well-equipped to understand and talk about the sports industry's different facets in Arabic.

We must note, however, that the list of sports and topics covered in this unit is not exhaustive. For example, culturally significant sports like Camel Racing and Equestrian Sports have been omitted due to space constraints, despite their deep roots and popularity in Arab culture. Motorsports, too, which have gained traction in recent years, especially with events like Formula 1 races in Bahrain, have not been included.

In most units of this book, we have been meticulous about avoiding the repetition of keywords across multiple subsections, opting to place each vocabulary item in just one relevant category. This approach is intended to offer a streamlined learning experience by reducing redundancy. However, in the Sports unit, you will encounter an exception to this rule. Some keywords appear in more than one section, even when their meaning remains consistent. This intentional repetition serves a specific purpose: to allow you to see how a term is used in different sporting contexts. This strategy aims to provide you with a more nuanced understanding of the term's application, making it easier for you to engage with Arabic sports commentary and reporting that spans various athletic disciplines.

By mastering the vocabulary and context presented in this unit, you will be better equipped to understand and engage with Arabic media's coverage of sports, thereby deepening your insight into the social and cultural fabric of the Arab world.

6.1 Ball Sports

6.1.1 Soccer (Football)

Track **53**

booking — **إِنْذارٌ لِلاعِبٍ**

أَصْدَرَ الحَكَمُ إِنْذارًا لِلّاعِبِ بِسَبَبِ تَصَرُّفِهِ العَنيفِ خِلالَ المُباراةِ.

The referee issued a booking [yellow card] to the player due to his aggressive behavior during the match.

possession — **اِسْتِحْواذٌ**

اِسْتَحْوَذَ الفَريقُ المُنافِسُ عَلى الكُرَةِ لِمُدَّةٍ طَويلَةٍ خِلالَ الشَّوْطِ الأَوَّلِ.

The opposing team had long possession of the ball during the first half.

to retire — **اِعْتَزَلَ** • اِعْتِزالٌ

أَعْلَنَ النَّجْمُ العالَمِيُّ عَنِ اعْتِزالِهِ لِكُرَةِ القَدَمِ بَعْدَ مَسيرَةٍ حافِلَةٍ بِالْإِنْجازاتِ.

The global star announced his retirement from soccer after a career filled with achievements.

red card — **بِطاقَةٌ حَمْراءُ**

بِسَبَبِ تَدَخُّلِهِ الخَشِنِ، تَلَقّى اللّاعِبُ بِطاقَةً حَمْراءَ وَطُرِدَ مِنَ المُباراةِ.

Due to his rough tackle, the player received a red card and was expelled from the match.

yellow card — **بِطاقَةٌ صَفْراءُ**

نَظَرًا لِالْتِحامِهِ غَيْرِ القانونِيِّ، أَظْهَرَ الحَكَمُ لِلْمُدافِعِ بِطاقَةً صَفْراءَ.

Due to his illegal clash, the referee showed the defender a yellow card.

بُطولَةٌ
tournament

فازَ فَريقُ بَرْشِلونَةْ بِالْبُطولَةِ الْأوروبِّيَّةِ لِكُرَةِ القَدَمِ بَعْدَ مُباراةٍ مُثيرَةٍ.

Barcelona team won the European soccer tournament after an exciting match.

تَدَرَّبَ
to train • تَدَرُّبٌ

يَتَدَرَّبُ اللّاعِبونَ بِجِدٍّ لِتَحْسينِ مَهاراتِهِمْ قَبْلَ المُباراةِ المُقْبِلَةِ.

The players are training hard to improve their skills before the upcoming match.

تَدْريبٌ
training

تَمَّ تَأْجيلُ جَلْسَةِ التَّدْريبِ اليَوْمَ بِسَبَبِ الأَحْوالِ الجَوِّيَّةِ السَّيِّئَةِ.

Today's training session was postponed due to bad weather.

تَسْديدَةٌ
shot

خِلالَ الشَّوْطِ الثّاني، أَطْلَقَ اللّاعِبُ تَسْديدَةً قَوِيَّةً جِدًّا، أَذْهَلَتِ الحارِسَ وَاسْتَقَرَّتْ في الشِّباكِ، مُحْرِزًا بِذَلِكَ الهَدَفَ الثّاني لِفَريقِهِ.

During the second half, the player launched a powerful shot that astonished the goalkeeper and ended up in the net, scoring his team's second goal.

تَسَلُّلٌ
offside

رَغْمَ احْتِجاجاتِ اللّاعِبينَ، أَكَّدَ الحَكَمُ أَنَّ الهَدَفَ تَمَّ في وَضْعِ تَسَلُّلٍ.

Despite the players' protests, the referee confirmed that the goal was offside.

تَشْكيلٌ
formation

أَعْلَنَ المُدَرِّبُ عَنْ تَشْكيلِ الفَريقِ قَبْلَ بِدايَةِ المُباراةِ.

The coach announced the team's formation before the start of the match.

تَصَدٍّ لِهَدَفٍ
save (for goalkeeper)

أَظْهَرَتْ حارِسَةُ المَرْمى مَهارَةً رائِعَةً في تَصَدّيها لِلْهَدَفِ.

The goalkeeper showed great skill in her save.

You might come across different terms for the same concept in various media outlets. For instance, تَصَدٍّ لِهَدَفٍ is often also called إِنْقاذُ هَدَفٍ.

tie, draw **تَعادُلٌ**

إِنْتَهَتِ المُباراةُ بِتَعادُلٍ سَلْبِيٍّ بَيْنَ الفَريقَيْنِ.

The match ended in a goalless draw between the two teams.

VAR (video assistant referee) **تِقْنِيَّةُ الفيدْيو**

تَمَّ اسْتِخْدامُ تِقْنِيَّةِ الفيدْيو لِتَحْديدِ صِحَّةِ الهَدَفِ.

Video Assistant Referee technology was used to determine the validity of the goal.

GLT (goal-line technology) **تِقْنِيَّةُ خَطِّ المَرْمى**

أَكَّدَتْ تِقْنِيَّةُ خَطِّ المَرْمى أَنَّ الكُرَةَ كانَتْ قَدِ اجْتازَتِ الخَطَّ بِالْكامِلِ.

Goal-line technology confirmed that the ball had fully crossed the line.

tactic **تَكْتيكٌ**

التَّكْتيكُ الَّذي اتَّبَعَهُ المُدَرِّبُ كانَ مِفْتاحًا لِلْفَوْزِ في المُباراةِ.

The tactic adopted by the coach was key to winning the match.

positioning **تَمَرْكُزٌ**

كانَ تَمَرْكُزُ اللاعِبينَ في المَلْعَبِ مِثالِيًّا، مِمّا سَمَحَ لِلْفَريقِ بِالفَوْزِ.

The players' positioning on the field was perfect, allowing the team to win.

pass **تَمْريرَةٌ**

قامَ اللّاعِبُ بِتَمْريرَةٍ طَويلَةٍ نَحْوَ الجَناحِ الأَيْمَنِ.

The player made a long pass towards the right wing.

حارِسُ مَرْمًى • حُرّاسٌ **goalkeeper, goalie**

أَظْهَرَ حارِسُ المَرْمى مَهاراتٍ رائِعَةً في صَدِّ الكُراتِ الخَطِرَةِ.

The goalkeeper showed excellent skills in blocking dangerous balls.

حامِلُ الرّايَةِ **assistant referee; linesman**

أَشارَ حامِلُ الرّايَةِ إِلى أَنَّ الكُرَةَ خَرَجَتْ عَنِ الخَطِّ.

The assistant referee signaled that the ball had gone out of line.

حامِيَ السّاقِ • حُماةٌ **shin guards**

يَرْتَدي جَميعُ اللّاعِبينَ حامِيَ السّاقِ لِلْحِمايَةِ خِلالَ المُباراةِ.

All players wear shin guards for protection during the match.

حِذاءٌ • أَحْذِيَةٌ **cleats, boots**

اِشْتَرى اللّاعِبُ حِذاءَ كُرَةِ قَدَمٍ جَديدٍ لِيُحَسِّنَ مِنْ أَدائِهِ.

The player bought new soccer cleats to improve his performance.

In Arabic, the word حِذاءٌ is grammatically singular but actually refers to a pair of shoes. For multiple pairs or shoes in general, the plural form أَحْذِيَةٌ is used. It's worth noting that this term is a general word for 'shoes' and is not specifically used for soccer cleats.

حَرَسَ مَرْمًى • حِراسَةٌ **to guard the goal**

حَرَسَ الحارِسُ المَرْمى بِكُلِّ تَرْكيزٍ لِمَنْعِ الفَريقِ المُنافِسِ مِنَ التَّسْجيلِ.

The goalkeeper guarded the goal with full concentration to prevent the opposing team from scoring.

حَكَمُ مُباراةٍ • حُكّامٌ **referee**

كانَ الحَكَمُ صارِمًا وَعادِلًا في قَراراتِهِ خِلالَ المُباراةِ.

The referee was firm and fair in his decisions during the match.

حَلْقُ المَرْمى • حُلوقٌ / أَحْلاقٌ **goal mouth**

حاوَلَ اللّاعِبُ التَّسْجيلَ، لَكِنَّ الكُرَةَ مَرَّتْ فَوْقَ حَلْقِ المَرْمى.

The player tried to score, but the ball went over the goal mouth.

خَسارَةٌ • خَسائِرُ **loss**

تَلَقّى الفَريقُ خَسارَةً قاسِيَةً في المُباراةِ الأَخيرَةِ.

The team suffered a crushing loss in the last match.

خَطُّ التَّماسِّ • خُطوطٌ **touchline, sideline**

اِسْتَلَمَ اللّاعِبُ الكُرَةَ قُرْبَ خَطِّ التَّماسِّ لِيُعيدَها إلى اللَّعِبِ.

The player received the ball near the touchline to put it back into play.

خَطُّ دِفاعٍ **back line**

كانَ خَطُّ دِفاعِ الفَريقِ غَيْرَ قابِلٍ لِلاِخْتِراقِ طَوالَ المُباراةِ.

The team's back line was unpenetrable throughout the match.

خَطُّ هُجومٍ **front line**

قَرَّرَ المُدَرِّبُ إِجْراءَ بَعْضِ التَّغْييراتِ عَلى خَطِّ الهُجومِ في الفَريقِ لِزِيادَةِ القُوَّةِ الهُجومِيَّةِ.

The coach decided to make some changes to the team's front line to increase attacking potency.

خَطُّ وَسَطٍ **halfway line**

خِلالَ المُباراةِ، اِعْتَمَدَ نَجاحُ الْفَريقِ بِشَكْلٍ كَبيرٍ عَلى أَداءِ لاعِبِ خَطِّ الوَسَطِ الماهِرِ.

During the match, the team's success relied heavily on the performance of their skilled halfway line player.

خَطَأٌ • أَخْطاءٌ **foul**

أَعْلَنَ الحَكَمُ عَنْ خَطَأٍ ضِدَّ الفَريقِ المُضيفِ، مِمّا أَثارَ اسْتِياءَ الجَماهيرِ.

The referee called a foul against the home team, much to the fans' displeasure.

خَطَأٌ is a term often used in sports, and it's also commonly referred to as فاوِلْ (taken from English). While مُخالَفَة is another synonym, you'll hear خَطَأٌ much more frequently.

دائِرَةُ الوَسَطِ • دَوائِرُ **center circle**

بَدَأَتِ المُباراةُ بِرَكْلَةٍ قَوِيَّةٍ مِنْ دائِرَةِ الوَسَطِ.

The match started with a strong kick from the center circle.

دِفاعٌ **defense**

تَمَيَّزَ الفَريقُ بِدِفاعِهِ القَوِيِّ وَالمُتَناسِقِ.

The team was distinguished by its strong and coordinated defense.

دِفاعٌ مُحْكَمٌ **solid defense**

بِفَضْلِ دِفاعِهِمِ المُحْكَمِ، تَمَكَّنوا مِنَ الحِفاظِ عَلى شِباكِهِمْ نَظيفَةً.

Thanks to their solid defense, they were able to keep their goal clean.

دِفاعِيٌّ **defensive**

اِعْتَمَدَ الفَريقُ اسْتِراتيجِيَّةً دِفاعِيَّةً لِمَنْعِ الفَريقِ الخَصْمِ مِنَ التَّسْجيلِ.

The team adopted a defensive strategy to prevent the opposing team from scoring.

دَوْرِيٌّ **league**

حَقَّقَ فَريقُ النّادي الأَهْلي الفَوْزَ في الدَّوْرِيِّ السُّعودِيِّ هَذا العامَ.

Al-Ahli Club team achieved victory in the Saudi League this year.

دَوْرِيُّ أَبْطالِ أوروبّا **UEFA Champions League**

تَأَهَّلَ فَريقُ مانْشِسْتَرْ يونايْتِدْ لِلْمَرْحَلَةِ القادِمَةِ مِنْ دَوْرِيِّ أَبْطالِ أوروبّا.

Manchester United team qualified for the next stage of the UEFA Champions League.

رَأْسُ حَرْبَةٍ • رُؤوسٌ **striker**

سَجَّلَ رَأْسُ الحَرْبَةِ هَدَفًا رائِعًا في الدَّقائِقِ الأَخيرَةِ مِنَ المُباراةِ.

The striker scored a fantastic goal in the final minutes of the match.

to dribble • مُراوَغةٌ **راوَغَ بِالْكُرَةِ**

راوَغَتِ اللّاعِبَةُ بِالْكُرَةِ وَتَفَوَّقَتْ عَلى المُدافِعاتِ بِبَراعَةٍ.

The player dribbled the ball and skillfully outperformed the defenders.

corner flag **رايَةٌ رُكْنِيَّةٌ**

أَرْسَلَ اللّاعِبُ الكُرَةَ عالِيًا مِنْ عِنْدِ الرّايَةِ الرُّكْنِيَّةِ، مُحاوِلًا تَسْجيلَ هَدَفٍ.

The player sent the ball high from the corner flag, trying to score a goal.

man of the match • رِجالٌ **رَجُلُ المُباراةِ**

تَمَّ اخْتيارُ أَحْمَدَ كَرَجُلِ المُباراةِ بِفَضْلِ أَدائِهِ المُتَميِّزِ.

Ahmed was chosen as the man of the match thanks to his outstanding performance.

to kick • رَكْلٌ **رَكَلَ**

رَكَلَ اللّاعِبُ الكُرَةَ بِقُوَّةٍ نَحْوَ الشِّباكِ.

The player kicked the ball hard towards the net.

kick **رَكْلَةٌ**

حَصَلَ الفَريقُ عَلى رَكْلَةٍ حُرَّةٍ بَعْدَ تَدَخُّلٍ خَشِنٍ مِنَ الخَصْمِ.

The team got a free kick after a rough intervention from the opponent.

The noun رَكْلَةٌ (kick) is interchangeable with ضَرْبَةٌ (strike, hit) above and in the following expressions.

penalty shootout **رَكَلاتُ التَّرْجيحِ**

في نِهايَةٍ مُثيرَةٍ، حُسِمَتِ المُباراةُ بِرَكَلاتِ التَّرْجيحِ.

In a nail-biting finish, the soccer match was decided by a penalty shootout.

رَكَلاتُ التَّرْجيحِ can also be translated as رَكْلَةُ جَزاءٍ تَرْجيحيَّةٌ.

kick-off رَكْلَةُ البِدايَةِ

أَطْلَقَ الحَكَمُ صافِرَتَهُ، مُعْلِنًا عَنْ بِدايَةِ المُباراةِ بِرَكْلَةِ البِدايَةِ.

The referee blew his whistle, signaling the start of the match with the kickoff.

penalty kick رَكْلَةُ جَزاءٍ

أَحْرَزَ اللاعِبُ هَدَفًا مِنْ رَكْلَةِ جَزاءٍ في الدَّقيقَةِ الأَخيرَةِ مِنَ الوَقْتِ الإضافِيِّ.

The player scored a goal from a penalty kick in the final minute of extra time.

free kick رَكْلَةٌ حُرَّةٌ

سَجَّلَ اللاعِبُ هَدَفًا رائِعًا مِنْ رَكْلَةٍ حُرَّةٍ.

The player scored a fantastic goal from a direct kick.

direct free kick رَكْلَةٌ حُرَّةٌ مُباشِرَةٌ

مَنَحَ الحَكَمُ الفَريقَ الخَصْمَ رَكْلَةً حُرَّةً مُباشِرَةً بَعْدَ تَعَرُّضِهِ لِخَطَأٍ قَريبٍ مِنْ مِنْطَقَةِ الجَزاءِ.

The referee awarded a direct free kick to the opposing team after a foul near the penalty box.

corner kick رَكْلَةٌ رُكْنِيَّةٌ

أَدَّى اللاعِبُ رَكْلَةً رُكْنِيَّةً ناجِحَةً أَدَّتْ إِلى هَدَفٍ.

The player executed a successful corner kick leading to a goal.

رَكْلَةٌ (kick) is interchangeable with ضَرْبَةٌ (hit, strike) in soccer terminology, and you might encounter either term used to describe various types of kicks or strikes. For instance, رَكْلَةُ جَزاءٍ (penalty kick) can also be expressed as ضَرْبَةُ جَزاءٍ. Similarly, ضَرْبَةُ مَرْمًى (goal kick; p. 166) can be replaced with رَكْلَةُ مَرْمًى.

throw-in رَمْيَةُ تَماسٍّ

أُحْتُسِبَتْ رَمْيَةُ التَّماسِّ لِفَريقِ الخَصْمِ بَعْدَما لَمَسَتِ الكُرَةُ يَدَ أَحَدِ لاعِبي الفَريقِ المُنافِس.

A throw-in was awarded to the opposing team after one of the opposing players touched the ball with their hand.

زِيٌّ • أَزْياءٌ **uniform, kit**

أظْهَرَ الفَريقُ زِيَّهُم الجَديدَ لِلْمَوْسِمِ القادِمِ.

The team showcased their new uniform for the upcoming season.

سَجَّلَ هَدَفًا • تَسْجيلٌ **to score a goal**

سَجَّلَتِ اللّاعِبَةُ هَدَفًا مُثيرًا لِلاهْتِمامِ في الدَّقائِقِ الأَخيرَةِ مِنَ المُباراةِ.

The player scored an exciting goal in the last minutes of the match.

سَدَّدَ • تَسْديدٌ **to shoot**

سَدَّدَ لاعِبُ الوَسَطِ الكُرَةَ بِقُوَّةٍ نَحْوَ المَرْمى، لَكِنَّ الحارِسَ شَتَّتَها بِبَراعَةٍ.

The midfielder shot the ball powerfully towards the goal, but the goalkeeper skillfully deflected it.

شِباكٌ نَظيفَةٌ **clean sheet**

حافَظَ الحارِسُ عَلى شِباكِهِ نَظيفَةً خِلالَ المُباراةِ بِأَكْمَلِها، مانِعًا أَيَّ تَسْجيلٍ مِنَ الخَصْمِ.

The goalkeeper kept a clean sheet throughout the match, preventing any scoring from the opponent.

صافِرَةٌ **whistle**

عِنْدَما سَمِعَ اللّاعِبونَ صافِرَةَ الحَكَمِ، اِنْتَهَتِ المُباراةُ وَبَدَأَ الاِحْتِفالُ.

When the players heard the referee's whistle, the match ended and the celebration began.

ضَرْبَةٌ **kick**

اِسْتَعَدَّ اللّاعِبُ لِتَوْجيهِ ضَرْبَةِ الجَزاءِ، وَحَبَسَ الحُضورُ في الاِسْتادِ أَنْفاسَهُمْ.

The player prepared to take the penalty kick, and everyone in the stadium was holding their breath.

ضَرْبَةُ رَأْسٍ **header**

نَفَّذَ اللّاعِبُ ضَرْبَةَ رَأْسٍ مِثالِيَّةً، أَرْسَلَتِ الكُرَةَ مُباشَرَةً إِلى الشِّباكِ.

The player executed a perfect header, sending the ball directly into the net.

In the previous expression, ضَرْبَةٌ is not interchangeable with رَكْلَةٌ because it refers to a strike with the head rather than a kick with the foot.

goal kick ضَرْبَةٌ مَرْمًى

أعادَ حارِسُ المَرْمى الكُرَةَ إلى اللَّعِبِ بضَرْبَةِ مَرْمًى بَعْدَ تَوَقُّفِ اللَّعِبِ.

The goalkeeper returned the ball into play with a goal kick after a stoppage in play.

crossbar عارِضَةٌ

اِرْتَدَّتِ الكُرَةُ عَنِ العارِضَةِ بَعْدَ تَسْديدَةٍ قَوِيَّةٍ مِنَ اللّاعِبِ.

The ball rebounded off the crossbar after a powerful shot by the player.

cross عَرْضِيَّةٌ

سَدَّدَ اللّاعِبُ رَكْلَةً عَرْضِيَّةً رائِعَةً، تَمَكَّنَ مِنْ خِلالِها زَميلُهُ مِنْ تَسْجيلِ الهَدَفِ.

The player delivered an excellent cross, through which his teammate managed to score a goal.

to win فازَ • فَوْزٌ

فازَ فَريقُ بَرْشلونَةْ بِالْمُباراةِ بِثَلاثَةِ أَهْدافٍ مُقابِلَ هَدَفٍ واحِدٍ.

Barcelona team won the match by three goals to one.

team فَريقٌ • فِرَقٌ

واجَهَ اليوفِنْتوسْ فَريقَ روما في المُباراةِ النِّهائِيَّةِ لِلدَّوْرِيِّ الإيطالِيِّ.

Juventus faced Roma in the final match of the Italian league.

olympic team فَريقٌ أولِمْبِيٌّ • فِرَقٌ

تَمَّ اخْتيارُ مُحَمَّد لِلانْضِمامِ إلى الفَريقِ الأولِمْبِيِّ السُّعودِيِّ لِكُرَةِ القَدَمِ.

Mohamed was selected to join the Saudi Olympic soccer team.

youth team فَريقُ الشَّبابِ

قادَ فَريقُ الشَّبابِ الفَوْزَ في بُطولَةِ كَأْسِ الشَّبابِ الوَطَنِيَّةِ.

The youth team led the victory in the National Youth Cup Championship.

junior team **فَريقُ النّاشِئينَ**

تَأَهَّلَ فَريقُ النّاشِئينَ لِلدَّوْرِ الثّاني بَعْدَ فَوْزِهِمِ الكَبيرِ في المُباراةِ الأولى.

The junior team advanced to the second round after their big win in the first match.

away team **فَريقٌ ضَيْفٌ**

اِسْتَضافَ فَريقُ بَرْشِلونَةْ فَريقَ الرِّيالْ مَدْريدْ كَفَريقٍ ضَيْفٍ في كامْبْ نو.

Barcelona hosted Real Madrid as an away team at Camp Nou.

home team **فَريقٌ مُضيفٌ**

فازَ الفَريقُ المُضيفُ مانْشِسْتَرْ يونايْتِدْ عَلى الفَريقِ الضَّيْفِ تشيلْسي بِنَتيجَةِ 2-1.

The home team, Manchester United, beat the away team, Chelsea, with a score of 2-1.

captain **قائِدُ الفَريقِ** • قادَةٌ

كانَ قائِدُ الفَريقِ، لِيونيلْ ميسّي، اللّاعِبَ الأَكْثَرَ تَأْثيرًا في المُباراةِ.

The captain, Lionel Messi, was the most influential player in the match.

goalpost **قائِمٌ** • قَوائِمُ

أَصابَتِ الكُرَةُ الْقائِمَ الْأَيْمَنَ لِلْمَرمى بَعْدَ تَسْديدَةٍ قَوِيَّةٍ مِنَ اللّاعِبَةِ.

The ball hit the right goalpost after a powerful shot from the player.

FIFA World Cup **كَأْسُ العالَمِ لِكُرَةِ القَدَمِ** • كُؤوسٌ

بَدَأَتِ التَّحْضيراتُ لِكَأْسِ العالَمِ لِكُرَةِ القَدَمِ 2026، وَالجَماهيرُ في تَرَقُّبٍ شَديدٍ.

Preparations for the 2026 FIFA World Cup have begun, and fans are eagerly anticipating.

captain **كابْتِنْ**

كابْتِنُ الفَريقِ، كِريسْتيانو رونالْدو، قادَ فَريقَهُ إِلى الفَوْزِ.

The team captain, Cristiano Ronaldo, led his team to victory.

The terms قائِدُ الفَريقِ (literally, 'team leader') and كابْتِنْ (from the English 'captain') are interchangeable. You might encounter either of these terms in sports contexts, and they carry the same meaning, designating the person who leads and represents the team.

soccer, football كُرَةُ القَدَمِ

تُعْتَبَرُ كُرَةُ القَدَمِ أَكْثَرَ الرِّياضاتِ شَعْبِيَّةً حَوْلَ العالَمِ.

Soccer is considered the most popular sport around the world.

soccer ball, football كُرَةُ قَدَمٍ

إِسْتَلَمَ اللّاعِبُ كُرَةَ القَدَمِ وَرَكَضَ نَحْوَ الهَدَفِ.

The player received the soccer ball and ran towards the goal.

Of course, in context, it generally suffices to simply say كُرَةٌ (ball).

player لاعِبٌ

وَقَّعَ اللّاعِبُ الشّابُّ عَقْدًا جَديدًا مَعَ ناديه.

The young player signed a new contract with his club.

midfielder لاعِبُ وَسَطٍ

كانَ لاعِبُ الوَسَطِ مَسْؤولًا عَنْ تَوْزيعِ الكُراتِ وَتَنْظيمِ الهَجَماتِ.

The midfielder was responsible for distributing the balls and organizing the attacks.

to play لَعِبَ • لَعِبٌ

لَعِبَ فَريقُ الأَهلي مُباراةً قَوِيَّةً ضِدَّ فَريقِ الزَّمالِكْ.

Al Ahli played a strong match against Al Zamalek.

fair play لَعِبٌ نَظيفٌ

شَهِدَتِ المُباراةُ لَعِبًا نَظيفًا مِنَ الفَريقَيْنِ، مِمّا أَدّى إِلى مُباراةٍ مُمْتِعَةٍ.

The match saw fair play from both teams, leading to an enjoyable match.

friendly match **مُباراةٌ وِدِّيَّةٌ**

اِسْتَضافَ نادي الأَرْسنالْ فَريقَ مانْشِسْتَرْ سيتي في مُباراةٍ وِدِّيَّةٍ اسْتِعْدادًا لِلْمَوْسِمِ الجَديدِ.

Arsenal hosted Manchester City in a friendly match in preparation for the new season.

defender **مُدافِعٌ**

أَظْهَرَ المُدافِعُ مَهاراتِهِ الدِّفاعِيَّةَ المُمْتازَةَ طَوالَ المُباراةِ.

The defender showed his excellent defensive skills throughout the match.

coach **مُدَرِّبٌ**

قَرَّرَ المُدَرِّبُ إِجْراءَ تَغْييراتٍ اسْتِراتيجِيَّةٍ في الشَّوْطِ الثّاني.

The coach decided to make strategic changes in the second half.

marking **مُراقَبَةُ لاعِبٍ**

كانَتْ مُراقَبَةُ اللّاعِبِ مِنْ قِبَلِ الدِّفاعِ أَمْرًا حاسِمًا في مَنْعِ الأَهْدافِ.

The player marking by the defense was crucial in preventing goals.

to pass • تَمْريرٌ **مَرَّرَ**

مَرَّرَتِ اللّاعِبَةُ الكُرَةَ إِلى زَميلَتِها في الفَريقِ، الَّتي سَجَّلَتِ الهَدَفَ.

The player passed the ball to her teammate, who scored the goal.

goal • مَرامٍ **مَرْمًى**

اِسْتَهْدَفَ اللّاعِبُ المَرْمى بِتَسْديدَةٍ قَوِيَّةٍ، لَكِنَّها ارْتَدَّتْ مِنَ القائِمِ.

The player targeted the goal with a powerful shot, but it bounced off the post.

مَرْمًى (goal) is the physical structure, consisting of the metal posts and the net. Compare this to هَدَفٌ (goal), which is the instance of scoring.

assistant referee; linesman **مُساعِدُ حَكَمٍ**

أَشارَ مُساعِدُ الحَكَمِ إِلى خَطِّ الجانِبِ لِتَحْديدِ التَّسَلُّلِ.

The assistant referee pointed to the sideline to determine the offside.

supporter, fan **مُشَجِّعٌ**

تَواجَدَ مُشَجِّعو نادي تشيلْسي في المُدَرَّجاتِ لِتَشْجيعِ فَريقِهِمْ.

Chelsea's supporters were in the stands to cheer on their team.

hooligan **مُشَجِّعٌ مُتَعَصِّبٌ**

تَمَّ القَبْضُ عَلى المُشَجِّعِ المُتَعَصِّبِ بَعْدَ أَنْ أَثارَ أَعْمالَ شَغَبٍ في المُباراةِ.

The hooligan was arrested after he instigated riots in the match.

IMS (International Match Standard) *pl.* **مَعاييرُ المُبارَياتِ الدَّوْلِيَّةِ**

أُقيمَتِ المُباراةُ وَفْقًا لِمَعاييرِ المُبارَياتِ الدَّوْلِيَّةِ المُعْتَمَدَةِ مِنَ الفيفا.

The match was held according to the IMS (International Match Standard) approved by FIFA.

substitutes' bench • مَقاعِدُ **مَقْعَدُ البُدَلاءِ**

اِسْتَبْدَلَ المُدَرِّبُ اللّاعِبَ المُصابَ بِلاعِبٍ آخَرَ مِنْ مَقْعَدِ البُدَلاءِ.

The coach replaced the injured player with another from the substitutes' bench.

field, pitch • مَلاعِبُ **مَلْعَبٌ**

لَعِبَ الفَريقانِ المُباراةَ عَلى مَلْعَبِ ويمْبِلي الشَّهيرِ.

The two teams played the match on the famous Wembley pitch.

penalty area • مَناطِقُ **مِنْطَقَةُ جَزاءٍ**

تَعَرَّضَ الـمُهاجِمُ لِمُخالَفَةٍ داخِلَ مِنطَقَةِ الجَزاءِ، مِمّا أَدّى إِلى رَكْلَةِ جَزاءٍ.

The striker was fouled inside the penalty area, leading to a penalty kick.

forward **مُهاجِمٌ**

سَجَّلَ المُهاجِمُ هَدَفًا رائِعًا مِنْ مُنْتَصَفِ المَلْعَبِ.

The forward scored a fantastic goal from the middle of the pitch.

half time | **نِصْفُ الوَقْتِ** • أَنْصاف

فِي نِصْفِ الوَقْتِ، كانَتِ النَّتيجَةُ تَعادُلًا بَيْنَ الفَريقَيْنِ.

At half time, the score was a draw between the two teams.

World Cup finals | **نِهائِيّاتُ كَأْسِ العالَمِ** pl.

تَأَهَّلَتِ الأَرْجَنْتينُ وَفَرَنْسا لِنِهائِيّاتِ كَأْسِ العالَمِ.

Argentina and France qualified for the World Cup finals.

full time | **نِهايَةُ المُباراةِ**

عِنْدَ نِهايَةِ المُباراةِ، فازَ فَريقُ ليفِرْبول بِالْمُباراةِ بِثَلاثَةِ أَهْدافٍ مُقابِلَ هَدَفٍ.

At full time, Liverpool team won the match by three goals to one.

hat-trick | **هاتْريكْ**

سَجَّلَ المُهاجِمُ هاتْريكْ خِلالَ الشَّوْطِ الثّاني مِنَ المُباراةِ.

The striker scored a hat-trick during the second half of the match.

offense | **هُجومٌ**

شَنَّ الفَريقُ هُجومًا قَوِيًّا فِي الدَّقائِقِ الأَخيرَةِ مِنَ المُباراةِ.

The team launched a strong offense in the last minutes of the match.

cohesive offense | **هُجومٌ مُتَماسِكٌ**

قامَ الفَريقُ بِتَنْظيمِ هُجومٍ مُتَماسِكٍ ضِدَّ الخَصْمِ.

The team organized a cohesive offense against the opponent.

offensive | **هُجومِيٌّ**

اِعْتَمَدَ الفَريقُ الأَحْمَرُ اسْتِراتيجِيَّةً هُجومِيَّةً خِلالَ المُباراةِ.

The red team adopted an offensive strategy during the match.

هَدَفٌ • أَهْدافٌ **goal**

سَجَّلَ الفريقُ الأَزْرَقُ هَدَفَ التَّعادُلِ في الدَّقيقَةِ الأَخيرَة.

The blue team scored the equalizing goal in the last minute.

هَدَفٌ بِالْخَطَأ في مَرْمى الفريقِ نَفْسِهِ **own goal**

أَحْرَزَ لاعِبُ الوَسَطِ هَدَفًا بِالْخَطَأ في مَرْمى فَريقِهِ.

The midfielder scored an own goal.

وَقْتٌ إِضافِيٌّ • أَوْقاتٌ **extra time**

بِسَبَبِ الإِصاباتِ، أَضافَ الحَكَمُ خَمْسَ دَقائِقَ مِنَ الوَقْتِ الإِضافِيِّ.

Due to injuries, the referee added five minutes of extra time.

وَقْتٌ مُحْتَسَبٌ بَدَلَ ضائِعٍ **added time, injury time, stoppage time**

بَعْدَ وَقْتٍ طَويلٍ مُحْتَسَبٍ بَدَلَ ضائِعٍ، تَمَكَّنَ الفريقُ الضَّيْفُ مِنْ تَسْجيلِ هَدَفِ الفَوْزِ.

After a long injury time, the away team managed to score the winning goal.

6.1.1.1 Mini-Articles

Track **54**

في بُطولَةِ الدَّوْرِيِّ الأوروبِّيِّ لِكُرَةِ القَدَمِ، نَجَحَ فَريقُ "الأَبْطالِ" في الفَوْزِ عَلى فَريقِ "النُّجومِ". حَقَّقَ اللّاعِبُ أَحْمَد عَبْد العَزيز "هاتْريك"، وَسَجَّلَ هَدَفًا رابِعًا مُثيرًا بِضَرْبَةِ رَأْسٍ، مِمّا جَعَلَهُ رَجُلَ المُباراة. رَغْمَ تَلَقّيهِ بِطاقَةً صَفْراءَ في الشَّوْطِ الثّاني، ظَلَّ خَطُّ دِفاعِهِمْ مُحْكَمًا وَحافَظوا عَلى شِباكٍ نَظيفَةٍ حَتّى نِهايَةِ المُباراة.

In the European Football League Championship, the team Al-Abtal (the Heroes) succeeded in defeating the team Al-Nujoom (the Stars). Player Ahmed Abdel Aziz achieved a "hat-trick" and scored a thrilling fourth goal with a header, making him the man of the match. Despite receiving a yellow card in the second half, their solid defense remained impenetrable, keeping a clean sheet until the end of the game.

بَعْدَ مُرورِ أَسابيعَ مِنَ التَّدْريبِ المُكَثَّفِ وَالتَّكْتيكِيِّ، تَأَهَّلَ فَريقُ "النُّسورِ السَّوْداءِ" لِلنِّهائِيّاتِ في كَأْسِ العالَمِ لِكُرَةِ القَدَمِ. في المُباراةِ القادِمَةِ ضِدَّ "النُّجومِ البرونْزِيَّةِ"، يُتَوَقَّعُ أَنْ يَقودَ قائِدُ الفَريقِ مُحَمَّد الشَّرْقاوي، الَّذي اشْتُهِرَ بِتَمْريراتِهِ الدَّقيقَةِ وَتَمَرْكُزِهِ الإِسْتراتيجِيِّ، فَريقَهُ نَحْوَ النَّصْرِ.

After weeks of intensive and tactical training, the team Al-Nusoor Al-Sawdaa (Black Eagles) qualified for the finals in the FIFA World Cup. In the upcoming match against Al-Nujoom Al-Bronziyya (Bronze Stars), the team captain, Mohamed Al-Sharqawi, known for his precise passes and strategic positioning, is expected to lead his team to victory.

يَشْهَدُ دَوْرِيُّ الشَّبابِ لِكُرَةِ القَدَمِ هَذا العامَ مُنافَسَةً شَديدَةً بَيْنَ فَريقَيْ "العَمالِقَةِ الصِّغارِ" وَ "الصُّقورِ الجَديدَةِ". في المُباراةِ الأَخيرَةِ، أَظْهَرَ اللاّعِبُ يوسُف عَلي تِقْنِيَّةً مُذْهِلَةً لِلرَّكْلَةِ الحُرَّةِ المُباشِرَةِ أَسْفَرَتْ عَنْ هَدَفٍ، بَيْنَما أَظْهَرَ حارِسُ مَرْمى العَمالِقَةِ، حُسَيْن رَبيع، مَهاراتٍ رائِعَةً في التَّصَدّي لِلْهَدَفِ، وَأَنْقَذَ فَريقَهُ مِنَ الخَسارَةِ بِتَصَدّيه لِرَكْلَةِ جَزاءٍ في الوَقْتِ المُحْتَسَبِ بَدَلَ ضائِعٍ.

This year's youth football league is witnessing fierce competition between the teams Al-Amaliqah Al-Sighar (Young Giants) and Al-Suquor Al-Jadida (New Falcons). In the last match, player Youssef Ali showcased an amazing direct free-kick technique resulting in a goal, while the goalkeeper of Al-Amaliqah Al-Sighar, Hussein Rabie, demonstrated fantastic skills in saving a penalty kick in injury time, saving his team from a loss.

في المُباراةِ الحاسِمَةِ لِلدَّوْرِيِّ الدَّوْلِيِّ، نَجَحَ فَريقُ "الرِّياحِ الصّاعِقَةِ" في تَحْقيقِ الفَوْزِ عَلى "الأَبْطالِ الحَديدِيّينَ". تَمَكَّنَ اللاّعِبُ الواعِدُ عَلي حَسَن مِنْ تَسْجيلِ هَدَفَيْنِ وَتَقْديمِ تَمْريرَةٍ حاسِمَةٍ، مِمّا جَعَلَهُ بِلا شَكٍّ رَجُلَ المُباراةِ. بِفَضْلِ حِراسَةِ المَرْمى الرّائِعَةِ لِأَحْمَد رَجَب، تَمَكَّنَ الفَريقُ مِنَ الحِفاظِ عَلى شِباكٍ نَظيفَةٍ حَتّى نِهايَةِ اللِّقاءِ، رَغْمَ الضَّغْطِ الكَبيرِ مِنَ الفَريقِ المُنافِسِ.

In the decisive match of the international league, the team Al-Riyah Al-Sa'iqah (Thundering Winds) managed to secure a victory against Al-Abtal Al-Hadidiyyin (Iron Champions). The promising player Ali Hassan scored two goals and provided a crucial assist, making him undoubtedly the man of the match. Thanks to the excellent goalkeeping of Ahmed Ragab, the team maintained a clean sheet until the end of the game despite significant pressure from the opposing team.

اِسْتَطاعَ فَريقُ "الأُسودِ المَلَكِيَّةِ" تَحْقيقَ الفَوْزِ في مُباراةِ نِصْفِ النِّهائِيِّ، وَبِالتّالي تَأَهَّلَ لِلْمُباراةِ النِّهائِيَّةِ في بُطولَةِ كَأْسِ العالَمِ. كانَ اللاّعِبُ النَّجْمُ مَحْمود سُلَيْمان، قائِدُ الفَريقِ، عُنْصُرًا حاسِمًا في الفَوْزِ. سَجَّلَ هَدَفًا رائِعًا بَعْدَ تَمْريرَةٍ مُذْهِلَةٍ مِنْ زَميلِهِ في الفَريقِ.

The team Al-Aswad Al-Malakiyya (Royal Blacks) achieved victory in the semi-final, thus qualifying for the final match in the World Cup tournament. Star player Mahmoud Suleiman, the team captain, played a vital role in the victory. He scored a brilliant goal after an amazing pass from his teammate.

فازَ فَريقُ "الأَمَلِ الشّابِّ" بِالْمُباراةِ الحاسِمَةِ في دَوْرِيِّ الأَبْطالِ لِفِرَقِ الشَّبابِ. كانَ اللاّعِبُ الشّابُّ عُمَر يوسُف البالِغُ مِنَ العُمْرِ سَبْعَةَ عَشَرَ عامًا، وَالَّذي يَلْعَبُ كَمُهاجِمٍ، بارِعًا في اخْتِراقِ خَطِّ دِفاعِ الخَصْمِ وَسَجَّلَ هَدَفًا بَعْدَ رَكْلَةٍ حُرَّةٍ مُباشِرَةٍ. في الوَقْتِ ذاتِهِ، أَظْهَرَ حارِسُ المَرْمى، طارِقُ عادِل، أَداءً اسْتِثْنائِيًّا، حَيْثُ تَمَكَّنَ مِنَ التَّصَدّي لِثَلاثَةِ أَهْدافٍ مُحَقَّقَةٍ وَحافَظَ عَلى شِباكِهِ نَظيفَةً.

The team Al-Amal Al-Shabbi (Young Hope) won the decisive match in the Champions League for youth teams. The young player Omar Youssef, who is seventeen years old and plays as a forward, showed remarkable skills in breaking through the opponent's defense and scored a goal from a direct free kick. At the same time, goalkeeper Tarek Adel delivered an exceptional performance, saving three clear goals and maintaining a clean sheet.

6.1.1.2 Informative Article: The Evolution of Soccer

Track **55**

تَطَوُّرُ كُرَةِ القَدَمِ: اِسْتِراتيجِيّاتٌ تَكْتيكِيَّةٌ وَتِقْنِيّاتٌ حَديثَةٌ

كُرَةُ القَدَمِ لَيْسَتْ مُجَرَّدَ لُعْبَةٍ تُلْعَبُ عَلى أَرْضِيَّةِ المَلْعَبِ، بَلْ هِيَ نَتيجَةٌ لِتَطَوُّرِ اسْتِراتيجِيّاتٍ تَكْتيكِيَّةٍ خِلالَ العُقودِ القَليلَةِ الماضِيَةِ. عِنْدَ النَّظَرِ إِلى اللُّعْبَةِ كَما كانَتْ في العَقْدِ الأَوَّلِ مِنَ القَرْنِ العِشْرينَ، سَنَجِدُ أَنَّ التَّكْتيكاتِ وَالأَدْوارَ قَدْ تَطَوَّرَتْ بِشَكْلٍ كَبيرٍ.

كانَ تَشْكيلُ الفِرَقِ في السّابِقِ عادَةً 2 - 3 - 5، وَهُوَ نِظامٌ كانَ يَعْتَمِدُ بِشَكْلٍ أَساسِيٍّ عَلى الهُجومِ بِخَمْسَةِ لاعِبينَ في خَطِّ الهُجومِ. وَلَكِنْ، مَعَ مُرورِ الوَقْتِ، بَدَأَتِ الفِرَقُ في تَبَنّي تَكْتيكاتٍ أَكْثَرَ تَعْقيدًا، كَنِظامِ 4 - 4 - 2 الَّذي يَعْتَمِدُ عَلى خَطِّ دِفاعٍ قَوِيٍّ وَخَطِّ وَسَطٍ يَسْتَطيعُ التَّحَوُّلَ بَيْنَ الدِّفاعِ وَالهُجومِ بِسَلاسَةٍ.

كَما تَغَيَّرَتْ أَدْوارُ اللّاعِبينَ بِشَكْلٍ كَبيرٍ. في الماضي، كانَ دَوْرُ حارِسِ المَرْمى يَقْتَصِرُ بِشَكْلٍ أَساسِيٍّ في مَنْعِ الكُرَةِ مِنْ دُخولِ المَرْمى. وَلَكِنِ الآنَ، أَصْبَحَ الحارِسُ جُزْءًا أَساسِيًّا مِنَ الفَريقِ، حَيْثُ يَبْدَأُ الهَجَماتِ وَيُشارِكُ في التَّمَرْكُزِ الدِّفاعِيِّ. كَذَلِكَ أَصْبَحَتِ الأَدْوارُ الهُجومِيَّةُ أَكْثَرَ تَعْقيدًا، مَعَ الاعْتِمادِ عَلى اللّاعِبينَ في خَلْقِ الفُرَصِ بِالْإِضافَةِ إِلى تَسْجيلِ الأَهْدافِ.

وَمِنَ الجَديرِ بِالذِّكْرِ أَنَّ التِّكْنولوجْيا أَثَّرَتْ أَيْضًا في تَطَوُّرِ التَّكْتيكاتِ في كُرَةِ القَدَمِ. تِقْنِيَّةُ الفيدْيو(VAR) ، وَتِقْنِيَّةُ خَطِّ المَرْمى هِيَ أَمْثِلَةٌ عَلى ذَلِكَ. لَقَدْ أَصْبَحَ ال VAR أَداةً مُهِمَّةً في تَحْديدِ القَراراتِ الصَّعْبَةِ كالتَّسَلُّلِ وَرَكَلاتِ الجَزاءِ، مِمّا يُؤَدّي إِلى تَغْييرِ كَيْفِيَّةِ تَنْظيمِ الفَريقِ وَتَكْتيكاتِهِ خِلالَ المُباراةِ. وَتِقْنِيَّةُ خَطِّ المَرْمى أَيْضًا أَثَّرَتْ عَلى اللُّعْبَةِ، فَهِيَ تُحَدِّدُ بِدِقَّةٍ مَتى تَكونُ الكُرَةُ قَدِ اجْتازَتْ خَطَّ المَرْمى بِالْكامِلِ، مِمّا يُساعِدُ الحَكَمَ عَلى اتِّخاذِ القَرارِ الصَّحيحِ في حالاتِ الأَهْدافِ المُثيرَةِ لِلْجَدَلِ.

بِالرَّغْمِ مِنَ التَّطَوُّراتِ في التَّكْتيكاتِ وَالأَدْوارِ، هُناكَ شَيْءٌ واحِدٌ في كُرَةِ القَدَمِ لَمْ يَتَغَيَّرْ، وَهُوَ الحُبُّ وَالشَّغَفُ الَّذي يُكِنُّهُ اللّاعِبونَ وَالمُشَجِّعونَ لِلُعْبَةِ. بِغَضِّ النَّظَرِ عَنِ التَّطَوُّراتِ الحَديثَةِ في اللُّعْبَةِ، تَبْقى كُرَةُ القَدَمِ في جَوْهَرِها لُعْبَةً تَعْتَمِدُ عَلى التَّنْسيقِ، القُوَّةِ، وَالإِبْداعِ. تِلْكَ هِيَ القِيَمُ الَّتي تَجْعَلُ كُرَةَ القَدَمِ تَجْرِبَةً مُشَوِّقَةً لا تُقاوَمُ، لَيْسَ فَقَطْ لِلّاعِبينَ، وَلَكِنْ أَيْضًا لِمَلايينِ المُشَجِّعينَ حَوْلَ العالَمِ.

Soccer is not just a game played on the field; it is the result of tactical evolution over the past few decades. When looking at the game as it was in the early 20th century, we find that tactics and roles have evolved significantly.

Previously, team formations were usually 2-3-5, a system heavily focused on attacking with five players positioned in the forward line. However, over time, teams began adopting more complex tactics, such as the 4-4-2 system, which emphasizes a strong defensive line and a midfield capable of smoothly transitioning between defense and attack.

The roles of players have also changed significantly. In the past, the goalkeeper's role was primarily limited to preventing the ball from entering the goal. But now, the goalkeeper has become an integral part of the team, initiating attacks, and participating in defensive positioning. Similarly, offensive roles have become more intricate, with players involved in creating opportunities in addition to scoring goals.

It's worth noting that technology has also impacted the development of soccer tactics. Video Assistant Referee (VAR) and goal-line technology are examples of this. VAR has become an important tool in determining challenging decisions such as offsides and penalty kicks, leading to changes in how teams organize and implement tactics during the match. Goal-line technology, too, has influenced the game by accurately determining when the ball has completely crossed the goal line, helping the referee make the correct decisions in contentious goal situations.

Despite the developments in tactics and roles, there is one thing in soccer that has not changed, and that is the love and passion players and fans have for the game. Regardless of modern advancements in the sport, soccer remains at its core a game built on coordination, strength, and creativity. These are the values that make soccer an irresistible and thrilling experience, not only for players but also for millions of fans around the world.

6.1.1.3 Article: A Rising Star

Track **56**

النَّجْمُ الصّاعِدُ: مِنْ فَريقِ الشَّبابِ إِلى السّاحَةِ العالَمِيَّةِ

يَبْدو أَنَّ اللّاعِبَ المِصْرِيَّ الشّابَّ، مُحَمَّد أَحْمَد، يَتَجاوَزُ جَميعَ التَّوَقُّعاتِ في عالَمِ كُرَةِ القَدَمِ. بَدَأَ مُحَمَّد، الَّذي يَبْلُغُ مِنَ العُمْرِ 19 عامًا الآنَ، مَسيرَتَهُ الكُرَوِيَّةَ في فَريقِ الشَّبابِ بِنادي الأَهْلي، وَسُرْعانَ ما بَرَزَ كَمُهاجِمٍ مَوْهوبٍ.

لَطالَما كانَ مُحَمَّد يَتَدَرَّبُ بِجِدٍّ، مُسْتَخْدِمًا كُلَّ حِذاءٍ لَدَيْهِ حَتّى يَبْلى. نَشَأَ وَسَطَ عائِلَةٍ تَعْشَقُ كُرَةَ القَدَمِ، حَيْثُ كانَ وَالِدُهُ حارِسَ مَرْمىً في نادٍ مَحَلِّيٍّ، وَقَدْ وَرِثَ مُحَمَّد شَغَفَهُ مِنْهُ. لَكِنَّهُ لَمْ يَكُنْ يَتَخَيَّلُ أَنَّهُ سَيُحَقِّقُ هَذِهِ النَّجاحاتِ الهائِلَةَ في وَقْتٍ مُبَكِّرٍ مِنْ حَياتِهِ.

مُنْذُ انْضمامِهِ إلى فَريقِ الأَهْلي الأَوَّل، أَظْهَرَ مُحَمَّد قُدْرَةً غَيْرَ عادِيَّةٍ عَلى تَسْجيلِ الأَهْدافِ وَمُراقَبَةِ اللّاعِبينَ. في مُباراةٍ حاسِمَةٍ ضِدَّ الزَّمالِك، سَجَّلَ هَدَفَيْنِ وَقَدَّمَ تَمْريرَةً حاسِمَةً أَدَّتْ إلى الفَوْزِ بِالْمُباراة. في ذَلِكَ اليَوْمِ، أَصْبَحَ رَجُلَ المُباراةِ، وَأَذاقَ الجَماهيرَ طَعْمَ الانْتِصارِ.

لَكِنَّ اللَّحْظَةَ الَّتي أَذْهَلَتِ الجَميعَ كانَتْ عِنْدَما سَجَّلَ هاتْريك في نِصْفِ نِهائِيّاتِ دَوْرِيِّ أَبْطالِ إِفْريقْيا. أَثارَ هَذا الإِنْجازُ الرّائِعُ اهْتِمامَ العَديدِ مِنَ الأَنْدِيَةِ الأوروبِّيَّةِ الكُبْرى، الَّتي بَدَأَتْ في التَّفاوُضِ لِضَمِّ النَّجْمِ المِصْرِيِّ الصّاعِدِ.

تَأْتي هَذِهِ النَّجاحاتُ كَنَتيجَةٍ لِسَنَواتٍ مِنَ العَمَلِ الشّاقِّ وَالتَّدْريبِ المُكَثَّفِ، وَدَعْمِ العائِلَةِ وَالأَصْدِقاءِ. مَعَ الوَقْتِ، سَتَزْدادُ خِبْراتُ مُحَمَّد وَمَهاراتُهُ، وَسَيُصْبِحُ لاعِبًا أَساسِيًّا في كُلِّ مُباراةٍ يُشارِكُ فيها.

مُحَمَّد أَحْمَد هُوَ دَليلٌ عَلى أَنَّ الشَّغَفَ وَالتَّدْريبَ الشّاقَّ يُمْكِنُ أَنْ يُؤَدِّيا إلى نَتائِجَ مُذْهِلَةٍ. فَهُوَ بِالْفِعْلِ نَجْمٌ صاعِدٌ بِسُرْعَةٍ، وَيَبْدو أَنَّ مُسْتَقْبَلَهُ في كُرَةِ القَدَمِ سَيَكونُ باهِرًا. مَعَ اسْتِمْرارِهِ في تَحْقيقِ النَّجاحِ، يَظَلُّ مُحَمَّد مَصْدَرَ إِلْهامٍ لِكُلِّ لاعِبٍ شابٍّ يَحْلُمُ بِاللَّعِبِ في أَكْبَرِ السّاحاتِ الكُرَوِيَّةِ.

The Rising Star: From Youth Team to the Global Arena

It seems that the young Egyptian player, Mohamed Ahmed, is surpassing all expectations in the world of football. Mohamed, who is now 19 years old, began his football journey in the youth team of Al-Ahly Club, and quickly emerged as a talented striker.

Mohamed has always trained diligently, using every pair of shoes he had until they were worn out. He grew up in a football-loving family, with his father being a goalkeeper in a local club, and Mohamed inherited his passion from him. However, he could never have imagined achieving such tremendous success at an early stage of his life.

Since joining the senior team of Al-Ahly, Mohamed has displayed an extraordinary ability to score goals and control the game. In a crucial match against Al-Zamalek, he scored two goals and provided a decisive assist that led to victory. On that day, he became the man of the match, giving the fans a taste of triumph.

But the moment that astonished everyone was when he scored a hat-trick in the semi-finals of the CAF Champions League. This remarkable achievement caught the attention of several top European clubs, which began negotiating to sign the promising Egyptian star.

These successes are the result of years of hard work and intensive training, as well as the support of family and friends. With time, Mohamed's experiences and skills will continue to grow, making him a crucial player in every match he participates in.

Mohamed Ahmed is proof that passion and hard work can lead to astounding results. He is already a rapidly rising star, and his future in football seems brilliant. As he continues to achieve success, Mohamed remains an inspiration for every young player dreaming of playing on the biggest football arenas.

6.1.2 Basketball

Track **57**

to block • اِعْتِراضٌ **اِعْتَرَضَ مَسارَ الكُرَةِ**

اِعْتَرَضَ اللاعِبُ مَسارَ الكُرَةِ، مِمّا مَنَعَ الخَصْمَ مِنَ التَّسْجيلِ.

The player blocked the ball's path, preventing the opponent from scoring.

ball handling **التَّحَكُّمُ بِالْكُرَةِ**

كانَتْ مَهاراتُ اللاعِبِ في التَّحَكُّمِ بِالْكُرَةِ مُدْهِشَةً، فَقَدْ أَظْهَرَ تَفَوُّقًا واضِحًا في المَلْعَبِ.

The player's ball handling skills were amazing, showing clear superiority on the court.

power forward **الجَناحُ (طَويلُ القامَةِ)**

كانَ الجَناحُ طَويلُ القامَةِ لِفَريقِ لوس أَنْجِلوس ليكَرْزْ النَّجْمَ المُتَأَلِّقَ في المُباراةِ.

The power forward from the Los Angeles Lakers was the shining star in the match.

small forward **الجَناحُ (قَصيرُ القامَةِ)**

فازَ الجَناحُ قَصيرُ القامَةِ بِجائِزَةِ أَفْضَلِ لاعِبٍ في البُطولَةِ.

The small forward won the award for best player in the tournament.

basket • سِلالٌ **السَّلَّةُ**

سَجَّلَتِ اللّاعِبَةُ هَدَفًا رائِعًا في السَّلَّةِ مِنْ مَسافَةٍ بَعيدَةٍ.

The player scored a fantastic basket from a long distance.

> Literally 'a goal in the basket,' as سَلَّةٌ is the physical basket (hoop and net), while هَدَفٌ is the instance of scoring.

shooting guard **المُسَدِّدُ**

قادَ المُسَدِّدُ فَريقَهُ إِلى الفَوْزِ بِتَسْجيلِهِ لِأَكْثَرِ النِّقاطِ.

The shooting guard led his team to victory by scoring the most points.

shot — **تَصويبَةٌ**

كانَتْ تَصويبَةُ اللّاعِبِ دَقيقَةً وَمِثالِيَّةً، حَيْثُ أَسْقَطَ الكُرَةَ في السَّلَّةِ بِسُهولَةٍ وَسَجَّلَ النُّقْطَةَ الحاسِمَةَ لِفَريقِهِ.

The player's shot was accurate and perfect, as he smoothly dropped the ball into the basket and scored the crucial point for his team.

three-pointer — **تَصويبَةٌ ثُلاثِيَّةٌ**

سَجَّلَ اللّاعِبُ تَصويبَةً ثُلاثِيَّةً قَوِيَّةً.

The player scored a powerful three-pointer shot.

pass — **تَمْريرٌ**

قامَتِ اللّاعِبَةُ بِتَمْريرِ الكُرَةِ بِسَلاسَةٍ لِزَميلَتِها الَّتي سَجَّلَتِ الهَدَفَ.

The player smoothly passed the ball to her teammate who made the basket.

bounce pass — **تَمْريرَةٌ مُرْتَدَّةٌ**

اِسْتَعْمَلَ اللّاعِبُ تَمْريرَةً مُرْتَدَّةً لِتَجَنُّبِ الدِّفاعِ.

The player used a bounce pass to avoid the defense.

bounce — **تَنْطيطُ الكُرَةِ (اِرْتِدادٌ)**

كانَ تَنْطيطُ الكُرَةِ أَمْرًا طَبيعِيًّا لِلّاعِبِ خِلالَ المُباراةِ.

Bouncing the ball was natural for the player during the match.

to dribble — **حاوَرَ** • مُحاوَرَةٌ

تَمَكَّنَ اللّاعِبُ مِنَ المُحاوَرَةِ بِالْكُرَةِ بِمَهارَةٍ عالِيَةٍ.

The player was able to dribble the ball with high skill.

boundary lines *pl.* — **حُدُوْدُ المَلْعَبِ**

سَجَّلَ اللّاعِبُ الهَدَفَ بَعْدَ الِانْطِلاقِ مِنْ داخِلِ حُدودِ المَلْعَبِ.

The player scored the basket after launching from within the boundary lines.

sneakers حِذاءٌ رِياضِيٌّ • أَحْذِيَةٌ

كانَ اللّاعِبُ يَرْتَدي حِذاءً رِياضِيًّا مِنَ العَلامَةِ التِّجارِيَّةِ نايْكي.

The player was wearing sneakers from the Nike brand.

referee حَكَمٌ • حُكّامٌ

تَدَخَّلَ الحَكَمُ لِتَوْضيحِ القَواعِدِ بَعْدَ حُدوثِ الِاعْتِراضِ.

The referee intervened to clarify the rules after the objection occurred.

hoop حَلْقَةُ الشَّبَكَةِ

إِجْتازَتِ الكُرَةُ حَلْقَةَ الشَّبَكَةِ بِسَلاسَةٍ بَعْدَ رَمْيَةٍ مُتْقَنَةٍ.

The ball passed through the hoop smoothly after a well-executed throw.

three-point line خَطُّ الثُّلاثِيَّةِ • خُطوطٌ

مِنْ خَلْفِ خَطِّ الثُّلاثِيَّةِ، سَجَّلَ اللّاعِبُ نِقاطًا مُهِمَّةً لِلْفَريقِ.

From behind the three-point line, the player scored important points for the team.

free-throw line خَطُّ الرَّمْيَةِ الحُرَّةِ

أَشارَ الحَكَمُ إِلى خَطِّ الرَّمْيَةِ الحُرَّةِ بَعْدَ أَنِ ارْتَكَبَ اللّاعِبُ خَطَأً.

The referee pointed to the free-throw line after the player committed a foul.

foul خَطَأٌ • أَخْطاءٌ

بَعْدَ خَطَأٍ مِنْ لاعِبِ الخَصْمِ، تَحَصَّلَ لاعِبُنا عَلى فُرْصَةٍ لِتَنْفيذِ رَمْيَةٍ حُرَّةٍ.

After a foul by an opposing player, our player got a chance to execute a free throw.

man to man دِفاعُ رَجُلٍ لِرَجُلٍ

اِعْتَمَدَ الفَريقُ دِفاعَ رَجُلٍ لِرَجُلٍ لِإِحْباطِ هَجَماتِ الخَصْمِ.

The team adopted man-to-man defense to thwart the opponent's attacks.

zone defense دِفاعُ مِنْطَقَةٍ

اِسْتَخْدَمَ المُدَرِّبُ دِفاعَ المِنْطَقَةِ لِتَحْقيقِ التَّوازُنِ بَيْنَ الهُجومِ وَالدِّفاعِ.

The coach used zone defense to achieve balance between offense and defense.

tip-off رَمْيَةُ بِدايَةِ المُباراةِ

بَدَأَتِ المُباراةُ بِرَمْيَةِ بِدايَةٍ مِنَ الحَكَمِ.

The match started with a tip-off from the referee.

free throw رَمْيَةٌ حُرَّةٌ

بَعْدَ تَعَرُّضِهِ لِلْعَرْقَلَةِ، أَحْرَزَ اللّاعِبُ نُقْطَتَيْنِ مِنْ رَمْيَةٍ حُرَّةٍ.

After being fouled, the player scored two points from a free throw.

layup رَمْيَةٌ خَفيفَةٌ

قامَ اللّاعِبُ بِتَنْفيذِ رَمْيَةٍ خَفيفَةٍ لِتَجاوُزِ دِفاعِ الخَصْمِ.

The player executed a layup to bypass the opponent's defense.

uniform زِيٌّ رِياضِيٌّ • أَزْياءٌ

كانَ الفَريقُ يَرْتَدي زِيَّهُ الرِّياضِيَّ الأَزْرَقَ الجَديدَ في المُباراةِ.

The team was wearing their new blue sports uniform in the match.

to dunk سَدَّدَ رَمْيَةً ساحِقَةً • تَسْديدٌ

سَدَّدَ اللّاعِبُ رَمْيَةً ساحِقَةً مُبْهِرَةً جَعَلَتِ الجَماهيرَ تَنْفَجِرُ بِالتَّصْفيقِ.

The player dunked a smashing throw that made the crowd burst into applause.

point guard صانِعُ الأَلْعابِ

صانِعُ الأَلْعابِ في فَريقِ السِّلْتِكس كانَ يَتَحَكَّمُ في مَجْرى اللَّعِبِ بِمَهارَةٍ.

The point guard on the Celtics team was skillfully controlling the course of the game.

to shoot • تَصْويبٌ **صَوَّبَ**

صَوَّبَ اللّاعِبُ الكُرَةَ بِقُوَّةٍ نَحْوَ السَّلَّةِ، مُحْرِزًا ثَلاثَ نِقاطٍ.

The player shot the ball hard towards the basket, scoring three points.

slam dunk **رَمْيَةٌ ساحِقَةٌ**

سَجَّلَ اللّاعِبُ رَمْيَةً ساحِقَةً رائِعَةٍ.

The player made a fantastic slam dunk.

to steal • قَطْعٌ **قَطَعَ الكُرَةَ**

تَمَكَّنَتِ اللّاعِبَةُ مِنْ قَطْعِ الكُرَةِ مِنَ الخَصْمَةِ بِمَهارَةٍ.

The player skillfully stole the ball from the opponent.

basketball **كُرَةُ السَّلَّةِ**

كُرَةُ السَّلَّةِ هيَ واحِدَةٌ مِنْ أَكْثَرِ الرِّياضاتِ شَعْبِيَّةً في العالَمِ.

Basketball is one of the most popular sports in the world.

ball out of bounds **كُرَةٌ خارِجَ الحُدودِ**

أَخْرَجَ اللّاعِبُ الكُرَةَ خارِجَ الحُدودِ بِطَريقِ الخَطَأِ، وَمَنَحَ الحَكَمُ الكُرَةَ لِلْفَريقِ المُنافِسِ.

The player mistakenly knocked the ball out of bounds, and the referee awarded the ball to the opposing team.

basketball **كُرَةُ سَلَّةٍ**

نَجَحَ في تَنْفيذِ تَسْديدَةٍ لا تُصَدَّقُ مِنْ مُنْتَصَفِ المَلْعَبِ، حَيْثُ وَضَعَ كُرَةَ السَّلَّةِ في السَّلَّةِ بِسَلاسَةٍ وَدِقَّةٍ، مُحَطِّمًا كُلَّ التَّوَقُّعاتِ .

He successfully executed an incredible half-court shot, smoothly putting the basketball through the hoop with precision, shattering all expectations.

Notice that the name of the sport is always definite كُرَةُ السَّلَّةِ (basketball) in Arabic, while the term to reference the ball can be definite كُرَةُ السَّلَّةِ (the basketball) or indefinite كُرَةُ سَلَّةٍ (a basketball).

rebound كُرَةٌ مُرْتَدَّةٌ

اللّاعِبُ الَّذي حَصَلَ عَلى أَكْبَرِ عَدَدٍ مِنَ الكُراتِ المُرْتَدَّةِ كانَ عامِلًا رَئيسِيًّا في فَوْزِ الفَريقِ.

The player who got the most rebounds was a major factor in the team's victory.

center لاعِبُ ارْتِكازٍ

كانَتْ لاعِبَةُ الِارْتِكازِ حاسِمَةً في الدِّفاعِ عَنِ السَّلَّةِ.

The center (player) was crucial in defending the basket.

to rebound لَعِبَ كُرَةً مُرْتَدَّةً • لَعِبٌ

عِنْدَما سَقَطَتِ الكُرَةُ مِنَ السَّلَّةِ، نَجَحَ اللّاعِبُ في لَعِبِ كُرَةٍ مُرْتَدَّةٍ.

When the ball fell from the basket, the player managed to rebound.

backboard لَوْحَةُ السَّلَّةِ / اللَّوْحَةُ الخَلْفِيَّةُ

اِصْطَدَمَتِ الكُرَةُ بِلَوْحَةِ السَّلَّةِ قَبْلَ أَنْ تَدْخُلَ السَّلَّةَ.

The ball hit the backboard before it went into the basket.

coach مُدَرِّبٌ

وَضَعَ المُدَرِّبُ خُطَّةً مُمْتازَةً أَدَّتْ إِلى فَوْزِ الفَريقِ.

The coach put in place an excellent plan that led to the team's victory.

to pass مَرَّرَ • تَمْريرٌ

مَرَّرَ اللّاعِبُ الكُرَةَ لِزَميلِهِ الَّذي كانَ في مَوْقِعٍ أَفْضَلَ لِلتَّسْديدِ.

The player passed the ball to his teammate who was in a better position to shoot.

center مَرْكَزٌ • مَراكِزُ

المَرْكَزُ في كُرَةِ السَّلَّةِ يَلْعَبُ دَوْرًا مُهِمًّا في الدِّفاعِ وَالهُجومِ.

The center in basketball plays an important role in both defense and offense.

مَلْعَبٌ • مَلاعِبُ **court**

جَميعُ المُبارَياتِ في بُطولَةِ كُرَةِ السَّلَّةِ الدَّوْلِيَّةِ أُقيمَتْ في هَذا المَلْعَبِ.

All matches in the international basketball championship were held on this court.

مُنْتَصَفُ الوَقْتِ **half time**

بِنِهايَةِ مُنْتَصَفِ الوَقْتِ، كانَتِ النَّتيجَةُ التَّعادُلَ بَيْنَ الفَريقَيْنِ.

At half time, the score was tied between the two teams.

هُجومٌ خاطِفٌ **fast break**

اِسْتَغَلَّ الفَريقُ الفُرْصَةَ لِتَنْفيذِ هُجومٍ خاطِفٍ، مُحْرِزًا نِقاطًا سَريعَةً.

The team took advantage of a fast break, scoring quick points.

وَقْتٌ إِضافِيٌّ • أَوْقاتٌ **extra time**

عِنْدَما انْتَهَتِ المُباراةُ بِالتَّعادُلِ، كانَ عَلى الفَريقَيْنِ أَنْ يَلْعَبا وَقْتًا إِضافِيًّا.

When the match ended in a draw, the teams had to play extra time.

وَقْتٌ مُسْتَقْطَعٌ • أَوْقاتٌ **timeout**

طَلَبَ المُدَرِّبُ وَقْتًا مُسْتَقْطَعًا لِمُناقَشَةِ اسْتِراتيجِيَّةٍ جَديدَةٍ مَعَ الفَريقِ.

The coach requested a timeout to discuss a new strategy with the team.

6.1.2.1 Mini-Articles

Track **58**

في اللَّيْلَةِ الماضِيَةِ، في المَلْعَبِ الرَّئيسِيِّ، أَظْهَرَ اللّاعِبُ الشّابُّ حَسَن، الجَناحُ القَصيرُ لِفَريقِ الأَقْصى، أَداءً مُتَمَيِّزًا في مُباراةِ كُرَةِ السَّلَّةِ المُحْتَدِمَةِ. مُرْتَدِيًا حِذاءَهُ الرِّياضِيَّ الجَديدَ، تَحَكَّمَ حَسَنْ بِالْكُرَةِ بِمَهارَةٍ عالِيَةٍ وَقامَ بِتَمْريراتٍ مُذْهِلَةٍ إِلى زُمَلائِهِ في الفَريقِ. وَفي الدَّقائِقِ الأَخيرَةِ، أَظْهَرَ قُوَّتَهُ في دِفاعِ المِنْطَقَةِ وَتَمَكَّنَ مِنَ اعْتِراضِ مَسارِ الكُرَةِ عِدَّةَ مَرّاتٍ، مُحافِظًا عَلى فُرْصَةِ الفَوْزِ لِفَريقِهِ.

Last night, at the main stadium, the young player Hassan, the short winger from Al-Aqsa (The Maximum) team, demonstrated an outstanding performance in the intense basketball match. With his new sports shoes, Hassan skillfully controlled the ball and delivered astonishing passes to his teammates. In the final minutes, he showcased his defensive strength in the zone, intercepting the ball multiple times, ensuring the chance for victory for his team.

بِالأَمْسِ، فازَ فَريقُ النُّجومِ عَلى الهِلالِ فِي مُباراةٍ شَهِدَتِ الكَثيرَ مِنَ التَّوَتُّرِ وَالإثارَةِ. كانَ صانِعُ الأَلْعابِ مَحْمود الخالِدي في مَرْكَزِ الدِّفاعِ الصَّلْبِ. قَدَّمَ الخالِدي أَداءً بارِعًا بِالمُراوَغَةِ بِالكُرَةِ عَبْرَ المَلْعَبِ، مُناوِرًا الدِّفاعَ اللَّصيقَ لِلْخَصْمِ. وَفي الوَقْتِ الإِضافِيِّ، أَطْلَقَ الخالِدِيُّ تَصويبَةً ثُلاثِيَّةً مِنْ خَطِّ الثُّلاثِيَّةِ، سَدَّدَها بِسَلاسَةٍ في حَلْقَةِ الشَّبَكَةِ، مُحْرِزًا النِّقاطَ الثَّلاثَةَ الفاصِلَةَ لِلْمُباراةِ.

Yesterday, the team Al-Nujoom (the Stars) won against Al-Hilal (the Crescent) in a match that witnessed a lot of tension and excitement. Point guard Mahmoud Al-Khaldi was in a solid defensive position. Al-Khaldi delivered a brilliant performance, dribbling the ball across the court, and outmaneuvering the opponents' sticky defense. In overtime, Al-Khaldi took a smooth three-point shot from the three-point line, effortlessly swishing it into the net, securing the decisive three points for the match.

خِلالَ اللَّيْلَةِ الماضِيَةِ، قَدَّمَ فَريقُ الهِلالِ أَداءً رائِعًا فِي النِّصْفِ الثّاني مِنَ المُباراةِ بَعْدَ أَنْ كانوا مُتَأَخِّرينَ بِشَكْلٍ كَبيرٍ في مُنْتَصَفِ الوَقْتِ. بِقِيادَةِ مُدَرِّبِهِمِ الجَديدِ، قَدَّمَ صانِعُ الأَلْعابِ الثّاني، عُمَر الحُسَيْن، عَرْضًا رائِعًا في التَّصْويبِ، مُسَجِّلًا العَديدَ مِنَ التَّصْويباتِ الثُّلاثِيَّةِ. وَبِفَضْلِ تَمْريراتِهِ الرّائِعَةِ وَقُدْرَتِهِ عَلى قَطْعِ الكُراتِ، اِسْتَطاعَ الفَريقُ أَنْ يُنَفِّذَ هُجومًا خاطِفًا مُذْهِلًا وَأَنْ يُسَجِّلَ رَمْيَةً ساحِقَةً فِي اللَّحَظاتِ الأَخيرَةِ، مُحَقِّقًا فَوْزًا مُذْهِلًا.

During the past night, the team Al-Hilal (the Crescent) displayed a fantastic performance in the second half of the match after being significantly behind at halftime. Led by their new coach, the second playmaker, Omar Al-Hussein, put on a splendid shooting display, scoring several three-pointers. With his excellent passes and ball-stealing ability, the team executed a stunning comeback and scored a decisive buzzer-beater, achieving an amazing victory.

6.1.2.2 Informative Article: Basketball Basics

Track **59**

أَساسِيّاتُ لُعْبَةِ كُرَةِ السَّلَّةِ: المُقَدِّمَةُ الشّامِلَةُ

كُرَةُ السَّلَّةِ هِيَ واحِدَةٌ مِنَ الرِّياضاتِ الأَكْثَرِ شَعْبِيَّةً حَوْلَ العالَمِ، وَهِيَ تَجْمَعُ بَيْنَ القُوَّةِ وَالسُّرْعَةِ وَالمَهارَةِ الاِسْتِراتيجِيَّةِ. إِلَيْكَ بَعْضُ الأَساسِيّاتِ لِفَهْمِ هَذِهِ اللُّعْبَةِ المُثيرَةِ.

بِدايَةً، تَتَكَوَّنُ كُرَةُ السَّلَّةِ مِنْ فَريقَيْنِ، كُلٌّ مِنْهُما يَضُمُّ خَمْسَةَ لاعِبينَ. الهَدَفُ الرَّئيسِيُّ مِنَ اللُّعْبَةِ هُوَ إِحْرازُ النِّقاطِ عَبْرَ إِدْخالِ الكُرَةِ فِي السَّلَّةِ المُعَلَّقَةِ عَلى ارْتِفاعِ 10 أَقْدامٍ عَلى اللَّوْحَةِ الخَلْفِيَّةِ في نِهايَةِ المَلْعَبِ.

تَتَنَوَّعُ الطُّرُقُ الَّتي يُمْكِنُ مِنْ خِلالِها إِحْرازُ النِّقاطِ. يُمْكِنُ لِلّاعِبِ أَنْ يُحْرِزَ نُقْطَتَيْنِ عَنْ طَريقِ تَصْويبِ الكُرَةِ فِي السَّلَّةِ مِنْ داخِلِ خَطِّ الثُّلاثِيَّةِ، وَثَلاثَ نِقاطٍ عِنْدَ التَّصْويبِ مِنْ خارِجِهِ. أَمّا الرَّمْيَةُ الحُرَّةُ، فَتُقَدِّمُ نُقْطَةً واحِدَةً، وَتُمْنَحُ لِلّاعِبِ عِنْدَ ارْتِكابِ خَطَأٍ ضِدَّهُ مِنْ قِبَلِ الفَريقِ المُنافِسِ.

تَبْدأُ المُباراةُ بِما يُسَمّى بـ "رَمْيَةِ بِدايَةِ المُباراةِ" أَوْ "tip-off" حَيْثُ يَرْمي الحَكَمُ الكُرَةَ في الهَواءِ بَيْنَ لاعِبَيْنِ مِنَ الفَريقَيْنِ في وَسَطِ المَلْعَبِ، وَالهَدَفُ مِنْ ذَلِكَ هُوَ الاِسْتِحْواذُ عَلى الكُرَةِ.

تَتَضَمَّنُ مَراكِزُ اللّاعِبينَ الأَساسِيَّةُ "لاعِبَ الهُجومِ الخَلْفِيَّ"، "المُدافِعَ مُسَدِّدَ الهَدَفِ"، "الجَناحَ قَصيرَ القامَةِ"، "الجَناحَ طَويلَ القامَةِ" وَ "لاعِبَ الاِرْتِكازِ". يَتَحَكَّمُ لاعِبُ الهُجومِ الخَلْفِيُّ بِالْكُرَةِ وَيَقودُ الهَجَماتِ، في حينِ يَكونُ الجَناحُ الطَّويلُ وَلاعِبُ الاِرْتِكازِ في الغالِبِ مِنْ بَيْنِ اللّاعِبينَ الأَطْوَلِ في الفَريقِ، وَهُمْ يَتَعامَلونَ بِشَكْلٍ أَساسِيٍّ مَعَ الكُراتِ المُرْتَدَّةِ وَالتَّصْويباتِ القَريبَةِ مِنَ السَّلَّةِ.

تَعْتَمِدُ كُرَةُ السَّلَّةِ عَلى مَجْموعَةٍ مِنَ القَواعِدِ الأَساسِيَّةِ. يَجِبُ عَلى اللّاعِبِ أَنْ يُنَطِّطَ الكُرَةَ بِيَدِهِ أَثْناءَ الجَرْيِ، وَهُوَ ما يُعْرَفُ بِالمُحاوَرَةِ. إذا انْتَهَكَ لاعِبٌ هَذِهِ القاعِدَةَ، يُمْكِنُ أَنْ يُؤَدِّيَ ذَلِكَ إلى خَطَأٍ تِقْنِيٍّ يُعْرَفُ بـ "المَشْيِ بِالكُرَةِ"، مِمّا يُعْطي الكُرَةَ لِلْفَريقِ الخَصْمِ. وَفي الدِّفاعِ، يَجِبُ عَلى اللّاعِبينَ تَجَنُّبُ الاِتِّصالِ الجَسَدِيِّ العَنيفِ مَعَ الخَصْمِ، وَإلّا يُمْكِنُ أَنْ يُؤَدِّيَ ذَلِكَ إلى خَطَأٍ شَخْصِيٍّ يُمْكِنُ أَنْ يُؤَدِّيَ إلى مَنْحِ الفَريقِ الخَصْمِ رَمْيَةً حُرَّةً أَوْ حُكْمٍ بِالاِسْتِحْواذِ على الكُرَةِ.

إنَّ مَعْرِفَةَ أَساسِيّاتِ لُعْبَةِ كُرَةِ السَّلَّةِ هِيَ الخُطْوَةُ الأولى لِاسْتِمْتاعِكَ بِاللُّعْبَةِ، سَواءٌ كُنْتَ تُشاهِدُها أَوْ تُشارِكُ فيها. تَتَطَلَّبُ اللُّعْبَةُ مَهارَةً وَتَنْسيقًا وَفَهْمًا اسْتِراتيجِيًّا، لَكِنَّها في المَقامِ الأَوَّلِ مُمْتِعَةٌ وَمُثيرَةٌ. أَحْضِرْ كُرَةً وَاسْتَمْتِعْ بِاللَّعِبِ!

Basketball Basics: A Comprehensive Introduction

Basketball is one of the most popular sports around the world, combining strength, speed, and strategic skills. Here are some basics to understand this exciting game.

To begin with, basketball consists of two teams, each with five players. The main goal of the game is to score points by putting the ball in the basket hanging at a height of 10 feet on the backboard at the end of the court.

There are various ways to score points. A player can score two points by shooting the ball into the basket from inside the three-point line, and three points when shooting from beyond it. Free throws, on the other hand, contribute one point and are awarded to a player when the opposing team commits a foul against them.

The game starts with what is known as the "tip-off," where the referee tosses the ball into the air between players from each team at the center of the court, and the goal is to gain possession of the ball.

Last night, in an exciting women's volleyball match, the game between the Roses and the Jasmines ended in a draw after five highly competitive sets. During the match, the middle blocker from the Roses, Fatimah Abdullah, showcased a remarkable performance with her powerful spikes, while the Jasmines' defender, Sarah Al-Hashim, shone with her saves at the net. Play stopped several times for brief periods, adding a strategic element and creating tension in the atmosphere.

Basketball relies on a set of basic rules. A player must dribble the ball while running, known as dribbling. If a player violates this rule, it can result in a technical foul called "traveling," giving the ball to the opposing team. In defense, players must avoid excessive physical contact with the opponent, or it can result in a personal foul, leading to free throws or turnover of possession.

Understanding the basics of basketball is the first step to enjoying the game, whether you're watching or participating. The game requires skill, coordination, and strategic understanding, but it is primarily fun and thrilling. Grab a ball and enjoy playing!

6.1.3 Volleyball

Track **60**

serve — **إِرْسالٌ**

بَدَأَتِ اللّاعِبَةُ المُباراةَ بِإِرْسالٍ قَوِيٍّ أَصابَ الخَصْمَ بِالْمُفاجَأَةِ.

The player started the match with a strong serve that surprised the opponent.

ace — **إِرْسالٌ ساحِقٌ**

بَعْدَ تَحْضيرٍ مُمْتازٍ مِنَ المُحَضِّرِ، قامَ اللّاعِبُ بِإِرْسالٍ ساحِقٍ.

After an excellent set by the setter, the player made an ace serve.

volleyball — **الكُرَةُ الطّائِرَةُ**

تُعْتَبَرُ الكُرَةُ الطّائِرَةُ واحِدَةً مِنَ الرِّياضاتِ المَشْهورَةِ جِدًّا، وَتُلْعَبُ بَيْنَ فَريقَيْنِ، كُلُّ فَريقٍ يَتَأَلَّفُ مِنْ سِتَّةِ لاعِبينَ.

Volleyball is one of the most popular sports and is played between two teams, each consisting of six players.

libero — **اللّاعِبُ الحُرُّ**

يَقومُ اللّاعِبُ الحُرُّ في فَريقِنا بِدَوْرٍ حاسِمٍ في الدِّفاعِ.

The libero on our team plays a crucial role in defense.

setter — **المُحَضِّرُ**

تَحْضيرُ الكُرَةِ لِلضَّرْبَةِ القَوِيَّةِ هوَ واحِدٌ مِنَ المَهاراتِ الأَساسِيَّةِ لِلْمُحَضِّرِ.

Setting the ball for the strong hit is one of the fundamental skills of the setter.

تَصَدٍّ أَرْضِيٌّ — dig

أَنْقَذَ تَصَدٍّ أَرْضِيٌّ رائعٌ الفَريقَ مِنْ خَطَأٍ مُحْتَمَلٍ.

A fantastic dig by the player saved the team from a potential error.

تَصَدٍّ عَلى الشَّبَكَةِ — block

قامَتِ اللّاعِبَةُ بِتَصَدٍّ رائعٍ عَلى الشَّبَكَةِ، مِمّا أَدّى إلى نُقْطَةٍ لِفَريقِها.

The player made a great block at the net, leading to a point for her team.

تَصَدّى عَلى الشَّبَكَةِ • تَصَدٍّ — to block

تَصَدَّتِ اللّاعِبَةُ عَلى الشَّبَكَةِ بِقُوَّةٍ، مانِعَةً الخَصْمَ مِنَ التَّسْجيلِ.

The player blocked powerfully at the net, preventing the opponent from scoring.

تَمْريرٌ — pass, bump

التَّمْريرُ الجَيِّدُ هُوَ أَساسُ اللُّعْبَةِ في الكُرَةِ الطّائِرَةِ.

Good passing is the foundation of the game in volleyball.

حَضَّرَ • تَحْضيرٌ — to set

بَعْدَ تَحْضيرِ الكُرَةِ بِمَهارَةٍ، سَدَّدَ اللّاعِبُ ضَرْبَةً قَوِيَّةً.

After setting the ball skillfully, the player made a strong spike.

حَكَمٌ • حُكّامٌ — referee

قامَ الحَكَمُ بِإِلْغاءِ النُّقْطَةِ بَعْدَ اكْتِشافِ خَطَأٍ في تَنْفيذِ اللّاعِبينَ خِلالَ مُباراةِ الكُرَةِ الطّائِرَةِ .

The referee canceled the point after discovering an error in the players' execution during the volleyball match.

خَطَأٌ — foul

أَطْلَقَ الحَكَمُ صافِرَتَهُ بَعْدَ أَنِ ارْتَكَبَ اللّاعِبُ خَطَأً خِلالَ مُباراةِ الكُرَةِ الطّائِرَةِ .

The referee blew the whistle after the player committed a foul during the volleyball match.

زِيٌّ رِياضِيٌّ • أَزْياءٌ

uniform

كانَ الزِّيُّ الرِّياضِيُّ لِلْفَريقِ لافِتًا لِلنَّظَرِ بِأَلْوانِهِ الزّاهِيَةِ.

The team's uniform was eye-catching with its bright colors.

شَبَكَةٌ • شِباكٌ

net

اِرْتَطَمَتِ الكُرَةُ بِالشَّبَكَةِ قَبْلَ أَنْ تَعْبُرَ إِلى الجانِبِ الآخَرِ.

The ball hit the net before it crossed over to the other side.

شَوْطٌ • أَشْواطٌ

set

فازَ الفَريقُ بِالشَّوْطِ الأَوَّلِ بِنَتيجَةِ 25 - 20.

The team won the first set with a score of 25-20.

ضَرَبَ • ضَرْبٌ

to spike

بَعْدَ تَمْريرَةٍ مِثالِيَّةٍ مِنْ زَميلِهِ، قامَ اللّاعِبُ بِضَرْبَةٍ قَوِيَّةٍ نَحْوَ الخَصْمِ.

After a perfect pass from his teammate, the player made a strong spike towards the opponent.

ضَرْبَةٌ

spike, hit

كانَتْ ضَرْبَةُ اللّاعِبِ قَوِيَّةً جِدًّا، مِمّا أَدّى إِلى نُقْطَةٍ مُباشِرَةٍ لِلْفَريقِ.

The player's spike was so strong, it led to a direct point for the team.

قامَ بِتَصَدٍّ أَرْضِيٍّ • قِيامٌ

to dig

عِنْدَما سَقَطَتِ الكُرَةُ بِسُرْعَةٍ، قامَتِ اللّاعِبَةُ بِتَصَدٍّ أَرْضِيٍّ مُدْهِشٍ.

When the ball fell quickly, the player made an amazing dig.

Sometimes a straightforward term in English might not have a direct equivalent in Arabic. In such cases, a more descriptive phrase is often used in Arabic to convey the same meaning.

كُرَةٌ طائِرَةٌ

volleyball

تَمَّ تَبادُلُ التَّمْريرَةِ بِنَجاحٍ بَيْنَ اللاعِبَيْنِ، قَبْلَ أَنْ يَضْرِبَ لاعِبٌ ثالِثٌ الكُرَةَ الطّائِرَةَ فَوْقَ الشَّبَكَةِ .

The pass was successfully exchanged between the players before a third player spiked the volleyball over the net.

Notice that the name of the sport is always definite الكُرَةُ الطّائِرَةُ (volleyball) in Arabic, while the term to reference the ball can be definite الكُرَةُ الطّائِرَةُ (the volleyball) or indefinite كُرَةٌ طائِرَةٌ (a volleyball).

middle blocker/hitter **لاعِبُ الوَسَطِ**

يَتَمَيَّزُ لاعِبُ الوَسَطِ في فَريقِنا بِقُوَّتِهِ وَقُدْرَتِهِ عَلى التَّصَدّي لِلضَّرَباتِ القَوِيَّةِ.

Our middle blocker is distinguished by his strength and ability to block powerful spikes.

to serve • لَعِبَ **لَعِبَ الإِرْسالَ**

بَدَأَتِ اللّاعِبَةُ المُباراةَ بِلَعِبِ إِرْسالٍ قَوِيٍّ.

The player started the match by serving powerfully.

match **مُباراةٌ**

كانَتْ مُباراةُ الكُرَةِ الطّائِرَةِ مَليئَةً بِالْإِثارَةِ وَالتَّوَتُّرِ.

The volleyball match was filled with excitement and tension.

coach **مُدَرِّبٌ**

كانَتِ المُدَرِّبَةُ فَخورَةً بِأَداءِ الفَريقِ في المُباراةِ.

The coach was proud of the team's performance in the match.

court • مَلاعِبُ **مَلْعَبٌ**

كانَ المَلْعَبُ مُمْتَلِئًا بِالْمُشَجِّعينَ الَّذينَ جاؤوا لِمُشاهَدَةِ المُباراةِ.

The court was full of fans who came to watch the match.

outside hitter **مُهاجِمٌ خارِجِيٌّ**

قَدَّمَ مُهاجِمُنا الخارِجِيُّ أَداءً اسْتِثْنائِيًّا في المُباراةِ.

Our outside hitter delivered an exceptional performance in the match.

timeout • أَوْقاتٌ وَقْتٌ مُسْتَقْطَعٌ

أَخَذَ المُدَرِّبُ وَقْتًا مُسْتَقْطَعًا لِإعادَةِ تَنْظيمِ الفَريقِ وَتَقْديمِ بَعْضِ التَّعْليماتِ.

The coach took a timeout to reorganize the team and provide some instructions.

6.1.3.1 Mini-Articles

Track **61**

في مُباراةٍ رائِعَةٍ وَتَفاعُلِيَّةٍ لِلْكُرَةِ الطّائِرَةِ أَمْسِ، تَفَوَّقَ فَريقُ النَّوارِسِ عَلى الصُّقورِ بِثَلاثَةِ أَشْواطٍ نَظيفَةٍ. كانَ المُحَضِّرُ يوسُف الخَيْر في قَلْبِ الأَحْداثِ، حَيْثُ قامَ بِتَمْريراتٍ مُدْهِشَةٍ إِلى مُهاجِمِهِ الخارِجِيِّ عَلَي الرّاشِد، الَّذي نَفَّذَ العَديدَ مِنَ الضَّرَباتِ القَوِيَّةِ الَّتي لَمْ يَسْتَطِعِ الخَصْمُ التَّصَدِّيَ لَها. كانَ اللّاعِبُ الحُرُّ عَبْد الرَّحْمَن الشّامي لا يُصَدَّقُ في الدِّفاعِ، حَيْثُ تَمَكَّنَ مِنْ تَنْفيذِ تَصَدِّياتٍ أَرْضِيَّةٍ مُدْهِشَةٍ.

In a fantastic and interactive volleyball match yesterday, Team Nawaris (Seagulls) outperformed Team Suqour (Falcons), winning three clean sets. The setter, Youssef Al-Khair, was at the heart of the action, delivering amazing passes to his outside hitter, Ali Al-Rashed, who executed numerous powerful hits that the opponent couldn't defend. The libero, Abdulrahman Al-Shami, was unbelievable in defense, making incredible floor saves.

اللَّيْلَةَ الماضِيَةَ، في مُباراةٍ مُثيرَةٍ لِلْكُرَةِ الطّائِرَةِ النِّسائِيَّةِ، اِنْتَهَتِ المُباراةُ بَيْنَ فَريقَي الوُرودِ وَالْياسَمينِ بِالتَّعادُلِ بَعْدَ خَمْسَةِ أَشْواطٍ شَديدَةِ التَّنافُسِ. خِلالَ المُباراةِ، أَظْهَرَتْ لاعِبَةُ الوَسَطِ لِفَريقِ الوُرودِ، فاطِمَة العبدالله، أَداءً رائِعًا بِتَنْفيذِها لِعِدَّةِ ضَرَباتٍ ساحِقَةٍ، بَيْنَما كانَتْ مُدافِعَةُ الياسَمينِ، سارَّة الهاشِم، مُتَأَلِّقَةً بِتَصَدِّياتِها عَلى الشَّبَكَةِ. تَوَقَّفَ اللَّعِبُ في العَديدِ مِنَ المَرّاتِ لِوَقْتٍ مُسْتَقْطَعٍ، مِمّا أَضافَ عُنْصُرًا اسْتراتيجِيًّا وَأَحْدَثَ تَوَتُّرًا في الأَجْواءِ.

Last night, in an exciting women's volleyball match, the game between Team Wurood (Roses) and Team Yasamin (Jasmines) ended in a draw after five highly competitive sets. During the match, the middle blocker from Team Wurood, Fatimah Abdullah, showcased a remarkable performance with her powerful spikes, while Team Yasamin's defender, Sarah Al-Hashim, shone with her saves at the net. Play stopped several times for brief periods, adding a strategic element and creating tension in the atmosphere.

مَعَ بِدايَةِ اللَّيْلَةِ، لَمْ يَكُنْ أَحَدٌ يَتَوَقَّعُ أَنْ تَنْتَهِيَ أَوَّلُ مُباراةٍ لِلْمُدَرِّبِ الجَديدِ لِفَريقِ النُّسورِ، سَعيد العُتَيْبي، بِنَتائِجَ رائِعَةٍ. وَلَكِنْ، تَحْتَ إِرْشاداتِ العُتَيْبي، قَدَّمَ الفَريقُ أَداءً قَوِيًّا في المَلْعَبِ. قامَ اللّاعِبُ عَبْد اللهِ العُمَرِيّ بِإِرْسالاتٍ قَوِيَّةٍ وَتَمَكَّنَ مِنْ تَحْقيقِ عِدَّةِ إِرْسالاتٍ ساحِقَةٍ. بِالْإِضافَةِ إِلى ذَلِكَ، كانَتِ التَّمْريراتُ الرّائِعَةُ وَالتَّصَدّي الأَرْضِيُّ المُذْهِلُ مِنَ اللّاعِبِ الحُرِّ ناصِر البَلَوي نُقْطَةَ التَّحَوُّلِ في المُباراةِ. بِفَضْلِ هَذا المَجْهودِ الجَماعِيِّ، فازَ النُّسورُ بِالْمُباراةِ بِثَلاثَةِ أَشْواطٍ مُقابِلَ شَوْطَيْنِ.

As the night began, no one expected the first match under the guidance of the new coach for the team Al-Nusoor (the Eagles), Saed Al-Otaibi, to result in such impressive outcomes. However, under Al-Otaibi's guidance, the team delivered a strong performance on the court. The player, Abdullah Al-Omari, sent powerful serves and managed to achieve several overwhelming aces. Additionally, the excellent sets and astonishing floor saves from the libero, Nasser Al-Balawi, became a turning point in the game. Thanks to this collective effort, Al-Nusoor (the Eagles) won the match with three sets against two.

6.1.3.2 Interview with a Women's Volleyball Team Coach

Track **62**

مُقابَلَةٌ مَعَ مُدَرِّبَةِ فَريقِ الكُرَةِ الطّائِرَةِ النِّسائِيِّ

المُراسِلُ: مَرْحَبًا يا كابْتِنْ زَيْنَب، شُكْرًا لَكِ عَلى وَقْتِك. هَلْ يُمْكِنُكِ أَنْ تُحَدِّثينا بِإيجازٍ عَنِ الأَداءِ العامِّ لِلْفَريقِ في المُباراةِ الأَخيرَةِ؟

كابْتِنْ زَيْنَب: مَرْحَبًا، بِالطَّبْعِ، أَعْتَقِدُ أَنَّ الفَريقَ أَدّى بِشَكْلٍ رائِع. كانَتْ مُباراةً قَوِيَّةً وَتَنافُسِيَّةً، وَرَأَيْنا التِزامَ كُلِّ اللّاعِباتِ بِاللَّعِبِ الجَماعِيِّ وَالتَّكْتيكاتِ الَّتي تَمَّ تَطْبيقُها.

المُراسِلُ: لَقَدْ كانَتْ فاطِمَة العبد الله، لاعِبَةُ الوَسَطِ، في حالَةٍ رائِعَةٍ. كَيْفَ أَضافَ أَداؤُها لِلْفَريقِ؟

كابْتِنْ زَيْنَب: بِالتَّأْكيدِ، فاطِمَة كانَتْ مُتَأَلِّقَةً. كانَتْ ضَرَباتُها القَوِيَّةُ حاسِمَةً، وَهَذا ما كُنّا نَحْتاجُهُ لِلسَّيْطَرَةِ عَلى المُباراةِ. وَلَيْسَ ذَلِكَ فَحَسْبُ، بَلْ كانَتْ أَيْضًا رائِعَةً في الدِّفاعِ وَالتَّمْريراتِ.

المُراسِلُ: وَماذا عَنْ سارَّة الهاشِم؟ كانَتْ تَصَدِّياتُها عَلى الشَّبَكَةِ مُدْهِشَةً.

كابْتِنْ زَيْنَب: نَعَمْ، سارَّة هِيَ إِحْدى أَقْوى اللّاعِباتِ في الدِّفاعِ. لَدَيْها حِسٌّ رائِعٌ لِلْكُرَةِ وَتَتَمَكَّنُ مِنَ التَّصَدّي بِشَكْلٍ فَعّالٍ عَلى الشَّبَكَةِ. بِالتَّأْكيدِ، كانَتْ واحِدَةً مِنَ الأَسْبابِ الَّتي أَدَّتْ إِلى تَحْقيقِنا لِهَذا التَّعادُلِ.

المُراسِلُ: كانَ هُناكَ الكَثيرُ مِنَ الأَوْقاتِ المُسْتَقْطَعَةِ خِلالَ اللَّعِبِ، كَيْفَ اسْتَخْدَمْتِ هَذِهِ الفَتَراتِ لِصالِحِ الفَريقِ؟

كابْتِنْ زَيْنَب: الأَوْقاتُ المُسْتَقْطَعَةُ مُهِمَّةٌ لِلتَّواصُلِ مَعَ الفَريقِ وَإِعادَةِ تَرْتيبِ أَفْكارِنا. نَسْتَخْدِمُها لِلنِّقاشِ حَوْلَ التَّكْتيكاتِ وَالإِجْراءاتِ الَّتي يَجِبُ تَغْييرُها أَوِ الاِسْتِمْرارُ فيها. أَعْتَقِدُ أَنَّنا اسْتَفَدْنا بِشَكْلٍ جَيِّدٍ مِنْ هَذِهِ الأَوْقاتِ المُسْتَقْطَعَةِ خِلالَ المُباراةِ.

المُراسِلُ: شُكْرًا لَكِ عَلى وَقْتِكِ، كابْتِنْ زَيْنَب. نَتَمَنّى لَكِ وَلِلْفَريقِ التَّوْفيقَ في المُباراةِ القادِمَةِ.

كابْتِنْ زَيْنَب: شُكْرًا لَكَ. نَتَطَلَّعُ إِلى المُباراةِ القادِمَةِ وَنَعِدُ جَماهيرَنا بِأَداءٍ قَوِيٍّ.

Interview with a Women's Volleyball Team Coach

Reporter: Hello, Coach Zainab, thank you for your time. Can you briefly tell us about the team's overall performance in the last match?

Coach Zainab: Hello, of course! I believe the team performed exceptionally well. It was a strong and competitive match, and we saw all the players committed to teamwork and the implemented tactics.

Reporter: Fatimah Abdullah, the middle blocker, was in excellent form. How did her performance contribute to the team?

Coach Zainab: Certainly, Fatimah was on fire. Her powerful hits were decisive, and that's what we needed to gain control of the game. Not only that, but she was also outstanding in defense and passing.

Reporter: And what about Sarah Al-Hashim? Her saves at the net were amazing.

Coach Zainab: Yes, Sarah is one of the strongest defensive players. She has a great sense of the ball and effectively blocks at the net. She was definitely one of the reasons we achieved this tie.

Reporter: There were many timeouts during the game. How did you use these periods to the team's advantage?

Coach Zainab: Timeout periods are essential for communication with the team and reorganizing our thoughts. We use them to discuss tactics and decide on changes or continuations in our approach. I believe we made good use of these timeouts during the match.

Reporter: Thank you for your time, Coach Zainab. We wish you and the team the best of luck in the upcoming match.

Coach Zainab: Thank you. We look forward to the next match and promise our fans a strong performance.

6.1.4 Handball

Track **63**

أَمْسَكَ • إِمْساكٌ **to catch**

أَمْسَكَ الحارِسُ الكُرَةَ بِبَراعَةٍ، مانِعًا تَسْجيلَ الفَريقِ المُنافِسِ لِلْهَدَفِ.

The goalkeeper skillfully caught the ball, preventing the opposing team from scoring a goal.

إِمْساكٌ **catch**

قامَ اللاعِبُ بِإِمْساكٍ رائِعٍ، حَيْثُ تَدَحْرَجَ وَتَصَدّى لِلْكُرَةِ لِإِنْقاذِها مِنَ السُّقوطِ عَلى الأَرْضِ .

The player made a spectacular catch, diving to save the ball from hitting the ground.

تَمْريرَةٌ **pass**

خِلالَ المُباراةِ، كانَتْ تَمْريراتُ اللاعِبينَ سَريعَةً وَدَقيقَةً.

During the match, the players' passes were fast and accurate.

حارِسُ مَرْمًى • حُرّاسٌ **goalkeeper**

أَبْدَعَ حارِسُ المَرْمى في فَريقِنا في صَدِّهِ لِلْكُراتِ.

Our goalkeeper excelled in blocking the balls.

حَكَمٌ • حُكّامٌ **referee**

اِتَّخَذَ حَكَمُ المُباراةِ قَراراتٍ حاسِمَةً وَعادِلَةً.

The referee of the match made decisive and fair decisions.

خَطَأٌ • أَخْطاءٌ **foul**

اِحْتَجَّ اللّاعِبُ عَلى الخَطَأِ الَّذي أَعْلَنَهُ الحَكَمُ.

The player objected to the foul that the referee announced.

دَورانٌ حَوْلَ المِحْوَرِ **pivot**

بَيْنَما اقْتَرَبَ المُدافِعُ، اِسْتَخْدَمَ اللّاعِبُ الماهِرُ حَرَكَةَ الدَّورانِ حَوْلَ المِحْوَرِ لِتَغْييرِ اتِّجاهِهِ وَإيجادِ مِساحَةٍ لِلتَّسْديدِ نَحْوَ المَرْمى.

As the defender closed in, the skillful player used a pivot move to change direction and create space for a shot on goal.

راوَغَ • مُراوَغَةٌ **to dribble**

راوَغَ اللّاعِبُ خَصْمَهُ بِمَهارَةٍ قَبْلَ أَنْ يَرْمِيَ الكُرَةَ.

The player skillfully dribbled past his opponent before throwing the ball.

رَمى • رَمْيٌ **to throw**

رَمَتِ اللّاعِبَةُ الكُرَةَ بِقُوَّةٍ نَحْوَ المَرْمى.

The player threw the ball powerfully towards the goal.

رَمْيَةٌ **throw**

نَفَّذَ اللّاعِبُ رَمْيَةً مُتْقَنَةً، مُحَقِّقًا هَدَفًا مُثيرًا لِلْفَريقِ.

The player made a skillful throw, scoring an exciting goal for the team.

رَمْيَةُ البِدايَةِ **throw-off**

بَدَأَتِ المُباراةُ بِرَمْيَةِ البِدايَةِ مِنَ الفَريقِ المُضيفِ.

The match started with a throw-off from the home team.

زِيٌّ رِياضِيٌّ • أَزْياءٌ **uniform**

كانَ الزِّيُّ الرِّياضِيُّ لِلْفَريقِ النِّسائِيِّ مُتَمَيِّزًا وَجَذّابًا.

The women's team's sports uniform was distinctive and attractive.

to shoot • تَسْديدٌ **سَدَّدَ**

سَدَّدَ اللاعِبُ بِقُوَّةٍ وَأَحْرَزَ هَدَفًا مُهِمًّا لِلفريقِ.

The player shot powerfully and scored an important goal for the team.

to block • صَدٌّ **صَدَّ**

صَدَّ الحارِسُ الكُرَةَ بِنَجاحٍ، مانِعًا الفَريقَ المُنافِسَ مِنْ تَسْجيلِ هَدَفٍ.

The goalkeeper successfully blocked the ball, preventing the opposing team from scoring a goal.

block **صَدَّةٌ**

تَمَكَّنَتِ الحارِسَةُ مِنْ صَدَّةٍ مُذْهِلَةٍ، مَنَعَتْ بِها الهَدَفَ.

The goalkeeper managed an amazing block, preventing a goal.

left back • ظَهائِرُ **ظَهيرٌ أَيْسَرُ**

قامَ الظَّهيرُ الأَيْسَرُ بِصَدِّ هَجْمَةٍ قَوِيَّةٍ مِنَ الفَريقِ المُنافِسِ.

The left back blocked a strong attack from the opposing team.

right back **ظَهيرٌ أَيْمَنُ**

أَظْهَرَ الظَّهيرُ الأَيْمَنُ أَداءً قَوِيًّا خِلالَ اللِّقاءِ.

The right back showed a strong performance during the match.

handball **كُرَةُ اليَدِ**

يُظْهِرُ الفَريقُ النِّسائِيُّ لِكُرَةِ اليَدِ تَقَدُّمًا مَلْحوظًا هَذا المَوْسِمَ.

The women's handball team is showing notable progress this season.

handball **كُرَةُ يَدٍ**

تَدَحْرَجَتْ كُرَةُ اليَدِ خارِجَ الحُدودِ، الأَمْرَ الَّذي مَنَحَ الاِسْتِحْواذَ لِلْفَريقِ الخَصْمِ .

The handball rolled out of bounds, giving possession to the opposing team.

wing player لاعِبُ جَناحٍ

قامَ لاعِبُ الجَناحِ بِتَمْريرَةٍ مُتْقَنَةٍ إلى المُدافعِ الأَيْمَنِ.

The wing player made a skillful pass to the right back.

center back مُدافِعُ خَطِّ الوَسَطِ

كانَ مُدافِعُ خَطِّ الوَسَطِ عُنْصُرًا حاسِمًا في فَوْزِ الفَريقِ.

The center back was a crucial element in the team's victory.

coach مُدَرِّبٌ

اِسْتَخْدَمَ مُدَرِّبُ الفَريقِ وَقْتًا مُسْتَقْطَعًا لِتَجْميعِ أَفْكارِ الفَريقِ وَتَوْجيهِهِمْ.

The team coach used a timeout to gather the team's thoughts and guide them.

dribble مُراوَغَةٌ

واجَهَتِ اللّاعِبَةُ خَصْمَتَها بِمُراوَغَةٍ مَهارِيَّةٍ، ثُمَّ أَحْرَزَتْ هَدَفًا.

The player confronted her opponent with skillful dribbling, then scored a goal.

goal مَرْمًى • مَرامٍ

تَمَّ التَّصَدّي لِلْكُرَةِ بِنَجاحٍ قَبْلَ أَنْ تَصِلَ إلى المَرْمى.

The ball was successfully intercepted before it reached the goal.

court مَلْعَبٌ • مَلاعِبُ

كانَ مَلْعَبُ المُباراةِ في حالَةٍ مُمْتازَةٍ وَجاهِزًا لِلْمُنافَسَةِ .

The match court was in excellent condition and ready for competition.

half time اِسْتِراحَةُ ما بَيْنَ الشَّوْطَيْنِ • أَنْصافٌ

اِسْتَغَلَّ الفَريقُ اِسْتِراحَةَ مابَيْنَ الشَّوْطَيْنِ لِإعادَةِ تَنْظيمِ اسْتراتيجِياتِهِمْ وَتَقْديمِ التَّوْجيهاتِ الأَخيرَةِ قَبْلَ بِدايَةِ الشَّوْطِ الثّاني.

The team utilized the halftime break to reorganize their strategies and provide final instructions before the start of the second half.

وَقْتٌ مُسْتَقْطَعٌ • أَوْقاتٌ **timeout**

بَعْدَ اسْتِخْدامِ وَقْتٍ مُسْتَقْطَعٍ، أَظْهَرَ الفَريقُ تَحَسُّنًا مَلْحوظًا في أَدائِهِ.

After using a timeout, the team showed a noticeable improvement in their performance.

6.1.4.1 Mini-Articles

Track **64**

أَبْهَرَ نادي الوُرودِ الجَماهيرَ في بُطولَةِ كُرَةِ اليَدِ النِّسائِيَّةِ، حَيْثُ حَقَّقَ فَوْزًا مُسْتَحَقًّا عَلى نادي الرِّياحِ .أَظْهَرَتِ البِدايَةُ القَوِيَّةُ لِلاعِبَةِ الوُرودِ، سَمَر الشَّهْري، أَنَّ الفَريقَ مُسْتَعِدٌّ لِلْمُنافَسَةِ بِقُوَّةٍ. اِسْتَقْبَلَتْ حارِسَةُ مَرْمى الرِّياحِ، مَها الزَّهْرانِيّ، عِدَّةَ رَمْياتٍ قَوِيَّةٍ، وَلَكِنَّ دِفاعَ الوُرودِ كانَ قَوِيًّا جِدًّا.

The Al-Worood (The Roses) team impressed the audience in the women's handball championship, achieving a well-deserved victory against the Al-Riyaah (The Winds) team. The powerful start by Al-Worood's player, Samar Al-Shahri, indicated that the team was ready to compete fiercely. The Al-Riyaah goalkeeper, Maha Al-Zahrani, faced several strong shots, but Al-Worood's defense was very strong.

حَقَّقَ فَريقُ السِّهامِ فَوْزًا مُثيرًا عَلى فَريقِ الصُّقورِ في مُباراةِ الأَمْسِ لِكُرَةِ اليَدِ. اِسْتَمْتَعَ المُشاهِدونَ بِالأَداءِ المُذْهِلِ لِحارِسِ مَرْمى السِّهامِ، أَحْمَد الخالِدي، الَّذي قامَ بِصَدّاتٍ مُدْهِشَةٍ ضِدَّ الرَّمْياتِ القَوِيَّةِ لِلصُّقورِ. المُدافِعُ الأَيْمَنُ، سَعْد السَّهْلي، كانَ نَجْمَ اللِّقاءِ، حَيْثُ قامَ بِتَمْريراتٍ فَعّالَةٍ وَسَجَّلَ عَدَدًا مِنَ الأَهْدافِ الرّائِعَةِ.

The Al-Siham (The Arrows) team achieved an exciting victory against the Al-Suqoor (The Falcons) team in yesterday's handball match. The viewers enjoyed the amazing performance of Al-Siham's goalkeeper, Ahmed Al-Khalidi, who made incredible saves against the powerful shots from Al-Suqoor. The right defender, Saad Al-Sahli, was the star of the match, providing effective passes and scoring several fantastic goals.

يَتَدَرَّبُ فَريقُ الجَوارِحِ لِلرِّجالِ بِجِدٍّ لِلْبُطولَةِ القادِمَةِ لِكُرَةِ اليَدِ، حَيْثُ يَتَوَقَّعونَ المُنافَسَةَ مَعَ أَقْوى الفِرَقِ. المُدَرِّبُ، مَحْمود بن صالِح، واثِقٌ في قُدْرَةِ لاعِبيهِ عَلى تَقْديمِ أَفْضَلِ ما لَدَيْهِمْ. يُعْتَبَرُ لاعِبُ الجَناحِ، فارِس بْنُ خالِد، واحِدًا مِنَ اللّاعِبينَ المُمَيَّزينَ في الفَريقِ، الَّذينَ يَتَطَلَّعونَ لِلتَّأَلُّقِ في البُطولَةِ القادِمَةِ.

The Al-Jawarih (The Predators) men's team is training hard for the upcoming handball championship, expecting tough competition with the strongest teams. The coach, Mahmoud bin Saleh, is confident in his players' ability to perform their best. The winger, Fares bin Khalid, is considered one of the standout players in the team, eager to shine in the upcoming championship.

فِي لِقاءٍ شَديدِ الإِثارَةِ فِي الدَّوْرِيِّ المَحَلِّيِّ لِكُرَةِ اليَدِ، تَقابَلَ فَريقا الجِبالِ وَالوِدْيانِ. كانَتِ الأَضْواءُ مُسَلَّطَةً عَلى الحَكَمِ الَّذي اتَّخَذَ قَراراتٍ حاسِمَةً فِي المُباراةِ. بَعْدَ العَديدِ مِنَ الأَخْطاءِ النّاجِمَةِ عَنْ تَمْريراتِ الفَريقَيْنِ، أَعْلَنَ الحَكَمُ وَقْتًا مُسْتَقْطَعًا، مِمّا أَضْفى عَلى اللِّقاءِ جَوًّا مِنَ التَّوَتُّرِ.

In a thrilling encounter in the local handball league, the Al-Jibal (the Mountains) and Al-Wadiyan (the Valleys) teams faced each other. The spotlight was on the referee, who made decisive calls during the match. After several errors resulting from both teams' passes, the referee announced extra time, adding tension to the game.

اِنْتَهَتْ مُباراةُ الجَوارِحِ وَالنُّسورِ فِي كُرَةِ اليَدِ بِالتَّعادُلِ بَعْدَ وَقْتٍ إِضافِيٍّ اتَّسَمَ بِالتَّنافُسِ الشَّديدِ. لَعِبَ لاعِبُ جَناحِ النُّسورِ، يوسُف الشَّهْرِيّ، دَوْرًا حاسِمًا فِي اللِّقاءِ، حَيْثُ قامَ بِعِدَّةِ مُراوَغاتٍ ناجِحَةٍ صَوْبَ الخَصْمِ. لاعِبُ جَناحِ الجَوارِحِ، أَحْمَد العَنْزِيّ، أَظْهَرَ مَهارَةً مُذْهِلَةً فِي التَّسْديدِ وَالتَّمْريرِ، مِمّا جَعَلَ المُباراةَ أَكْثَرَ إِثارَةً وَتَنافُسًا.

The match between the Al-Jawarih (the Predators) and the Al-Nasoor (the Eagles) women's handball teams ended in a draw after a highly competitive extra time. Al-Nasoor's winger, Yousef Al-Shahri, played a crucial role in the game with successful dribbles towards the opponent. Al-Jawarih's winger, Ahmed Al-Anzi, displayed remarkable shooting and passing skills, making the match more thrilling and competitive.

حَقَّقَ فَريقُ الفَراشاتِ أَوَّلَ فَوْزٍ لَهُ فِي الدَّوْرِيِّ النِّسائِيِّ لِكُرَةِ اليَدِ بِفَضْلِ الأَداءِ المُتَمَيِّزِ لِمُدافِعَتِهِ، نورَة العَسيري. اِسْتَعْرَضَتْ نورَة مَهاراتِها فِي الدِّفاعِ وَالتَّمْريرِ، بَيْنَما قَدَّمَتِ الحارِسَةُ لَمْياء الهاجِرِيّ أَداءً مُمْتازًا فِي الصَّدِّ، مِمّا ساهَمَ فِي تَحْقيقِ الفَوْزِ لِلْفَريقِ.

The Al-Farashat (the Butterflies) team secured their first victory in the women's national handball league thanks to the outstanding performance of their defender, Nora Al-Asiri. Nora displayed her defensive and passing skills effectively, while goalkeeper Lamia Al-Hajri delivered an excellent performance in blocking, contributing to the team's victory.

فازَ فَريقُ الأُسودِ لِلرِّجالِ بِبُطولَةِ كُرَةِ اليَدِ الوَطَنِيَّةِ بَعْدَ مُباراةٍ مُثيرَةٍ مَعَ فَريقِ النُّمورِ. فِي الدَّقائِقِ الأَخيرَةِ مِنَ المُباراةِ، قامَ مُدافِعُ الأُسْوَدِ الأَيْمَنُ، مُحَمَّد بِنْ عَبْدِ العَزيز، بِتَمْريرِ كُرَةٍ حاسِمَةٍ إِلى لاعِبِ جَناحِ الفَريقِ، عُمَر بِنْ فَهْد، الَّذي نَجَحَ فِي إِحْرازِ هَدَفِ الفَوْزِ.

The Al-Usuud men's team won the national handball championship after an exciting match against the Al-Numuur (the Tigers) team. In the final minutes of the game, Al-Usuud's right defender, Mohammed bin Abdulaziz, made a crucial pass to the team's winger, Omar bin Fahd, who successfully scored the winning goal.

في مُباراةٍ مَلْحَمِيَّةٍ بَيْنَ فَريقَي النُّسورِ وَالجِبالِ النِّسائِيِّ، اِنْتَهى اللِّقاءُ بِالتَّعادُلِ بَعْدَ مُباراةٍ شَديدَةِ التَّنافُسِ. اِسْتَعْرَضَتِ اللّاعِبَةُ الحُرَّةُ في النُّسورِ، أَمَل الغامِدِيّ، مَهاراتِها في المُراوَغَةِ وَتَمْريرِ الكُرَةِ بِدِقَّةٍ. بِالرَّغْمِ مِنَ الصَّدّاتِ المُمْتازَةِ مِنْ حارِسَةِ مَرْمى الجِبالِ، رانْيا الفَيْفي، فَقَدِ اسْتَطاعَ فَريقُ النُّسورِ الحِفاظَ عَلى التَّعادُلِ.

In an epic match between the Al-Nusoor (the Eagles) and the Al-Jibal women's handball teams, the game ended in a draw after a fiercely competitive match. Al-Nusoor's libero, Amal Al-Ghamdi, showcased her skills in dribbling and precise passing. Despite the excellent saves by the Mountains' goalkeeper, Rania Al-Faifi, the Al-Nusoor team managed to maintain the tie.

أَحْرَزَ فَريقُ الصُّقورِ الرِّجالِيُّ مَرْكَزًا مُتَقَدِّمًا في بُطولَةِ العالَمِ لِكُرَةِ اليَدِ، الَّتي واجَهَ فيها أَقْوى الفِرَقِ العالَمِيَّةِ. بِفَضْلِ الأَداءِ الاِسْتِثْنائِيِّ لِحارِسِ المَرْمى، أَحْمَد سالِم، وَقُدْرَتِهِ عَلى الصَّدِّ بِبَراعَةٍ، تَمَكَّنَ الفَريقُ مِنَ الحِفاظِ عَلى شَبَكَتِهِم نَظيفَةً في أَغْلَبِ أَوْقاتِ المُباراةِ.

The Al-Suqoor (the Falcons) men's team achieved an advanced position in the World Handball Championship, competing against the strongest global teams. Thanks to the exceptional performance of their goalkeeper, Ahmed Salem, and his skillful saves, the team managed to keep their net clean for most of the match.

6.1.5 Tennis

Track **65**

serve — **إِرْسالٌ**

بَدَأَتِ اللّاعِبَةُ المُباراةَ بِإِرْسالٍ قَوِيٍّ.

The player started the match with a powerful serve.

ace — **إِرْسالٌ ساحِقٌ**

بِإِرْسالٍ ساحِقٍ مِنْ روجِر فيدْرِر، اِنْتَهَتِ النُّقْطَةُ في غَمْضَةِ عَيْنٍ.

An ace from Roger Federer, the point ended in the blink of an eye.

break — **اِسْتِراحَةٌ**

خِلالَ فَتْرَةِ الاِسْتِراحَةِ، شَرِبَتِ اللّاعِبَةُ المِياهَ وَتَلَقَّتِ التَّعْليماتِ مِنْ مُدَرِّبِها .

During the break, the players rehydrated and received instructions from her coach.

التِّنِسْ **tennis**

نَبَأٌ عاجِلٌ: سيرينا وِلْيامْزْ تَتَأَهَّلُ إِلى النِّهائِيّاتِ في التِّنِس.

Breaking news: Serena Williams advances to the finals in tennis.

الخَطُّ الزَّوْجِيُّ **doubles line**

لامَسَتِ الكُرَةُ الخَطَّ الزَّوْجِيَّ، ما أَكَّدَ أَنَّها ضَرْبَةٌ داخِلَ المَلْعَبِ .

The ball brushed the doubles line, confirming it as an in-bounds shot.

الخَطُّ الفَرْدِيُّ **singles line**

عَلى الرَّغْمِ مِنَ الضَّغْطِ، اِسْتَطاعَ اللّاعِبُ أَنْ يُحافِظَ عَلى تَرْكيزِهِ وَيُحَقِّقَ النِّقاطَ عَلى الخَطِّ الفَرْدِيِّ.

Despite the pressure, the player was able to maintain his focus and score points on the singles line.

المِنْطَقَةُ اليُسْرى مِنَ المَلْعَبِ (مِنْطَقَةُ الأَفْضَلِيَّةِ) • مَناطِقُ **advantage court**

لَعِبَ اللّاعِبُ الإِرْسالَ مِنَ المِنْطَقَةِ اليُسْرى مِنَ المَلْعَبِ.

The player served from the advantage court.

المِنْطَقَةُ اليُمْنى مِنَ المَلْعَبِ **deuce court**

أَخْطَأَ اللّاعِبُ في الإِرْسالِ مِنَ المِنْطَقَةِ اليُمْنى مِنَ المَلْعَبِ.

The player made a mistake in serving from the deuce court.

تَعادُلٌ **deuce**

وَصَلَتِ المُباراةُ إِلى حالَةِ التَّعادُلِ بَعْدَ مَجْموعَةٍ تَنافُسِيَّةٍ.

The match reached a deuce after a competitive set.

تِقْنِيَّةُ عَيْنِ الصَّقْرِ **Hawk-Eye technology**

اِسْتَخْدَمَ اللّاعِبُ تِقْنِيَّةَ عَيْنِ الصَّقْرِ لِلتَّحَقُّقِ مِنْ صِحَّةِ القَرارِ.

The player used the Hawk-Eye technology to verify the decision.

ball boy/girl جامِعُ / جامِعَةُ الكُراتِ

كانَ جامِعُ الكُراتِ سَريعًا وَمُتَفانِيًا في عَمَلِه.

The ball boy was quick and dedicated in his job.

umpire, referee حَكَمٌ • حُكّامٌ

أَصْدَرَ حَكَمُ المُباراةِ قَراراتٍ عادِلَةً وَمُنْصِفَةً.

The match referee issued fair and just decisions.

line judge حَكَمُ الخَطِّ

أَكَّدَ حَكَمُ الخَطِّ أَنَّ الكُرَةَ خارِجَ الخَطِّ.

The line judge confirmed that the ball was out of line.

baseline خَطُّ القاعِدَةِ

سَدَّدَ اللّاعِبُ الكُرَةَ بِقُوَّةٍ مِنْ خَطِّ القاعِدَةِ.

The player hit the ball hard from the baseline.

service line خَطُّ الإِرْسالِ • خُطوطٌ

بَدَأَتِ اللّاعِبَةُ الجَوْلَةَ بِإِرْسالٍ قَوِيٍّ عَلى خَطِّ الإِرْسالِ.

The player started the round with a strong serve on the service line.

fault خَطَأٌ • أَخْطاءٌ

أَخْطَأَ اللّاعِبُ في تَقْديرِ مَكانِ الكُرَةِ، مِمّا أَدّى إِلى خَطَأٍ .

The player made a mistake in estimating the location of the ball, leading to a fault.

side spin دَورانٌ جانِبِيٌّ

نَفَّذَ اللّاعِبُ دَوَرانًا جانِبِيًّا مُعَقَّدًا لِلْكُرَةِ، مِمّا أَدّى إِلى صُعوبَةِ اسْتِقْبالِها مِنْ قِبَلِ الخَصْمِ.

The player executed a complex side spin on the ball, making it difficult for the opponent to receive it.

دَورانٌ سُفْلِيٌّ لِلْكُرَة
back spin

أَظْهَرَتِ اللّاعِبَةُ مَهارَةً في تَنْفيذِ الدَّورانِ السُّفْلِيِّ لِلْكُرَة، مِمّا أَدّى إلى فَوْزِها بِالنُّقْطَةِ.

The player showed skill in back spinning the ball, leading to her winning the point.

دَورانٌ عُلْوِيٌّ لِلْكُرَة
top spin

باسْتِخْدامِ الدَّورانِ العُلْوِيِّ لِلْكُرَة، نَجَحَ اللّاعِبُ في خِداعِ خَصْمِهِ وَفازَ بِالنُّقْطَةِ.

Using a top spin on the ball, the player succeeded in deceiving his opponent and won the point.

شَبَكَةٌ
net • شِباكٌ

لَمْ يَتَمَكَّنِ اللّاعِبُ مِنْ تَجاوُزِ الشَّبَكَةِ في الضَّرْبَةِ الأَخيرَة، مِمّا أَدّى إلى خَسارَتِهِ لِلنُّقْطَةِ.

The player was unable to overcome the net in the last shot, leading to him losing the point.

شَريكٌ زَوْجِيٌّ
doubles partner • شُرَكاءُ

أَعْلَنَتِ اللّاعِبَةُ عَنِ اخْتيارِها لِشَريكٍ زَوْجِيٍّ جَديدٍ لِلْمَوْسِمِ القادِمِ مِنَ البُطولاتِ.

The player announced her choice of a new doubles partner for the upcoming tournament season.

صِفْرٌ
love • أَصْفارٌ

بَعْدَ مَجْموعَةٍ شاقَّةٍ، كانَتِ النَّتيجَةُ صِفْرًا لِكِلا اللّاعِبَيْنِ، مِمّا أَظْهَرَ التَّوَتُّرَ وَالتَّحَدِّيَ بَيْنَهُما.

After a tough set, the score was love-all, showing the tension and challenge between them.

ضَرَبَ
to hit • ضَرْبٌ

واصَلَ اللّاعِبُ ضَرْبَ الكُرَةِ بِقُوَّةٍ وَدِقَّةٍ، مِمّا أَدّى إلى تَقَدُّمِهِ في المُباراةِ.

The player continued to hit the ball with strength and precision, leading to his advancement in the match.

ضَرْبَةٌ أَمامِيَّةٌ
forehand

كانَتِ الضَّرْبَةُ الأَمامِيَّةُ لِلّاعِبَةِ مِثالِيَّةً، مِمّا أَدّى إلى تَسْجيلِها لِنُقْطَةٍ.

The player's forehand shot was perfect, resulting in her scoring a point.

backhand ضَرْبَةٌ خَلْفِيَّةٌ

أَظْهَرَ اللّاعِبُ مَهارَةً في الضَّرْبَةِ الخَلْفِيَّةِ، مِمّا سَمَحَ لَهُ بِاسْتِعادَةِ التَّحَكُّمِ في المُباراةِ.

The player demonstrated skill in the backhand shot, allowing him to regain control of the match.

smash ضَرْبَةٌ ساحِقَةٌ

في اللَّحْظَةِ المُناسِبَةِ، سَدَّدَ اللّاعِبُ ضَرْبَةً ساحِقَةً، مِمّا أَدّى إلى فَوْزِهِ في المُباراةِ.

At the right moment, the player hit a smash, leading to his victory in the match.

drop shot ضَرْبَةٌ ساقِطَةٌ

أَلْقَتِ اللّاعِبَةُ بِالْكُرَةِ بِلُطْفٍ في ضَرْبَةٍ ساقِطَةٍ، مِمّا أَدّى إلى فَوْزِها بِالنُّقْطَةِ.

The player gently tossed the ball in a drop shot, leading to her winning the point.

volley ضَرْبَةٌ طائِرَةٌ

أَظْهَرَ اللّاعِبُ قُدْرَةً مُدْهِشَةً عَلى تَنْفيذِ ضَرْبَةٍ طائِرَةٍ حاسِمَةٍ، مِمّا ساعَدَهُ في الفَوْزِ بِالنُّقْطَةِ.

The player showed an impressive ability to execute a decisive volley, which helped him win the point.

slice ضَرْبَةٌ قاطِعَةٌ

أَدَّتِ الضَّرْبَةُ القاطِعَةُ الَّتي نَفَّذَها اللّاعِبُ إلى تَغْييرِ وَتيرَةِ المُباراةِ.

The player's slice shot led to a change in the pace of the match.

lob ضَرْبَةٌ مُقوَّسَةٌ

نَجَحَتِ اللّاعِبَةُ في تَنْفيذِ ضَرْبَةٍ مُقوَّسَةٍ عالِيَةٍ، مِمّا أَدّى إلى تَسْجيلِها لِلنُّقْطَةِ.

The player succeeded in executing a high lob shot, leading to her scoring a point.

half volley ضَرْبَةٌ نِصْفُ طائِرَةٍ

حاوَلَ اللّاعِبُ تَنْفيذَ ضَرْبَةٍ نِصْفِ طائِرَةٍ، لَكِنَّ الكُرَةَ لَمْ تَصِلْ إلى الشَّبَكَةِ.

The player attempted to execute a half volley, but the ball did not reach the net.

tennis **كُرَةُ المِضْرَبِ**

عَلى الرَّغْمِ مِنَ الصُّعوباتِ، اِسْتَطاعَ اللّاعِبُ الفَوْزَ بِمُباراةِ كُرَةِ المِضْرَبِ.

Despite the difficulties, the player was able to win the tennis match.

> The sport is also commonly referred to by its international name التِّنِسْ.

tennis ball **كُرَةُ مِضْرَبٍ**

عِنْدَما ضَرَبَتْ كُرَةُ المِضْرَبِ مِضْرَبَ اللّاعِبِ، اِرْتَدَّتْ بِسُرْعَةٍ وَتَجاوَزَتِ الشَّبَكَةَ، مِمّا أَدّى إِلى فَوْزِهِ بِالنُّقْطَةِ.

When the tennis ball hit the player's racket, it rebounded quickly and crossed the net, leading to his winning of the point.

tiebreak **كَسْرُ التَّعادُلِ**

كانَ كَسْرُ التَّعادُلِ مُثيرًا لِلْغايَةِ وَانْتَهى بِفَوْزِ اللّاعِبِ الشّابِّ.

The tiebreak was extremely exciting and ended with the young player's victory.

player **لاعِبٌ**

في نِهائِيّاتِ بُطولَةِ وِيمْبِلْدونْ، أَبْدَعَ اللّاعِبُ في اسْتِعْراضِ مَهاراتِهِ وَتَفَوَّقَ عَلى مُنافِسِهِ بِثَلاثِ مَجْموعاتٍ مُتَتالِيَةٍ.

In the Wimbledon finals, the player brilliantly showcased his skills and outperformed his opponent with three consecutive sets.

to serve **لَعِبَ الإِرْسالَ** • لَعِبٌ

اِسْتَعَدَّ اللّاعِبُ لِلَعِبِ الإِرْسالِ بِتَرْكيزٍ عالٍ وَثِقَةٍ في النَّفْسِ.

The player prepared to serve with high concentration and self-confidence.

> When talking about actions like 'to serve,' 'to volley,' or 'to smash' in Arabic, the common approach is to use لَعِبَ or ضَرَبَ followed by the action's masdar (verbal noun). For example, instead of saying أَرْسَلَ, you would say لَعِبَ الإِرْسالَ.

to smash **لَعِبَ ضَرْبَةً ساحِقَةً** • لَعِبٌ

فاجَأَ اللّاعِبُ الجَميعَ عِنْدَما لَعِبَ ضَرْبَةً ساحِقَةً وَفازَ بِالنُّقْطَةِ.

The player surprised everyone when he played a smash and won the point.

game — **لُعْبَةٌ**

نَفَّذَتِ اللاعِبَةُ إِرْسالًا قاضِيًا لِتَحْسِمِ اللُّعْبَةَ في كُرَةِ المِضْرَبِ .

The player served an ace to clinch the game in tennis.

match — **مُباراةٌ**

كانَتِ المُباراةُ شَديدَةَ الإِثارَةِ وَكُلُّ لَحْظَةٍ كانَتْ مَصيرِيَّةً.

The match was extremely exciting, and every moment was decisive.

set — **مَجْموعَةٌ**

لَقَدْ أَظْهَرَتِ المَجْموعَةُ الأَخيرَةُ مِنَ المُباراةِ مَدى تَفَوُّقِ اللّاعِبِ.

The last set of the match showed the player's superiority.

let — **مُرورُ الكُرَةِ مَعَ لَمْسِ الشَّبَكَةِ أَثْناءَ أَداءِ الإِرْسالِ**

خِلالَ الإِرْسالِ، مَرَّتِ الكُرَةُ وَلَمَسَتِ الشَّبَكَةَ، مِمّا أَدّى إِلى إِعادَةِ الإِرْسالِ وَفْقًا لِقاعِدَةِ ال let.

During the serve, the ball touched the net, leading to a re-serve according to the let rule.

> In sports, sometimes there's no exact Arabic word for a certain action or technique. In these cases, the English term is usually used. Even when Arabic terms do exist, English words are often still used.

racket — **مِضْرَبٌ** • مَضارِبُ

خِلالَ اللُّعْبَةِ، تَعَرَّضَ المِضْرَبُ لِلْكَسْرِ بَعْدَ أَنْ ضَرَبَ اللّاعِبُ الكُرَةَ بِقُوَّةٍ شَديدَةٍ.

During the game, the racket broke after the player hit the ball with extreme force.

court — **مَلْعَبٌ** • مَلاعِبُ

كانَتْ جَوْدَةُ المَلْعَبِ مِثالِيَّةً وَمُناسِبَةً لِلْمُباراةِ.

The quality of the court was perfect and suitable for the match.

advantage — **مَيْزَةٌ / أَفْضَلِيَّةٌ**

بَعْدَ سِلْسِلَةٍ طَويلَةٍ مِنَ الأَشْواطِ المُتَقارِبَةِ، حَصَلَ اللّاعِبُ عَلى المَيزَةِ وَفازَ بِالْجَوْلَةِ.

After a long series of close games, the player got the advantage and won the round.

to volley • ضَرْبٌ **نَفَّذَ ضَرْبَةً طائِرَةً**

حاوَلَ اللاعِبُ تَنْفيذَ ضَرْبَةٍ طائِرَةٍ، لَكِنَّ الكُرَةَ سَقَطَتْ قَبْلَ الشَّبَكَةِ.

The player attempted to volley, but the ball dropped before the net.

6.1.5.1 Mini-Articles

Track **66**

تَمَكَّنَ نَجْمُ التِّنِسِ السُّعودِيُّ، سَعيد القَحْطاني، مِنْ تَحْقيقِ فَوْزٍ مُذْهِلٍ في نِهائِيِّ بُطولَةِ الجرانْدْ سْلام. قَدَّمَ القَحْطاني أداءً مُتَمَيِّزًا في مَلْعَبِ التِّنِسِ مُسَجِّلًا عَدَدًا مِنَ الإِرْسالاتِ السّاحِقَةِ وَالضَّرَباتِ السّاقِطَةِ الَّتي أَبْهَرَتِ الجُمْهورَ. فازَ بِالْمُباراةِ بِثَلاثِ مَجْموعاتٍ نَظيفَةٍ وَأَثْبَتَ أَنَّهُ يَمْتَلِكُ ما يُؤَهِّلُهُ لِلتَّتْويجِ في أَكْبَرِ البُطولاتِ العالَمِيَّةِ.

Saudi tennis star, Sa'id Al-Qahtani, managed to achieve a stunning victory in the Grand Slam final. Al-Qahtani delivered an outstanding performance on the tennis court, scoring several powerful serves and impressive drop shots that amazed the audience. He won the match in three clean sets, proving that he has what it takes to be crowned in the biggest global tournaments.

في مُباراةٍ حاسِمَةٍ في الدَّوْرِ الرّابِعِ لِبُطولَةِ ويمْبِلْدون، اِسْتَعانَ الحَكَمُ بِتِقْنِيَّةِ عَيْنِ الصَّقْرِ لِتَحْديدِ ما إذا كانَتِ الكُرَةُ داخِلَ أَوْ خارِجَ خَطِّ الإِرْسالِ. بَعْدَ الاِسْتِعانَةِ بِالتِّقْنِيَّةِ، تَمَّ تَأْكيدُ أَنَّ الكُرَةَ كانَتْ في الدّاخِلِ، وَبِالتّالي تَمَّ مَنْحُ اللّاعِبَةِ السُّعودِيَّةِ، رَجاء السُّلَيْمان، النُّقْطَةَ، وَبِالتّالي الفَوْزَ بِالْمَجْموعَةِ الأولى.

In a crucial match in the fourth round of Wimbledon, the referee used Hawk-Eye technology to determine whether the ball was in or out of the service line. After consulting the technology, it was confirmed that the ball was in, and thus the Saudi player, Rajaa' Al-Sulaiman, was awarded the point and subsequently won the first set.

تَأَهَّلَ الثُّنائِيُّ السُّعودِيُّ المُكَوَّنُ مِنْ مُحَمَّد النَّعيم وَفَهْد السَّعْدي لِلدَّوْرِ النِّهائِيِّ في بُطولَةِ التِّنِسِ الزَّوْجِي. يَشْتَهِرُ الثُّنائِيُّ بِتَنْسيقِهِما العالي وَتَمْريراتِهِما الدَّقيقَةِ، وَقَدْ أَظْهَرا هَذِهِ المَهاراتِ مَرَّةً أُخْرى في مُباراةِ الأَمْسِ. فازَ الثُّنائِيُّ بِالْمُباراةِ بِنَتيجَةِ 6 - 3 , 7 - 6 بَعْدَ كَسْرِ التَّعادُلِ في المَجْموعَةِ الثّانِيَةِ.

The Saudi duo composed of Mohammed Al-Naim and Fahd Al-Saadi advanced to the finals in the doubles tennis championship. The pair is known for their excellent coordination and precise passing, and they showcased these skills once again in yesterday's match. They won the match with a score of 6-3, 7-6 after breaking the tie in the second set.

6.1.5.2 Article: The Highly Anticipated Final

Track **67**

النِّهائيُّ المُرْتَقَبُ: عَبْد الرَّحْمن السَّلامي يُواجِهُ أَنْدريهْ روسّو في مَعْرَكَةِ الأَبْطالِ بِبُطولَةِ ويمْبِلْدونْ

تَجْري الاِسْتِعْداداتُ عَلى قَدَمٍ وَساقٍ في أَحَدِ أَشْهَرِ المَلاعِبِ العالَمِيَّةِ لِلتِّنِسِ اسْتِعْدادًا لِلْمُباراةِ النِّهائِيَّةِ في بُطولَةِ ويمْبِلْدونْ، حَيْثُ سَيَتَواجَهُ في النِّهائِيِّ اللّاعِبُ السُّعودِيُّ الشّابُّ، عَبْد الرَّحْمن السَّلامي، وَالنَّجْمُ العالَمِيُّ الشَّهيرِ، أَنْدريهْ روسّو.

مُنْذُ بِدايَةِ البُطولَةِ، أَظْهَرَ السَّلامي مُسْتَوىً اسْتِثْنائِيًّا في لَعِبِ الإِرْسالِ، حَيْثُ كانَتْ إِرسالاتُهُ قَوِيَّةً في مُعْظَمِ الأَوْقاتِ، ما مَنَحَهُ العَديدُ مِنَ النِّقاطِ. كَما كانَ دِفاعُهُ جَيِّدًا عِنْدَ خَطِّ القاعِدَةِ وَالشَّبَكَةِ، وَاسْتَخْدَمَ الضَّرْبَةَ الخَلْفِيَّةَ وَالأَمامِيَّةَ بِمَهارَةٍ في تَقْديمِ ضَرَباتٍ صَعْبَةٍ عَلى خَصْمِهِ.

في نِصْفِ النِّهائِيِّ، كانَ لابُدَّ لَهُ مِنَ الاِسْتِعانَةِ بِكُلِّ مَهاراتِهِ لِكَسْرِ التَّعادُلِ مَعَ اللّاعِبِ المُنافِسِ. لَقَدْ أَظْهَرَ القُوَّةَ في تَسْديدِ الضَّرَباتِ السّاحِقَةِ، وَكَذَلِكَ القُدْرَةَ عَلى إِرْسالِ الكُرَةِ بِضَرْبَةٍ مُقَوَّسَةٍ بَعيدًا عَنْ مُتَناوَلِ خَصْمِهِ. وَقَدْ ساعَدَهُ تَمَكُّنُهُ مِنَ الضَّرَباتِ الأَمامِيَّةِ وَالخَلْفِيَّةِ في تَحْقيقِ هَذا النَّجاحِ.

في الجِهَةِ الأُخْرى مِنَ المَلْعَبِ، يَتَمَتَّعُ روسّو بِخِبْرَةٍ كَبيرَةٍ في عالَمِ التِّنِسِ. كَما إِنَّهُ مَعْروفٌ بِقُوَّتِهِ في الضَّرَباتِ الطّائِرَةِ وَالقاطِعَةِ. كَما يَمْتازُ بِالْقُدْرَةِ عَلى تَغْييرِ مَسارِ الكُرَةِ بِفَضْلِ الدَّورانِ الجانِبِيِّ وَالعُلْوِيِّ وَالسُّفْلِيِّ لِلْكُرَةِ. كَما إِنَّهُ يُتْقِنُ كُلَّ مِنَ اللَّعِبِ الدِّفاعِيِّ وَالهُجومِيِّ، وَلَدَيْهِ القُدْرَةُ عَلى الاِنْتِقالِ بِسَلاسَةٍ مِنْ خَطِّ القاعِدَةِ إِلى الشَّبَكَةِ.

في النِّهايَةِ، يَتَعَيَّنُ عَلى كُلٍّ مِنَ اللّاعِبَيْنِ التَّرْكيزُ عَلى الاِسْتراتيجِيَّةِ وَالتَّحَكُّمِ في المُباراةِ. سَيَكونُ الحَكَمُ وَحَكَمُ الخَطِّ في مَوْقِعِ الحَدَثِ، مُسْتَعِدَّيْنِ لِاسْتِخْدامِ تِقْنِيَّةِ عَيْنِ الصَّقْرِ إِذا اقْتَضَتِ الحاجَةُ.

مِنَ المُنْتَظَرِ أَنْ تَكونَ المُباراةُ حافِلَةً بِالإِثارَةِ وَالتَّشْويقِ، حَيْثُ تَلْتَقي الخِبْرَةُ وَالشَّبابُ، وَنَحْنُ نَتَطَلَّعُ إِلى مُشاهَدَةِ مُباراةِ تِنِسٍ مُمْتِعَةٍ وَمُثيرَةٍ.

The Highly Anticipated Final: Abdulrahman Al-Salami Faces Andre Russo in the Battle of Champions at Wimbledon

Preparations are in full swing at one of the world's most renowned tennis courts, Wimbledon, ahead of the final match. In the final, the young Saudi player, Abdulrahman Al-Salami, will go head-to-head against the world-famous star, Andre Russo.

Since the beginning of the tournament, Al-Salami has showcased exceptional performance in serving, with his serves proving to be powerful most of the time, earning him numerous points. His defense at the baseline and net has been strong, and he skillfully utilizes both his backhand and forehand to deliver challenging shots to his opponent.

In the semifinal, he had to rely on all his skills to break the tie with his competitive opponent. He demonstrated strength in powerful shots and the ability to send the ball in a curving trajectory, beyond his opponent's reach. His proficiency in both forehand and backhand contributed to his success.

On the other side of the court, Russo boasts significant experience in the world of tennis. He is well-known for his strength in volley and slice shots. Additionally, he excels at changing the ball's trajectory with side spin, topspin, and backspin. He is adept at both defensive and offensive play, smoothly transitioning from the baseline to the net.

In the end, both players must focus on strategy and game control. The umpire and line judge will be present at the event, ready to employ Hawk-Eye technology if necessary.

The match is expected to be filled with excitement and suspense, as experience meets youth. We look forward to witnessing an enjoyable and thrilling tennis match.

6.2 Athletics and Olympic Sports

6.2.1 Track and Field

Track **68**

athletics *pl.* **أَلْعابُ القُوى**

تُعْتَبَرُ أَلْعابُ القُوى إِحْدى أَبْرَزِ الفَعاليّاتِ فِي الأَلْعابِ الأولِمْبِيَّةِ.

Athletics is one of the most prominent events in the Olympics.

track and field sports **أَلْعابُ المِضْمارِ وَالمَيْدانِ**

تُعْتَبَرُ أَلْعابُ المِضْمارِ وَالمَيْدانِ مِنْ أَكْثَرِ الأَلْعابِ شَعْبِيَّةً فِي الأَلْعابِ الأولِمْبِيَّةِ، وَتَشْمَلُ فَعاليّاتِ الجَرْيِ وَالقَفْزِ وَالرَّمْيِ.

Track and field are among the most popular sports in the Olympics, encompassing running, jumping, and throwing events.

Olympic **أولِمْبِيٌّ**

سَيُشارِكُ اللّاعِبُ فِي الأَلْعابِ الأولِمْبِيَّةِ لِأَوَّلِ مَرَّةٍ هَذا العامَ.

The player will participate in the Olympics for the first time this year.

cross-country running | **اِخْتِراقُ الضّاحِيَةِ**

حَقَّقَ اللّاعِبُ فَوْزًا مُسْتَحَقًّا في سِباقِ اخْتِراقِ الضّاحِيَةِ.

The player achieved a well-deserved victory in the cross-country running race.

heptathlon | **السُّباعِيُّ**

فازَتِ الرِّياضِيَّةُ البِريطانِيَّةُ في السُّباعِيِّ في الأَلْعابِ الأولِمْبِيَّةِ.

The British athlete won the heptathlon in the Olympics.

running | **العَدْوُ / الجَرْيُ / الرَّكْضُ**

أَثْناءَ الْمُنافَسَةِ القَوِيَّةِ في سِباقِ الْعَدْوِ في الأولِمْبِياد، تَأَلَّقَتِ الْبَطَلَةُ وَحَقَّقَتِ المَرْكَزَ الأَوَّلَ بِفارِقٍ كَبيرٍ .

During the fierce competition in the Olympic running race, the champion excelled and achieved the first-place position with a significant lead.

decathlon | **العُشارِيُّ / ديكاثلون**

سَيُشارِكُ الرِّياضِيُّ في العُشارِيِّ في الأَلْعابِ الأولِمْبِيَّةِ القادِمَةِ.

The athlete will participate in the decathlon in the upcoming Olympics.

pole vault | **القَفْزُ بِالزّانَةِ**

حَطَّمَ الرِّياضِيُّ الفَرَنْسِيُّ الرَّقْمَ القِياسِيَّ في القَفْزِ بِالزّانَةِ.

The French athlete broke the record in the pole vault.

jumping | **الوَثْبُ**

حَقَّقَ الرِّياضِيُّ المِصْرِيُّ نَجاحًا كَبيرًا في مَجالِ الوَثْبِ العالي.

The Egyptian athlete achieved great success in the field of high jumping.

triple jump | **الوَثْبُ الثُّلاثِيُّ**

اِسْتَطاعَ الرِّياضِيُّ المَغْرِبِيُّ الفَوْزَ بِالْميدالْيَةِ الذَّهَبِيَّةِ في الوَثْبِ الثُّلاثِيِّ.

The Moroccan athlete managed to win the gold medal in the triple jump.

الوَثْبُ الطَّويلُ — **long jump**

أَظْهَرَ الرِّياضِيُّ المِصْرِيُّ مَهاراتٍ مُذْهِلَةً في الوَثْبِ الطَّويلِ.

The Egyptian athlete demonstrated amazing skills in the long jump.

الوَثْبُ العالي — **high jump**

اِحْتَلَّ الوَثْبُ العالي مَكانَةً كَبيرَةً في الأَلْعابِ الأولِمْبِيَّةِ.

The high jump occupied a prominent place in the Olympics.

بِدايَةٌ غَيْرُ صَحيحَةٍ — **false start**

تَمَّ اسْتِبْعادُ الرِّياضِيِّ مِنَ السِّباقِ بِسَبَبِ بِدايَةٍ غَيْرِ صَحيحَةٍ.

The athlete was disqualified from the race due to a false start.

بَطيءٌ — **slow**

كانَتْ وَتيرَةُ السِّباقِ بَطيئَةً في البِدايَةِ.

The pace of the race was slow at the beginning.

ثَقيلٌ — **heavy**

أَطْلَقَ الرِّياضِيُّ رَمْيَةً قَوِيَّةً وَدَقيقَةً، دافِعًا المِطْرَقَةَ الثَّقيلَةَ لِمَسافَةٍ مُبْهِرَةٍ في مُسابَقَةِ رَمْيِ المِطْرَقَةِ.

The athlete unleashed a powerful and precise throw, propelling the heavy hammer to an impressive distance

حِذاءُ سِباقٍ • أَحْذِيَةٌ — **spikes**

اِسْتَخْدَمَ العَدّاءُ حِذاءَ جَرْيٍ خاصٍّ لِتَحْسينِ أَدائِهِ.

The runner used special running spikes to improve his performance.

حَواجِزُ *pl.* — **hurdles**

تُعْتَبَرُ الحَواجِزُ واحِدَةً مِنَ الفَعالِيّاتِ الأَكْثَرِ تَحَدِّيًا في الأَلْعابِ الأولِمْبِيَّةِ.

Hurdles are one of the most challenging events in the Olympics.

خَطُّ البِدايَةِ • خُطوطٌ **start line**

كانَ جَميعُ العَدّائينَ عَلى خَطِّ البِدايَةِ جاهِزينَ لِلسِّباقِ.

All the runners were ready at the start line.

خَطُّ النِّهايَةِ **finish line**

بَعْدَ سِباقٍ مُثيرٍ، تَجاوَزَ العَدّاءُ خَطَّ النِّهايَةِ وَاحْتَفَلَ بِالْفَوْزِ.

After an exciting race, the runner crossed the finish line and celebrated the victory.

خَفيفُ الحَرَكَةِ **light-footed**

خِلالَ السِّباقِ، يَجِبُ أَنْ يَكونَ العَدّاءُ خَفيفَ الحَرَكَةِ.

During the race, a runner must be light-footed.

رَقْمٌ قِياسِيٌّ • أَرْقامٌ **record**

حَطَّمَ العَدّاءُ الإِثْيوبِيُّ الرَّقْمَ القِياسِيَّ في العَدْوِ الطَّويلِ.

The Ethiopian runner broke the record in long distance running.

رَقْمٌ قِياسِيٌّ شَخْصِيٌّ **personal best**

حَقَّقَ الرِّياضِيُّ رَقْمًا قِياسِيًّا شَخْصِيًّا في السِّباقِ.

The athlete achieved a personal best in the race.

رَقْمٌ قِياسِيٌّ عالَمِيٌّ • أَرْقامٌ **world record**

سَجَّلَ العَدّاءُ الجامايْكِيُّ رَقْمًا قِياسِيًّا عالَمِيًّا في سِباقِ الأَلْفِ مِتْرٍ.

The Jamaican runner set a world record in the thousand-meter race.

رَكَضَ • رَكْضٌ **to run**

رَكَضَ العَدّاءُ بِسُرْعَةٍ فائِقَةٍ لِلْفَوْزِ بِالسِّباقِ.

The runner ran at a super fast pace to win the race.

archery رِمايَةُ القَوْسِ وَالسَّهْمِ

تُعَدُّ رِمايَةُ القَوْسِ وَالسَّهْمِ مِنَ الرِّياضاتِ الَّتي تَتَطَلَّبُ التَّرْكيزَ وَالدِّقَّةَ.

Archery is one of the sports that require concentration and precision.

to throw رَمى • رَمْيٌ

أَخَذَ الرِّياضِيُّ الرُّمْحَ وَقامَ بِرَمْيِهِ بِقُوَّةٍ لا تُصَدَّقُ .

The athlete picked up the javelin and threw it with incredible force.

javelin throw رَمْيُ الرُّمْحِ

أَظْهَرَ الرِّياضِيُّ مَهاراتٍ رائِعَةً في رَمْيِ الرُّمْحِ.

The athlete showed amazing skills in javelin throw.

discus throw رَمْيُ القُرْصِ

حَقَّقَ الرِّياضِيُّ الفَوْزَ في رَمْيِ القُرْصِ في الأَلْعابِ الأولِمْبِيَّةِ.

The athlete won the discus throw in the Olympics.

shot put رَمْيُ الكُرَةِ الحَديدِيَّةِ / رَمْيُ الجُلَّةِ

أَظْهَرَ الرِّياضِيُّ مَهارَةً عالِيَةً في رَمْيِ الكُرَةِ الحَديدِيَّةِ.

The athlete showed high skill in shot put.

hammer throw رَمْيُ المِطْرَقَةِ

سَجَّلَ الرِّياضِيُّ الرّوسِيُّ رَقْمًا قِياسِيًّا في رَمْيِ المِطْرَقَةِ.

The Russian athlete set a record in the hammer throw.

throw رَمْيَةٌ

نَفَّذَ الرِّياضِيُّ رَمْيَةً قَوِيَّةً لِيَفوزَ بِالمُسابَقَةِ.

The athlete made a strong throw to win the competition.

Olympic sports *pl.* **رِياضاتٌ أولِمْبِيَّةٌ**

تَتَضَمَّنُ الرِّياضاتُ الأولِمْبِيَّةُ مَجْموعَةً مُتَنَوِّعَةً مِنَ الفَعالِيّاتِ، مِثْلَ الجَرْيِ وَالرَّمْيِ والقَفْزِ.

The Olympic sports include a variety of events such as running, throwing, and jumping.

jumping sports *pl.* **رِياضاتُ القَفْزِ / رِياضاتُ الوَثْبِ**

تَحْظى رِياضاتُ القَفْزِ بِشَعْبِيَّةٍ كَبيرَةٍ في الأَلْعابِ الأولِمْبِيَّةِ.

Jumping sports are very popular in the Olympics.

race **سِباقٌ**

فازَ العَدّاءُ الكينِيُّ في سِباقِ العَدْوِ الطَّويلِ.

The Kenyan runner won the long-distance race.

cross-country race **سِباقُ اخْتِراقِ الضّاحِيَةِ**

يُعْتَبَرُ سِباقُ اخْتِراقِ الضّاحِيَةِ تَحَدِّيًا كَبيرًا لِلْقُدْرَةِ عَلى التَّحَمُّلِ.

The cross-country race is a major challenge for endurance.

relay race **سِباقُ التَّتابُعِ**

فازَ الفَريقُ المِصْرِيُّ في سِباقِ التَّتابُعِ في الأَلْعابِ الأولِمْبِيَّةِ.

The Egyptian team won the relay race in the Olympics.

sprint **سِباقُ السُّرْعَةِ**

يَتَطَلَّبُ سِباقُ السُّرْعَةِ تَدْريبًا عالِيَ الكَفاءَةِ وَسُرْعَةَ اسْتِجابَةٍ.

The sprint race requires highly efficient training and quick response.

road running **سِباقُ الطُّرُقاتِ**

يُفَضِّلُ بَعْضُ العَدّائينَ سِباقَ الطُّرُقاتِ بِسَبَبِ التَّغْييرِ في المَناظِرِ وَالتَّضاريسِ.

Some runners prefer road running due to the change in scenery and terrain.

سَريعٌ
fast

اِسْتَعْرَضَ العَدّاءُ الجامايْكِيُّ سُرْعَتَهُ الفائِقَةَ عِنْدَما هَزَمَ جَميعَ المُنافِسينَ في سِباقِ 100 مِتْرٍ.

The Jamaican runner showcased his super-fast speed when he beat all competitors in the 100m race.

عَدّاءٌ
runner

في سِباقِ ال 800 مِتْرٍ، تَفَوَّقَ العَدّاءُ المَغْرِبِيُّ عَلى جَميعِ المُنافِسينَ لِيُحَقِّقَ الذَّهَبِيَّةَ.

In the 800m race, the Moroccan runner surpassed all competitors to clinch the gold.

عَصا التَّتابُعِ • عِصِيٌّ
baton

في الأَلْعابِ الأولِمْبِيَّةِ، نَجَحَ العَدّاءُ الكينِيُّ في تَمْريرِ عَصا التَّتابُعِ بِبَراعَةٍ لِزَميلِهِ.

In the Olympics, the Kenyan runner succeeded in skillfully passing the relay baton to his teammate.

قَفَزَ • قَفْزٌ
to jump

أَظْهَرَ العَدّاءُ التّونِسِيُّ قُدْرَةً اسْتِثْنائِيَّةً عَلى القَفْزِ عِنْدَما حَقَّقَ رَقْمًا قِياسِيًّا جَديدًا في القَفْزِ العالي.

The Tunisian runner showed exceptional jumping ability when he set a new record in high jump.

The masdar (verbal noun) describes the action or sport of jumping, as in 'high jump.' In Arabic grammar, you can create an 'instance noun' by adding a ة to the masdar, as we see below. This instance noun signifies a single occurrence of the action, such as 'a jump.'

قَفْزَةٌ
jump

كانَتِ القَفْزَةُ النِّهائِيَّةُ لِلْعَدّاءِ الأَمْريكِيِّ كافِيَةً لِتَأْمينِ مَكانِهِ في المَرْكَزِ الأَوَّلِ.

The American runner's final jump was enough to secure his place in first position.

ماراثونْ
marathon

فازَ العَدّاءُ الإِثْيوبِيُّ في ماراثونْ بوسْطِنْ بَعْدَ سِباقٍ شاقٍّ اسْتَمَرَّ لِأَكْثَرَ مِنْ ساعَتَيْنِ.

The Ethiopian runner won the Boston Marathon after a grueling race that lasted for over two hours.

long distance pl. **مَسافاتٌ طَويلَةٌ**

نَجَحَ العَدّاءُ العِراقِيُّ في تَحْطيمِ الرَّقْمِ القِياسِيِّ العالَمِيِّ في سِباقِ المَسافاتِ الطَّويلَةِ.

The Iraqi runner succeeded in breaking the world record in long-distance racing.

middle distance pl. **مَسافاتٌ مُتَوَسِّطَةٌ**

في الألْعابِ الأولِمْبِيَّةِ، حَقَّقَ العَدّاءُ الإيطاليُّ زَمَنًا رائِعًا في سِباقِ المَسافاتِ المُتَوَسِّطَةِ.

In the Olympics, the Italian runner achieved a great time in the middle-distance race.

track • مَضاميرُ **مِضْمارٌ**

أَظْهَرَ العَدّاءُ السّوريُّ مَهاراتٍ مُذْهِلَةً في المِضْمارِ، مُحَطِّمًا الرَّقْمَ القِياسِيَّ الأوروبِّيَّ.

The Syrian runner displayed amazing skills on the track, smashing the European record.

field • مَيادينُ **مَيْدانٌ**

تَمَّ تَجْهيزُ المَيْدانِ بِأَحْدَثِ الأَجْهِزَةِ لِاسْتِضافَةِ مُنافَساتِ الأَلْعابِ الأولِمْبِيَّةِ.

The field was equipped with the latest facilities to host the Olympic Games competitions.

6.2.1.1 Mini-Articles

Track **69**

أَظْهَرَ العَدّاءُ الكُوَيْتِيُّ سَعْد العَجَمي أَداءً مُمْتازًا في الأَلْعابِ الأولِمْبِيَّةِ اليَوْمَ، حَيْثُ حَطَّمَ الرَّقْمَ القِياسِيَّ العالَمِيَّ في الوَثْبِ الطَّويلِ. بَعْدَ بِدايَةٍ غَيْرِ صَحيحَةٍ في أَوَّلِ مُحاوَلَةٍ، تَمَكَّنَ العَجَمي مِنَ القَفْزِ مَسافَةَ 8.5 مِترٍ في المُحاوَلَةِ الثّانِيَةِ، مُتَجاوِزًا الرَّقْمَ القِياسِيَّ السّابِقَ بِ 2 سم. فَرْحَةُ العَجَمي كانَتْ واضِحَةً حينَ حَقَّقَ هَذا الإِنْجازَ الهائِلَ.

Kuwaiti athlete Saad Al-Ajmi showed an excellent performance in the Olympics today, breaking the world record in the long jump. After a false start in his first attempt, Al-Ajmi managed to jump a distance of 8.5 meters in his second attempt, surpassing the previous record by 2 centimeters. Al-Ajmi's joy was evident when he achieved this incredible feat.

اِنْطَلَقَتْ صَباحَ اليَوْمِ سِباقاتُ ماراثونِ الرِّياضِ، حَيْثُ شارَكَ الآلافُ مِنَ العَدّائينَ وَالعَدّاءاتِ مِنْ جَميعِ أَنْحاءِ العالَمِ. السِّباقُ، الَّذي يَبْدَأُ وَيَنْتَهي عِنْدَ خَطِّ النِّهايَةِ في وَسَطِ مَدينَةِ الرِّياضِ، يُعْتَبَرُ مِنْ أَبْرَزِ الأَحْداثِ الرِّياضِيَّةِ في المَمْلَكَةِ. كانَ الفائِزُ في سِباقِ الرِّجالِ العَدّاءَ الإِثْيوبِيُّ كيبيروارکو، بَيْنَما حَقَّقَتِ الكينِيَّةُ مارْيامْ كيبْكوتِ الفَوْزَ في سِباقِ السَّيِّداتِ.

The Riyadh Marathon races kicked off this morning, with thousands of runners from all around the world participating. The race, starting and ending at the finish line in the heart of Riyadh, is one of the most prominent sporting events in the kingdom. The winner in the men's race was Ethiopian runner Kibiro Warko, while the Kenyan Maryam Kibkot claimed victory in the women's race.

أَبْهَرَ الفَريقُ السُّعوديُّ لِسباقِ التَّتابُعِ الجُمْهورَ في الأَلْعابِ الأولِمْبِيَّةِ، حَيْثُ حَقَّقوا الفَوْزَ بِالْميداليَةِ الذَّهَبِيَّةِ. الفَريقُ، الَّذي يَتَأَلَّفُ مِنَ العَدّائينَ أَحْمَد الحَمْدان، خالِد الشَّريف، ماجِد الصّالح وَسُلْطان الدّوسَري، أَظْهَروا تَواصُلًا رائِعًا وَسُرْعَةً اسْتِثْنائِيَّةً. كانَتْ عَصا التَّتابُعِ تَنْتَقِلُ بِسَلاسَةٍ بَيْنَ العَدّائينَ، مِمّا ساعَدَهُمْ عَلى تَحْقيقِ رَقْمٍ قِياسِيٍّ شَخْصِيٍّ جَديدٍ وَالفَوْزِ بِالْميداليَةِ الذَّهَبِيَّةِ.

The Saudi relay team impressed the audience at the Olympics, winning the gold medal. The team, consisting of runners Ahmed Al-Hamdani, Khalid Al-Sharif, Majed Al-Saleh, and Sultan Al-Dosari, showed excellent teamwork and exceptional speed. The baton passed smoothly between the runners, helping them achieve a new personal best and secure the gold medal.

قَدَّمَ العَدّاءُ التّونِسِيُّ، عادِل بِنْ عَلِيّ، أَداءً مُتَمَيِّزًا في سِباقِ الحَواجِزِ 110 مِترٍ في الأَلْعابِ الأولِمْبِيَّةِ. بَعْدَ بِدايَةٍ سَريعَةٍ وَمُتْقَنَةٍ، اِسْتَطاعَ بِنْ عَلِيّ الحِفاظَ عَلى الوَتيرَةِ وَتَجاوُزَ الحَواجِزِ بِسَلاسَةٍ، مُحَقِّقًا رَقْمًا قِياسِيًّا شَخْصِيًّا جَديدًا وَفازَ بِالْميداليَةِ البُرونْزِيَّةِ.

Tunisian athlete Adel Ben Ali delivered an outstanding performance in the 110-meter hurdles at the Olympics. After a fast and precise start, Ben Ali maintained the pace and smoothly cleared the hurdles, achieving a new personal best and winning the bronze medal.

أَثْبَتَ الرُّماةُ المِصْرِيّونَ، أَمْجَد الزُّهَيْري وَنورهان العيسَوي، مُسْتَوىً عالٍ مِنَ الكَفاءَةِ في مُسابَقَةِ رَمْيِ الرُّمْحِ خِلالَ أولِمْبِيادِ طوكْيو. بِفَضْلِ أَدائِهِ المُتَمَيِّزِ، تَمَكَّنَ الزُّهَيْري مِنْ حَجْزِ مَكانٍ في النِّهائِيّاتِ وَاحْتَلَّ المَرْكَزَ الثّاني، بَيْنَما نَجَحَتِ العيسَوي في الوُصولِ إِلى المَرْكَزِ الثّالِثِ، مُحَقِّقَةً رَقْمًا قِياسِيًّا شَخْصِيًّا جَديدًا في فِئَتِها.

Egyptian archers Amjad Al-Zuhairi and Norhan Al-Ayissawi demonstrated a high level of competence in the javelin throw competition at the Tokyo Olympics. Thanks to their outstanding performance, Al-Zuhairi secured a place in the finals and took the second position, while Al-Ayissawi reached the third position, setting a new personal record in her category.

تَأَلَّقَ الفَريقُ اللُّبْنانِيُّ لِلْوَثْبِ العالي في الأَلْعابِ الأولِمْبِيَّةِ، حَيْثُ تَمَكَّنَ كُلٌّ مِنْ ريما نَصّر وَمُحَمَّد سُلَيْمان مِنَ الوُصولِ إِلى النِّهائِيّاتِ. بَرَزَتْ نَصّر بِشَكْلٍ خاصٍّ بِتَحْقيقِها رَقْمًا قِياسِيًّا شَخْصِيًّا جَديدًا وَحُصولِها عَلى المَرْكَزِ الرّابِعِ، بَيْنَما حَقَّقَ سُلَيْمان المَرْكَزَ الخامِسَ في مُنافَساتِ الرِّجالِ.

The Lebanese high jump team shined at the Olympics, with both Rima Nassar and Mohammed Suleiman reaching the finals. Nassar, in particular, stood out by achieving a new personal best and securing the fourth position, while Suleiman claimed the fifth position in the men's competition.

فازَ العَدّاءُ الجَزائِريُّ ياسين مَرزوق بِالْميداليَةِ الذَّهَبِيَّةِ في الدّيكاثلون في الأَلْعابِ الأولِمْبِيَّةِ. أَثْبَتَ مَرزوق مَهاراتِهِ في العَديدِ مِنَ الرِّياضاتِ، الَّتي شَمِلَتِ الجَرْيِ، الوَثْبَ العالِيَ، رَمْيَ القُرْصِ، وَالوَثْبَ الطَّويلَ، لِيُتَوَّجَ بِاللَّقَبِ الأولِمْبِيِّ.

Algerian athlete Yassine Merzouk won the gold medal in the decathlon at the Olympics. Merzouk showcased his skills in various sports, including running, high jump, discus throw, and long jump, to clinch the Olympic title.

اِسْتَمَرَّتْ سَيْطَرَةُ المَغْرِبِ عَلى سِباقاتِ المَسافاتِ الطَّويلَةِ في الأَلْعابِ الأولِمْبِيَّةِ، حَيْثُ حَقَّقَ العَدّاءُ حُسَيْن بوجْنان المَرْكَزَ الأَوَّلَ في سِباقِ 10,000 مِتْرٍ. في الوَقْتِ نَفْسِهِ، حَقَّقَتِ العَدّاءَةُ نورا المِريني رَقْمًا قِياسِيًّا شَخْصِيًّا جَديدًا في سِباقِ 5000 مِتْرٍ، مُحَقِّقَةً المَرْكَزَ الثّاني وَميداليَةً فِضِّيَّةً لِلْمَغْرِبِ.

Morocco's dominance in long-distance races at the Olympics continued, as athlete Hussein Bujnan claimed the first position in the 10,000-meter race. At the same time, runner Nora Merini achieved a new personal best in the 5000-meter race, securing the second position and a silver medal for Morocco.

6.2.2 Gymnastics

Track **70**

leotard — **بَذْلَةُ جُمْبازٍ**

في المُسابَقَةِ، اِرْتَدَتْ لاعِبَةُ الجُمْبازِ السّورِيَّةُ بَذْلَةَ جُمْبازٍ زَرْقاءَ مُذْهِلَةً.

In the competition, the Syrian gymnast wore an amazing blue leotard.

to flip — **تَشَقْلَبَ** • تَشَقْلُبٌ

خِلالَ المُسابَقَةِ، قامَتْ لاعِبَةُ الجُمْبازِ الكَنَدِيَّةُ بِتَشَقْلُبٍ مُدْهِشٍ حَقَّقَتْ بِهِ النِّقاطَ الكامِلَةَ.

During the competition, the Canadian gymnast did an amazing flip that earned her full points.

floor exercise — **تَمرينٌ أَرْضِيٌّ / جُمْبازٌ أَرْضِيٌّ** pl.

في التَّمرينِ الأَرْضِيِّ، تَعَثَّرَ لاعِبُ الجُمْبازِ الأَمْريكِيُّ، وَلَكِنَّهُ اسْتَعادَ تَوازُنَهُ بِسُرْعَةٍ.

In the floor exercise, the American gymnast stumbled, but he quickly regained his balance.

to balance — **تَوازَنَ** • تَوازُنٌ

بِدِقَّةٍ وَتَحَكُّمٍ لافِتٍ، قامَتْ لاعِبَةُ الجُمْبازِ بِالتَّوازُنِ عَلَى القُضْبانِ غَيْرِ المُتَساوِيَةِ، مُظْهِرَةً إِتْقانَها لِلْمَهارَةِ .

With incredible precision and control, the gymnast balanced on the uneven bars, showcasing her mastery of the skill.

جُمْبازٌ
gymnastics

شَهِدَتْ بُطولَةُ الجُمْبازِ أَداءً مُذْهِلًا مِنَ الرِّياضِيِّينَ حَوْلَ العالَمِ.

The gymnastics championship witnessed breathtaking performances from athletes around the world.

جُمْبازٌ إيقاعِيٌّ
rhythmic gymnastics

سِحْرُ أَداءِ الجُمْبازِ الإيقاعِيِّ أَسَرَ الجُمْهورَ في المُسابَقَةِ الدَّوْلِيَّةِ .

The mesmerizing grace of rhythmic gymnastics captivated the audience at the international competition.

جِهازُ الحَلْقِ • أَجْهِزَةٌ
still rings

عَلى جِهازِ الحَلْقِ، أَبْهَرَتْ لاعِبَةُ الجُمْبازِ المِصْرِيَّةُ الجُمْهورَ بِأَدائِها الرّائِع.

On the still rings, the Egyptian gymnast amazed the audience with her fantastic performance.

جِهازُ القُضْبانِ غَيْرِ المُتَساوِيَةِ
uneven bars

أَدّى لاعِبُ الجُمْبازِ الأَلْمانِيُّ تَمارينَ مُدْهِشَةً عَلى جِهازِ القُضْبانِ غَيْرِ المُتَساوِيَةِ، مُتْقِنًا كُلَّ حَرَكَةٍ.

The German gymnast performed amazing exercises on the uneven bars, mastering each move.

جِهازُ المُتَوازي • أَجْهِزَةٌ
parallel bars

خِلالَ المُسابَقَةِ، أَظْهَرَ لاعِبُ الجُمْبازِ اللُّبْنانِيُّ مَهاراتِهِ الرّائِعَةَ عَلى جِهازِ المُتَوازي.

During the competition, the Lebanese gymnast showcased his remarkable skills on the parallel bars.

حِصانُ الحَلْقِ
pommel horse

تَمَكَّنَ لاعِبُ الجُمْبازِ اليابانِيُّ مِنْ تَنْفيذِ تَمارينَ مُعَقَّدَةٍ عَلى حِصانِ الحَلْقِ.

The Japanese gymnast managed to perform complex exercises on the pommel horse.

routine رُوتِينٌ

قَدَّمَتْ لاعِبَةُ الجُمْبازِ الأَمْريكِيَّةُ روتينًا مُثيرًا لِلإِعْجابِ في مُنافَسَةِ الجُمْبازِ.

The American gymnast presented an impressive routine in the gymnastics competition.

flip شَقْلَبَةٌ

في تَمارينِ الجُمْبازِ، قامَ لاعِبُ الجُمْبازِ الأوكرانِيُّ بشَقْلَبَةٍ مُثيرَةٍ لِلإِعْجابِ.

In the gymnastics exercises, the Ukrainian gymnast made an impressive flip.

cartwheel شَقْلَبَةٌ جانِبِيَّةٌ

نَفَّذَتْ لاعِبَةُ الجُمْبازِ التّونِسِيَّةُ شَقْلَبَةً جانِبِيَّةً مِثالِيَّةً خِلالَ المُسابَقَةِ.

The Tunisian gymnast executed a perfect cartwheel during the competition.

somersault شَقْلَبَةٌ هَوائِيَّةٌ

أَبْهَرَتْ لاعِبَةُ الجُمْبازِ الكَنَدِيَّةُ الجُمْهورَ بشَقْلَبَةٍ هَوائِيَّةٍ رائِعَةٍ.

The Canadian gymnast amazed the audience with a fantastic somersault.

mount صُعودٌ

تَمَكَّنَ لاعِبُ الجُمْبازِ الفَرَنْسِيُّ مِنَ الصُّعودِ عَلى العارِضَةِ بِسَلاسَةٍ.

The French gymnast managed to mount the beam smoothly.

balance beam عارِضَةُ التَّوازُنِ • عَوارِضُ

فاجَأَتْ لاعِبَةُ الجُمْبازِ المِصْرِيَّةُ الجَميعَ بِأَدائِها الرّائِعِ عَلى عارِضَةِ التَّوازُنِ.

The Egyptian gymnast surprised everyone with her superb performance on the balance beam.

split فَتْحُ الحَوْضِ

خِلالَ العَرْضِ، قامَتْ لاعِبَةُ الجُمْبازِ الصّينِيَّةُ بِفَتْحِ حَوْضٍ مُذْهِلٍ أَثارَ تَصْفيقَ الجُمْهورِ.

During the display, the Chinese gymnast performed a stunning split that provoked applause from the audience.

قَفَزَ • قَفْزٌ **to leap**

قَفَزَتْ لاعِبَةُ الجُمْبازِ بِبَراعَةٍ عَلى جِهَازِ حِصانِ الحَلْقِ خِلالَ مُنافَسَةِ الجُمْبازِ.

The gymnast leaped gracefully onto the pommel horse during the gymnastics competition.

قَفَزَ • قَفْزٌ **to vault**

في روتينِها النِّهائِيِّ، قَفَزَتْ لاعِبَةُ الجُمْبازِ بِثِقَةٍ فَوْقَ طاوِلَةِ القَفْزِ، مُبْهِرَةً الحُكّامَ بِارْتِفاعِها وَهَيْئَتِها .

In her final routine, the gymnast confidently vaulted over the vaulting table, impressing the judges with her height and form.

In English gymnastics terminology, 'to leap' and 'to vault' are distinct actions. 'To vault' specifically refers to jumping or leaping over a barrier, often with the support of the hands on that barrier. In Arabic, however, the same verb قَفَزَ is commonly used to express both actions.

قَفْزَةٌ **vault, jump**

أَدّى لاعِبُ الجُمْبازِ الإِنْجليزِيُّ قَفْزَةً مُثيرَةً لِلْإِعْجابِ خِلالَ المُسابَقَةِ.

The English gymnast performed an impressive vault during the competition.

لاعِبُ جُمْبازٍ **gymnast**

أَظْهَرَتْ لاعِبَةُ الجُمْبازِ السّودانِيَّةُ مُسْتَوًى عالٍ مِنَ الرَّشاقَةِ وَالتَّناسُقِ خِلالَ الأَداءِ.

The Sudanese gymnast showed a high level of agility and coordination during her performance.

لَفَّةٌ **twist**

في نِهايَةِ روتينِهِ، نَفَّذَ لاعِبُ الجُمْبازِ الإِسْبانِيُّ لَفَّةً مُعَقَّدَةً وَرَشيقَةً.

At the end of his routine, the Spanish gymnast executed a complex and agile twist.

نَتيجَةٌ • نَتائِجُ **score**

بَعْدَ أَداءٍ مُمْتازٍ، حَصَلَتْ لاعِبَةُ الجُمْبازِ البُرْتُغالِيَّةُ عَلى نَتيجَةٍ عالِيَةٍ.

After an excellent performance, the Portuguese gymnast received a high score.

dismount **نُزولٌ**

بَعْدَ الأَداءِ الرّائِعِ، نَزَلَ لاعِبُ الجُمْبازِ النِّمْساوِيُّ مِنَ العارِضَةِ بِكُلِّ أَناقَةٍ.

After the fantastic performance, the Austrian gymnast dismounted from the beam with grace.

handstand **وُقوفٌ عَلى اليَدَيْنِ**

أَظْهَرَ لاعِبُ الجُمْبازِ الأُرْدُنِّيُّ مَهارَةً فائِقَةً في وُقوفِهِ عَلى اليَدَيْنِ خِلالَ التَّمارينِ الأَرْضِيَّةِ.

The Jordanian gymnast demonstrated superb skill in his handstand during the floor exercise.

6.2.2.1 Mini-Articles

Track **71**

في مُنافَساتِ الجُمْبازِ الأولِمْبِيِّ، حَقَّقَتِ اللاعِبَةُ السُّعودِيَّةُ نادِيَة العيسى فَوْزًا مُذْهِلًا في التَّمارينِ الأَرْضِيَّةِ. بَدَأَتْ نادِيَة بِلَفَّةٍ مُثيرَةٍ لِلْإِعْجابِ، ثُمَّ قامَتْ بِتَنْفيذِ عِدَّةِ شَقْلَباتٍ جانِبِيَّةٍ وَهَوائِيَّةٍ بِمَهارَةٍ فائِقَةٍ. حَتّى إِنَّ تَعَثُّرَها لَمْ يَكُنْ كافِيًا لِتَقْويضِ أَدائِها، حَيْثُ اسْتَعادَتِ التَّوازُنَ واسْتَكْمَلَتِ الرّوتينَ مُرْتَدِيَةً بَذْلَةَ جُمْبازٍ رائِعَةً. نَتيجَتُها المُذْهِلَةُ ضَمِنَتْ لَها المَرْكَزَ الأَوَّلَ في المُسابَقَةِ.

In the Olympic gymnastics competitions, Saudi athlete Nadia Al-Issa achieved a stunning victory in the floor exercises. She started with an impressive twist and executed several skillful cartwheels and sommersaults. Even her stumble was not enough to undermine her performance, as she regained balance and continued the routine with a fantastic leotard. Her amazing result secured her the first place in the competition.

اللّاعِبُ الكُوَيْتِيُّ عُمَر العُتَيْبي أَظْهَرَ تَمَكُّنًا رائِعًا في أَداءِ الجُمْبازِ في جِهازِ الحَلَقِ. تَمَكَّنَ مِنَ الحِفاظِ عَلى التَّوازُنِ المِثالِيِّ طَوالَ الرّوتينِ، وَقامَ بِتَنْفيذِ شَقْلَباتٍ مُذْهِلَةٍ وَقَوِيَّةٍ. عَلى الرَّغْمِ مِنْ صُعوبَةِ نُزولِهِ مِنَ الجِهازِ في النِّهايَةِ، لَكِنَّ العُتَيْبي أَكْمَلَ روتينَهُ بِثَباتٍ وَقُوَّةٍ. تُظْهِرُ النَّتائِجُ أَنَّ عَمَلَهُ الشّاقَّ وَالتَّدْريبَ المُكَثَّفَ قَدْ أَثْمَرا، حَيْثُ حَقَّقَ العُتَيْبي نَتيجَةً مُرْتَفِعَةً في المُسابَقَةِ.

Kuwaiti athlete Omar Al-Otaibi showed remarkable proficiency in gymnastics on the still rings. He managed to maintain perfect balance throughout the routine and executed incredible and powerful flips. Despite the difficulty in dismounting from the apparatus in the end, Al-Otaibi completed his routine with poise and strength. The results indicate that his hard work and intense training have paid off, as Al-Otaibi achieved a high score in the competition.

حَقَّقَتِ اللّاعِبَةُ الإِماراتِيَّةُ رُؤى العَسّاف الميدالِيَةَ الذَّهَبِيَّةَ في مُسابَقَةِ الجُمْبازِ الإيقاعِيِّ. تَناسَبَ أَداؤُها الرّائِعُ في الجُمْبازِ مَعَ الرّوتينِ الَّذي قَدَّمَتْهُ، حَيْثُ بَدَأَتْ بِقَفْزَةٍ مُثيرَةٍ لِلْإِعْجابِ ثُمَّ تَبِعَتْها بِعِدَّةِ شَقْلَباتٍ هَوائِيَّةٍ وَفَتَحاتٍ

حَوْض. خِتامُ العَرْضِ كانَ بِلَفَّةٍ مُذْهِلَةٍ وَنُزولٍ بالغِ الرَّوْعَةِ. بَذَلَتِ العَسّاف كُلَّ جُهْدِها وَاسْتَحَقَّتِ الذَّهَبَ، وَهِيَ الآنَ تَتَطَلَّعُ إِلى المَزيدِ مِنَ النَّجاحِ في الأولِمْبِيادِ القادِمِ.

Emirati athlete Ruaa Al-Asaf won the gold medal in rhythmic gymnastics. Her fantastic gymnastics performance perfectly matched the routine she presented. She started with an impressive jump, followed by several skillful aerial flips and splits. The finale of her performance was a breathtaking roll and a graceful descent. Al-Asaf gave her all and deserved the gold, and now she is looking forward to more success in the upcoming Olympics.

6.2.2.2 Article: Gymnastics at the 2023 Arab Games

Track **72**

الجُمْبازُ في دَوْرَةِ الأَلْعابِ العَرَبِيَّةِ 2023

أُقيمَتْ مُنافَساتُ الجُمْبازِ في دَوْرَةِ الأَلْعابِ العَرَبِيَّةِ 2023 في مُجَمَّعِ ميلودْ حَديفي الرِّياضِيِّ في بِئْرِ الجيرِ، وَهْرانْ، الجَزائِرِ، مِنْ 7 إِلى 10 يولْيو. شَمِلَتِ المُنافَسَةُ ما مَجْموعُهُ 13 حَدَثًا.

تَصَدَّرَتِ الدَّوْلَةُ المُضيفَةُ، الجَزائِرُ، جَدْوَلَ الميدالْياتِ بِمَجْموعِ 16 ميدالْيَةً، بِما في ذَلِكَ 6 ذَهَبِيّاتٍ، وَ 5 فِضِّيّاتٍ، وَ 5 بُرونْزِيّاتٍ. تَلَتْها سورْيا بِ 11 ميدالْيَةً، بِما في ذَلِكَ 4 ذَهَبِيّاتٍ، وَفِضِّيَّتانِ، وَ 5 بُرونْزِيّاتٍ. وَحَلَّتِ الأُرْدُنُّ في المَرْكَزِ الثّالِثِ بِمَجْموعِ ميدالْيَتَيْنِ ذَهَبِيَّتَيْنِ.

مُنافَساتُ الرِّجالِ

في المُنافَسَةِ الكُلِّيَّةِ لِلرِّجالِ، فازَ لَيْث نَجّار مِنْ سورْيا بِالْميدالْيَةِ الذَّهَبِيَّةِ، يَليه حَمْزَة الحُسَيْنِيّ مِنَ المَغْرِبِ وَعَبْدُ الرَّزّاق ناصِر مِنَ المَغْرِبِ، اللَّذانِ فازا بِالْفِضِّيَّةِ وَالبُرونْزِيَّةِ عَلى التَّوالي. وَفازَتِ الجَزائِرُ بِمُنافَسَةِ الفِرَقِ، في حينِ حَصَلَتِ المَغْرِبُ وَسورْيا عَلى الميدالْياتِ الفِضِّيَّةِ وَالبُرونْزِيَّةِ.

في مُنافَساتِ الأَجْهِزَةِ الفَرْدِيَّةِ، فازَ أَحْمَد سامي مُحَمَّد أبو السُّعود مِنَ الأُرْدُنِّ بِجائِزَةِ حِصانِ الحَلَقِ، وَفازَ هِلال مَتيجوي مِنَ الجَزائِرِ في جِهازِ الْحَلَقِ، وَفازَ لَيْث نَجّار مِنْ سورْيا في التَّمارينِ الأَرْضِيَّةِ، وَفازَ أَحْمَد رياض عِليوات مِنَ الجَزائِرِ بِجائِزَةِ الْقَفْزِ، وَحَمْزَة الحُسَيْنِيّ مِنَ المَغْرِبِ في الْمُتَوازي.

مُنافَساتُ النِّساءِ

في المُنافَسَةِ الكُلِّيَّةِ لِلنِّساءِ، فازَتْ سُلاف حَسَن مِنْ سورْيا بِالْميدالْيَةِ الذَّهَبِيَّةِ، تَلَتْها فاطِمَة سَعيد مِنَ الجَزائِرِ وَلَطيفَة سالِم مِنَ الجَزائِرِ، اللَّتانِ فازَتا بِالْفِضِّيَّةِ وَالبُرونْزِيَّةِ عَلى التَّوالي.

فِي أَحْداثِ الأَجْهِزَةِ الفَرْدِيَّةِ، فازَتْ سُلاف حَسَن مِنْ سورْيا فِي القُضْبانِ غَيْرِ المُتَساوِيَةِ، وَفازَتْ رُبا أُسامَة حَمْزَة مِنَ الأُرْدُنِّ فِي القَفْزِ، وَفازَتْ مَلَك رِزوقي مِنَ الجَزائِرِ فِي التَّمارينِ الأَرْضِيَّةِ، وَفازَتْ لَطيفَة سالِم مِنَ الجَزائِرِ بِعارِضَةِ التَّوازُنِ.

شَكَّلَتِ الأَلْعابُ العَرَبِيَّةُ 2023 لَحْظَةً هامَّةً لِلْجُمْبازِ فِي العالَمِ العَرَبِيِّ، مَعَ تَأَلُّقِ جَميعِ الدُّوَلِ المُشارِكَةِ.

Gymnastics at the 2023 Arab Games

The gymnastics competitions at the 2023 Arab Games were held at the Miloud Hadefi Sports Complex in Bir El Djir, Oran, Algeria, from July 7th to 10th. The competition included a total of 13 events.

The host country, Algeria, topped the medal table with a total of 16 medals, including 6 golds, 5 silvers, and 5 bronzes. Syria followed with 11 medals, including 4 golds, 2 silvers, and 5 bronzes. Jordan secured the third place with a total of 2 gold medals.

Men's Events

In the all-around event for men, Lais Najar from Syria won the gold medal, followed by Hamza Al-Husseini from Morocco and Abdelrazzak Nasser from Morocco, who won the silver and bronze medals, respectively. Algeria won the team event, while Morocco and Syria took the silver and bronze medals.

In the individual apparatus events, Ahmed Sami Mohammed Abu Al-Saud from Jordan won the pommel horse, while Hilal Matigui from Algeria won the still rings. Lais Najar from Syria won the floor exercise, Ahmed Riad Aliwat from Algeria won the vault, and Hamza Al-Husseini from Morocco won the parallel bars.

Women's Events

In the all-around event for women, Sulaf Hassan from Syria won the gold medal, followed by Fatima Saeed from Algeria and Latifa Salem from Algeria, who won the silver and bronze medals, respectively.

In the individual apparatus events, Sulaf Hassan from Syria won the uneven bars, Ruba Osama Hamza from Jordan won the vault, Malak Rezgui from Algeria won the floor exercise, and Latifa Salem from Algeria won the balance beam.

The 2023 Arab Games marked an important moment for gymnastics in the Arab world, with all participating countries showcasing their excellence.

6.2.3 Weightlifting

Track **73**

weights *pl.* **أَثْقالٌ**

كانَتْ أَثْقالُ الرَّبّاعِ اليونانيِّ ثَقيلَةً لِلْغايَةِ، لَكِنَّهُ أَظْهَرَ قُوَّةً لا تُصَدَّقُ.

The Greek weightlifter's weights were very heavy, but he showed incredible strength.

personal best **أَفْضَلُ رَقْمٍ شَخْصِيٍّ**

تَحَدّى الرَّبّاعُ الأَلْمانِيُّ نَفْسَهُ وَحَقَّقَ أَفْضَلَ رَقْمٍ شَخْصِيٍّ لَهُ في المُنافَسَةِ الأَخيرَةِ.

The German weightlifter challenged himself and achieved his personal best in the last competition.

weight plates *pl.* **أَقْراصُ رَفْعِ الأَثْقالِ**

قَرَّرَ النّادي الرِّياضِيُّ الِاسْتِثْمارَ في شِراءِ مَجْموعَةٍ جَديدَةٍ مِنْ أَقْراصِ رَفْعِ الأَثْقالِ لِغُرْفَةِ رَفْعِ الأَثْقالِ.

The sports club decided to invest in buying a new set of plates for the weightlifting room.

barbell **البارْ**

رَفَعَ الرَّبّاعُ الرّوسِيُّ البارَ بِقُوَّةٍ مُدْهِشَةٍ خِلالَ التَّدْريبِ.

The Russian weightlifter powerfully lifted the barbell during training.

repetition or rep **تِكْرارٌ**

أَدّى الرَّبّاعُ الفَرَنْسِيُّ عِدَّةَ تِكْراراتٍ في رَفْعِ الأَثْقالِ لِلْحِفاظِ عَلى لِياقَتِهِ البَدَنِيَّةِ.

The French weightlifter performed several repetitions in weightlifting to maintain his physical fitness.

weightlifting belt • أَحْزِمَةٌ **حِزامُ رَفْعِ الأَثْقالِ**

يُعْتَبَرُ حِزامُ رَفْعِ الأَثْقالِ أَداةً ضَرورِيَّةً في رَفْعِ الأَثْقالِ، وَاللّاعِبُ الصّينِيُّ دائِمًا يَتَأَكَّدُ مِنَ ارْتِدائِهِ.

The weightlifting belt is an essential tool in weightlifting, and the Chinese athlete always makes sure to wear it.

snatch خَطْفٌ

قامَ الرَّبّاعُ الأَمْريكيُّ بِتَحْطيمِ أَفْضَلِ رَقْمٍ شَخْصيٍّ لَهُ في الخَطْفِ.

The American weightlifter smashed his personal best in the snatch.

weightlifter رَبّاعٌ

حَقَّقَ الرَّبّاعُ الجَزائِرِيُّ الفَوْزَ في بُطولَةِ رَفْعِ الأَثْقالِ الدَّوْلِيَّةِ.

The Algerian weightlifter won the international weightlifting championship.

to lift رَفَعَ • رَفْعٌ

رَفَعَ الرَّبّاعُ الجَزائِرِيُّ البارَ بِقُوَّةٍ غَيْرِ عادِيَّةٍ.

The Algerian weightlifter lifted the bar with extraordinary strength.

weightlifting رَفْعُ الأَثْقالِ

أَظْهَرَتْ بُطولَةُ رَفْعِ الأَثْقالِ الإِسْبانِيَّةُ الكَثيرَ مِنَ المَواهِبِ الجَديدَةِ.

The Spanish weightlifting championship showcased a lot of new talents.

lift رَفْعَةٌ

كانَتْ رَفْعَةُ الرَّبّاعِ المِصْرِيِّ أَحَدَ الأَحْداثِ الرّائِعَةِ في البُطولَةِ.

The Egyptian weightlifter's lift was one of the spectacular events in the championship.

failed lift رَفْعَةٌ فاشِلَةٌ

أَخْفَقَ الرَّبّاعُ البَرازيلِيُّ في رَفْعَةٍ خِلالَ المُنافَسَةِ، مِمّا أَدّى إِلى رَفْعَةٍ فاشِلَةٍ.

The Brazilian weightlifter failed a lift during the competition, leading to a failed lift.

world record رَقْمٌ قِياسِيٌّ عالَمِيٌّ

نَجَحَ الرَّبّاعُ الإِيرانِيُّ في رَفْعَةٍ ضَخْمَةٍ، مُحَطِّمًا بِذَلِكَ الرَّقْمَ القِياسِيَّ العالَمِيَّ.

The Iranian weightlifter succeeded in a massive lift, thereby breaking the world record.

مَجْموعَةٌ

set

تَتَكَوَّنُ كُلُّ مَجْموعَةٍ مِنْ ثَلاثِ تِكْراراتٍ، حَيْثُ يَقومُ الرَّبّاعُ الأُسْتُرالِيُّ بِثَلاثِ مُحاوَلاتٍ لِرَفْعِ البارِ.

Each set consists of three repetitions, where the Australian lifter makes three attempts to lift the barbell.

نَتْرٌ

clean and jerk

اِسْتَعَدَّ الرَّبّاعُ البِريطانِيُّ لِرَفْعَةِ النَّتْرِ، مُرَكِّزًا بِكُلِّ قُوَّتِهِ عَلى البارِ.

The British weightlifter prepared for the clean and jerk, focusing all his strength on the barbell.

6.2.3.1 Mini-Articles

Track **74**

في أَحْدَثِ أَخْبارِ رَفْعِ الأَثْقالِ، تَمَكَّنَ الرَّبّاعُ الشّابُّ أَحْمَد البَكْر مِنْ تَحْطيمِ الرَّقْمِ القِياسِيِّ العالَمِيِّ في رَفْعَةِ النَّتْرِ. في المُنافَسَةِ الَّتي أُقيمَتْ يَوْمَ الأَحَدِ، رَفَعَ البَكْر البارَ المُحَمَّلَ بِالأَوْزانِ الثَّقيلَةِ بِكُلِّ قُوَّةٍ، وَسَطَ تَشْجيعٍ حَماسِيٍّ مِنَ الجُمْهورِ. أَظْهَرَ قُوَّةَ بِنْيَتِهِ وَمَهارَتَهُ، مُسْتَخْدِمًا حِزامَ رَفْعِ الأَثْقالِ الخاصَّ بِهِ لِتَقْديمِ أَداءٍ مُذْهِلٍ.

In the latest weightlifting news, the young weightlifter Ahmed Al-Bakr managed to break the world record in the snatch lift. In the competition held on Sunday, Al-Bakr lifted the heavily loaded barbell with great strength, amid enthusiastic cheering from the audience. He demonstrated his strong physique and skill, using his weightlifting belt to deliver an impressive performance.

في الأَلْعابِ الأولِمْبِيَّةِ الأَخيرَةِ، تَأَلَّقَ الرَّبّاعُ فَتْحي المَهْدي وَحَصَلَ عَلى الميدالِيَّةِ الذَّهَبِيَّةِ في فِئَةِ وَزْنِ 77 كيلوغْرامًا. لَقَدْ أَدّى أَداءً مُتَمَيِّزًا في رَفْعَةِ النَّتْرِ، حَيْثُ رَفَعَ بارًا يَزِنُ 205 كيلوغْرامًا، وَهُوَ رَقْمٌ يَتَجاوَزُ الرَّقْمَ القِياسِيَّ السّابِقَ. بَذَلَ المَهْدي جُهْدًا كَبيرًا، وَأَظْهَرَ قُوَّةً هائِلَةً وَتَحَمُّلًا رائِعًا، لِيُحَقِّقَ هَذا الإِنْجازَ الهائِلَ.

In the last Olympic Games, weightlifter Fathi Al-Mahdi excelled and won the gold medal in the 77 kg weight category. He delivered an outstanding performance in the snatch lift, lifting a barbell weighing 205 kilograms, a number that surpassed the previous world record. Al-Mahdi exerted significant effort, displaying tremendous strength and remarkable endurance to achieve this remarkable feat.

في أَخْبارٍ مُشَوِّقَةٍ مِنْ عالَمِ رَفْعِ الأَثْقالِ، تَمَكَّنَتْ ماريا الحَمَد، الرَّبّاعَةُ الواعِدَةُ، مِنْ تَحْقيقِ رَقْمٍ قِياسِيٍّ شَخْصِيٍّ جَديدٍ. خِلالَ الجَلَساتِ التَّدْريبِيَّةِ الأَخيرَةِ، قامَتِ الحَمَد بِرَفْعِ البارِ المُحَمَّلِ بِأَثْقالٍ تَجاوَزَتْ وَزْنَها، وَهُوَ إِنْجازٌ اسْتِثْنائِيٌّ بِحَقٍّ. لَقَدْ بَذَلَتْ مَجْهودًا جَبّارًا في تَنْفيذِ الرَّفْعَةِ، مُعَزِّزَةً بِذَلِكَ مَكانَتَها كَرَبّاعَةٍ قَوِيَّةٍ.

In exciting news from the world of weightlifting, promising weightlifter Maria Al-Hamad achieved a new personal record. During the last training sessions, Al-Hamad lifted a barbell that exceeded her weight, a truly exceptional feat. She exerted tremendous effort in executing the lift, solidifying her position as a strong weightlifter.

فِي جَلْسَةٍ تَدْرِيبِيَّةٍ لِرَفْعِ الأَثْقالِ أَمْسِ، أَظْهَرَ مُحَمَّد السَّعيد بَراعَةً كَبيرَةً فِي رَفْعَةِ الخَطْفِ. بَعْدَ تَنْفيذِ عِدَّةِ مَجْموعاتٍ مِنَ الرَّفْعاتِ، اِسْتَطاعَ السَّعيد تَحْقيقَ الرَّقْمِ الأَعْلى لَهُ فِي رَفْعِ الأَثْقالِ، حَيْثُ تَجاوَزَ الوَزْنَ الَّذي رَفَعَهُ فِي السّابِقِ بِمَراحِلَ. رَغْمَ بَعْضِ المُحاوَلاتِ الفاشِلَةِ، فَإِنَّهُ اسْتَمَرَّ فِي الضَّغْطِ عَلى نَفْسِهِ حَتّى تَفَوَّقَ عَلى نَفْسِهِ. بِفَضْلِ هَذا الأَداءِ، يَبْدو مُسْتَقْبَلُ السَّعيد فِي رَفْعِ الأَثْقالِ واعِدًا.

In yesterday's weightlifting training session, Mohammed Al-Saeed showcased great skill in the clean and jerk lift. After several sets of lifts, Al-Saeed managed to achieve his personal best in weightlifting, surpassing the weight he previously lifted by leaps and bounds. Despite some failed attempts, he continued to push himself until he exceeded his limits. Thanks to this performance, Al-Saeed's future in weightlifting seems promising.

فِي المُنافَسَةِ الشَّرِسَةِ فِي الأَلْعابِ الأولِمْبِيَّةِ، فازَ الرَّبّاعُ المَوْهوبُ، نادِر العَبْد، بِالْميدالْيَةِ الفِضِّيَّةِ فِي فِئَةِ الوَزْنِ الخَفيفِ (69 كيلوغْرامًا). رَفَعَ العَبْد بارًا يَزِنُ 210 كيلوغْرامًا فِي رَفْعَةِ النَّتْرِ، وَهُوَ إِنْجازٌ مُبْهِرٌ. بِالرَّغْمِ مِنْ تَحْقيقِهِ لِلْميدالْيَةِ الفِضِّيَّةِ فَقَطْ، فَإِنَّ أَداءَ العَبْد كانَ أَكْثَرَ مِنْ مُثيرٍ لِلْإِعْجابِ، وَأَظْهَرَ قُوَّةً هائِلَةً وَتَحَمُّلًا مُذْهِلًا.

In the fierce competition at the Olympics, talented weightlifter Nader Al-Abd won the silver medal in the lightweight category (69 kilograms). Al-Abd lifted a barbell weighing 210 kilograms in the snatch lift, an impressive feat. Despite achieving only the silver medal, Al-Abd's performance was more than admirable, showing incredible strength and remarkable endurance.

أَضافَتِ الرَّبّاعَةُ فَرَح الحُسَيْن الميدالْيَةَ البُرونْزِيَّةَ إِلى مَجْموعَةِ ميدالْياتِها الأولِمْبِيَّةِ، وَذَلِكَ فِي فِئَةِ الوَزْنِ الثَّقيلِ (فَوْقَ 75 كيلوغْرامًا). قامَتِ الحُسَيْن بِرَفْعِ بارٍ يَزِنُ 185 كيلوغْرامًا فِي رَفْعَةِ الخَطْفِ، وَهُوَ ما تَفَوَّقَتْ بِهِ عَلى العَديدِ مِنَ المُنافِسينَ الأَقْوِياءِ. بِالرَّغْمِ مِنْ أَنَّها لَمْ تُحَقِّقِ الذَّهَبَ، فَإِنَّ الحُسَيْن أَظْهَرَتْ قُدْرَةً مُدْهِشَةً وَقُوَّةَ تَحَمُّلٍ لا مَثيلَ لَها.

Weightlifter Farah Al-Hussein added the bronze medal to her Olympic medal collection in the heavyweight category (over 75 kilograms). Hussein lifted a barbell weighing 185 kilograms in the clean and jerk lift, surpassing many strong competitors. Although she didn't win the gold, Hussein demonstrated an amazing ability and unparalleled endurance.

6.3 Combat Sports

6.3.1 Wrestling

Track **75**

to escape إفْلاتٌ • **أَفْلَتَ**

فِي مُباراةٍ حَماسِيَّةٍ، تَمَكَّنَ المُصارِعُ الشّابُّ مِنَ الإفْلاتِ مِنْ وَضْعِ الإمْساكِ الَّذي وَضَعَهُ فيه خَصْمُهُ.

In an exciting match, the young wrestler managed to escape the hold placed on him by his opponent.

takedown **إسْقاطٌ**

فازَ المُصارِعُ المُخَضْرَمُ بِواسِطَةِ الإسْقاطِ المُفاجِئِ الَّذي أَذْهَلَ الجَماهيرَ.

The veteran wrestler won with a surprising takedown that amazed the audience.

hold **إمْساكٌ**

تَفَوَّقَتْ مَهاراتُ المُصارِعِ في الإمْساكِ، مِمّا أَدّى إلى اسْتِسْلامِ خَصْمِهِ.

The wrestler's hold skills prevailed, leading to his opponent's submission.

to submit اِسْتِسْلامٌ • **اِسْتَسْلَمَ**

في نِهايَةِ مُباراةِ المُصارَعَةِ الحَماسِيَّةِ، أَجْبَرَ المُصارِعُ خَصْمَهُ عَلى الاِسْتِسْلامِ بَعْدَ حَرَكَةٍ قَوِيَّةٍ وَمُحْكَمَةٍ.

At the end of the exciting wrestling match, the wrestler forced his opponent to submit after a strong and precise move.

wrestling; grappling **المُصارَعَةُ**

تَنافَسَ العَديدُ مِنَ المُصارِعينَ البارِزينَ في بُطولَةِ المُصارَعَةِ الحُرَّةِ الدَّوْلِيَّةِ هَذا العامَ.

Several prominent wrestlers competed in this year's international freestyle wrestling championship.

freestyle wrestling **المُصارَعَةُ الحُرَّةُ**

تَشْهَدُ البُطولاتُ الوَطَنِيَّةُ مُنافَسَةً شَرِسَةً، حَيْثُ يَعْرِضُ الرِّياضِيّونَ مَهاراتِهِمْ في المُصارَعَةِ الحُرَّةِ.

National championships witness fierce competition as athletes showcase their skills in freestyle wrestling.

to pin • تَثْبيتٌ **ثَبَّتَ**

فِي الدَّقائِقِ الأَخيرَةِ مِنَ المُباراةِ، ثَبَّتَ المُصارِعُ خَصْمَهُ عَلى حَصيرَةِ المُصارَعَةِ.

In the final minutes of the match, the wrestler managed to pin his opponent on the wrestling mat.

wrestling shoes • أَحْذِيَةٌ **حِذاءُ مُصارَعَةٍ**

اِرْتَدى المُصارِعُ حِذاءَ المُصارَعَةِ الجَديدَ الَّذي مَنَحَهُ تَوازُنًا أَكْثَرَ عَلى الحَصيرَةِ.

The wrestler wore the new wrestling shoes that gave him more balance on the mat.

wrestling mat • حَصائِرُ \ حَصْرٌ **حَصيرَةُ مُصارَعَةٍ**

قَبْلَ بَدْءِ مُباراةِ المُصارَعَةِ، يَتَأَكَّدُ الحَكَمُ مِنْ أَنَّ حَصيرَةَ المُصارَعَةِ نَظيفَةٌ وَآمِنَةٌ لِلْمُصارِعينَ.

Before the wrestling match begins, the referee ensures that the wrestling mat is clean and safe for the wrestlers.

referee • حُكّامٌ **حَكَمٌ**

وَقَفَ الحَكَمُ بِجانِبِ الحَصيرَةِ، مُراقِبًا النِّزالَ بَيْنَ المُصارِعَيْنِ بِعِنايَةٍ.

The referee stood beside the mat, carefully watching the match between the wrestlers.

singlet **سِنْجِلِت / زِيُّ المُصارَعَةِ**

اِرْتَدى المُصارِعُ الشّابُّ زِيَّ المُصارَعَةِ الجَديدَ خِلالَ بُطولَةِ المُصارَعَةِ الأَخيرَةِ.

The young wrestler wore the new singlet during the last wrestling tournament.

to wrestle, grapple • مُصارَعَةٌ **صارَعَ**

قَدَّمَ المُصارِعُ المُتَمَرِّسُ عَرْضًا رائِعًا، حَيْثُ صارَعَ بِبَراعَةٍ وَدِقَّةٍ اسْتِراتيجِيَّةٍ عالِيَةٍ.

The seasoned wrestler put on a great show as he wrestled with skill and high strategic precision.

wrestler **مُصارِعٌ**

أَثارَ المُصارِعُ الشّابُّ إِعْجابَ الجَماهيرِ بِأَدائِهِ القَوِيِّ وَالحاسِمِ فِي مُبارَياتِهِ.

The young wrestler impressed the crowd with his strong and decisive performance in his matches.

professional wrestling / pro-wrestling **مُصارَعَةُ المُحْتَرِفينَ**

صارَعَ المُصارِعُ الخَبيرُ خَصْمَهُ بِبَراعَةٍ، مِمّا أدّى إلى فَوْزِهِ في بُطولَةِ مُصارَعَةِ المُحْتَرِفينَ.

The expert wrestler grappled his opponent skillfully, leading to his victory in the professional wrestling championship.

6.3.1.1 Mini-Articles

Track **76**

في مُباراةٍ مُثيرَةٍ لِلْمُصارَعَةِ الحُرَّةِ، حَقَّقَ سَلْمان الحَرْبي فَوْزًا كَبيرًا عَلى مُنافِسِهِ خالِد الفايِز. كانَ الحَرْبي قَدْ صارَعَ بِمَهارَةٍ وَقُوَّةٍ، حَيْثُ نَجَحَ في تَنْفيذِ عِدَّةِ إِسْقاطاتٍ ناجِحَةٍ. في نِهايَةِ المُباراةِ، نَجَحَ الحَرْبي في تَثْبيتِ الفايِز عَلى حَصيرَةِ المُصارَعَةِ، مِمّا أدّى إلى حُكْمٍ بِلَمْسِ الأكْتافِ وَإِعْلانِ الحَرْبي فائِزًا. كانَ الفايِز قَدْ حاوَلَ الإِفْلاتَ، لَكِنَّ جُهودَهُ لَمْ تَكُنْ كافِيَةً.

In an exciting wrestling match, Salman Al-Harbi achieved a significant victory over his opponent, Khalid Al-Fayez. Al-Harbi wrestled with skill and strength, executing several successful takedowns. In the end, Al-Harbi managed to pin Al-Fayez on the wrestling mat, leading to a pinfall victory and declaring Al-Harbi the winner. Al-Fayez tried to escape, but his efforts were not enough.

مِنْ غَيْرِ المَأْلوفِ أَنْ يَظْهَرَ نَجْمٌ جَديدٌ في عالَمِ مُصارَعَةِ المُحْتَرِفينَ بِسُرْعَةٍ كَمُحَمَّد الشَّهْري. بَعْدَ سِلْسِلَةٍ مِنَ الانْتِصاراتِ السّاحِقَةِ، أَصْبَحَ الشَّهْري واحِدًا مِنْ أَكْثَرِ المُصارِعينَ المُحْتَرِفينَ إِثارَةً لِلإِعْجابِ. يَتَمَيَّزُ الشَّهْري بِقُوَّتِهِ وَقُدْرَتِهِ عَلى الإِمْساكِ القَوِيِّ وَالإِسْقاطاتِ المُحْكَمَةِ. وَقَدْ أَثارَ إِعْجابَ الجُمْهورِ وَالمُشَجِّعينَ بِأُسْلوبِهِ المُمَيَّزِ في المُصارَعَةِ.

It's unusual for a new star to emerge in the world of professional wrestling as quickly as Mohammed Al-Shahri. After a series of overwhelming victories, Al-Shahri has become one of the most impressive professional wrestlers. He is known for his strength and ability to execute powerful holds and precise takedowns. The audience and fans have been impressed by his distinctive wrestling style.

في أَحْدَثِ المُبارَياتِ في عالَمِ المُصارَعَةِ، اِسْتَسْلَمَ البَطَلُ السّابِقُ فَهْد العُتَيْبي أَمامَ المُصارِعِ الصّاعِدِ أَحْمَد الجَمايْعَة. بَدَأَ الجَمايْعَة المُباراةَ بِقُوَّةٍ، حَيْثُ قامَ بِتَنْفيذِ عِدَّةِ إِسْقاطاتٍ مُذْهِلَةٍ. بَعْدَ مَجْموعَةٍ مِنَ التَّحَرُّكاتِ المُحْكَمَةِ، نَجَحَ الجَمايْعَة في الإِمْساكِ بِالْعُتَيْبي بِقَبْضَةٍ لا يُمْكِنُ الهُروبُ مِنْها، مِمّا دَفَعَ العُتَيْبي لِإِعْلانِ الاِسْتِسْلامِ. أَظْهَرَ الجَمايْعَة طُموحَهُ وَقُوَّتَهُ في هَذِهِ المُباراةِ، مُعْلِنًا عَنْ نَفْسِهِ كَنَجْمٍ واعِدٍ في عالَمِ المُصارَعَةِ.

In the latest matches in the world of wrestling, former champion Fahad Al-Otaibi surrendered to the rising wrestler Ahmed Al-Jumay'a. Al-Jumay'a started the match with strength, executing several amazing takedowns. After a series of well-executed moves, Al-Jumay'a managed to lock Al-Otaibi in an inescapable grip, leading Al-Otaibi to declare submission. Al-Jumay'a showcased his ambition and strength in this match, announcing himself as a promising star in the world of wrestling.

6.3.2 Boxing

Track **77**

boxing **المُلاكَمَةُ**

تُعْتَبَرُ المُلاكَمَةُ مِنَ الرِّياضاتِ القِتالِيَّةِ الأَكْثَرِ شَعْبِيَّةً في العالَمِ.

Boxing is considered one of the most popular combat sports in the world.

to dodge • تَفادٍ **تَفادى**

في الجَوْلَةِ الثّالِثَةِ، تَفادى المُلاكِمُ المِصْرِيُّ الضَّرْبَةَ القاضِيَةَ بِبَراعَةٍ.

In the third round, the Egyptian boxer skillfully dodged the knockout punch.

to counter • مُجابَهَةٌ **جابَهَ**

لَمْ يَتَمَكَّنِ المُلاكِمُ المِصْرِيُّ مِنْ مُجابَهَةِ الهَجْمَةِ القَوِيَّةِ لِخَصْمِهِ.

The Egyptian boxer could not counter the strong offense of his opponent.

to block • حَجْبٌ **حَجَبَ**

حَجَبَ المُلاكِمُ الأَمْريكِيُّ جَميعَ اللَّكَماتِ الَّتي وَجَّهَها المُنافِسُ نَحْوَهُ.

The American boxer blocked all the punches that his opponent directed at him.

referee • حُكّامٌ **حَكَمٌ**

بِناءً عَلى قَرارِ الحَكَمِ، فازَ المُلاكِمُ البِريطانِيُّ بِالْمُباراةِ.

Based on the referee's decision, the British boxer won the match.

boxing ring **حَلْبَةُ مُلاكَمَةٍ**

تَحَوَّلَتْ حَلْبَةُ المُلاكَمَةِ إِلى ساحَةِ حَرْبٍ حَقيقِيَّةٍ خِلالَ النِّزالِ.

The boxing ring turned into a real battleground during the fight.

hand wrap رِباطُ اليَدِ • أَرْبِطَةٌ

بِفَضْلِ رِباطِ اليَدِ، كانَ المُلاكِمُ قادِرًا عَلى حِمايَةِ مِعْصَمِهِ مِنَ الإِصابَةِ.

Thanks to the hand wrap, the boxer was able to protect his wrist from injury.

corner رُكْنٌ • أَرْكانٌ

في الرُّكْنِ الأَزْرَقِ، أَرْهَقَ المُلاكِمُ المَكْسيكِيُّ مُنافِسَهُ بِسِلْسِلَةٍ مِنَ الضَّرَباتِ القَوِيَّةِ.

In the blue corner, the Mexican boxer wore out his opponent with a series of strong punches.

boxing trunks سِرْوالُ مُلاكَمَةٍ • سَراويلُ

في سِرْوالِ المُلاكَمَةِ الأَحْمَرِ، بَدا المُلاكِمُ الكوبِيُّ واثِقًا وَجاهِزًا لِلنِّزالِ.

In his red boxing trunks, the Cuban boxer looked confident and ready for the fight.

knockout (KO) ضَرْبَةٌ قاضِيَةٌ

بَعْدَ تَوْجيهِ ضَرْبَةٍ قاضِيَةٍ، أَصْبَحَ المُلاكِمُ المَغْرِبِيُّ بَطَلَ العالَمِ.

After delivering a knockout punch, the Moroccan boxer became a world champion.

technical knockout (TKO) ضَرْبَةٌ قاضِيَةٌ فَنِّيَّةٌ

نَتيجَةً لِلإِصابَةِ الشَّديدَةِ، أَعْلَنَ الحَكَمُ نِهايَةَ المُباراةِ بِضَرْبَةٍ قاضِيَةٍ فَنِّيَّةٍ.

As a result of the severe injury, the referee declared the match over by technical knockout.

(a pair of) boxing gloves قُفّازٌ

كانَ قُفّازُ المُلاكِمِ النَّيْجيرِيِّ مَليئًا بِالدِّماءِ بَعْدَ الجَوْلَةِ الأَخيرَةِ.

The Nigerian boxer's gloves were full of blood after the last round.

As with حِذاءٌ (see p. 160), قُفّازٌ refers to 'a pair'.

to punch لَكَمَ • لَكْمٌ

في الجَوْلَةِ الرّابِعَةِ، لَكَمَ المُلاكِمُ الرّوسِيُّ خَصْمَهُ بِقُوَّةٍ شَديدَةٍ، مِمّا أَدّى إِلى إِسْقاطِهِ عَلى الأَرْضِ.

In the fourth round, the Russian boxer punched his opponent hard, causing him to fall to the ground.

punch لَكْمَةٌ

فِي الجَوْلَةِ الأَخيرَةِ، تَمَكَّنَ المُلاكِمُ مِنْ تَوْجيهِ لَكْمَةٍ قَوِيَّةٍ لِخَصْمِهِ.

In the last round, the boxer managed to deliver a strong punch to his opponent.

jab لَكْمَةٌ أَمامِيَّةٌ مُسْتَقيمَةٌ

كانَتْ لَكْمَةُ المُلاكِمِ الأَرْجَنْتينِيِّ الأَمامِيَّةُ المُسْتَقيمَةُ سَريعَةً جِدًّا وَفَعّالَةً.

The Argentine boxer's straight jab was very fast and effective.

hook لَكْمَةٌ خُطّافِيَّةٌ

نَجَحَ المُلاكِمُ الإِسْبانِيُّ فِي تَوْجيهِ لَكْمَةٍ خُطّافِيَّةٍ قَوِيَّةٍ لِخَصْمِهِ.

The Spanish boxer succeeded in delivering a powerful hook to his opponent.

uppercut لَكْمَةٌ صاعِدَةٌ

تَسَبَّبَتِ اللَّكْمَةُ الصّاعِدَةُ القَوِيَّةُ فِي إِسْقاطِ المُلاكِمِ البَرازيلِيِّ عَلَى الأَرْضِ.

The powerful uppercut caused the Brazilian boxer to fall to the ground.

cross لَكْمَةٌ عَكْسِيَّةٌ

بِفَضْلِ تَوْجيهِهِ لَكْمَةً عَكْسِيَّةً مُفاجِئَةً، فازَ المُلاكِمُ الرّومانِيُّ بِالنِّزالِ.

Thanks to his unexpected cross punch, the Romanian boxer won the bout.

boxer مُلاكِمٌ

قامَ المُدَرِّبُ بِتَحْسينِ تِقْنِيّاتِ المُلاكِمِ وَتَعْزيزِ لِياقَتِهِ البَدَنِيَّةِ.

The coach worked on improving the boxer's techniques and enhancing his physical fitness.

to weave ناوَرَ • مُناوَرَةٌ

ناوَرَ المُلاكِمُ الفَرَنْسِيُّ بِمَهارَةٍ عالِيَةٍ لِتَجَنُّبِ اللَّكَماتِ القَوِيَّةِ لِخَصْمِهِ.

The French boxer weaved with high skill to avoid his opponent's strong punches.

mouthguard **واقي الفَمِ**

قَبْلَ بِدايَةِ النِّزالِ، وَضَعَ المُلاكِمُ المِصْرِيُّ واقِيَ الفَمِ لِحِمايَةِ أَسْنانِه.

Before the start of the fight, the Egyptian boxer put on a mouthguard to protect his teeth.

6.3.2.1 Mini-Articles

Track **78**

في لَيْلَةٍ مَليئَةٍ بِالْإِثارَةِ وَالتَّشْويقِ، نَجَحَ عادِل العَمْري في تَحْقيقِ فَوْزٍ مُذْهِلٍ عَلى مُنافِسِهِ رَشاد الجابِر في مُباراةِ المُلاكَمَةِ. بَعْدَ عِدَّةِ جَوْلاتٍ مُتَوَتِّرَةٍ، أَصابَ العَمْري الجابِر بِلَكْمَةٍ صاعِدَةٍ قَوِيَّةٍ أَدَّتْ إِلى ضَرْبَةٍ قاضِيَةٍ، مِمّا أَنْهى المُباراةَ. أَوْقَفَ الحَكَمُ النِّزالَ وَأَعْلَنَ العَمْري فائِزًا، في حينِ لَمْ يَسْتَطِعِ الجابِر الوُقوفَ مِنْ جَديدٍ.

In a thrilling and suspenseful night, Adel Al-Amri achieved a stunning victory over his opponent Rashad Al-Jaber in the boxing match. After several tense rounds, Al-Amri landed a powerful upward punch that delivered a knockout blow, ending the match. The referee stopped the fight and declared Al-Amri the winner, while Al-Jaber couldn't stand up again.

في مُباراةِ مُلاكَمَةٍ مُثيرَةٍ، أَظْهَرَ المُلاكِمُ مَحْمود الرِّفاعي مَهاراتِهِ في التَّفادي وَالمُناوَرَةِ. اِسْتَطاعَ الرِّفاعي تَفادِيَ العَديدِ مِنْ لَكَماتِ مُنافِسِهِ عادِل العيسى وَرَدَّ عَلَيْها بِلَكَماتٍ خُطّافِيَّةٍ وَعَكْسِيَّةٍ سَريعَةٍ. وَقَدْ أَدَّتْ هَذِهِ التَّكْتيكاتُ النّاجِحَةُ إِلى فَوْزِ الرِّفاعي بِعِدَّةِ نِقاطٍ.

In an exciting boxing match, boxer Mahmoud Al-Rifa'i showcased his skills in evading and maneuvering. Al-Rifa'i managed to dodge many punches from his opponent Adel Al-Issa and responded with quick hook and counter punches. These successful tactics led to Al-Rifa'i winning by points.

بَعْدَ سِلْسِلَةٍ مِنَ الاِنْتِصاراتِ القَوِيَّةِ، أَصْبَحَ المُلاكِمُ جابِر الخالِدي البَطَلَ الجَديدَ في عالَمِ المُلاكَمَةِ. في مُباراتِهِ الأَخيرَةِ، كانَتْ لَكَماتُ الخالِدي الأَمامِيَّةُ المُسْتَقيمَةُ وَلَكَماتُهُ العَكْسِيَّةُ القَوِيَّةُ أَكْثَرَ مِمّا يَسْتَطيعُ مُنافِسُهُ تَحَمُّلَهُ، مِمّا أَدّى إِلى ضَرْبَةٍ قاضِيَةٍ فَنِّيَّةٍ وَتَمَّ الإِعْلانُ عَنِ الخالِدي بَطَلًا جَديدًا. يَبْدو أَنَّ المُسْتَقْبَلَ مُشْرِقٌ لِهَذا البَطَلِ الجَديدِ.

After a series of strong victories, boxer Jaber Al-Khaldi has become the new champion in the world of boxing. In his latest match, Al-Khaldi's powerful straight punches and effective counter punches proved too much for his opponent to handle, leading to a technical knockout, and Al-Khaldi was declared the new champion. The future looks bright for this new champion.

6.3.3 Martial Arts

Track **79**

submission اِسْتِسْلامٌ

أَثْناءَ المُنافَسَةِ، قَدَّمَ المُصارِعُ البَرازيلِيُّ تِقْنِيَّةَ الِاسْتِسْلامِ الفَعّالَةِ الَّتي تَمَكَّنَتْ مِنَ السَّيْطَرَةِ عَلى المُباراةِ.

During the competition, the Brazilian wrestler executed an effective submission technique that managed to control the match.

Another common term for 'submission' in martial arts is إِخْضاعٌ.

gi (uniform) الجي

خِلالَ التَّدْريبِ، يَرْتَدي المُتَدَرِّبونَ في الجودو الزِّيَّ التَّقْليدِيَّ الَّذي يُعْرَفُ بِاسْمِ الجي.

During training, Judo practitioners wear the traditional uniform known as a gi.

grappling المُصارَعَةُ

حَقَّقَ المُصارِعُ المِصْرِيُّ الشّابُّ فَوْزًا مُهِمًّا في بُطولَةِ المُصارَعَةِ العالَمِيَّةِ، مُثْبِتًا أَنَّهُ واحِدٌ مِنَ النُّجومِ الصّاعِدَةِ في هَذِهِ الرِّياضَةِ.

The young Egyptian wrestler achieved a significant victory in the world wrestling championship, proving that he is one of the rising stars in this sport.

taekwondo تّايكوِنْدو

أَحْرَزَتْ ماريا، البالِغَةُ مِنَ العُمْرِ 15 عامًا، حِزامًا أَسْوَدَ في الجودو وَالتّايكوِنْدو، مُثْبِتَةً بِذَلِكَ قُدُراتِها الِاسْتِثْنائِيَّةَ في الفُنونِ القِتالِيَّةِ.

At the age of 15, Maria has earned a black belt in Judo and Taekwondo, proving her exceptional skills in martial arts.

to parry • تَفادٍ تَفادى

في المُباراةِ الأَخيرَةِ، تَفادى جونِ الضَّرْبَةَ القَوِيَّةَ مِنْ خَصْمِهِ وَرَدَّ بِلَكْمَةٍ مُرْتَدَّةٍ أَسْفَرَتْ عَنْ فَوْزِهِ في الجَوْلَةِ.

In the last match, John parried the strong punch from his opponent and countered with a rebound punch that resulted in his round victory.

جابَهَ • مُجابَهَةٌ **to counter**

بَعْدَ أَنْ جابَهَ خَصْمَهُ بِضَرْبَةٍ قَوِيَّةٍ، كانَ لِزامًا عَلى أَليكْس تَقْييمُ الوَضْعِ وَتَغْييرُ اسْتِراتيجِيَّتِه.

After his opponent countered with a strong punch, it was imperative for Alex to assess the situation and change his strategy.

جوجيتْسو بَرازيلِيٌّ **Brazilian jiu-jitsu**

أَثْناءَ التَّدْريبِ، يَجِبُ عَلى المُقاتِلينَ في الجوجيتْسو البَرازيلِيِّ تَعَلُّمُ فَنِّ المُصارَعَةِ وَتِقْنِيّاتِهِ المُخْتَلِفَة.

During training, fighters in Brazilian Jiu-Jitsu must learn the art of grappling and its various techniques.

جودو **judo**

واجَهَ المُتَسابِقُ في الجودو صُعوبَةً في التَّغَلُّبِ عَلى الحَجْبِ المُفاجِئِ لِخَصْمِه.

The judo competitor had difficulty overcoming his opponent's sudden block.

حَجَبَ • حَجْبٌ **to block**

في مُباراةِ البارِحَةِ، حَجَبَ المُقاتِلُ البَرازيلِيُّ جَميعَ الهَجَماتِ الوارِدَةِ بِمَهارَةٍ عالِيَةٍ.

In last night's match, the Brazilian fighter skillfully blocked all incoming attacks.

حِزامٌ أَسْوَدُ • أَحْزِمَةٌ **black belt**

حَقَّقَ لاعِبُ الفُنونِ القِتالِيَّةِ الشّابُّ الحِزامَ الأَسْوَدَ بَعْدَ سَنَواتٍ مِنَ التَّدْريبِ وَالتَّعَب.

The young martial artist achieved the black belt after years of training and hard work.

دافَعَ • دِفاعٌ / مُدافَعَةٌ **to defend**

في التَّدْريبِ الصَّباحِيِّ، دافَعَ المُقاتِلُ السّورِيُّ بِشَكْلٍ مِثالِيٍّ عَنْ نَفْسِهِ ضِدَّ هَجَماتِ المُعَلِّم.

During the morning training, the Syrian fighter defended himself perfectly against the teacher's attacks.

دوجو **dojo** (training hall)

يَتَدَرَّبُ المُقاتِلونَ كُلَّ يَوْمٍ في الدوجو لِتَحْسينِ مَهاراتِهِمْ في الفُنونِ القِتالِيَّة.

Fighters train every day in the dojo to improve their martial arts skills.

to kick • رَكْلٌ **رَكَلَ**

رَكَلَ المُقاتِلُ الجَديدُ خَصْمَهُ بِقُوَّةٍ، مُسْقِطًا إِيّاهُ عَلى الأَرْضِ.

The new fighter kicked his opponent hard, knocking him to the ground.

kick **رَكْلَةٌ**

أَطْلَقَ المُقاتِلُ الأَمْريكِيُّ رَكْلَةً قَوِيَّةً نَحْوَ خَصْمِهِ، لَكِنَّها لَمْ تُصِبِ الهَدَفَ.

The American fighter launched a strong kick towards his opponent, but it didn't hit the target.

to throw • رَمْيٌ **رَمى**

في الجَوْلَةِ الثّالِثَةِ، رَمى المُقاتِلُ الصّينِيُّ خَصْمَهُ عَلى الأَرْضِ بِطَريقَةٍ مُثيرَةٍ لِلْإِعْجابِ.

In the third round, the Chinese fighter impressively threw his opponent to the ground.

sensei, master **سينساي / مُعَلِّمٌ**

يُعْتَبَرُ السّينْساي ياماموتو أَحَدَ أَبْرَزِ المُعَلِّمينَ في فُنونِ القِتالِ اليابانِيَّةِ.

Sensei Yamamoto is considered one of the foremost teachers in Japanese martial arts.

to grapple • مُصارَعَةٌ **صارَعَ**

في الجَوْلَةِ الأَخيرَةِ، صارَعَ المُقاتِلُ الكورِيُّ خَصْمَهُ بِقُوَّةٍ وَسَيْطَرَةٍ فائِقَةٍ.

In the final round, the Korean fighter grappled his opponent with great strength and control.

to strike • ضَرْبٌ **ضَرَبَ**

ضَرَبَ المُقاتِلُ البِريطانِيُّ خَصْمَهُ بِقُوَّةٍ، مِمّا أَدّى إِلى إِنْهاءِ المُباراةِ مُبَكِّرًا.

The British fighter struck his opponent hard, resulting in an early end to the match.

strike **ضَرْبَةٌ**

تَمَكَّنَتْ لاعِبَةُ الفُنونِ القِتالِيَّةِ مِنْ إِطْلاقِ ضَرْبَةٍ مُفاجِئَةٍ أَدَّتْ إِلى فَوْزِها بِالْمُباراةِ.

The martial artist managed to launch a surprise strike that led to her winning the match.

عَرْقَلَ • عَرْقَلَةٌ **to sweep**

فِي الدَّوْرَةِ الأولِمْبِيَّةِ الأَخيرَةِ، نَفَّذَ الرِّياضِيُّ اليابانِيُّ عَرْقَلَةً مُذْهِلَةً أَبْهَرَتِ الجُمْهورَ.

In the last Olympic Games, the Japanese athlete executed an amazing sweep that awed the audience.

فُنونٌ قِتالِيَّةٌ *pl.* **martial arts**

تُعْتَبَرُ الفُنونُ القِتالِيَّةُ جُزْءًا مُهِمًّا مِنَ التَّدْريبِ الرِّياضِيِّ فِي العَديدِ مِنَ الثَّقافاتِ حَوْلَ العالَمِ.

Martial arts are an important part of athletic training in many cultures around the world.

كاراتيهْ **karate**

يُعْتَبَرُ الكاراتيهْ مِنَ الفُنونِ القِتالِيَّةِ الأَكْثَرِ شُهْرَةً وانْتِشارًا فِي العالَمِ.

Karate is considered one of the most famous and widespread martial arts in the world.

لاعِبُ الفُنونِ القِتالِيَّةِ **martial artist**

يُعْتَبَرُ لاعِبُ الفُنونِ القِتالِيَّةِ الرّوسِيُّ أَحَدَ أَبْرَزِ الأَسْماءِ فِي عالَمِ الفُنونِ القِتالِيَّةِ.

The Russian martial artist is considered one of the leading names in the world of martial arts.

لَكَمَ • لَكْمٌ **to punch**

خِلالَ المُباراةِ، لَكَمَ المُلاكِمُ خَصْمَهُ مَرّاتٍ عِدَّةً، لَكِنَّهُ لَمْ يَتَمَكَّنْ مِنْ إِسْقاطِهِ.

During the match, the boxer punched his opponent several times, but was unable to knock him down.

لَكْمَةٌ **punch**

نَفَّذَتِ اللّاعِبَةُ المِصْرِيَّةُ لَكْمَةً قَوِيَّةً أَدَّتْ إِلى إِسْقاطِ خَصْمَتِها عَلى الحَلْبَةِ.

The Egyptian player landed a powerful punch that knocked her opponent down in the ring.

موي تايْ / المُلاكَمَةُ التّايلانْدِيَّةُ **Muay Thai**

يَشْتَهِرُ الرِّياضِيُّ التّايلانْدِيُّ بِتَفَوُّقِهِ فِي الموي تايْ، وَهُوَ نَوْعٌ مِنَ الفُنونِ القِتالِيَّةِ التَّقْليدِيَّةِ.

The Thai athlete is known for his excellence in Muay Thai, a type of traditional martial arts.

6.3.3.1 Mini-Articles

Track **80**

فِي بُطولَةِ الكاراتيهِ الوَطَنِيَّةِ الأَخيرَةِ، أَثْبَتَ اللاعِبُ غالِب العبد الله أَنَّهُ يَسْتَحِقُّ الحِزامَ الأَسْوَدَ الَّذي يَرْتَديهِ. نَفَّذَ رَكَلاتٍ وَلَكَماتٍ قَوِيَّةً وَدَقيقَةً، مُظْهِرًا التَّدْريبَ الشّاقَّ الَّذي خَضَعَ لَهُ فِي الدوجو. تَمَكَّنَ العبد الله مِنْ تَفادي الضَّرَباتِ المُتَكَرِّرَةِ مِنْ مُنافِسِهِ، وَقابَلَها بِضَرَباتٍ مُضادَّةٍ فَعّالَةٍ، مِمّا أَدّى إِلى فَوْزِهِ فِي المُباراةِ.

In the recent national karate championship, the fighter Ghalib Al-Abdullah proved that he deserved the black belt he wears. He delivered powerful and precise kicks and punches, showcasing the rigorous training he underwent in the dojo. Al-Abdullah managed to evade his opponent's repeated strikes and countered them effectively, leading to his victory in the match.

عَلى مَدارِ الأَشْهُرِ السِّتَّةِ الماضِيَةِ، قادَ المُعَلِّمُ عَبْد الرَّحْمَن بَرْنامَجًا مُتَقَدِّمًا لِلتَّدْريبِ عَلى الفُنونِ القِتالِيَّةِ. اِسْتَمَرَّ التَّدْريبُ فِي الدوجو الَّذي يُعْتَبَرُ مَكانًا مُقَدَّسًا لِلتَّعَلُّمِ وَالنُّمُوِّ. تُرَكِّزُ الدُّروسُ عَلى مَهاراتِ الدِّفاعِ وَالهُجومِ وَكَذَلِكَ الاِحْتِرامِ وَالتَّأْديبِ. الآنَ، يُظْهِرُ الطُّلّابُ تَقَدُّمًا كَبيرًا فِي مَهاراتِ الرَّكْلِ، والضَّرْبِ، وَالمُصارَعَةِ.

Over the past six months, Sensei Abdulrahman has been leading an advanced martial arts training program. The training took place in the dojo, which is considered a sacred place for learning and growth. The lessons focused on defensive and offensive skills, as well as respect and discipline. Now, the students are showing significant progress in kicking, striking, and grappling techniques.

حَقَّقَ اللاعِبُ حَمَد النّاصِر نَجاحًا كَبيرًا فِي البُطولَةِ الوَطَنِيَّةِ لِلْجوجيتْسو البَرازيلِيِّ. اِعْتَمَدَ النّاصِر عَلى مَهاراتِ المُصارَعَةِ القَوِيَّةِ لِلسَّيْطَرَةِ عَلى مُنافِسِهِ. فِي النِّهايَةِ، أَجْبَرَ مُنافِسَهُ عَلى الاِسْتِسْلامِ بَعْدَ تَنْفيذِ حَرَكَةِ قَفْلِ الرَّقَبَةِ بِبَراعَةٍ. هَذا الفَوْزُ الكَبيرُ لِلنّاصِر جَعَلَ الجَميعَ يَتَطَلَّعونَ إِلى ما يَحْمِلُهُ المُسْتَقْبَلُ لِهَذا اللاعِبِ الواعِدِ.

The fighter Hamad Al-Nasser achieved great success in the national Brazilian Jiu-Jitsu championship. Al-Nasser relied on his strong grappling skills to control his opponent. In the end, he forced his opponent to submit after executing a skillful neck lock. This significant win for Al-Nasser has everyone looking forward to what the future holds for this promising fighter.

6.3.3.2 Descriptions of Various Martial Arts

Track **81**

نَظْرَةٌ عامَّةٌ عَلى فُنونِ القِتالِ المُخْتَلِفَةِ

التّايكونْدو: هُوَ فَنٌّ قِتالِيٌّ أَصْلُهُ مِنْ كورْيا، يُرَكِّزُ بِشَكْلٍ خاصٍّ عَلى الرَّكَلاتِ عالِيَةِ السُّرْعَةِ. يَشْتَهِرُ التّايْكونْدو بِالرَّكَلاتِ المَصْحوبَةِ بِالدَّورانِ وَالقَفْزِ، وَالَّتي تَتَطَلَّبُ التَّوازُنَ، المُرونَةَ، وَالتَّنْسيقَ. بِالإِضافَةِ إِلى الرَّكَلاتِ، يَتَضَمَّنُ التّايْكونْدو أَيْضًا بَعْضَ التِّقْنِيّاتِ اليَدَوِيَّةِ مِثْلَ اللَّكَماتِ وَالضَّرَباتِ وَالحَجْبِ.

الجوجيتْسو البَرازيلِيُّ: هُوَ فَنٌّ قِتاليٌّ يُرَكِّزُ بِشَكْلٍ رَئيسِيٍّ عَلى المُصارَعَةِ وَالإِخْضاعِ. نَشَأَ في اليابانِ، لَكِنَّهُ طُوِّرَ بِشَكْلٍ مَلْحوظٍ في البَرازيلِ. يُشَجِّعُ الجوجيتْسو البَرازيلِيُّ اللاعِبينَ عَلى اسْتِخْدامِ التِّقْنِيّاتِ لِلتَّغَلُّبِ عَلى القُوَّةِ الخامِ، مَعَ التَّرْكيزِ بِشَكْلٍ خاصٍّ عَلى الخَنْقِ وتَثْبيتِ المَفاصِلِ.

الجودو: هُوَ فَنٌّ قِتاليٌّ يابانِيٌّ يُرَكِّزُ عَلى الطَّرْحِ أَرْضًا وَالمُصارَعَةِ. يَتَمَيَّزُ الجودو بِمَجْموعَةٍ واسِعَةٍ مِنَ التِّقْنِيّاتِ، الَّتي تَشْمَلُ الرَّمْياتِ، القَفْلَ، وَالتَّثْبيتَ. الهَدَفُ في الجودو هُوَ إِلْقاءُ الخَصْمِ أَرْضًا، شَلُّ حَرَكَتِهِ، أَوْ إِخْضاعُهُ عَنْ طَريقِ القَفْلِ أَوِ الخَنْقِ.

كاراتيهْ: هُوَ فَنٌّ قِتاليٌّ يابانِيٌّ يَتَضَمَّنُ الضَّرْبَ بِالْيَدَيْنِ وَالقَدَمَيْنِ. يَشْتَهِرُ الكاراتيهْ بِاللَّكَماتِ القَوِيَّةِ وَالرَّكَلاتِ وَضَرَباتِ الرُّكْبَةِ وَالكوعِ، فَضْلًا عَنِ التِّقْنِيّاتِ الدِّفاعِيَّةِ مِثْلِ الحَجْبِ وَالتَّفادي. الهَدَفُ في الكاراتيهْ هُوَ التَّحَكُّمُ في الخَصْمِ عَبْرَ الضَّرَباتِ القَوِيَّةِ وَالدَّقيقَةِ.

المَوايْ تايْ (المُلاكَمَةُ التّايْلانْدِيَّةُ): هُوَ فَنٌّ قِتاليٌّ تايْلانْدِيٌّ يَشْتَهِرُ بِكَوْنِهِ "فَنَّ الأَطْرافِ الثَّمانِيَةِ"، الَّذي تُسْتَخْدَمُ فيه القَدَمانِ، اليَدانِ، الرُّكْبَتانِ، وَالكوعانَ. تُعْتَبَرُ الضَّرَباتُ بِالرُّكْبَةِ وَالكوعِ مِنْ تِقْنِيّاتِ المَوايْ تايِ الأَكْثَرِ فَتْكًا، وَلَكِنَّ الفَنَّ يَتَضَمَّنُ أَيْضًا القَبَضاتِ، الرَّكَلاتِ، وَالحَجْبَ.

An Overview of the Different Martial Arts

Taekwondo: A martial art originating from Korea that focuses primarily on high-speed kicks. Taekwondo is renowned for its spinning and jumping kicks, which require balance, flexibility, and coordination. In addition to kicks, Taekwondo also incorporates some hand techniques such as punches, strikes, and blocks.

Brazilian Jiu-Jitsu: A martial art that primarily focuses on grappling and submissions. It originated in Japan but has notably developed in Brazil. Brazilian Jiu-Jitsu encourages fighters to use techniques to overcome raw strength, with a particular emphasis on chokes and joint locks.

Judo: A Japanese martial art that emphasizes throwing and grappling. Judo is characterized by a wide range of techniques, including throws, locks, and holds. The goal in Judo is to throw the opponent to the ground, immobilize them, or gain submission through a lock or choke.

Karate: A Japanese martial art that involves striking with the hands and feet. Karate is known for powerful punches, kicks, knee strikes, and elbow strikes, as well as defensive techniques like blocks and evasions. The aim in Karate is to control the opponent through powerful and precise strikes.

Muay Thai (Thai Boxing): A Thai martial art known as the "Art of Eight Limbs," which employs the feet, hands, knees, and elbows. Knees and elbows are considered some of the most lethal Muay Thai techniques, but the art also includes clinching, kicks, and blocks.

6.4 Sports Culture and Industry

6.4.1 Sports Events

Track **82**

to host • اِسْتِضافَةٌ **اِسْتَضافَ**

تَمَّ اخْتيارُ دُبَيَّ مُؤَخَّرًا لِاسْتِضافَةِ البُطولَةِ العالَمِيَّةِ لِكُرَةِ القَدَمِ في العامِ القادِمِ.

Dubai was recently chosen to host the World Football Championship next year.

playoffs *pl.* **الأَدْوارُ الإِقْصائِيَّةُ**

فازَ فَريقُ بوسطِنْ في الأَدْوارِ الإِقْصائِيَّةِ، مِمّا أَهَّلَهُ لِلدَّوْرِ النِّهائِيِّ في بُطولَةِ الدَّوْرِيِّ الأَمْريكِيِّ لِكُرَةِ السَّلَّةِ.

The Boston team won in the playoffs, qualifying them for the finals in the American Basketball Championship.

the Olympic games *pl.* **الأَلْعابُ الأولِمْبِيَّةُ**

سَيَشْهَدُ العامُ القادِمُ إِقامَةَ الأَلْعابِ الأولِمْبِيَّةِ في باريس، وَيُتَوَقَّعُ حُضورُ الآلافِ مِنَ الرِّياضِيّينَ.

The coming year will see the Olympic Games held in Paris, with thousands of athletes expected to attend.

the Winter Olympics *pl.* **الأَلْعابُ الأولِمْبِيَّةُ الشِّتْوِيَّةُ**

شَهِدَتِ الأَلْعابُ الأولِمْبِيَّةُ الشِّتْوِيَّةُ في بِكينْ مُنافَساتٍ شَرِسَةً وَأَرْقامًا قِياسِيَّةً مُتَمَيِّزَةً.

The Winter Olympics in Beijing witnessed fierce competitions and outstanding records.

the Summer Olympics *pl.* **الأَلْعابُ الأولِمْبِيَّةُ الصَّيْفِيَّةُ**

سَتَكونُ الأَلْعابُ الأولِمْبِيَّةُ الصَّيْفِيَّةُ القادِمَةُ في لوسْ أَنْجِلوسْ هِيَ الأَكْبَرَ في تاريخِ الأَلْعابِ.

The upcoming Summer Olympics in Los Angeles will be the largest in the history of the Games.

the Paralympics *pl.* **الأَلْعابُ البارالِمْبِيَّةُ**

تُعَدُّ الأَلْعابُ البارالِمْبِيَّةُ فُرْصَةً لِلرِّياضِيّينَ ذَوي الإِعاقَةِ لِإِظْهارِ مَهاراتِهِمْ وَتَحْقيقِ النَّجاحِ.

The Paralympics provide an opportunity for disabled athletes to showcase their skills and achieve success.

الأولِمْبِيادُ **the Olympics**

مِنَ المُتَوَقَّعِ أَنْ يَشْهَدَ الأولِمْبِيادُ القادِمُ في باريسَ تَواجُدَ ما يَزيدُ عَنْ 200 دَوْلَةٍ.

The upcoming Olympics in Tokyo are expected to see the presence of more than 200 countries.

الحَلَقاتُ الأولِمْبِيَّةُ *pl.* **Olympic rings**

رُفِعَتِ الحَلَقاتُ الأولِمْبِيَّةُ خِلالَ حَفْلِ الاِفْتِتاحِ، مِمّا أَثارَ حَماسَ الجَماهيرِ.

The Olympic rings were raised during the opening ceremony, exciting the crowd.

الدَّوْرِيُّ الجَزائِرِيُّ لِلْمُحْتَرِفينَ **Algerian Ligue Professionnelle**

بَدَأَتِ المُبارَياتُ الأولى لِلدَّوْرِيِّ الجَزائِرِيِّ لِلْمُحْتَرِفينَ، وَيَتَطَلَّعُ الجُمْهورُ بِفارِغِ الصَّبْرِ لِمُشاهَدَةِ مُنافَساتٍ قَوِيَّةٍ.

The first matches of the Algerian Ligue Professionnelle have started, and the audience is eagerly looking forward to watching strong competitions.

الدَّوْرِيُّ السُّعودِيُّ لِلْمُحْتَرِفينَ **Saudi Professional League**

أَعْلَنَتِ الهَيْئَةُ الرِّياضِيَّةُ في السُّعودِيَّةِ عَنْ بَدْءِ الدَّوْرِيِّ السُّعودِيِّ لِلْمُحْتَرِفينَ في الأُسْبوعِ القادِمِ.

The Saudi Sports Authority announced the start of the Saudi Professional League next week.

الدَّوْرِيُّ العِراقِيُّ المُمْتازُ لِكُرَةِ القَدَمِ **Iraqi Premier League**

سَجَّلَ فَريقُ الزَّوْراءِ فَوْزًا مُثيرًا في الدَّوْرِيِّ العِراقِيِّ المُمْتازِ لِكُرَةِ القَدَمِ.

Al-Zawraa team recorded an exciting win in the Iraqi Premier League for soccer.

الدَّوْرِيُّ المِصْرِيُّ المُمْتازُ **Egyptian Premier League**

سَيَتَقابَلُ فَريقا الأَهْلي وَالزَّمالِكِ في المُباراةِ القادِمَةِ ضِمْنَ الدَّوْرِيِّ المِصْرِيِّ المُمْتازِ.

Al-Ahly and Zamalek teams will face each other in the upcoming match in the Egyptian Premier League.

الشُّعْلَةُ الأولِمْبِيَّةُ **the Olympic torch**

تَمَّ تَمْريرُ الشُّعْلَةِ الأولِمْبِيَّةِ مِنْ يَدٍ لِأُخْرى في مَراسِمَ مَهيبَةٍ احتِفالًا بِبِدايَةِ الأَلْعابِ.

The Olympic torch was passed from hand to hand in a grand ceremony that marked the beginning of the Games.

القَرْيَةُ الأولِمْبِيَّةُ • قُرًى — **the Olympic village**

تَمَّ تَجْهيزُ القَرْيَةِ الأولِمْبِيَّةِ لِاسْتِقْبالِ الرِّياضِيِّينَ مِنْ جَميعِ أَنْحاءِ العالَمِ.

The Olympic village has been prepared to welcome athletes from all around the world.

القَسَمُ الأولِمْبِيُّ — **Olympic Oath**

أَلْقى الرِّياضِيُّ الشّابُّ القَسَمَ الأولِمْبِيَّ، مُتَعَهِّدًا بِاللَّعِبِ بِروحٍ رِياضِيَّةٍ وَنَزاهَةٍ.

The young athlete recited the Olympic Oath, pledging to play with sportsmanship and integrity.

المَدينَةُ المُضيفَةُ • مُدُنٌ — **host city**

تَسْتَعِدُّ المَدينَةُ المُضيفَةُ، باريس، لِاسْتِقْبالِ الأَلْعابِ الأولِمْبِيَّةِ القادِمَةِ.

The host city, Paris, is preparing to welcome the upcoming Olympic Games.

اِنْتِقاءٌ — **draft**

أَعْلَنَ الفَريقُ أَنَّهُمْ قَدِ انتَقَوا لاعِبًا جَديدًا في الاِنْتِقاءِ السَّنَوِيِّ لِلدَّوْرِيِّ الوَطَنِيِّ لِكُرَةِ القَدَمِ الأَمْريكِيَّةِ.

The team announced that they have drafted a new player in the annual NFL draft.

بُطولَةٌ — **championship, tournament**

تُقامُ بُطولَةُ رولانْ غاروسْ لِلتِّنِسِ كُلَّ عامٍ في باريس.

The Roland Garros Tennis Championship is held every year in Paris.

بُطولَةُ العالَمِ — **world championship**

تَحَقَّقَ حُلْمُ اللاعِبِ بِالتَّأَهُّلِ لِبُطولَةِ العالَمِ بَعْدَ تَحْقيقِهِ سِلْسِلَةٍ مِنَ الاِنْتِصاراتِ المُذْهِلَةِ في المُنافَساتِ المُؤَهِّلَةِ .

The player's dream came true as he qualified for the World Championship after achieving a series of stunning victories in the qualifying competitions.

بَلَدٌ مُضيفٌ • بِلادٌ / بُلْدانٌ — **host country**

قَرَّرَتِ اللَّجْنَةُ الأولِمْبِيَّةُ الدَّوْلِيَّةُ أَنْ تَكونَ اليابانُ هِيَ البَلَدَ المُضيفَ لِلأَلْعابِ الأولِمْبِيَّةِ 2024.

The International Olympic Committee decided that Japan will be the host country for the 2024 Olympic Games.

تَأَهُّلٌ

qualification

بَعْدَ مُباراةٍ حاسِمَةٍ، تَأَهَّلَ الفَريقُ البَرازيلِيُّ لِلدَّوْرِ النِّهائِيِّ في كَأْسِ العالَمِ.

After a decisive match, the Brazilian team qualified for the final round in the World Cup.

تَبادُلٌ

trade

نَجَحَ فَريقُ البيسْبولْ في تَبادُلِ لاعِبِهِ الرَّئيسِيِّ مُقابِلَ لاعِبَيْنِ اثْنَيْنِ مِنَ الفَريقِ الخَصْمِ.

The baseball team succeeded in trading their main player for two players from the opposing team.

تَرْتيبٌ

standings

في التَّرْتيبِ الحالِيِّ لِلدَّوْرِيِّ، يَتَصَدَّرُ فَريقُ الرِّيالْ مَدْريد القائِمَةَ.

In the current league standings, Real Madrid team tops the list.

تَصْفِياتٌ مُؤَهِّلَةٌ

qualifiers *pl.*

تَسْتَعِدُّ الفِرَقُ لِلتَّصْفِياتِ المُؤَهِّلَةِ لِكَأْسِ العالَمِ 2026.

Teams are preparing for the qualifiers for the 2026 World Cup.

جَوْلَةٌ

round

بَعْدَ الجَوْلَةِ الأَخيرَةِ مِنَ المُبارَياتِ، تَمَّ تَحْديدُ الفِرَقِ الثَّمانِيَةِ الَّتي سَتُنافِسُ في الأَدْوارِ الإِقْصائِيَّةِ.

After the last round of matches, the eight teams that will compete in the playoffs have been determined.

حَدَثٌ • أَحْداثٌ

event

يُعَدُّ حَدَثُ ماراثونِ بوسْطِنْ مِنْ أَكْبَرِ الأَحْداثِ الرِّياضِيَّةِ السَّنَوِيَّةِ في الوِلاياتِ المُتَّحِدَةِ.

The Boston Marathon event is considered one of the biggest annual sports events in the United States.

opening ceremony **حَفْلُ افْتِتاحٍ**

أَبْهَرَ حَفْلُ افْتِتاحِ دَوْرَةِ الأَلْعابِ الأولِمْبيَّةِ الشَّتْويَّةِ الجَماهيرَ بِعُروضِهِ المُتَأَلِّقَة.

The opening ceremony of the Winter Olympics amazed the audience with its dazzling performances.

medal ceremony **حَفْلُ تَوْزيعِ الميدالْياتِ**

خِلالَ حَفْلِ تَوْزيعِ الميدالْياتِ، أَحْرَزَ الرِّياضِيُّ الكَنَدِيُّ الميدالْيَةَ الذَّهَبِيَّةَ في مُنافَساتِ التَّزَلُّجِ السَّريعِ.

During the medal ceremony, the Canadian athlete won the gold medal in speed skating competitions.

closing ceremony **حَفْلُ خِتامٍ**

عَرَضَ حَفْلُ الخِتامِ لِلْأَلْعابِ الأولِمْبِيَّةِ الصَّيْفِيَّةِ مَجْموعَةً مِنَ العُروضِ الفَنِّيَّةِ المُتَنَوِّعَةِ.

The closing ceremony of the Summer Olympics showcased a range of diverse artistic performances.

league **دَوْرِيٌّ**

يُعَدُّ دَوْرِيُّ الدَّرَجَةِ الأولى الإِنْجليزِيُّ مِنْ أَفْضَلِ البُطولاتِ الكُرَوِيَّةِ في العالَمِ.

The English Premier League is considered one of the best soccer leagues in the world.

Saudi Pro League **الدَّوْرِيُّ السُّعودِيُّ لِلْمُحْتَرِفينَ**

اِسْتِمْرارًا لِمَوْسِمِهِ النّاجِحِ، فازَ الهِلالُ في الدَّوْرِيِّ السُّعودِيِّ لِلْمُحْتَرِفينَ.

Continuing its successful season, Al Hilal won in the Saudi Pro League.

Arabian Gulf League **دَوْرِيُّ الخَليجِ العَرَبِيِّ**

حَقَّقَ فَريقُ الجَزيرَةِ الفَوْزَ في مُباراةٍ حاسِمَةٍ بِدَوْرِيِّ الخَليجِ العَرَبِيِّ.

Al-Jazira team achieved a victory in a decisive match in the Arabian Gulf League.

Qatar Stars League **دَوْرِيُّ النُّجومِ القَطَرِيُّ**

تَعَدَّدَتِ التَّوَقُّعاتُ حَوْلَ الفَريقِ الَّذي سَيَحْصُدُ اللَّقَبَ في دَوْرِيِّ النُّجومِ القَطَرِيِّ هَذا العامَ.

There were multiple predictions about which team would win the title in the Qatar Stars League this year.

سِباقٌ
race

يَجْذِبُ سِباقُ موناكو الكَبيرُ لِلفورْمولا 1 عُشّاقَ الرِّياضَةِ مِنْ جَميعِ أَنْحاءِ العالَمِ.

The Monaco Grand Prix race for Formula 1 attracts sports fans from all over the world.

فَريقٌ • فِرَقٌ
team

فازَ الفَريقُ الإِسْبانِيُّ بِنِهائِيّاتِ كَأْسِ الأُمَمِ الأوروبِّيَّةِ بَعْدَ مُباراةٍ مُثيرَةٍ.

The Spanish team won the European Nations Cup finals after an exciting match.

كَأْسٌ • كُؤوسٌ
trophy

سَيُمْنَحُ الفائِزُ في بُطولَةِ ويمْبِلْدونْ لِلتِّنِسِ كَأْسًا فِضِّيًّا.

The winner of the Wimbledon Tennis Championship will be awarded a silver trophy.

كَأْسُ العالَمِ
the World Cup

يَنْتَظِرُ المَلايينُ مِنْ عُشّاقِ كُرَةِ القَدَمِ بِشَغَفٍ بَدْءَ كَأْسِ العالَمِ، حَيْثُ سَتَتَنافَسُ أَفْضَلُ الفِرَقِ العالَمِيَّةِ عَلى اللَّقَبِ .

Millions of football fans eagerly await the start of the World Cup, where top teams from around the globe will battle for the title.

كَأْسُ العَرَبِ
the Arab Cup

مِنَ المُقَرَّرِ أَنْ تَكونَ النُّسْخَةُ القادِمَةُ مِنْ كَأْسِ العَرَبِ في قَطَرْ في نوفَمْبِرَ 2023.

The next edition of the Arab Cup is set to be in Jordan in 2024.

لاعِبٌ
player

حَصَلَ اللّاعِبُ الأَرْجَنْتينِيُّ ليونيل ميسّي عَلى جائِزَةِ الكُرَةِ الذَّهَبِيَّةِ هَذا العامَ.

Argentine player Lionel Messi received the Ballon d'Or this year.

game **مُباراةٌ**

كانَتِ المُباراةُ مَليئَةً بِالْإثارَةِ وَالتَّوَتُّرِ حَتّى الدَّقائِقِ الأَخيرَةِ.

The game was filled with excitement and tension until the last minutes.

match, game **مُباراةٌ**

في المُباراةِ القادِمَةِ، سَيُواجِهُ فَريقُ بَرْشلونَةْ فَريقَ رِيالْ مَدْريدْ.

In the next match, Barcelona team will face Real Madrid team.

all-star game **مُباراةُ كُلِّ النُّجومِ**

سَتُقامُ مُباراةُ كُلِّ النُّجومِ لِدَوْرِيِّ كُرَةِ السَّلَّةِ الأَمْريكِيِّ في مَدينَةِ لوسْ أَنْجِلوسْ.

The All-Star Game for the American Basketball League will be held in Los Angeles.

coach **مُدَرِّبٌ**

اِسْتَدْعى المُدَرِّبُ الجَديدُ لاعِبينَ شَبابَ لِتَعْزيزِ الفَريقِ.

The new coach called up young players to bolster the team.

podium **مِنَصَّةٌ**

بَعْدَ السِّباقِ، صَعِدَ الرِّياضِيّونَ الفائِزونَ عَلى المِنَصَّةِ لِتَلَقّي ميدالْياتِهِمْ.

After the race, the winning athletes climbed onto the podium to receive their medals.

season **مَوْسِمٌ** • مَواسِمُ

خِلالَ المَوْسِمِ الرِّياضِيِّ، تَتَواجَهُ الفِرَقُ في العَديدِ مِنَ المُبارَياتِ.

During the sports season, teams face off in numerous matches.

medal **ميدالْيَةٌ**

فازَتِ السَّبّاحَةُ الأُسْتُرالِيَّةُ بِالْميدالْيَةِ الذَّهَبِيَّةِ في الأَلْعابِ الأولِمْبِيَّةِ.

The Australian swimmer won the gold medal at the Olympics.

In the context of the Olympics, the Arabic terms for the levels of medals are: الذَّهَبِيَّةُ for Gold, الفِضِّيَّةُ for Silver, and البُرونْزِيَّةُ for Bronze.

semifinals **نِصْفُ نِهائِيٍّ**

فِي الدَّوْرِ نِصْفِ النِّهائِيِّ مِنَ البُطولَةِ، تَأَهَّلَ الفَريقُ البَرازيلِيُّ لِلنِّهائِيّاتِ.

In the semifinals of the tournament, the Brazilian team qualified for the finals.

to organize تَنْظيمٌ • **نَظَّمَ**

نَظَّمَ الِاتِّحادُ الدَّوْلِيُّ لِكُرَةِ القَدَمِ بُطولَةَ كَأْسِ العالَمِ في قَطَرَ.

The International Football Federation organized the World Cup tournament in Qatar.

finals *pl.* **نِهائِيّاتٌ**

تَتَواجَهُ الفِرَقُ الفائِزَةُ فِي النِّهائِيّاتِ لِتَحْديدِ بَطَلِ الدَّوْرِيِّ هَذا العامَ.

The winning teams are facing off in the finals to determine this year's league champion.

6.4.1.1 Mini-Articles

Track **83**

اِنْتَهَتِ الأَلْعابُ الأولِمْبِيَّةُ الصَّيْفِيَّةُ بِحَفْلِ خِتامٍ مُذْهِلٍ فِي المَدينَةِ المُضيفَةِ طوكْيو. كانَ حَفْلُ الخِتامِ مَليئًا بِالأَلْوانِ وَالأَضْواءِ، وَعُرِضَتْ فيهِ العَديدُ مِنَ العُروضِ الرّاقِصَةِ وَالموسيقِيَّةِ. تَمَّ تَوْزيعُ الميدالْياتِ وَإِطْفاءُ الشُّعْلَةِ الأولِمْبِيَّةِ، لِتَنْتَهِيَ هَذِهِ الأَلْعابُ بِطَريقَةٍ مُذْهِلَةٍ.

The Summer Olympics concluded with a spectacular closing ceremony in the host city, Tokyo. The closing ceremony was filled with colors and lights, featuring numerous dance and musical performances. The final medals were awarded, and the Olympic flame was extinguished, bringing these games to an amazing end.

تَسْتَعِدُّ العاصِمَةُ القَطَرِيَّةُ الدَّوْحَةُ لِاسْتِضافَةِ بُطولَةِ العالَمِ لِكَأْسِ العَرَبِ الشَّهْرَ القادِمَ. مِنَ المُتَوَقَّعِ أَنْ تُشارِكَ فِي البُطولَةِ فِرَقٌ مِنْ جَميعِ أَنْحاءِ العالَمِ العَرَبِيِّ. سَيَجْري افْتِتاحُ البُطولَةِ بِحَفْلِ افْتِتاحٍ كَبيرٍ يَتَضَمَّنُ عُروضًا موسيقِيَّةً وَراقِصَةً مِنَ الثَّقافَةِ العَرَبِيَّةِ. يَتَطَلَّعُ الجَميعُ بِشِدَّةٍ إِلى هَذا الحَدَثِ الرِّياضِيِّ الكَبيرِ.

The Qatari capital, Doha, is preparing to host the Arab Cup World Championship next month. Teams from all around the Arab world are expected to participate in the tournament. The championship will open with a grand opening ceremony showcasing music and dance from Arab culture. Everyone is eagerly looking forward to this major sporting event.

يَعودُ الحَماسُ وَالإثارَةُ مَعَ انْطِلاقَةِ مَوْسِمٍ جَديدٍ مِنَ مِنَ الدَّوْرِيِّ السُّعودِيِّ لِلْمُحْتَرِفينَ. تَتَطَلَّعُ الفِرَقُ المُشارِكَةُ في الدَّوْرِيِّ هَذا العامَ إلى تَقْديمِ أداءٍ مُمَيَّزٍ يَسُرُّ جَماهيرَهُمْ. المَوْسِمُ القادِمُ يَعِدُ بِمُنافَساتٍ شَرِسَةٍ وَمُبارَياتٍ مُثيرَةٍ.

Excitement and thrill return with the start of a new season of the Saudi Professional League. Participating teams in the league this year are eager to deliver outstanding performances to please their fans. The upcoming season promises intense competition and thrilling matches.

بَعْدَ عَقْدَيْنِ مِنَ الزَّمَنِ، تَعودُ بُطولَةُ العالَمِ لِلْمُلاكَمَةِ إلى القاهِرَةِ. تَعْتَزِمُ القاهِرَةُ اسْتِضافَةَ البُطولَةِ في المَدينَةِ الرِّياضِيَّةِ الأولِمْبِيَّةِ، حَيْثُ سَيَتَنافَسُ المُلاكِمونَ مِنْ جَميعِ أَنْحاءِ العالَمِ عَلى اللَّقَبِ.

After two decades, the World Boxing Championship returns to Cairo. Cairo is set to host the championship at the Olympic Sports City, where boxers from all over the world will compete for the title.

يَعودُ الحَماسُ وَالمُنافَسَةُ الشَّرِسَةُ الشَّهْرَ المُقْبِلَ مَعَ انْطِلاقِ بُطولَةِ الدَّوْرِيِّ العِراقِيِّ المُمْتازِ لِكُرَةِ القَدَمِ. يَتَطَلَّعُ الجُمْهورُ العِراقِيُّ العَريضُ إلى مُتابَعَةِ المُبارَياتِ حامِيَةِ الوَطيسِ وَالتَّشْجيعِ الحَماسِيِّ لِفِرَقِهِمِ المُفَضَّلَةِ.

Next month, enthusiasm and fierce competition return with the start of the Iraqi Premier League in football. The vast Iraqi audience is looking forward to following intense matches and passionately supporting their favorite teams.

مَعَ نِهايَةِ الألْعابِ الأولِمْبِيَّةِ الشَّتْوِيَّةِ، يَحْتَفِلُ الرِّياضِيّونَ مِنْ جَميعِ أَنْحاءِ العالَمِ بِإِنْجازاتِهِمْ. واحِدَةٌ مِنْ أَبْرَزِ الانْتِصاراتِ كانَتْ لِلْفَريقِ اللُّبْنانِيِّ الَّذي حَقَّقَ نَجاحًا غَيْرَ مَسْبوقٍ في تاريخِهِ الأولِمْبِيِّ.

With the end of the Winter Olympics, athletes from all over the world celebrate their achievements. One of the most notable victories was achieved by the Lebanese team, who achieved unprecedented success in their Olympic history.

6.4.2 Sports Business and Economy

Track **84**

economic impact — **أَثَرٌ اقْتِصادِيٌّ**

أَدَّتِ اسْتِضافَةُ الألْعابِ الأولِمْبِيَّةِ إلى أَثَرٍ اقْتِصادِيٍّ كَبيرٍ عَلى البِلادِ مِنْ خِلالِ تَعْزيزِ السِّياحَةِ وَالتِّجارَةِ.

Hosting the Olympic Games had a significant economic impact on the country by boosting tourism and trade.

branding — **إِدْراجُ عَلامَةٍ تِجارِيَّةٍ**

عَمِلَتِ الشَّرِكَةُ عَلى إِدْراجِ عَلامَةٍ تِجارِيَّةٍ جَديدَةٍ لِلْفَريقِ لِزِيادَةِ شَعْبِيَّتِهِ وَجاذِبِيَّتِه.

The company worked on branding a new logo for the team to increase its popularity and appeal.

إيرادٌ
revenue

يُعْتَبَرُ بَيْعُ التَّذاكِرِ، وَالتِّلْفازُ، وَالإِعْلاناتُ، مَصادِرَ الإِيرادِ الرَّئيسِيَّةَ لِلْأَنْدِيَةِ الرِّياضِيَّةِ.

Ticket sales, television, and advertising are the main sources of revenue for sports clubs.

اِسْتادٌ
stadium, arena

سَيَتِمُّ بِناءُ اسْتادٍ جَديدٍ بِتَمْويلٍ مِنَ الاِسْتِثْمارِ الخاصِّ لِاسْتِضافَةِ بُطولاتٍ كُبْرى.

A new stadium will be built with private investment funding to host major tournaments.

اِسْتِثْمارٌ
investment

جَذَبَتِ الفُرَصُ الرِّياضِيَّةُ النّاشِئَةُ اسْتِثْماراتٍ كَبيرَةً مِنَ الشَّرِكاتِ العالَمِيَّةِ.

Emerging sports opportunities have attracted significant investment from global corporations.

اِسْتِغْلالُ العَلامَةِ التِّجارِيَّةِ
merchandising

كَجُزْءٍ مِنَ اسْتِغْلالِ العَلامَةِ التِّجارِيَّةِ، أَصْدَرَ النّادي مَجْموعَةً مِنَ المُنْتَجاتِ الرِّياضِيَّةِ بِالشِّعارِ الجَديدِ.

As part of merchandising, the club released a range of sports products with the new logo.

اِقْتِصادِيّاتُ الرِّياضَةِ
sports economics *pl.*

تُعْتَبَرُ اقْتِصادِيّاتُ الرِّياضَةِ مَجالًا هامًّا مِنْ حَيْثُ تَحْليلِ الأَثَرِ المالِيِّ لِلرِّياضَةِ عَلى الاِقْتِصادِ العامِّ.

Sports economics is an important field in terms of analyzing the financial impact of sports on the overall economy.

الإِعْلانُ
advertising

تُواصِلُ الشَّرِكاتُ اسْتِغْلالَ الإِعْلانِ في الأَحْداثِ الرِّياضِيَّةِ لِزِيادَةِ الوَعْيِ بِمُنْتَجاتِها وَخِدْماتِها.

Companies continue to leverage advertising in sporting events to increase awareness of their products and services.

الحَدُّ الأَقْصى لِلْأُجورِ
salary cap

فَرْضُ الحَدِّ الأَقْصى لِلْأُجورِ في الدَّوْرِيّاتِ الرِّياضِيَّةِ يُساهِمُ في الحِفاظِ عَلى المُنافَسَةِ وَالتَّوازُنِ بَيْنَ الأَنْدِيَةِ.

The imposition of a salary cap in sports leagues contributes to maintaining competition and balance among clubs.

pay-per-view **الدَّفْعُ مُقابِلَ المُشاهَدَةِ**

أَصْبَحَتْ خِدْمَةُ الدَّفْعِ مُقابِلَ المُشاهَدَةِ شائِعَةً في البَثِّ الرِّياضِيِّ، مِمّا يُتيحُ لِلْمُعْجَبينَ مُشاهَدَةَ المُبارَياتِ المُفَضَّلَةِ لَهُمْ.

Pay-per-view service has become common in sports broadcasting, allowing fans to watch their favorite matches.

concession **تَوْكيلٌ**

تَمَّ تَجْديدُ تَوْكيلِ بَيْعِ الأَطْعِمَةِ وَالمَشْروباتِ في الإِسْتادِ لِلْمَوْسِمِ القادِمِ.

The concession for selling food and drinks in the stadium has been renewed for the coming season.

franchise **اِمْتيازٌ**

تَمَّ اقْتِناءُ امْتيازِ فَريقِ كُرَةِ القَدَمِ الشَّهيرِ مِنْ قِبَلِ رَجُلِ أَعْمالٍ ثَرِيٍّ.

A famous soccer team franchise was acquired by a wealthy businessman.

broadcasting **بَثٌّ**

أَصْبَحَ بَثُّ المُبارَياتِ الرِّياضِيَّةِ جُزْءًا حاسِمًا مِنَ الاِقْتِصادِ الرِّياضِيِّ.

Broadcasting sports matches has become a crucial part of the sports economy.

live streaming **بَثٌّ حَيٌّ**

اِكْتَسَبَ البَثُّ الحَيُّ لِلْمُبارَياتِ الرِّياضِيَّةِ شَعْبِيَّةً كَبيرَةً بَيْنَ المُشَجِّعينَ حَوْلَ العالَمِ.

Live streaming of sports matches has gained significant popularity among fans around the world.

infrastructure • بِنَى / بُنَى **بِنْيَةٌ تَحْتِيَّةٌ**

يُعَدُّ بِناءُ بِنْيَةٍ تَحْتِيَّةٍ رِياضِيَّةٍ جَيِّدَةٍ أَساسِيًّا لِنَجاحِ الأَحْداثِ الرِّياضِيَّةِ الكُبْرى.

Building good sports infrastructure is essential for the success of major sports events.

licensing — تَرْخيصٌ

يَعْتَمِدُ الفَريقُ عَلى تَرْخيصِ العَلامَةِ التِّجارِيَّةِ لِزِيادَةِ الإيراداتِ.

The team relies on licensing the brand to increase revenue.

sports marketing — تَسْويقُ الرِّياضَةِ

يَلْعَبُ تَسْويقُ الرِّياضَةِ دَوْرًا كَبيرًا في تَحْقيقِ نَجاحِ الأَحْداثِ وَالفِرَقِ الرِّياضِيَّةِ.

Sports marketing plays a big role in achieving success for sports events and teams.

media rights *pl.* — حُقوقُ بَثٍّ

أَصْبَحَتْ حُقوقُ البَثِّ مَصْدَرًا هامًّا لِلْإيراداتِ في قِطاعِ الرِّياضَةِ.

Media rights have become a significant source of revenue in the sports industry.

loss • خَسائِرُ — خَسارَةٌ

تَعَرَّضَتِ الشَّرِكَةُ الرِّياضِيَّةُ لِخَسارَةٍ مالِيَّةٍ كَبيرَةٍ بِسَبَبِ الإِغْلاقاتِ الَّتي تَسَبَّبَتْ فيها الجائِحَةُ.

The sports company suffered a significant financial loss due to the closures caused by the pandemic.

endorsement — دِعايَةٌ

وَقَّعَ الرِّياضِيُّ الشَّهيرُ صَفْقَةَ دِعايَةٍ مُرْبِحَةً مَعْ إِحْدى العَلاماتِ التِّجارِيَّةِ الرّائِدَةِ لِلْمَلابِسِ الرِّياضِيَّةِ.

The famous athlete signed a lucrative endorsement deal with a leading sportswear brand.

salary • رَواتِبُ — راتِبٌ

تَمَّ تَحْديدُ راتِبِ اللّاعِبِ الجَديدِ بَعْدَ مُفاوَضاتٍ طَويلَةٍ.

The new player's salary was set after long negotiations.

profit • أَرْباحٌ — رِبْحٌ

بِفَضْلِ اسْتِراتيجِيَّةٍ تَسْويقِيَّةٍ فَعّالَةٍ، حَقَّقَتِ الشَّرِكَةُ الرِّياضِيَّةُ رِبْحًا هائِلًا هَذا العامَ.

Thanks to an effective marketing strategy, the sports company made a huge profit this year.

transfer fee — رَسْمُ انْتِقالٍ • رُسومٌ

تَمَّ دَفْعُ رُسومِ انْتِقالٍ ضَخْمَةٍ لِنَقْلِ اللّاعِبِ إلى الفَريقِ الجَديدِ.

A huge transfer fee was paid to move the player to the new team.

sponsorship — رِعايَةٌ

اِكْتَسَبَ الفَريقُ رِعايَةً مِنْ شَرِكَةِ تِكْنولوجْيا كُبْرى لِلْمَوْسِمِ القادِمِ.

The team secured sponsorship from a major technology company for the coming season.

professional athlete — رِياضِيٌّ مُحْتَرِفٌ

حَقَّقَ الرِّياضِيُّ المُحْتَرِفُ عَقْدًا ضَخْمًا مَعَ فَريقٍ كَبيرٍ.

The professional athlete secured a massive contract with a big team.

stadium, arena — ساحَةٌ

تَمَّ افْتِتاحُ ساحَةٍ رِياضِيَّةٍ جَديدَةٍ ضَخْمَةٍ في العاصِمَةِ، تَسْتَوْعِبُ الآلافَ مِنَ المُشَجِّعينَ.

A new massive sports arena has been opened in the capital that accommodates thousands of fans.

share — سَهْمٌ • أَسْهُمٌ

اِشْتَرى المُسْتَثْمِرُ الكَبيرُ سَهْمًا كَبيرًا في النّادي الرِّياضِيِّ.

The major investor bought a large share in the sports club.

contract — عَقْدٌ • عُقودٌ

تَمَّ تَوْقيعُ عَقْدٍ جَديدٍ بَيْنَ اللّاعِبِ وَالنّادي لِمُدَّةِ ثَلاثَةِ أَعْوامٍ.

A new contract was signed between the player and the club for three years.

market value — قيمَةٌ سوقِيَّةٌ • قِيَمٌ

قُدِّرَتِ القيمَةُ السّوقِيَّةُ لِلّاعِبِ بِمَلايينِ الدّولاراتِ بِفَضْلِ أَدائِهِ المُمْتازِ.

The player was estimated to have a market value of millions of dollars thanks to his excellent performance.

ticket sales *pl.* **مَبيعاتُ تَذاكِرَ**

تُعْتَبَرُ مَبيعاتُ التَّذاكِرِ مَصْدَرًا هامًّا لِلْإيراداتِ لِلْعَديدِ مِنَ الأَنْدِيَةِ الرِّياضِيَّةِ.

Ticket sales are an important source of revenue for many sports clubs.

bonus **مُكافَأَةٌ**

بِناءً عَلى أَدائِهِ الرّائِعِ، تَمَّ مَنْحُ اللّاعِبِ مُكافَأَةً كَبيرَةً.

Based on his great performance, the player was granted a large bonus.

agent • وُكَلاءُ **وَكيلٌ**

تَوَلّى الوَكيلُ مُهِمَّةَ التَّفاوُضِ عَلى العُقودِ وَالرِّعايَةِ بِالنِّيابَةِ عَنِ الرِّياضِيِّ المُحْتَرِفِ.

The agent undertook the task of negotiating contracts and sponsorships on behalf of the professional athlete.

6.4.2.1 Mini-Articles

Track **85**

تَجْذِبُ الأَحْداثُ الرِّياضِيَّةُ الكُبْرى، كَكَأْسِ العالَمِ وَالأَلْعابِ الأولِمْبِيَّةِ، الِاهْتِمامَ العالَمِيَّ وَتَتْرُكُ أَثَرًا اقْتِصادِيًّا كَبيرًا عَلى البَلَدِ المُضيفِ. مِنْ خِلالِ تَحْسينِ البِنْيَةِ التَّحْتِيَّةِ، كَالْاِسْتاداتِ وَالمواصَلاتِ، وَزِيادَةِ السِّياحَةِ، يُمْكِنُ أَنْ تُحَقِّقَ هَذِهِ الأَحْداثُ عائِداتٍ كَبيرَةً وَتُحَفِّزَ النُّمُوَّ الاقْتِصادِيَّ لِلْبَلَدِ المُضيفِ.

Major sporting events, such as the World Cup and the Olympics, attract global attention and have a significant economic impact on the host country. By improving infrastructure, such as stadiums and transportation, and increasing tourism, these events can generate substantial revenue and drive economic growth for the host country.

حُقوقُ البَثِّ هِيَ مُكَوِّنٌ أَساسِيٌّ مِنَ الإيراداتِ الرِّياضِيَّةِ. حَيْثُ يَجْذِبُ البَثُّ الحَيُّ لِلْمُبارَياتِ وَالدَّفْعُ مُقابِلَ المُشاهَدَةِ جُمْهورًا واسِعًا وَيُقَدِّمانِ مَصْدَرًا هامًّا لِلْعائِداتِ. بِالْإِضافَةِ إِلى ذَلِكَ، فَإِنَّ التَّرْخيصَ لِلْبَثِّ يُساهِمُ أَيْضًا في تَعْزيزِ العَلامَةِ التِّجارِيَّةِ لِلْفِرَقِ وَالِاتِّحاداتِ الرِّياضِيَّةِ.

Broadcasting rights are a fundamental component of sports revenues. Live broadcasting of matches and pay-per-view attract a wide audience and provide a crucial source of revenue. Additionally, broadcasting licensing also contributes to enhancing the brand of sports teams and associations.

تُعْتَبَرُ الرِّعايَةُ الرِّياضِيَّةُ واحِدَةً مِنَ الاِسْتِثْماراتِ الأَكْثَرِ فَعالِيَّةً لِلشَّرِكاتِ الَّتي تَسْعى لِتَوْسيعِ تَواجُدِها العالَمِيِّ وَزِيادَةِ قاعِدَةِ عُمَلائِها. يُتيحُ الإِعْلانُ خِلالَ المُبارَياتِ الرِّياضِيَّةِ وَاسْتِغْلالُ العَلامَةِ التِّجارِيَّةِ لِلْفِرَقِ الرِّياضِيَّةِ الشَّهيرَةِ لِلشَّرِكاتِ فُرْصَةً لِتَعْزيزِ ظُهورِها وَالوُصولِ إِلى جُمْهورٍ عالَمِيٍّ أَكْبَرَ.

Sports sponsorship is considered one of the most effective investments for companies seeking to expand their global presence and increase their customer base. Advertising during sports matches and leveraging the brand of popular sports teams allows companies the opportunity to enhance their exposure and reach a larger global audience.

القيمَةُ السّوقِيَّةُ لِلْفِرَقِ الرِّياضِيَّةِ وَالرِّياضِيّينَ المُحْتَرِفينَ لا تَعْتَمِدُ فَقَطْ عَلى أَدائِهِم الرِّياضِيِّ، وَلَكِنْ أَيْضًا عَلى جاذِبِيَّتِهِم التِّجارِيَّةِ. يُمْكِنُ لِلّاعِبينَ المُحْتَرِفينَ تَحْقيقُ أَرْباحٍ كَبيرَةٍ مِنَ الرِّعايَةِ وَالتَّأْييدِ، بَيْنَما يُمْكِنُ لِلْفِرَقِ الرِّياضِيَّةِ زِيادَةُ إيراداتِها مِنْ خِلالِ مَبيعاتِ التَّذاكِرِ وَالتَّراخيصِ وَالاِسْتِثْماراتِ.

The market value of sports teams and professional athletes depends not only on their athletic performance but also on their commercial attractiveness. Professional athletes can generate significant profits from sponsorships and endorsements, while sports teams can increase their revenues through ticket sales, licensing, and investments.

في العَديدِ مِنَ الرِّياضاتِ الاِحْتِرافِيَّةِ، يوجَدُ سَقْفٌ لِلْأُجورِ لِلْحِفاظِ عَلى المُنافَسَةِ وَالعَدالَةِ. هَذا الحَدُّ الأَقْصى لِلْأُجورِ يُقَيِّدُ القُدْرَةَ عَلى دَفْعِ رَواتِبِ اللّاعِبينَ. وَمَعَ ذَلِكَ، يَجِبُ أَيْضًا أَنْ يَأْخُذَ اللّاعِبونَ في الاِعْتِبارِ مُكافَآتِ الأَداءِ وَالرِّعاياتِ التِّجارِيَّةِ عِنْدَ التَّفاوُضِ عَلى العُقودِ.

In many professional sports, there is a salary cap to maintain competitiveness and fairness. This salary ceiling restricts the ability to pay players' salaries. However, players should also consider performance bonuses and commercial endorsements when negotiating contracts.

لِلْوُكَلاءِ الرِّياضِيّينَ دَوْرٌ حَيَوِيٌّ في صِناعَةِ الرِّياضَةِ الاِحْتِرافِيَّةِ. إِنَّهُمْ يَعْمَلونَ عَلى تَمْثيلِ مَصالِحِ الرِّياضِيّينَ، سَواءٌ في التَّفاوُضِ عَلى العُقودِ أَوْ في إيجادِ فُرَصٍ لِلرِّعايَةِ وَالتَّأْييدِ. بِفَضْلِ خِبْرَتِهِمْ في القانونِ وَالأَعْمالِ التِّجارِيَّةِ، يُمْكِنُ لِلْوُكَلاءِ الرِّياضِيّينَ المُساعَدَةُ في التَّأَكُّدِ مِنْ أَنَّ الرِّياضِيّينَ يَتَلَقَّوْنَ القيمَةَ الحَقيقِيَّةَ لِمَهاراتِهِمْ وَأَدائِهِمْ.

Sports agents play a vital role in the professional sports industry. They represent the interests of athletes, whether in contract negotiations or in finding sponsorship and endorsement opportunities. With their expertise in law and business, sports agents can help ensure that athletes receive the true value for their skills and performance.

6.4.3 Sports Organizations and Governance

Track **86**

agenda أَجِنْدَةٌ

تَمَّ تَحْديدُ أَجِنْدَةِ الِاجْتِماعِ القادِمِ لِلاتِّحادِ الرِّياضِيِّ.

The agenda for the next meeting of the sports federation has been set.

ethics *pl.* أَخْلاقِيّاتٌ

تُعْتَبَرُ الأَخْلاقِيّاتُ في الرِّياضَةِ مَسْأَلَةً هامَّةً لِلْغايَةِ تُؤَثِّرُ عَلى سُلوكِ اللّاعِبينَ.

Ethics in sports is a very important matter that influences the behavior of the players.

general secretary أَمينٌ عامٌّ • أُمَناءُ

أَعْلَنَ الأَمينُ العامُّ لِلاتِّحادِ الأوروبِّيِّ لِكُرَةِ القَدَمِ عَنْ جَدْوَلٍ جَديدٍ لِلْمُبارَياتِ.

The General Secretary of the Union of European Football Associations announced a new schedule for the matches.

disqualification إِقْصاءٌ

أَدّى الإِخْفاقُ في اخْتِبارِ المُنَشِّطاتِ إلى إِقْصاءِ الرِّياضِيِّ مِنَ البُطولَةِ.

The athlete's failure in the doping test led to his disqualification from the championship.

United Arab Emirates Football Association (UAEFA) اِتِّحادُ الإماراتِ العَرَبِيَّةِ المُتَّحِدَةِ لِكُرَةِ القَدَمِ

بَعْدَ تَأْسيسِ اتِّحادِ الإماراتِ العَرَبِيَّةِ المُتَّحِدَةِ لِكُرَةِ القَدَمِ، أَصْبَحَتِ الإماراتُ مَكانًا مَرْكَزِيًّا لِكُرَةِ القَدَمِ في الخَليجِ.

After the establishment of the United Arab Emirates Football Association, the UAE has become a central place for soccer in the Gulf.

Union of Arab National Olympic Committees (UANOC) اِتِّحادُ اللِّجانِ الأولِمْبِيَّةِ الوَطَنِيَّةِ العَرَبِيَّةِ

سَعى اتِّحادُ اللِّجانِ الأولِمْبِيَّةِ الوَطَنِيَّةِ العَرَبِيَّةِ لِتَعْزيزِ التَّعاوُنِ الرِّياضِيِّ بَيْنَ الدُّوَلِ العَرَبِيَّةِ.

The Union of Arab National Olympic Committees sought to enhance sports cooperation among Arab countries.

اِتِّحادٌ رِياضِيٌّ
sports association, federation

يَهْدُفُ الاِتِّحادُ الرِّياضِيُّ الجَديدُ إِلى تَحْسينِ الرِّياضَةِ في المِنْطَقَةِ.

The new sports federation aims to improve sports in the region.

اِتِّحادُ غَرْبِ آسْيا لِكُرَةِ القَدَمِ
West Asian Football Federation (WAFF)

حَقَّقَتْ دُوَلُ اِتِّحادُ غَرْبِ آسْيا لِكُرَةِ القَدَمِ تَقَدُّمًا مَلْحوظًا في تَصْنيفِ الفيفا.

The countries of the West Asian Football Federation made notable progress in the FIFA ranking.

اِجْتِماعٌ عامٌّ سَنَوِيٌّ
annual general meeting

كانَ الاِجْتِماعُ العامُّ السَّنَوِيُّ لِلاتِّحادِ الرِّياضِيِّ فُرْصَةً لِمُناقَشَةِ الإِنْجازاتِ وَالتَّحَدِّياتِ.

The annual general meeting of the sports federation was an opportunity to discuss achievements and challenges.

اِخْتِبارُ مُنَشِّطاتٍ
doping test

تُجْرى اخْتِباراتُ المُنَشِّطاتِ بِانْتِظامٍ لِضَمانِ نَزاهَةِ الرِّياضَةِ.

Doping tests are conducted regularly to ensure the integrity of sports.

اِسْتِئْنافٌ
appeal

قَدَّمَ الرِّياضِيُّ اسْتِئْنافًا ضِدَّ قَرارِ الإِقْصاءِ مِنَ البُطولَةِ.

The athlete submitted an appeal against the disqualification decision from the championship.

Another common term for ‘appeal’ in martial arts is اِلْتِماسٌ.

الاِتِّحادُ الأوروبِّيُّ لِكُرَةِ القَدَمِ
Union of European Football Associations (UEFA)

الاِتِّحادُ الأوروبِّيُّ لِكُرَةِ القَدَمِ يَسْعى لِلْحِفاظِ عَلى النَّزاهَةِ وَالعَدالَةِ في كُرَةِ القَدَمِ الأوروبِّيَّةِ.

The Union of European Football Associations strives to maintain integrity and fairness in European soccer.

الاِتِّحادُ الجَزائِرِيُّ لِكُرَةِ القَدَمِ
Algerian Football Federation (AFF)

أَصْدَرَ الاِتِّحادُ الجَزائِرِيُّ لِكُرَةِ القَدَمِ قَرارًا بِتَأْجيلِ جَميعِ المُبارَياتِ بِسَبَبِ الظُّروفِ الجَوِّيَّةِ.

The Algerian Football Federation has issued a decision to postpone all matches due to weather conditions.

الاِتِّحادُ الدَّوْلِيُّ لِكُرَةِ القَدَمِ
Fédération Internationale de Football Association (FIFA)

أَعْلَنَ الاِتِّحادُ الدَّوْلِيُّ لِكُرَةِ القَدَمِ عَنِ اسْتِضافَةِ كَنَدا وَالمِكسيك وَالوِلاياتِ المُتَّحِدَةِ لِكَأْسِ العالَمِ 2026.

The Fédération Internationale de Football Association announced that Canada, Mexico, and the United States will host the 2026 World Cup.

الاِتِّحادُ السُّعودِيُّ لِكُرَةِ القَدَمِ
Saudi Arabian Football Federation (SAFF)

بَدَأَ الاِتِّحادُ السُّعودِيُّ لِكُرَةِ القَدَمِ تَنْفيذَ بَرْنامَجٍ تَدْريبِيٍّ جَديدٍ لِتَطْويرِ مَهاراتِ اللّاعِبينَ الشَّبابِ.

The Saudi Arabian Football Federation began implementing a new training program to develop the skills of young players.

الاِتِّحادُ العَرَبِيُّ لِكُرَةِ القَدَمِ
Arab Football Federation

تَعاوَنَ الاِتِّحادُ العَرَبِيُّ لِكُرَةِ القَدَمِ مَعَ الاِتِّحادِ الأوروبِّيِّ لِتَحْسينِ مُسْتَوى الكُرَةِ العَرَبِيَّةِ.

The Arab Football Federation collaborated with the European Union to improve the level of Arab football.

الاِتِّحادُ المِصْرِيُّ لِكُرَةِ القَدَمِ
Egyptian Football Association (EFA)

صَرَّحَ الاِتِّحادُ المِصْرِيُّ لِكُرَةِ القَدَمِ بِأَنَّهُ سَيَتِمُّ تَحْسينُ البِنْيَةِ التَّحْتِيَّةِ لِلْمَلاعِبِ.

The Egyptian Football Association announced that the infrastructure of the stadiums will be improved.

التَّحْكيمُ الرِّياضِيُّ
sports governance

يَتَطَلَّبُ التَّحْكيمُ الرِّياضِيُّ قَراراتٍ عادِلَةً وَنَزيهَةً لِلْحِفاظِ عَلى سُمْعَةِ الرِّياضَةِ.

Sports governance requires fair and honest decisions to maintain the reputation of the sport.

اللَّجْنَةُ الأولِمْبِيَّةُ الدَّوْلِيَّةُ • لِجانٌ **International Olympic Committee (IOC)**

صادَقَتِ اللَّجْنَةُ الأولِمْبِيَّةُ الدَّوْلِيَّةُ على تَضْمينِ رِياضَةٍ جَديدَةٍ في الألْعابِ الأولِمْبِيَّةِ القادِمَةِ.

The International Olympic Committee ratified the inclusion of a new sport in the upcoming Olympic Games.

الوِكالَةُ العالَمِيَّةُ لِمُكافَحَةِ المُنَشِّطاتِ **World Anti-Doping Agency (WADA)**

أَجْرَتِ الوِكالَةُ العالَمِيَّةُ لِمُكافَحَةِ المُنَشِّطاتِ فَحْصًا مُفاجِئًا لِفَريقِ الرَّكْضِ.

The World Anti-Doping Agency conducted a surprise test on the running team.

اِنْتِخاباتٌ *pl.* **election**

أَسْفَرَتِ انْتِخاباتُ الاِتِّحادِ الرِّياضِيِّ عَنْ فَوْزِ رَئيسٍ جَديدٍ.

The sports federation elections resulted in a new chairman.

Note that the masdar (verbal noun) اِنْتِخابٌ in singular form often refers to the act of electing (someone), whereas the plural اِنْتِخاباتٌ refers to the entire process.

تَحْكيمٌ **arbitration**

اِسْتَعانَتِ اللَّجْنَةُ المُنَظِّمَةُ لِلْبُطولَةِ بِجِهاتٍ خارِجِيَّةٍ لِلتَّحْكيمِ بِسَبَبِ التَّعْقيداتِ المُحْتَمَلَةِ.

The tournament organizing committee enlisted external parties for arbitration due to potential complexities.

تَعْليقٌ **suspension**

أَعْلَنَ الاِتِّحادُ الدَّوْلِيُّ لِكُرَةِ القَدَمِ تَعْليقَ أَحَدِ اللّاعِبينَ بِسَبَبِ تَلاعُبٍ في المُبارَياتِ.

The International Football Federation announced the suspension of a player due to match-fixing.

تَلاعُبٌ في المُبارَياتِ **match-fixing**

يَتَتَبَّعُ المُحَقِّقونَ ادِّعاءاتِ التَّلاعُبِ في المُبارَياتِ الَّتي تَوَرَّطَتْ فيها العَديدُ مِنَ الفِرَقِ الرَّئيسِيَّةِ.

Investigators are tracking match-fixing allegations involving several major teams.

حَظَرَ • حَظْرٌ **to ban**

حظَرَتِ اللَّجْنَةُ الأولِمْبِيَّةُ الدَّوْلِيَّةُ الرِّياضِيَّ الَّذي أَثْبَتَتِ الِاخْتِباراتُ اسْتِخْدامَهُ لِلْمُنَشِّطاتِ.

The International Olympic Committee banned the athlete who was proven to use doping.

حَكَمٌ • حُكّامٌ **referee, umpire**

اِسْتَعانَتِ اللَّجْنَةُ التَّحْكيمِيَّةُ بِحَكَمٍ ذي خِبْرَةٍ لِلْمُباراةِ النِّهائِيَّةِ.

The arbitration committee enlisted an experienced referee for the final match.

رَئيسٌ • رُؤَساءُ **chairman**

عَيَّنَ النّادي رَئيسًا جَديدًا لِلْمَجْلِسِ التَّنْفيذِيِّ.

The club appointed a new chairman for the executive board.

روحٌ رِياضِيَّةٌ **sportsmanship**

أَظْهَرَ اللّاعِبونَ روحًا رِياضِيَّةً عالِيَةً رَغْمَ التَّوَتُّرِ الشَّديدِ في المُباراةِ.

The players showed high sportsmanship despite the intense tension in the match.

سِياسَةٌ مُناهِضَةٌ لِلْمُنَشِّطاتِ **anti-doping policy**

إِنَّ الِاتِّحادَ صارِمٌ في تَطْبيقِ السِّياسَةِ المُناهِضَةِ لِلْمُنَشِّطاتِ لِلْحِفاظِ عَلى النَّزاهَةِ الرِّياضِيَّةِ.

The federation is strict in applying the anti-doping policy to maintain sports integrity.

شَفافِيَّةٌ **transparency**

شَدَّدَ الِاتِّحادُ عَلى شَفافِيَّةِ القَراراتِ لِلْحِفاظِ عَلى ثِقَةِ الأَعْضاءِ.

The federation emphasized the transparency of decisions to maintain the members' trust.

صَلاحِيَّةٌ **eligibility**

تَأَكَّدَتْ صَلاحِيَّةُ اللّاعِبِ لِلْمُشارَكَةِ في بُطولَةِ العالَمِ بَعْدَ اجْتِيازِهِ لِلْفَحْصِ الطِّبِّيِّ.

The player's eligibility to participate in the world championship was confirmed after he passed the medical examination.

to vote • تَصْويتٌ **صَوَّتَ**

اِجْتَمَعَتِ الجَمْعِيَّةُ العُمومِيَّةُ لِلنّادي لِلتَّصْويتِ عَلى التَّعْديلاتِ الجَديدَةِ في القَواعِدِ.

The club's general assembly gathered to vote on the new rule amendments.

membership **عُضْوِيَّةٌ**

بِسَبَبِ سُلوكِهِ غَيْرِ الأَخْلاقِيِّ، تَمَّ إِلْغاءُ عُضْوِيَّةِ اللّاعِبِ في النّادي.

Due to his unethical behavior, the player's membership in the club was cancelled.

corruption **فَسادٌ**

أَدّى الفَسادُ المُسْتَشْري في الاِتِّحادِ الرِّياضِيِّ إِلى طَلَباتٍ مُتَزايِدَةٍ لِلْإِصْلاحِ.

Rampant corruption in the sports federation has led to increasing demands for reform.

rules and regulations *pl.* **قَواعِدُ وَلَوائِحُ**

تَمَّ تَحْديثُ قَواعِدِ وَلَوائِحِ الدَّوْرِيِّ لِلْحَدِّ مِنَ الحَوادِثِ العَنيفَةِ الَّتي تَحْدُثُ خِلالَ المُبارَياتِ.

The league's rules and regulations have been updated to curb violent incidents that occur during matches.

disciplinary committee • لِجانٌ **لَجْنَةٌ تَأْديبِيَّةٌ**

حَرَصَتِ اللَّجْنَةُ التَّأْديبِيَّةُ عَلى تَطْبيقِ القَواعِدِ وَاللَّوائِحِ الخاصَّةِ بِالاِتِّحادِ بِكُلِّ صَرامَةٍ.

The disciplinary committee was keen on strictly enforcing the federation's rules and regulations.

board of directors • مَجالِسُ **مَجْلِسُ إِدارَةٍ**

اِجْتَمَعَ مَجْلِسُ الإِدارَةِ لِمُناقَشَةِ الخُطَطِ الجَديدَةِ لِتَحْسينِ البِنْيَةِ التَّحْتِيَّةِ لِلنّادي.

The board of directors met to discuss new plans to improve the club's infrastructure.

minutes • مَحاضِرُ **مَحْضَرُ اجْتِماعٍ**

اِجْتَمَعَ مَجْلِسُ إِدارَةِ النّادي لِمُراجَعَةِ مَحْضَرِ الاِجْتِماعِ الأَخيرِ.

The club's board of directors met to review the minutes of the last meeting.

Notice that, while the English term 'minutes' is always plural, the Arabic term is singular when referring to the minutes of one meeting.

مُدَوَّنَةُ سُلوكٍ

code of conduct

طَرَحَتِ الفِرَقُ الرِّياضِيَّةُ مُدَوَّنَةَ سُلوكٍ جَديدَةً لِضَمانِ الاِحْتِرامِ المُتَبادَلِ بَيْنَ اللّاعِبينَ.

Sports teams have introduced a new code of conduct to ensure mutual respect among players.

نَزاهَةٌ

integrity

أَصْدَرَ الاِتِّحادُ مُدَوَّنَةَ سُلوكٍ جَديدَةً لِتَعْزيزِ النَّزاهَةِ وَالشَّفافِيَّةِ.

The federation issued a new code of conduct to promote integrity and transparency.

نِقابَةُ الرِّياضِيّينَ

athletes' union

تَعاقَدَتِ اللّاعِبَةُ مَعَ نِقابَةِ الرِّياضِيّينَ لِحِمايَةِ حُقوقِها.

The player contracted with the athletes' union to protect her rights.

6.4.3.1 Mini-Articles

Track **87**

أَعْلَنَ اتِّحادُ الإِماراتِ العَرَبِيَّةِ المُتَّحِدَةِ لِكُرَةِ القَدَمِ عَنْ عَقْدِ اجْتِماعِهِ العامِّ السَّنَوِيِّ في الأُسْبوعِ القادِمِ. يُتَوَقَّعُ أَنْ يَشْهَدَ الاِجْتِماعُ مُناقَشَةَ عِدَّةِ قَضايا مُثيرَةٍ لِلْجَدَلِ تَتَعَلَّقُ بِقَواعِدِ وَلَوائِحِ اللُّعْبَةِ. وَسَيَتِمُّ خِلالَ الاِجْتِماعِ التَّصْويتُ عَلى العَديدِ مِنَ التَّغْييراتِ المُحْتَمَلَةِ.

The United Arab Emirates Football Association announced the holding of its annual general meeting next week. The meeting is expected to discuss several controversial issues related to the rules and regulations of the game. Several potential changes will be voted on during the meeting.

اليَوْمَ، أَعْلَنَتِ الوَكالَةُ العالَمِيَّةُ لِمُكافَحَةِ المُنَشِّطاتِ عَنْ حَظْرٍ جَديدٍ لِعَدَدٍ مِنَ الرِّياضِيّينَ بَعْدَ ظُهورِ نَتائِجَ إيجابِيَّةٍ لاخْتِباراتِ المُنَشِّطاتِ. يَأْتي هَذا الإِعْلانُ كَجُزْءٍ مِنَ السِّياسَةِ الصّارِمَةِ المُناهِضَةِ لِلْمُنَشِّطاتِ الَّتي تُطَبِّقُها الوَكالَةُ في مُحاوَلَةٍ لِلْحِفاظِ عَلى نَزاهَةِ وَشَفافِيَّةِ الرِّياضَةِ.

Today, the World Anti-Doping Agency announced a new ban on several athletes following positive doping test results. This announcement is part of the agency's strict anti-doping policy aimed at maintaining the integrity and transparency of sports.

فِي ظِلِّ استِمْرارِ تَقْديمِ العَطاءاتِ لِلْألْعابِ الأولِمْبِيَّةِ، قالَ الرَّئيسُ الجَديدُ لِلَّجْنَةِ الأولِمْبِيَّةِ الدَّوْلِيَّةِ إِنَّ اللَّجْنَةَ تَعْمَلُ عَلى تَعْزيزِ الشَّفافِيَّةِ وَمُكافَحَةِ الفَسادِ. يَأْتي هَذا بَعْدَ العَديدِ مِنَ الادِّعاءاتِ حَوْلَ تَلاعُبٍ فِي مُبارَياتٍ وَفَسادٍ داخِلَ اللَّجْنَةِ. سَيَكونُ مِنَ المُثيرِ لِلاهْتِمامِ رُؤْيَةُ كَيْفِيَّةِ تَنْفيذِ اللَّجْنَةِ لِهَذِهِ السِّياساتِ الجَديدَةِ فِي الأَشْهُرِ القادِمَةِ.

Amid the ongoing bidding for the Olympics, the new president of the International Olympic Committee stated that the committee is working to enhance transparency and combat corruption. This comes after multiple allegations of match-fixing and corruption within the committee. It will be interesting to see how the committee implements these new policies in the coming months.

أَعْلَنَ الاتِّحادُ الأوروبِّيُّ لِكُرَةِ القَدَمِ اليَوْمَ عَنْ إِطْلاقِ اتِّحادٍ رِياضِيٍّ جَديدٍ تَحْتَ مِظَلَّتِهِ، بِهَدَفِ تَوْفيرِ مِنَصَّةٍ أَكْبَرَ لِلّاعِبينَ الشَّبابِ. يَقومُ الاتِّحادُ الجَديدُ بِضَمانِ اسْتِمْرارِ الروحِ الرِّياضِيَّةِ وَتَعْزيزِ الأَخْلاقِيّاتِ الرِّياضِيَّةِ فِي الجيلِ القادِمِ مِنَ اللّاعِبينَ.

The European Football Association announced today the launch of a new sports union under its umbrella, with the aim of providing a larger platform for young players. The new union guarantees the continuation of the sportsmanship spirit and promotes sports ethics in the next generation of players.

فِي ضَوْءِ ادِّعاءاتِ تَلاعُبٍ مُحْتَمَلٍ فِي بَعْضِ مُبارَياتِ الدَّوْرِيِّ، أَعْلَنَ الاتِّحادُ السُّعوديُّ لِكُرَةِ القَدَمِ عَنْ فَتْحِ تَحْقيقٍ. فِي الوَقْتِ الحالِيِّ، تَمَّ تَعْليقُ الفِرَقِ المُتَّهَمَةِ حَتّى اكْتِمالِ التَّحْقيقِ. إِنَّ هَذا الأَمْرَ يُهَدِّدُ نَزاهَةَ الرِّياضَةِ، وَالاتِّحادُ مُلْتَزِمٌ بِالْقَضاءِ عَلى أَيِّ تَلاعُبٍ مُحْتَمَلٍ فِي المُبارَياتِ.

In light of allegations of possible match-fixing in some league matches, the Saudi Arabian Football Federation announced the opening of an investigation. Currently, the accused teams have been suspended until the investigation is completed. This is a matter that threatens the integrity of sports, and the federation is committed to eradicating any potential match-fixing in matches.

6.4.4 Sports Training and Health

Track **88**

warm-up — **إِحْماءٌ**

قَبْلَ بِدايَةِ المُباراةِ، قامَ اللّاعِبونَ بِتَمارينِ الإِحْماءِ لِتَجَنُّبِ الإِصاباتِ.

Before the start of the match, the players performed warm-up exercises to avoid injuries.

stretching — **إِطالَةٌ**

يَجِبُ أَنْ يَقومَ الرِّياضِيّونَ بِتَمارينِ الإِطالَةِ بِانْتِظامٍ لِزِيادَةِ مُرونَتِهِمْ.

Athletes should regularly perform stretching exercises to increase their flexibility.

to follow a diet اِتِّبَاعٌ • اِتَّبَعَ نِظامًا غِذائِيًّا

بَدَأَ اللاعِبُ يَتَّبِعُ نِظامًا غِذائِيًّا صارِمًا لِلْحِفاظِ عَلى وَزْنِهِ المِثالِيِّ.

The player has started to follow a strict diet to maintain his ideal weight.

taping اِسْتِخْدامُ اللّاصِقِ الطِّبِّيِّ

يَقومُ الطَّبيبُ الرِّياضِيُّ بِاسْتِخْدامِ اللّاصِقِ الطِّبِّيِّ لِتَوْفيرِ الدَّعْمِ وَتَقْليلِ الأَلَمِ لِلّاعِبِ المُصابِ.

The sports doctor is taping the injury site to provide support and reduce pain for the injured player.

strategy اِسْتِراتيجِيَّةٌ

وَضَعَ المُدَرِّبُ اسْتِراتيجِيَّةً جَديدَةً لِتَعْزيزِ أَداءِ الفَريقِ في المُبارَياتِ المُقْبِلَةِ.

The coach has devised a new strategy to boost the team's performance in the upcoming matches.

to regain physical fitness اِسْتِعادَةٌ • اِسْتَعادَ اللِّياقَةَ البَدَنِيَّةَ

بَعْدَ الإِصابَةِ، عَمِلَ اللاعِبُ بِجِدٍّ لِاسْتِعادَةِ لِياقَتِهِ البَدَنِيَّةِ.

After the injury, the player worked hard to regain his physical fitness.

to benefit اِسْتِفادَةٌ • اِسْتَفادَ

اِسْتَفادَ الفَريقُ كَثيرًا مِنَ التَّدْريباتِ الجَديدَةِ الَّتي قَدَّمَها المُدَرِّبُ.

The team greatly benefited from the new training drills introduced by the coach.

physical readiness الاِسْتِعْدادُ البَدَنِيُّ

مَعَ تَقَدُّمِ البُطولَةِ، أَصْبَحَ الاِسْتِعْدادُ البَدَنِيُّ لِلّاعِبينَ أَمْرًا حاسِمًا.

As the tournament progressed, the players' physical readiness became crucial.

injury prevention الوِقايَةُ مِنَ الإِصاباتِ

تُرَكِّزُ الجَلَساتُ التَّدْريبِيَّةُ لِلْفَريقِ عَلى الوِقايَةِ مِنَ الإِصاباتِ لِحِمايَةِ اللّاعِبينَ.

The team's training sessions focus on injury prevention to protect the players.

training program — **بَرْنامَجٌ تَدْريبِيٌّ** • بَرامِجُ

يَتْبَعُ اللّاعِبونَ بَرْنامَجًا تَدْريبِيًّا صارِمًا لِلْحِفاظِ عَلى مُسْتَواهم العالي.

The players follow a strict training program to maintain their high level.

concussion protocol — **بُروتوكولُ الارْتِجاجِ**

بَعْدَ التَّعَرُّضِ لِلارْتِجاجِ، خَضَعَ اللّاعِبُ لِبُروتوكولِ الارْتِجاجِ الصّارِمِ لِحِمايَةِ صِحَّتِه.

After experiencing a concussion, the player underwent a strict concussion protocol to protect his health.

protein — **بُروتينٌ**

بَعْدَ تَمْريناتِهِ، يَتَناوَلُ اللّاعِبُ وَجْبَةً غَنِيَّةً بِالْبُروتينِ لِلْمُساعَدَةِ في إعادَةِ بِناءِ العَضَلاتِ.

After his workouts, the player eats a protein-rich meal to help rebuild muscles.

strong build — **بِنْيَةٌ قَوِيَّةٌ**

اللّاعِبُ عِماد الدُّوْسَري، المَعْروفُ بِبِنْيَتِهِ القَوِيَّةِ، اِسْتَطاعَ السَّيْطَرَةَ عَلى الكُرَةِ وَالتَّغَلُّبَ عَلى دِفاعِ الخَصْمِ.

Player Imad Al-Dosari, known for his strong build, managed to control the ball and overcome the opponent's defense.

strength and conditioning — **تَأْهيلٌ**

عَمِلَ اللّاعِبُ مَعَ مُدَرِّبِ التَّأْهيلِ لِتَعْزيزِ قوَّتِهِ وَحالَتِهِ البَدَنِيَّةِ.

The player worked with the strength and conditioning coach to enhance his strength and physical condition.

rehabilitation — **تَأْهيلٌ**

بَعْدَ إصابَتِهِ الخَطيرَةِ، بَدَأَ اللّاعِبُ في عَمَلِيَّةِ التَّأْهيلِ لِاسْتِعادَةِ قُوَّتِهِ.

After his severe injury, the player began the rehabilitation process to regain his strength.

cool-down — **تَبْريدٌ**

يَقومُ اللّاعِبونَ بِجَلْسَةِ تَبْريدٍ بَعْدَ التَّدْريبِ لِتَجَنُّبِ تَيَبُّسِ العَضَلاتِ.

The players do a cool-down session after training to avoid muscle stiffness.

to train • تَدَرُّبٌ **تَدَرَّبَ**

يَتَدَرَّبُ اللّاعِبونَ كُلَّ يَوْمٍ لِلْحِفاظِ عَلى لِياقَتِهِم البَدَنِيَّةِ.

The players train every day to maintain their physical fitness.

to train regularly • تَدَرُّبٌ **تَدَرَّبَ بِانْتِظامٍ**

يَجِبُ أَنْ يَتَدَرَّبَ اللّاعِبونَ بِانْتِظامٍ لِضَمانِ اسْتِعْدادِهِمْ لِلْمُبارَياتِ.

Players need to train regularly to ensure they are ready for matches.

to train seriously • تَدَرُّبٌ **تَدَرَّبَ بِجِدِّيَّةٍ**

يَتَدَرَّبُ اللّاعِبُ بِجِدِّيَّةٍ لِلْفَوْزِ بِالْبُطولَةِ.

The player trains seriously to win the championship.

coaching **تَدْريبٌ**

لَقَدْ أَدّى التَّدْريبُ الفَنِّيُّ وَالتَّوْجيهُ الصّارِمُ مِنَ المُدَرِّبِ إِلى تَحْسينِ أَداءِ الفَريقِ.

The technical coaching and strict guidance from the coach led to an improvement in the team's performance.

training, exercise **تَدْريبٌ**

التَّدْريبُ اليَوْمِيُّ هُوَ مِفْتاحُ التَّحْضيرِ الجَيِّدِ لِلْبُطولاتِ الكَبيرَةِ.

Daily training is key to good preparation for major tournaments.

physical training **تَدْريبٌ بَدَنِيٌّ**

يَعْتَمِدُ التَّدْريبُ البَدَنِيُّ عَلى نَوْعِ الرِّياضَةِ الَّتي يُمارِسُها الرِّياضِيُّ.

The physical training depends on the type of sport the athlete practices.

mental training **تَدْريبٌ ذِهْنِيٌّ**

التَّدْريبُ الذِّهْنِيُّ جُزْءٌ أَساسِيٌّ مِنْ بَرْنامَجِ التَّدْريبِ، حَيْثُ يُساعِدُ اللّاعِبينَ عَلى تَعْزيزِ التَّرْكيزِ.

Mental training is a key part of the training program, helping players enhance focus.

resistance training — **تَدْريبُ مُقاوَمَةٍ**

يَسْتَهْدِفُ تَدْريبُ المُقاوَمَةِ بِناءَ قُوَّةِ العَضَلاتِ وَتَحْسينَ التَّحَمُّلِ.

Resistance training aims to build muscle strength and improve endurance.

cardiovascular training — *pl.* **تَدْريباتُ تَحْسينِ أَداءِ القَلْبِ**

إِنَّ تَدْريباتُ تَحْسينِ أَداءِ القَلْبِ جُزْءٌ أَساسِيٌّ مِنَ البَرْنامَجِ التَّدْريبِيِّ لِلْفَريقِ لِتَحْسينِ لِياقَتِهِم.

Cardiovascular training is a fundamental part of the team's training program to enhance their fitness.

massage — **تَدْليكٌ**

يَتَلَقَّى اللّاعِبونَ جَلَساتِ التَّدْليكِ بَعْدَ التَّدْريبِ لِتَخْفيفِ التَّوَتُّرِ العَضَلِيِّ.

The players receive massage sessions after training to alleviate muscle tension.

hydration — **تَرْطيبٌ**

لا يُمْكِنُ التَّقْليلُ مِنْ شَأْنِ أَهَمِّيَّةِ التَّرْطيبِ في الأَداءِ الرِّياضِيِّ.

The importance of hydration in athletic performance cannot be understated.

focus — **تَرْكيزٌ**

يَنْبَغي عَلى اللّاعِبينَ تَحْسينُ تَرْكيزِهِمْ خِلالَ اللُّعْبَةِ لِتَحْقيقِ الفَوْزِ.

The players need to improve their focus during the game to secure a win.

skill development — **تَطْويرُ مَهاراتٍ**

يَسْعى الفَريقُ لِتَطْويرِ مَهاراتِهِمْ عَلى أَساسٍ يَوْمِيٍّ مِنْ خِلالِ التَّدْريبِ الشّاقِّ.

The team seeks to develop their skills on a daily basis through rigorous training.

recovery — **تَعافي** • تعافٍ

بَعْدَ المُباراةِ الشّاقَّةِ، بَدَأَ اللّاعِبونَ في عَمَلِيَّةِ التَّعافي لِلتَّحْضيرِ لِلتَّدْريبِ التّالي.

After the intense match, the players began the recovery process to prepare for the next training.

تَغْذِيَةٌ

nutrition

يَتناوَلُ اللّاعِبونَ وَجَباتٍ غِذائِيَّةً مُتوازِنَةً لِلْحِفاظِ عَلى تَغْذِيَةٍ صِحِّيَّةٍ.

The players consume balanced meals to maintain healthy nutrition.

تَكْتيكٌ

tactic

يَسْتَخْدِمُ المُدَرِّبونَ تَكْتيكاتٍ مُعَيَّنَةً لِضَمانِ فَوْزِ فَريقِهِمْ.

The coaches employ certain tactics to ensure their team's victory.

تَمارينُ تَحْسينِ السُّرْعَةِ

speed improvement exercises *pl.*

تُمَثِّلُ تَمارينُ تَحْسينِ السُّرْعَةِ جُزْءًا أَساسِيًّا مِنَ التَّدْريباتِ لِلاعِبي كُرَةِ القَدَمِ.

Speed improvement exercises represent a crucial part of the training for soccer players.

تَمارينُ تَقْوِيَةِ العَضَلاتِ

muscle strengthening exercises *pl.*

تُساعِدُ تَمارينُ تَقْوِيَةِ العَضَلاتِ الرِّياضِيّينَ عَلى تَقْوِيَةِ أَجْسامِهِمْ وَزِيادَةِ تَحَمُّلِهِمْ.

Muscle strengthening exercises help athletes to fortify their bodies and increase their endurance.

تَمَرَّنَ

to exercise • تَمَرُّنٌ

مِنَ الضَّروريِّ أَنْ يَتَمَرَّنَ الرِّياضِيّونَ يَوْمِيًّا لِلْحِفاظِ عَلى صِحَّتِهِمْ وَلِياقَتِهِمْ.

It is essential for athletes to exercise daily to maintain their health and fitness.

تَمْرينٌ

workout, exercise, drill, training • تَمارينُ / تَمْريناتٌ

يَبْدَأُ اللّاعِبونَ يَوْمَهُمْ بِتَمْرينٍ شاقٍّ لِلْحِفاظِ عَلى لِياقَتِهِمْ.

The players start their day with a rigorous workout to maintain their fitness.

تَمْرينُ إِحْماءٍ

warm-up exercise

يُعَدُّ تَمْرينُ الإِحْماءِ خُطْوَةً أَساسِيَّةً قَبْلَ أَيِّ جُهْدٍ بَدَنِيٍّ كَبيرٍ.

The warm-up exercise is a fundamental step before any major physical effort.

stretching exercises **تَمْرينُ إطالَةٍ**

تُساهِمُ تَمارينُ الإطالَةِ في تَقْليلِ خَطَرِ الإصابَةِ وَزِيادَةِ المُرونَةِ.

Stretching exercises contribute to reducing the risk of injury and increasing flexibility.

physical exercise • تَمارينُ / تَمْريناتٌ **تَمْرينٌ بَدَنِيٌّ**

أَجْرى الفَريقُ تَمارينَ بَدَنِيَّةً شاقَّةً لِلْحِفاظِ عَلى لِياقَتِهِمْ.

The team performed intense physical exercises to maintain their fitness.

running exercise • تَمارينُ / تَمْريناتٌ **تَمْرينُ جَرْيٍ**

يُعْتَبَرُ تَمْرينُ الجَرْيِ واحِدًا مِنْ أَكْثَرِ التَّمارينِ شُمولِيَّةً لِتَحْسينِ اللِّياقَةِ البَدَنِيَّةِ.

Running exercise is one of the most comprehensive workouts to improve physical fitness.

group training **تَمْرينٌ جَماعِيٌّ**

يُمْكِنُ أَنْ يُساعِدَ التَّمْرينُ الجَماعِيُّ الرِّياضِيّينَ عَلى بِناءِ روحِ الفَريقِ وَتَحْسينِ التَّواصُلِ.

Group training can help athletes build team spirit and improve communication.

individual training **تَمْرينٌ فَرْدِيٌّ**

يُمْكِنُ أَنْ يَكونَ التَّمْرينُ الفَرْدِيُّ مُناسِبًا لِلرِّياضِيّينَ الَّذينَ يَرْغَبونَ في تَحْسينِ مَهاراتِهِمِ الخاصَّةِ.

Individual training can be suitable for athletes who wish to improve their specific skills.

jumping exercise **تَمْرينُ قَفْزٍ**

تَعْمَلُ تَمارينُ القَفْزِ عَلى تَقْوِيَةِ العَضَلاتِ وَزِيادَةِ القُدْرَةِ عَلى التَّحَمُّلِ.

Jumping exercises work on strengthening muscles and enhancing endurance.

ready, prepared **جاهِزٌ**

يَجِبُ أَنْ يَكونَ الرِّياضِيُّ جاهِزًا بَدَنِيًّا وَعَقْلِيًّا قَبْلَ المُشارَكَةِ في المُسابَقاتِ الرِّياضِيَّةِ.

The athlete should be physically and mentally ready before participating in sports competitions.

جَدْوَلُ تَدْريبٍ • جَداوِلُ **training schedule**

يَحْتاجُ الرِّياضِيّونَ إلى اتِّباعِ جَدْوَلِ تَدْريبٍ مُحَدَّدٍ لِلْحِفاظِ عَلى لِياقَتِهِمِ البَدَنِيَّةِ.

Athletes need to follow a specific training schedule to maintain their physical fitness.

جَلْسَةُ تَدْريبٍ **training session**

تَهْدُفُ جَلْسَةُ التَّدْريبِ إلى تَحْسينِ الأَداءِ الرِّياضِيِّ.

The training session aims to improve athletic performance.

حَسَّنَ • تَحْسينٌ **to improve**

واصَلَ الفَريقُ العَمَلَ الشّاقَّ لِتَحْسينِ أَدائِهِمْ قَبْلَ البُطولَةِ الكُبْرى.

The team continued to work hard to improve their performance ahead of the major tournament.

حَسَّنَ أَداءً • تَحْسينٌ **to improve performance**

يُطَبِّقُ اللّاعِبُ تَمارينَ جَديدَةً لِتَحْسينِ أَدائِهِ عَلى أَرْضِ المَلْعَبِ.

The player is implementing new exercises to improve his performance on the pitch.

حِصَّةٌ تَدْريبِيَّةٌ • حِصَصٌ **training session**

أَجْرى الفَريقُ حِصَّةً تَدْريبِيَّةً شاقَّةً صَباحَ اليَوْمِ اسْتِعْدادًا لِلْمُباراةِ الهامَّةِ القادِمَةِ.

The team conducted a rigorous training session this morning in preparation for the upcoming important match.

حَمّامُ ثَلْجٍ **ice bath**

تُسْتَخْدَمُ حَمّاماتُ الثَّلْجِ في بَعْضِ الأَحْيانِ كَجُزْءٍ مِنْ بَرْنامَجِ التَّعافي بَعْدَ التَّدْريبِ.

Ice baths are sometimes used as part of the recovery regimen post-training.

دُهونٌ *pl.* **fats**

تَلْعَبُ الدُّهونُ دَوْرًا مُهِمًّا في النِّظامِ الغِذائِيِّ الصِّحِّيِّ، لَكِنَّها يَجِبُ أَنْ تَكونَ بِكَمِّيّاتٍ مُحَدَّدَةٍ.

Fats play an important role in a healthy diet but should be in specified quantities.

fit — **ذو لِياقَةٍ**

يَجِبُ أَنْ يَكونَ الرِّياضِيُّ ذا لِياقَةٍ بَدَنِيَّةٍ جَيِّدَةٍ لِتَحْقيقِ أَداءٍ جَيِّدٍ.

An athlete should be fit to perform well.

rest — **راحَةٌ**

يَحْتاجُ الرِّياضِيّونَ إلى فَتَراتٍ مِنَ الرّاحَةِ لِلتَّعافي بَعْدَ التَّمْرينِ.

Athletes need periods of rest to recover after training.

athletic, sporty — **رِياضِيٌّ**

يُحافِظُ الشَّخْصُ الرِّياضِيُّ عَلى نَشاطِهِ وَلِياقَتِهِ البَدَنِيَّةِ بِشَكْلٍ مُنْتَظِمٍ.

An athletic person maintains his activity and physical fitness regularly.

athlete — **رِياضِيٌّ**

يُمْكِنُ لِلتَّشْجيعِ أَنْ يَلْعَبَ دَوْرًا هامًّا في تَحْفيزِ الرِّياضِيّينَ لِتَحْقيقِ أَفْضَلِ أَداءٍ.

Encouragement can play a key role in motivating athletes to achieve their best performance.

to assist in training — **ساعَدَ في تَدْريبٍ** • مُساعَدَةٌ

قامَ البَطَلُ العالَمِيُّ في فُنونِ القِتالِ المُخْتَلِطَةِ بِمُساعَدَةٍ في تَدْريبِ الرِّياضِيّينَ الشُّبّانِ، مُشارِكًا خِبْرَتَهُ وَمَهاراتِهِ لِتَطْويرِ مُسْتَواهُمْ .

The world champion in mixed martial arts assisted in training young athletes, sharing his expertise and skills to enhance their level.

to participate in training — **شارَكَ في تَدْريبٍ** • مُشارَكَةٌ

شارَكَ عَلِيُّ بْنُ حُسَيْنٍ في التَّدْريبِ الأَخيرِ لِلْفَريقِ، بَعْدَ تَعافيهِ مِنَ الإِصابَةِ الَّتي كانَتْ قَدْ أَبْعَدَتْهُ عَنِ المَلْعَبِ لِأَسابيعَ.

Ali bin Hussein participated in the team's last training session after recovering from the injury that had sidelined him for weeks.

شاقٌّ
difficult, hard

كانَتِ المُباراةُ شاقَّةً لِلْغايَةِ• وَلَكِنَّ الفَريقَ اسْتَطاعَ التَّغَلُّبَ عَلى التَّحَدِّياتِ وَالفَوْزَ في النِّهايَةِ.

The match was very difficult, but the team was able to overcome the challenges and win in the end.

شَجَّعَ • تَشْجيعٌ
to cheer

شَجَّعَتِ الجَماهيرُ الفَريقَ بِشِدَّةٍ طَوالَ المُباراةِ، مِمّا أَعْطى اللّاعِبينَ دافِعًا إِضافِيًّا لِلْأَداءِ بِشَكْلٍ أَفْضَلَ.

The fans strongly cheered the team throughout the match, giving the players an extra incentive to perform better.

ضَعيفٌ
weak

كانَ الفَريقُ ضَعيفًا في الدِّفاعِ خِلالَ الشَّوْطِ الأَوَّلِ، مِمّا سَمَحَ لِلْخَصْمِ بِتَسْجيلِ عِدَّةِ أَهْدافٍ.

The team was weak in defense during the first half, allowing the opponent to score several goals.

ضَغْطٌ
compression

تُساعِدُ المَلابِسُ الضّاغِطَةُ في الرِّياضَةِ عَلى التَّعافي، وَتُقَلِّلُ مَخاطِرَ الإِصاباتِ .

Compression garments in sports aid in recovery and reduce injury risks.

عَقارُ تَعْزيزِ الْأَداءِ • عَقاقيرُ
performance-enhancing drug

تُسْتَخْدَمُ عَقاقيرُ تَعْزيزِ الأَداءِ أَحْيانًا بِطُرُقٍ غَيْرِ قانونِيَّةٍ لِتَحْسينِ الأَداءِ الرِّياضِيِّ.

Performance-enhancing drugs are sometimes used illegally to improve sports performance.

عِلاجٌ طَبيعِيٌّ
physical therapy

يُمْكِنُ لِلْعِلاجِ الطَّبيعِيِّ أَنْ يُساعِدَ في التَّعافي مِنَ الإِصاباتِ الرِّياضِيَّةِ.

Physical therapy can assist in recovering from sports injuries.

عَلَّمَ • تَعْليمٌ
to teach

تَمَّ اسْتِدْعاءُ المُدَرِّبِ ذِي الخِبْرَةِ لِتَعْليمِ اسْتِراتيجِيّاتِ الدِّفاعِ المُتَقَدِّمَةِ لِفَريقِ كُرَةِ القَدَمِ.

he experienced coach was brought in to teach advanced defensive strategies to the soccer team.

فَريقٌ • فِرَقٌ **team**

إنَّ العَمَلَ كَفريقٍ هُوَ مِفْتاحُ النَّجاحِ في العَديدِ مِنَ الرِّياضاتِ.

Working as a team is the key to success in many sports.

فَعّالٌ **effective**

كانَتْ تَمارينُ الإحْماءِ فَعّالَةً في الحَدِّ مِنَ الإصاباتِ وَتَحْضيرِ اللّاعِبينَ لِلْمُباراةِ.

The warm-up exercises were effective in reducing injuries and preparing the players for the match.

فيتامينٌ **vitamin**

الفيتاميناتُ هِيَ مُكَمِّلاتٌ غِذائيَّةٌ ضَروريَّةٌ لِلصِّحَّةِ وَالأَداءِ الرِّياضيِّ.

Vitamins are essential dietary supplements for health and athletic performance.

قَويٌّ • أَقْوِياءُ **strong**

يَتَمَتَّعُ الرياضيُّ قَوِيُّ البِنْيَةِ بِعَضَلاتٍ قَويَّةٍ وَقُدْرَةٍ عاليَةٍ عَلى التَّحَمُّلِ.

An athlete who is strong in structure has strong muscles and high endurance capabilities.

كَرْبوهَيْدِراتْ *pl.* **carbohydrates**

الكَرْبوهَيْدِراتْ هِيَ مَصْدَرٌ أَساسِيٌّ لِلطّاقَةِ الَّتي يَحْتاجُها الرِّياضِيّونَ خِلالَ التَّدْريباتِ وَالمُنافَساتِ.

Carbohydrates are a primary source of energy that athletes need during training and competitions.

لاعِبٌ **player**

يَتَصَدَّرُ اللّاعِبُ المُحْتَرِفُ أَحْمَدُ العُمَري الأَخْبارَ مَرَّةً أُخْرى بَعْدَ أَدائِهِ المُذْهِلِ في المُباراةِ الأَخيرَةِ.

Professional player Ahmed Al-Omari is making headlines again after his stunning performance in the last match.

لِياقَةٌ بَدَنيَّةٌ **fitness**

يُحَقِّقُ الفَريقُ مَعاييرَ اللِّياقَةِ البَدَنيَّةِ العاليَةِ، مِمّا يَعْكِسُ التَّحْضيرَ الجَيِّدَ لِلْمَوْسِمِ الجَديدِ.

The team meets high fitness standards, reflecting good preparation for the new season.

مَادَّةٌ مَحْظورَةٌ • مَوادٌّ

banned substance

أَعْلَنَ الاِتِّحادُ الدَّوْلِيُّ لِأَلْعابِ القُوى عَنِ اكْتِشافِ اسْتِخْدامِ مَوادَّ مَحْظورَةٍ في الأَلْعابِ الأولِمْبِيَّةِ الأَخيرَةِ.

The International Athletics Federation announced the discovery of the use of banned substances in the latest Olympic Games.

مارَسَ الرِّياضَةَ • مُمارَسَةٌ

to practice sports

مارَسَ اللّاعِبُ مُحَمَّد أَحْمَد الرِّياضَةَ كَجُزْءٍ مِنْ روتينِهِ اليَوْمِيِّ لِلْحِفاظِ عَلى لِياقَتِهِ البَدَنِيَّةِ.

Player Mohammed Ahmed practiced sports as part of his daily routine to maintain his physical fitness.

مُتَدَرِّبٌ

trainee

قَدَّمَ المُتَدَرِّبُ فِراس السَّعيد أَداءً مُمْتازًا في التَّدْريبِ اليَوْمَ، وَيَبْدو أَنَّهُ مُسْتَعِدٌّ لِمُنافَسَةِ اللاعِبينَ الكِبارِ.

Trainee Feras Al-Saeed delivered an excellent performance in training today and looks ready to compete with the big players.

مُتَمَرِّنٌ

trainee

أَظْهَرَ المُتَمَرِّنُ يوسُف الرّاشِد تَحَسُّنًا كَبيرًا في أَدائِهِ خِلالَ الأَسابيعِ القَليلَةِ الماضِيَةِ.

Trainee Yusuf Al-Rashed has shown great improvement in his performance over the past few weeks.

مُدَرِّبٌ

coach

يَثِقُ المُدَرِّبُ عادِل فَهْد في قُدْرَةِ فَريقِهِ عَلى الفَوْزِ بِالْبُطولَةِ هَذا العامَ.

Coach Adel Fahd is confident in his team's ability to win the championship this year.

مُدَرِّبٌ مُؤَهَّلٌ

qualified coach

يَعْمَلُ المُدَرِّبُ المُؤَهَّلُ عِماد أَحْمَد عَلى تَطْويرِ اسْتِراتيجِيّاتٍ جَديدَةٍ لِتَحْسينِ أَداءِ الفَريقِ.

Qualified coach Emad Ahmed is working on developing new strategies to improve the team's performance.

assistant coach **مُدَرِّبٌ مُساعِدٌ**

لَعِبَ المُدَرِّبُ المُساعِدُ سَعيد القَحْطاني دَوْرًا حاسِمًا في تَنْسيقِ الدِّفاعِ خِلالَ المُباراة.

Assistant coach Saeed Al-Qahtani played a crucial role in coordinating the defense during the match.

mineral • مَعادِنُ **مَعْدِنٌ**

إنَّ المَعادِنَ، مِثْلَ الحَديدِ وَالزِّنْك، ضَرورِيَّةٌ لِلْحِفاظِ عَلى الصِّحَّةِ العامَّةِ وَالأَداءِ الرِّياضِيِّ.

Minerals like iron and zinc are necessary for maintaining general health and athletic performance.

supplement **مُكَمِّلٌ غِذائِيٌّ**

بَدَأَ اللّاعِبُ فَهْد أَحْمَد في تَناوُلِ مُكَمِّلٍ غِذائِيٍّ جَديدٍ لِتَحْسينِ نِسْبَةِ البُروتينِ في نِظامِهِ الغِذائِيِّ.

Player Fahd Ahmed started taking a new supplement to improve the protein ratio in his diet.

diet • أَنْظِمَةٌ **نِظامٌ غِذائِيٌّ**

يَتْبَعُ النَّجْمُ الرِّياضِيُّ حُسَيْن الجُمْعَة نِظامًا غِذائِيًّا صارِمًا لِلْحِفاظِ عَلى اللِّياقَةِ البَدَنِيَّةِ وَالتَّحَكُّمِ في الوَزْنِ.

Sports star Hussein Al-Juma is following a strict diet to maintain physical fitness and control weight.

6.4.4.1 Mini-Articles

Track **89**

أَعْلَنَ مَرْكَزُ التَّدْريبِ الرِّياضِيِّ الرّائِدُ عَنْ إِطْلاقِ بَرْنامَجٍ تَدْريبِيٍّ جَديدٍ يَهْدُفُ إِلى تَحْسينِ أَداءِ الرِّياضِيّينَ. يَتَضَمَّنُ البَرْنامَجُ تَمارينَ لِتَحْسينِ السُّرْعَةِ وَتَقْوِيَةِ العَضَلاتِ، بِالإِضافَةِ إِلى التَّدْريبِ الذِّهْنِيِّ. سَيَتْبَعُ الرِّياضِيّونَ أَيْضًا نِظامًا غِذائِيًّا مُتَوازِنًا يَضْمَنُ البُروتيناتِ وَالكَرْبوهَيْدراتِ وَالفيتاميناتِ الضَّرورِيَّةَ.

The leading sports training center has announced the launch of a new training program aimed at improving athletes' performance. The program includes exercises to enhance speed, strengthen muscles, and mental training. Athletes will also follow a balanced diet that ensures essential proteins, carbohydrates, and vitamins.

بَعْدَ فَتْرَةٍ طَويلَةٍ مِنَ التَّأْهيلِ، أَظْهَرَ الرِّياضِيُّ مُحَمَّد العابِد تَحَسُّنًا مَلْحوظًا في لِياقَتِهِ البَدَنِيَّةِ. خَضَعَ العابِد لِعِلاجٍ طَبيعِيٍّ مُكَثَّفٍ وَتَمْريناتٍ بَدَنِيَّةٍ مُنَظَّمَةٍ لِمُساعَدَتِهِ عَلى التَّعافي مِنْ إِصابَتِهِ. قالَ مُدَرِّبُهُ: "مُحَمَّد عَمِلَ بِجِدِّيَّةٍ وَاسْتَفادَ كَثيرًا مِنَ البَرْنامَجِ التَّدْريبِيِّ وَالنِّظامِ الغِذائِيِّ الَّذي اتَّبَعَهُ."

After a long period of rehabilitation, athlete Mohamed Al-Abid showed significant improvement in his physical fitness. Al-Abid underwent intensive physical therapy and organized exercises to aid his recovery from the injury. His coach said, “Mohamed worked diligently and benefited greatly from the training program and dietary regimen he followed.”

فِي الوَقْتِ الَّذي يَسْتَعِدُّ فيه الفَريقُ الوَطَنِيُّ لِلْمَوْسِمِ الرِّياضِيِّ الجَديدِ، أَصْبَحَتِ الوِقايَةُ مِنَ الإصاباتِ جُزْءًا أَساسِيًّا مِنْ بَرْنامَجِهِم التَّدْريبِيِّ. يَشْمَلُ هَذا تَمارينَ الإحْماءِ وَالإطالَةِ، بِالْإِضافَةِ إِلى تَعَلُّمِ التَّكْتيكاتِ الصَّحيحَةِ لِتَجَنُّبِ الإصاباتِ. بِالْإِضافَةِ إِلى ذَلِكَ، سَيَتِمُّ تَطْبيقُ بُروتوكولِ الارْتِجاجِ لِضَمانِ سَلامَةِ اللّاعِبينَ.

As the national team prepares for the new sports season, injury prevention has become an essential part of their training program. This includes warm-up and stretching exercises, in addition to learning proper tactics to avoid injuries. Furthermore, a concussion protocol will be implemented to ensure the safety of the players.

6.4.4.2 Interview with an Athlete

Track **90**

مُقابَلَةٌ مَعَ مُحَمَّد بَعْدَ فَتْرَةِ التَّأْهيلِ

المُقَدِّمُ: مَرْحَبًا مُحَمَّد، شُكْرًا لَكَ عَلى وَقْتِكَ. أَوَّلًا، كَيْفَ تَشْعُرُ بَعْدَ الإصابَةِ وَالفَتْرَةِ الطَّويلَةِ مِنَ التَّأْهيلِ؟

مُحَمَّد: مَرْحَبًا، شُكْرًا لَكَ. بِالطَّبْعِ، كانَتْ فَتْرَةً صَعْبَةً، لَكِنّي أَشْعُرُ الآنَ بِتَحَسُّنٍ كَبيرٍ. التَّأْهيلُ وَالتَّدْريبُ البَدَنِيُّ ساعَداني كَثيرًا في اسْتِعادَةِ قُوَّتي وَلِياقَتي البَدَنِيَّةِ.

المُقَدِّمُ: رائِعٌ! كَيْفَ كانَ بَرْنامَجُ التَّأْهيلِ الَّذي خُضْتَهُ؟

مُحَمَّد: كانَ بَرْنامَجُ التَّأْهيلِ مُكَثَّفًا وَلَكِنَّهُ فَعّالٌ. بَدَأْتُ بِتَمارينَ خَفيفَةٍ لِتَعْزيزِ المُرونَةِ وَالقُوَّةِ، ثُمَّ انْتَقَلْتُ تَدْريجِيًّا إِلى تَمارينَ أَكْثَرَ صُعوبَةً. كانَ العِلاجُ الطَّبيعِيُّ أَيْضًا جُزْءًا هامًّا مِنَ العَمَلِيَّةِ.

المُقَدِّمُ: أَظُنُّ أَنَّ النِّظامَ الغِذائِيَّ لَهُ دَوْرٌ كَبيرٌ أَيْضًا فِي التَّعافي، أَلَيْسَ كَذَلِكَ؟

مُحَمَّدُ: نَعَمْ، بِالطَّبْعِ. اتَّبَعْتُ نِظامًا غِذائِيًّا غَنِيًّا بِالْبُروتيناتِ وَالكَرْبوهَيْدراتِ وَالفيتاميناتِ لِمُساعَدَةِ جِسْمي عَلى الشِّفاءِ وَبِناءِ العَضَلاتِ. كانَ الأَمْرُ يَتَطَلَّبُ التِزامًا، لَكِنَّ النَّتائِجَ تَسْتَحِقُّ الجُهْدَ.

المُقَدِّمُ: هَلْ تَشْعُرُ بِأَنَّكَ مُسْتَعِدٌّ الآنَ لِلْعَوْدَةِ إِلى المَلاعِبِ؟

مُحَمَّد: أَشْعُرُ بِالتَّأْكِيدِ أَنَّني أَقْرَبُ بِكَثيرٍ إِلى ذَلِكَ الآنَ. أَنا أَتَدَرَّبُ بِجِدٍّ كُلَّ يَوْمٍ، وَأَتَطَلَّعُ إِلى اللَّحْظَةِ الَّتي أَسْتَطيعُ فيها العَوْدَةَ وَاللَّعِبَ بِشَكْلٍ كامِلٍ.

المُقَدِّمُ: هَذا رائِعٌ يا مُحَمَّد. نَتَمَنّى لَكَ العَوْدَةَ السَّريعَةَ إِلى المَلاعِبِ وَنَشْكُرُكَ عَلى وَقْتِكَ.

مُحَمَّدُ: شُكْرًا لَكَ.

Interview With Mohamed After the Rehabilitation Period

Interviewer: Hello Mohamed, thank you for your time. First of all, how do you feel after the injury and the long rehabilitation period?

Mohamed: Hello, thank you. Of course, it was a tough period, but I now feel a significant improvement. The rehabilitation and physical training have helped me a lot in regaining my strength and physical fitness.

Interviewer: That's great to hear! How was the rehabilitation program you went through?

Mohamed: The rehabilitation program was intense but effective. I started with light exercises to improve flexibility and strength, then gradually moved on to more challenging exercises. Physical therapy was also a crucial part of the process.

Interviewer: I believe the diet plays a significant role in recovery as well, doesn't it?

Mohamed: Yes, definitely. I followed a diet rich in proteins, carbohydrates, and vitamins to aid my body in healing and muscle building. It required commitment, but the results were worth the effort.

Interviewer: Do you feel you are now ready to return to the field?

Mohamed: I certainly feel much closer to that now. I am training hard every day, and I look forward to the moment when I can return and play to the fullest.

Interviewer: That's wonderful, Mohamed. We wish you a speedy return to the field, and thank you for your time.

Mohamed: Thank you.

6.4.5 Fan Culture and Supporters

Track **91**

أَنْشَدَ • إِنْشادٌ
to sing

بَعْدَ خَسارَةِ الفَريقِ المُحْبِطَةِ، أَنْشَدَ المُشَجِّعونَ أَغانيهِمِ الدّاعِمَةَ لِرَفْعِ مَعْنَوِيّاتِ اللّاعِبينَ.

After the team's disheartening loss, the fans sang their supportive songs to boost the players' morale.

بِطاقَةُ المُشَجِّعينَ
fan card

مِنَ الضَّروريِّ لِأَيِّ مُشَجِّعٍ رِياضِيٍّ أَنْ يَكونَ لَدَيْهِ بِطاقَةُ المُشَجِّعينَ لِلْحُصولِ عَلى مَيْزاتٍ خاصَّةٍ فِي المُبارَياتِ وَالأَحْداثِ الرِّياضِيَّةِ.

It is essential for any sports fan to have a fan card to get special benefits in matches and sports events.

تَحْريضُ الجَماهيرِ
inciting the crowd

تَمَّ القَبْضُ عَلى بَعْضِ المُشَجِّعينَ لِتَحْريضِ الجَماهيرِ وَإِثارَةِ الشَّغَبِ خِلالَ المُباراةِ.

Some fans were arrested for inciting the crowd and causing a riot during the match.

تَذْكِرَةٌ • تَذاكِرُ
ticket

يَتَطَلَّعُ الجَميعُ إِلى الحُصولِ عَلى تَذْكِرَةٍ لِنِهائِيّاتِ كَأْسِ العالَمِ، فَهِيَ مِنْ أَكْثَرِ الأَحْداثِ الرِّياضِيَّةِ شُهْرَةً.

Everyone is looking forward to getting a ticket to the World Cup finals, as it is one of the most famous sports events.

تَفاعَلَ • تَفاعُلٌ
to interact, engage (with)

يُشَجِّعُ النّادي المَحَلِّيُّ تَفاعُلَ الجُمْهورِ عَبْرَ الإِنْتَرْنِتْ، وَهُوَ يُحافِظُ عَلى تَحْديثِ صَفَحاتِهِ الاِجْتِماعِيَّةِ بِانْتِظامٍ.

The local club encourages fans to interact online, keeping their social pages regularly updated.

تَهَجَّمَ عَلى • تَهَجُّمٌ
to attack, assail

تَهَجَّمَ المُشَجِّعونَ عَلى الحَكَمِ بَعْدَ القَرارِ المُثيرِ لِلْجَدَلِ فِي الدَّقائِقِ الأَخيرَةِ مِنَ المُباراةِ.

The fans attacked the referee after the controversial decision in the last minutes of the match.

crowd, audience, spectators, fans • جَماهيرُ **جُمْهورٌ**

يُشَكِّلُ الجُمْهورُ جُزْءًا حَيَوِيًّا مِنْ أَيِّ مُباراةٍ رِياضِيَّةٍ، فَتَشْجيعُهُمْ يُعْطي اللّاعِبينَ دَفْعَةً مَعْنَوِيَّةً.

The crowd is a vital part of any sports match, as their cheering gives players a morale boost.

away fans **جُمْهورُ ضَيْفٍ**

كانَ جُمْهورُ الضَّيْفِ مُتَحَمِّسًا لِلْغايَةِ رَغْمَ كَوْنِهِمْ في أَرْضٍ غَريبَةٍ.

The away fans were very enthusiastic despite being on foreign ground.

passionate fanbase • جَماهيرُ **جُمْهورٌ مُتَعَصِّبٌ**

الجُمْهورُ المُتَعَصِّبُ لِلْفَريقِ يَعْتَبِرونَ نَفْسَهُمِ القَلْبَ النّابِضَ لِلنّادي.

The team's passionate fanbase consider themselves the beating heart of the club.

crowd attendance **حُضورٌ جَماهيرِيٌّ**

رَغْمَ الظُّروفِ الصَّعْبَةِ، كانَ حُضورُ الجَماهيرِ في المَلْعَبِ قَوِيًّا وَداعِمًا.

Despite tough circumstances, the crowd attendance at the stadium was strong and supportive.

team loss • خَسائِرُ **خَسارَةُ فَريقٍ**

بَعْدَ خَسارَةِ الفَريقِ الأَخيرَةِ، يَبْقى الدَّعْمُ مِنَ الجَماهيرِ أَكْثَرَ أَهَمِّيَّةً مِنْ أَيِّ وَقْتٍ مَضى.

After the team's latest loss, support from the fans remains more important than ever.

support **دَعْمٌ**

واصَلَ المُشَجِّعونَ دَعْمَ فَريقِهِمْ بِحَماسٍ، حَتّى بَعْدَ صافِرَةِ النِّهايَةِ.

The fans continued to passionately support their team, even after the final whistle.

fan support **دَعْمُ الجَماهيرِ**

رَغْمَ خَسارَةِ الفَريقِ، ظَلَّ دَعْمُ الجَماهيرِ قَوِيًّا وَثابِتًا.

Despite the team's loss, the fan support remained strong and constant.

رايَةٌ flag

تَمَّ تَزْيِينُ المَلْعَبِ براياتِ الفَريقِ، وَهِيَ تُرَفْرِفُ بِفَخْرٍ.

The stadium was decorated with the team's flags, fluttering proudly.

رَدَّدَ • تَرْديدٌ to chant

بَدَأَتِ الجَماهيرُ في تَرديدِ الأَغاني التَّقْليدِيَّةِ لِفَريقِها، مالِئَةً المَلْعَبَ بِالْهُتافاتِ.

The crowd began to chant their team's traditional songs, filling the stadium with cheers.

زَيَّنَ • تَزْيينٌ to decorate

زَيَّنَ المُشَجِّعونَ أَنْفُسَهُمْ بِأَلْوانِ الفَريقِ وَرُموزِهِ في دَعْمٍ قَوِيٍّ لِلّاعِبينَ.

The fans decorated themselves in the team's colors and symbols in strong support of the players.

شِعارُ فَريقٍ team logo

تَأَلَّقَ شِعارُ الفَريقِ عَلى القُمْصانِ وَالأَعْلامِ بِفَخْرٍ في المُدَرَّجاتِ.

The team's logo on the jerseys and flags shone proudly in the stands.

صَفَّقَ • تَصْفيقٌ to applaud

صَفَّقَ الجُمْهورُ بِحَماسٍ عِنْدَما سَجَّلَ الفَريقُ هَدَفَ التَّعادُلِ.

The crowd applauded enthusiastically when the team scored the equalizing goal.

فَوْزُ فَريقٍ team victory

تَعُمُّ الِاحْتِفالاتُ الشَّوارِعَ بَعْدَ فَوْزِ الفَريقِ في المُباراةِ النِّهائِيَّةِ لِلْبُطولَةِ.

Celebrations fill the streets after the team's victory in the final match of the tournament.

قاعِدَةٌ جَماهيرِيَّةٌ fanbase

أَسْعَدَ فَوْزُ الفَريقِ قاعِدَتَهُ الجَماهيرِيَّةَ بِشَكْلٍ كَبيرٍ.

The team's victory greatly pleased the fanbase.

team jersey • أَقْمِصَةٌ، قُمْصَانٌ **قَميصُ فَريقٍ**

كانَ قَميصُ الفَريقِ يَتَأَلَّقُ بَيْنَ الجَماهيرِ كَرَمْزٍ لِلْوَلاءِ وَالدَّعْمِ.

The team jersey shone among the crowd, as a symbol of loyalty and support.

smoke bomb • قَنابِلُ **قُنْبُلَةُ دُخانٍ**

اِسْتَخْدَمَ بَعْضُ المُشَجِّعينَ المُتَحَمِّسينَ قَنابِلَ الدُّخانِ لِلتَّعْبيرِ عَنْ حَماسِهِمْ.

Some of the passionate fans used smoke bombs to express their excitement.

banner **لافِتَةٌ**

رَفَعَ المُشَجِّعونَ لافِتاتٍ كَبيرَةً تَحْمِلُ شِعارَ الفَريقِ في المُدَرَّجاتِ المُكْتَظَّةِ.

The fans raised large banners bearing the team's logo in the packed stands.

enthusiastic **مُتَحَمِّسٌ**

المُشَجِّعونَ المُتَحَمِّسونَ يَأْتونَ مِنْ كُلِّ أَنْحاءِ البِلادِ لِدَعْمِ فَريقِهِمْ.

Enthusiastic fans come from all over the country to support their team.

fanatic **مُتَعَصِّبٌ**

نَظَرًا لِكَوْنِهِ مِنَ المُتَعَصِّبينَ لِفَريقِهِ، كانَ يَحْضُرُ كُلَّ مُباراةٍ بِغَضِّ النَّظَرِ عَنِ الظُّروفِ.

A fanatic of his team, he attended every match regardless of the circumstances.

dedicated, committed **مُتفانٍ**

يَشْهَدُ نادي المُشَجِّعينَ زِيادَةً في عَدَدِ الأَعْضاءِ المُتَفانينَ وَالمُلْتَزِمينَ.

The fan club is witnessing an increase in dedicated and committed members.

packed stands *pl.* **مُدَرَّجاتٌ مُكْتَظَّةٌ**

كانَتِ المُدَرَّجاتُ مُكْتَظَّةً بِالْمُشَجِّعينَ الَّذينَ جاؤوا لِمُشاهَدَةِ المُباراةِ المُرْتَقَبَةِ.

The stands were packed with fans who came to watch the anticipated match.

مُشَجِّعٌ **fan, supporter**

يَحْرِصُ المُشَجِّعونَ عَلى الهُتافِ بِكُلِّ قُوَّةٍ لِدَعْمِ فَريقِهِمْ.

The fans make sure to cheer loudly to support their team.

نادي المُشَجِّعينَ • نوادٍ **fan club**

تَجَمَّعَ أَعْضاءُ نادي المُشَجِّعينَ لِتَنْظيمِ حَدَثٍ خَيْرِيٍّ لِدَعْمِ الفَريقِ.

The fan club members gathered to organize a charity event in support of the team.

هُتافٌ **chant, cheer**

كانَتِ الهُتافاتُ مِنَ الجُمْهورِ الوَفِيِّ تَمْلَأُ الاِسْتادَ.

Chants from the loyal crowd filled the stadium.

هَتَفَ • هُتافٌ **to cheer**

هَتَفَ الجُمْهورُ بِأَعْلى صَوْتِهِمْ لِتَشْجيعِ فَريقِهِمْ خِلالَ المُباراةِ الحاسِمَةِ.

The crowd cheered at the top of their lungs to support their team during the crucial match.

وَفِيٌّ • أَوْفِياءُ **loyal**

عَلى الرَّغْمِ مِنَ التَّحَدِّياتِ، يُواصِلُ المُشَجِّعونَ الأَوْفِياءُ دَعْمَ فَريقِهِمْ.

Despite the challenges, the loyal fans continue to support their team.

يُشَجِّعُ • تَشْجيعٌ **to support, cheer on**

يُشَجِّعُ الجُمْهورُ المُتَحَمِّسُ فَريقَهُ بِحَماسَةٍ وَشَغَفٍ.

The enthusiastic crowd cheers on their team with fervor and passion.

6.4.5.1 Mini-Articles

Track **92**

رَغْمَ خَسارَةِ الفَريقِ في المُباراةِ الأَخيرَةِ، بَقِيَتْ قاعِدَةٌ جَماهيرِيَّةٌ وَفِيَّةٌ ومُتَفانِيَةٌ تَدْعَمُ فَريقَ النُّجومِ العَرَبِيَّةِ. يُرَدِّدُ المُشَجِّعونَ هُتافاتٍ مُتَعاطِفَةً وَيَهْتِفونَ لِلّاعِبينَ عَلى الرَّغْمِ مِنَ النَّتائِجِ. يُحَمِّسونَ الجَماهيرَ وَيُقَدِّمونَ دَعْمًا جَماهيرِيًّا لا يُعَدُّ وَلا يُحْصى. وَفي النِّهايَةِ، هَذا هُوَ الغَرَضُ الحَقيقِيُّ لِلرِّياضَةِ: تَوْحيدُ النّاسِ.

Despite the team's loss in the last match, a loyal and dedicated fan base remains to support the Arab Stars team. Fans chant sympathetic slogans and cheer for the players despite the results. They incite the crowd and provide countless fan support. Ultimately, this is the true purpose of sports: unifying people.

فِي مُباراةِ الأَمْسِ، كانَتِ المُدَرَّجاتُ مُكْتَظَّةً بِالْمُشَجِّعينَ المُتَحَمِّسينَ. كانوا يَمْلَأونَ المَلْعَبَ بِالْهُتافاتِ وَالأَغاني الَّتي رَدَّدَها الجَميعُ. كانوا يَرْتَدونَ قُمْصانَ الفَريقِ وَيَرْفَعونَ الرّاياتِ. حَتّى إِنَّ بَعْضَ المُشَجِّعينَ أَطْلَقوا قَنابِلَ الدُّخانِ لِإِضْفاءِ جَوٍّ احْتِفالِيٍّ عَلى المُباراةِ. هَذِهِ الثَّقافَةُ الجَماهيرِيَّةُ تُحَوِّلُ اللُّعْبَةَ إِلى أَكْثَرَ مِنْ مُجَرَّدِ رِياضَةٍ، بَلْ إِلى تَجْرِبَةٍ مُشْتَرَكَةٍ وَمُوَحَّدَةٍ لِلْمُجْتَمَعِ.

In yesterday's match, the stands were packed with enthusiastic fans. They filled the stadium with chants and songs that everyone echoed. They wore the team's jerseys and waved flags. Some fans even released smoke bombs to create a celebratory atmosphere during the match. This fan culture transforms the game into more than just a sport; it becomes a shared and unified experience for the community.

تَجْتَذِبُ بِطاقاتُ المُشَجِّعينَ الكَثيرَ مِنَ الأَتْباعِ، حَيْثُ تُوَفِّرُ لَهُمْ فُرْصَةً لِتَكْثيفِ دَعْمِهِمْ لِلْفَريقِ وَالتَّفاعُلِ مَعَهُ بِطُرُقٍ جَديدَةٍ. فَضْلًا عَنْ تَقْديمِ تَذاكِرَ مُخَفَّضَةٍ لِلْمُبارَياتِ، يَحْصُلُ أَعْضاءُ نادي المُشَجِّعينَ عَلى فُرْصَةٍ لِلِقاءِ اللّاعِبينَ وَالحُصولِ عَلى المَعْلوماتِ الحَصْرِيَّةِ. بِالنِّسْبَةِ لِلْكَثيرينَ، تِلْكَ البِطاقاتُ هِيَ وَسيلَةٌ لِلتَّعْبيرِ عَنِ التَّفاني وَالوَلاءِ لِلْفَريقِ الَّذي يُشَجِّعونَهُ.

Fan cards attract a large following, offering them the opportunity to intensify their support for the team and interact with it in new ways. In addition to providing discounted tickets to matches, fan club members have the chance to meet the players and receive exclusive information. For many, these cards are a means of expressing their dedication and loyalty to the team they support.

6.4.6 Sports Broadcasting and Commentary

Track **93**

أَجْرى مُقابَلَةً • إِجْراءٌ **to conduct an interview**

أَجْرى الصَّحَفِيُّ مُقابَلَةً مَعَ اللّاعِبِ المُتَأَلِّقِ بَعْدَ المُباراةِ.

The journalist conducted an interview with the outstanding player after the match.

أَحْرَزَ هَدَفًا • إِحْرازٌ **to score a goal**

تَمَكَّنَ اللاعِبُ الشّابُّ مِنْ إِحْرازِ هَدَفٍ رائِعٍ خِلالَ المُباراةِ النِّهائِيَّةِ، مِمّا ساهَمَ في فَوْزِ فَريقِهِ بِالبُطولَةِ.

The young player managed to score a fantastic goal during the final match, contributing to his team's victory in the championship.

to announce أَعْلَنَ • إِعْلانٌ

أَعْلَنَتِ الشَّبَكَةُ الرِّياضِيَّةُ عَنْ جَدْوَلِ البَثِّ لِلْمُبارَياتِ القادِمَةِ.

The sports network announced the broadcast schedule for the upcoming matches.

replay إِعادَةٌ

أَظْهَرَتِ الإِعادَةُ الهَدَفَ الرّائِعَ الَّذي سَجَّلَهُ اللّاعِبُ في الدَّقائِقِ الأَخيرَةِ.

The replay showed the great goal scored by the player in the last minutes.

broadcast, stream بَثٌّ

أَجْرَتِ الشَّبَكَةُ بَثًّا مُباشِرًا لِلْمُباراةِ الحاسِمَةِ.

The network conducted a live broadcast of the decisive match.

to broadcast, stream بَثَّ • بَثٌّ

سَيَتِمُّ بَثُّ المُباراةِ عَلى القَناةِ الرِّياضِيَّةِ الرَّئيسِيَّةِ.

The match will be broadcasted on the main sports channel.

live broadcast بَثٌّ مُباشِرٌ

إِنَّ مُشاهَدَةَ المُباراةِ في بَثٍّ مُباشِرٍ يَجْلِبُ الإِثارَةَ وَالتَّوَتُّرَ.

Watching the match on a live broadcast brings excitement and tension.

live streaming online بَثٌّ مُباشِرٌ عَلى الإِنْتَرْنِتْ

يُتيحُ البَثُّ المُباشِرُ عَلى الإِنْتَرْنِتْ لِلْمُشَجِّعينَ مِنْ جَميعِ أَنْحاءِ العالَمِ مُتابَعَةَ اللُّعْبَةِ.

Live streaming online allows fans from all over the world to follow the game.

to stream live بَثَّ مُباشَرَةً • بَثٌّ

سَتَبُثُّ القَناةُ الرِّياضِيَّةُ المُباراةَ مُباشَرَةً عَبْرَ الإِنْتَرْنِتْ.

The sports channel will stream the match live online.

analysis program • بَرامِجُ **بَرْنامَجٌ تَحْليلِيٌّ**

تابِع البَرْنامَجَ التَّحْليلِيَّ بَعْدَ المُباراةِ لِفَهْمٍ أَفْضَلَ لِلتَّكْتيكاتِ المُسْتَخْدَمَةِ.

Follow the analysis program after the match for a better understanding of the tactics used.

sports program • بَرامِجُ **بَرْنامَجٌ رِياضِيٌّ**

تَمَّ بَثُّ بَرْنامَجٍ رِياضِيٍّ مُمْتِعٍ يُرَكِّزُ عَلى تَحْليلِ أَحْدَثِ المُبارَياتِ فِي الدَّوْرِيِّ المَحَلِّيِّ.

An exciting sports program was broadcast, focusing on the analysis of the latest matches in the local league.

to talk about • تَحَدُّثٌ **تَحَدَّثَ عَنْ**

تَحَدَّثَ المُعَلِّقُ عَنْ تِقْنِيّاتِ الفَريقَيْنِ وَكَيْفِيَّةِ تَأْثيرِها عَلى نَتيجَةِ المُباراةِ.

The commentator talked about the teams' tactics and how they affected the match outcome.

analysis **تَحْليلٌ**

قَدَّمَ المُحَلِّلُ تَحْليلًا مُفَصَّلًا حَوْلَ أَداءِ اللّاعِبينَ خِلالَ المُباراةِ.

The analyst provided a detailed analysis of the players' performance during the match.

performance analysis **تَحْليلُ أَداءٍ**

أَجْرى المُحَلِّلُ تَحْليلَ أَداءٍ مُعَمَّقًا لِلْفَريقِ، مُرَكِّزًا عَلى تَمْريراتِهِمِ الدَّقيقَةِ وَسُرْعَةِ اسْتِجابَتِهِمْ.

The analyst conducted an in-depth performance analysis of the team, focusing on its accurate passes and quick responses.

strategic analysis **تَحْليلٌ اسْتِراتيجِيٌّ**

تَمَّ إِجْراءُ تَحْليلٍ اسْتِراتيجِيٍّ لِتَحَرُّكاتِ اللّاعِبينَ عَلى أَرْضِ المَلْعَبِ.

A strategic analysis was carried out on the movements of the players on the pitch.

sports analysis **تَحْليلٌ رِياضِيٌّ**

قَدَّمَ التَّحْليلُ الرِّياضِيُّ نَظْرَةً مُفَصَّلَةً عَلى الطُّرُقِ الَّتي اسْتَخْدَمَها الفَريقُ لِلتَّغَلُّبِ عَلى مُنافِسيهِ.

The sports analysis provided a detailed view of the strategies the team used to overcome their opponents.

تَحْليلُ ما بَعْدَ المُباراةِ
post-match analysis

قَدَّمَتْ قَناةُ الرِّياضَةِ تَحْليلَ ما بَعْدَ المُباراةِ، وَهُوَ يَعْرِضُ نِقاطَ القُوَّةِ وَالضَّعْفِ في أَداءِ كِلا الفَريقَيْنِ.

The sports channel offered a post-match analysis, highlighting the strengths and weaknesses in both teams' performances.

تَحْليلٌ مُفَصَّلٌ لِلْمُباراةِ
detailed analysis of the match

تَمَّ تَقْديمُ تَحْليلٍ مُفَصَّلٍ لِلْمُباراةِ، وَالَّذي أَبْرَزَ كُلَّ تَفاصيلِ اللُّعْبَةِ مِنَ البِدايَةِ حَتّى النِّهايَةِ.

A detailed analysis of the match was presented, which highlighted every detail of the game from start to finish.

تَعْليقٌ
commentary

كانَ تَعْليقُ المُعَلِّقِ الرِّياضِيِّ عَلى المُباراةِ مُثيرًا لِلْإِعْجابِ، حَيْثُ تَمَكَّنَ مِنْ تَوْصيلِ الإثارَةِ وَالتَّوَتُّرِ الَّذَيْنِ كانَ يَشْعُرُ بِهِما الجُمْهورُ إِلى المُشاهِدينَ.

The sports commentator's commentary on the match was impressive, as he was able to convey the excitement and tension felt by the audience to the viewers.

تَعْليقٌ مُباشِرٌ
live commentary

كانَ التَّعْليقُ المُباشِرُ لِلْمُباراةِ شَيِّقًا وَمُفيدًا، مَعَ تَوْفيرِ تَفاصيلَ دَقيقَةٍ عَنْ تَطَوُّرِ اللَّعِبِ.

The live commentary of the match was interesting and informative, providing intricate details of the play's development.

تَغْطِيَةٌ حَصْرِيَّةٌ
exclusive coverage

اِسْتَمْتَعَ المُشاهِدونَ بِتَغْطِيَةٍ حَصْرِيَّةٍ لِلْمُباراةِ عَلى قَناةِ الرِّياضَةِ المَحَلِّيَّةِ.

Viewers enjoyed exclusive coverage of the match on the local sports channel.

تَغْطِيَةٌ مُباشِرَةٌ لِلْمُباراةِ
live coverage of the match

بَدَأَتِ القَناةُ الرِّياضِيَّةُ تَغْطِيَتَها المُباشِرَةَ لِلْمُباراةِ الكَبيرَةِ.

The sports channel began its live coverage of the big match.

interview with players **حِوارٌ مَعَ لاعِبينَ**

قَدَّمَتِ القَناةُ الرِّياضِيَّةُ حِواراتٍ مُثيرَةً مَعَ اللّاعِبينَ، وَالَّتي أَعْطَتِ المُعْجَبينَ نَظْرَةً عَميقَةً عَلى الأَداءِ الرِّياضِيِّ.

The sports channel presented engaging interviews with the players, giving fans an in-depth look into athletic performance.

great **رائِعٌ**

كانَ أَداءُ الفَريقِ رائِعًا، وَهَذا ما أَشادَ بِهِ المُحَلِّلونَ بِشِدَّةٍ.

The team's performance was great, which was highly praised by the analysts.

interesting **شَيِّقٌ**

كانَتِ المُباراةُ شَيِّقَةً، وَكانَتْ كُلُّ لَحْظَةٍ مَليئَةً بِالْإِثارَةِ وَالتَّشْويقِ.

The match was interesting, and every moment was filled with thrill and excitement.

to film • تَصْويرٌ **صَوَّرَ**

تَمَّ تَصْويرُ المُباراةِ بِواسِطَةِ كاميراتٍ مُتَعَدِّدَةٍ لِتَوْفيرِ أَفْضَلِ تَغْطِيَةٍ مُمْكِنَةٍ لِلْحَدَثِ الرِّياضِيِّ.

The match was filmed with multiple cameras to provide the best possible coverage of the sporting event.

to show, display • عَرْضٌ **عَرَضَ**

عَرَضَتِ الشّاشَةُ لَقَطاتٍ مُثيرَةً لِأَبْرَزِ الأَهْدافِ في المُباراةِ.

The screen displayed thrilling shots of the most significant goals in the match.

to comment on, commentate • تَعْليقٌ **عَلَّقَ عَلى**

عَلَّقَ المُعَلِّقُ عَلى المُباراةِ بِحَماسَةٍ شَديدَةٍ، مِمّا زادَ مِنْ إِثارَةِ المُشاهِدينَ.

The commentator passionately commented on the match, increasing the viewers' excitement.

unclear **غَيْرُ واضِحٍ**

كانَتْ بَعْضُ القَراراتِ التَّحْكيمِيَّةِ غَيْرَ واضِحَةٍ خِلالَ المُباراةِ، مِمّا أَثارَ جَدَلًا بَيْنَ المُعَلِّقينَ.

Some of the refereeing decisions during the match were unclear, stirring controversy among commentators.

قَناةٌ رِياضِيَّةٌ • قَنَواتٌ
sports channel

تَمَّ بَثُّ المُباراةِ عَلى قَناةٍ رِياضِيَّةٍ مَعْروفَةٍ لِجَميعِ المُشَجِّعين.

The match was broadcasted on a well-known sports channel for all fans.

كاميرا
camera

حَرَصَ المُخْرِجُ عَلى اسْتِخْدامِ عِدَّةِ كاميراتٍ لِالْتِقاطِ أَفْضَلِ اللَّقَطاتِ مِنَ المُباراةِ.

The director made sure to use several cameras to capture the best shots of the match.

مُتَأَخِّرٌ
delayed

بِسَبَبِ مُشْكِلَةٍ فَنِّيَّةٍ، كانَ بَثُّ المُباراةِ مُتَأَخِّرًا بَعْضَ الشَّيْءِ.

Due to a technical issue, the broadcast of the match was somewhat delayed.

مُثيرٌ
thrilling

كانَتِ المُباراةُ مُثيرَةً وَمَليئَةً بِالأَحْداثِ الَّتي أَبْقَتِ الجُمْهورَ في أَعْلى دَرَجاتِ الإِثارَةِ.

The match was thrilling and full of events that kept the audience on high excitement.

مُثيرٌ لِلاهْتِمامِ
interesting

كانَتِ النِّهايَةُ المُثيرَةُ لِلْمُباراةِ مُثيرَةً لِلاهْتِمامِ بِشَكْلٍ خاصٍّ، حَيْثُ تَمَّ تَسْجيلُ هَدَفِ الفَوْزِ في الدَّقائِقِ الأَخيرَةِ.

The exciting end to the match was particularly interesting, as the winning goal was scored in the final minutes.

مُشَوِّقٌ
exciting

قَدَّمَتِ القَناةُ الرِّياضِيَّةُ تَغْطِيَةً مُشَوِّقَةً لِلْمُباراةِ، حَيْثُ اسْتَعْرَضَتِ اللَّقَطاتِ الأَكْثَرَ أَهَمِّيَّةً.

The sports channel gave an exciting coverage of the match, showcasing the most important shots.

مُعَلِّقٌ رِياضِيٌّ
sports commentator

لَمْ يُخْفِ المُعَلِّقُ الرِّياضِيُّ حَماسَهُ لِلْأَداءِ الرّائِعِ الَّذي قَدَّمَهُ الفَريقُ.

The sports commentator did not hide his enthusiasm for the great performance the team delivered.

interview **مُقابَلَةٌ**

خِلالَ المُقابَلَةِ، ناقَشَ الـمُدَرِّبُ اسْتِراتيجِيّاتِ الـفَريقِ للمُباراةِ الحاسِمَةِ ضِدَّ مُنافِسيهِمِ اللَّدودينَ .

During the interview, the coach discussed the team's strategies for the crucial match against their arch-rivals.

highlight reel **مُلَخَّصُ أَحْداثٍ**

شاهِدِ المُلَخَّصَ لِأَبْرَزِ الأَحْداثِ في المُباراةِ.

Watch the highlight reel for the most significant events in the match.

enjoyable **مُمْتِعٌ**

كانَتِ المُباراةُ مُمْتِعَةً وَمَليئَةً بِالأَهْدافِ الرّائِعَةِ الَّتي أَبْهَرَتِ الجُمْهورَ.

The match was enjoyable and full of great goals that wowed the crowd.

boring **مُمِلٌّ**

أَدّى الفَريقُ الضَّيْفُ أَداءً مُمِلًّا، مِمّا أَسْفَرَ عَنْ خَسارَةٍ مُذِلَّةٍ أَمامَ الفَريقِ المُضيفِ.

The visiting team performed boringly, resulting in a humiliating defeat to the host team.

sports debate **نِقاشٌ رِياضِيٌّ**

اِسْتَضافَ البَرْنامَجُ نِقاشًا رِياضِيًّا بَيْنَ عَدَدٍ مِنَ المُحَلِّلينَ لِتَحْليلِ أَداءِ الفِرَقِ.

The program hosted a sports debate among a number of analysts to analyze the teams' performances.

هَدَفُ الفَوْزِ • أَهْدافٌ

سَجَّلَ اللاعِبُ البارِزُ هَدَفَ الفَوْزِ الحاسِمَ في اللَّحَظاتِ الأَخيرَةِ مِنَ المُباراةِ، مِمّا مَنَحَ فَريقَهُ الانتِصارَ الغالِيَ.

The prominent player scored the decisive winning goal in the final moments of the match, granting his team the valuable victory.

هَزيمَةٌ مُذِلَّةٌ • هَزائِمُ **humiliating defeat**

كانَتِ الهَزيمَةُ مُذِلَّةً لِلْفَريقِ، حَيْثُ خَسِرَ بِفارِقِ خَمْسَةِ أَهْدافٍ دونَ رَدٍّ.

The defeat was humiliating for the team, losing by five goals to none.

واضِحٌ **clear**

كانَتْ تَفاصيلُ اسْتراتيجِيَّةِ الفَريقِ واضِحَةً مِنْ خِلالِ التَّنْفيذِ المُمْتازِ لِلْخُطَّةِ الهُجومِيَّةِ.

The team's strategic details were clear through the excellent execution of the offensive plan.

وافٍ **informative**

كانَ البَرْنامَجُ الرِّياضِيُّ الَّذي تَمَّ بَثُّهُ عَلى القَناةِ وافِيًا وَمُفيدًا، حَيْثُ قَدَّمَ تَحْليلاتٍ مُفَصَّلَةً لِكُلِّ جَوانِبِ المُباراةِ.

The sports program aired on the channel was informative and useful, providing detailed analyses of all aspects of the match.

وَصَفَ • وَصْفٌ **to describe**

وَصَفَ المُعَلِّقُ المُباراةَ بِأَنَّها كانَتْ واحِدَةً مِنْ أَرْوَعِ اللِّقاءاتِ الَّتي شَهِدَها الدَّوْرِيُّ هَذا المَوْسِمَ.

The commentator described the match as one of the most spectacular encounters the league has seen this season.

6.4.6.1 Mini-Articles

Track **94**

تَمَكَّنَ المُعَلِّقُ الرِّياضِيُّ المَعْروفُ، أَحْمَد الحَسَن، مِنْ تَوْقيعِ عَقْدٍ مَعَ قَناةِ الرِّياضَةِ الأولى لِتَقْديمِ التَّعْليقِ المُباشِرِ عَلى المُبارَياتِ الكُبْرى. وَلَطالَما كانَ الحَسَن مَعْروفًا بِتَعْليقاتِهِ المُثيرَةِ وَالْمُحَمَّلَةِ بِالْمَعْلوماتِ، وَتُعْتَبَرُ خِبْرَتُهُ الطَّويلَةُ في التَّحْليلِ الرِّياضِيِّ إِضافَةً قَوِيَّةً لِلْقَناةِ.

The well-known sports commentator, Ahmed Al-Hasan, has signed a contract with the first sports channel to provide live commentary on major matches. Al-Hasan has always been known for his exciting and informative commentary, and his extensive experience in sports analysis is a strong addition to the channel.

في بَرْنامَجٍ تَحْليلِيٍّ يُبَثُّ مُباشَرَةً عَلى الإِنْتَرْنِتْ، تَحَدَّثَ المُحَلِّلُ الرِّياضِيُّ سامي السَّعْدي عَنِ الأَداءِ الأَخيرِ لِفَريقِ الوَحْدَةِ في المُباراةِ الَّتي انْتَهَتْ بِخَسارَتِهِ. اِسْتَخْدَمَ السَّعْدي التَّحْليلَ الاِسْتراتيجِيَّ وَأَداءَ اللّاعِبينَ لِاسْتِخْلاصِ نَتائِجِهِ، مَعَ التَّرْكيزِ عَلى المَناطِقِ الَّتي يَجِبُ تَحْسينُها في الفَريقِ.

In an online live analysis program, sports analyst Sami Al-Saadi discussed the recent performance of Al-Wahda team in the match that ended in their loss. Al-Saadi used strategic analysis and player performance to reach his conclusions, focusing on areas that need improvement in the team.

أَعْلَنَتْ شَبَكَةُ الرِّياضَةِ المَرْكَزِيَّةُ أَنَّها سَتُقَدِّمُ تَغْطِيَةً حَصْرِيَّةً لِمُباراةِ القِمَّةِ بَيْنَ الهِلالِ وَالنَّصْرِ، وَالَّتي تُعْتَبَرُ مِنْ أَكْثَرِ المُبارَياتِ المُنْتَظَرَةِ في المَوْسِمِ. سَتَشْمَلُ التَّغْطِيَةُ تَعْليقًا مُباشِرًا، وتَحْليلًا لِما قَبْلَ المُباراةِ وَما بَعْدَ المُباراةِ، وَحِواراتٍ مَعَ اللّاعِبينَ.

The Central Sports Network announced that it will provide exclusive coverage of the summit match between Al-Hilal and Al-Nassr, which is one of the most anticipated matches of the season. The coverage will include live commentary, pre-match and post-match analysis, and interviews with the players.

Made in the USA
Coppell, TX
27 February 2024